Yale Broadway Masters

FORTHCOMING VOLUMES IN THE SERIES

Irving Berlin, BY JEFFREY MAGEE

Leonard Bernstein, BY CAROL OJA

George Gershwin, BY LARRY STARR

Jerome Kern, BY STEPHEN BANFIELD

Andrew Lloyd Webber, BY JOHN SNELSON

Frank Loesser, BY THOMAS L. RIIS

Cole Porter, BY PATRICK O'CONNOR

Sigmund Romberg, BY WILLIAM A. EVERETT

RICHARD RODGERS

GEOFFREY BLOCK

YALE UNIVERSITY PRESS   NEW HAVEN & LONDON

Frontispiece: Richard Rodgers composing "Bali Ha'i" (1948). This photo was the model for the official centennial portrait painted by Kim Beaty in 2001.

Designed by James J. Johnson and set in Electra Roman types by Tseng Information Systems, Inc.
Printed in the United States of America by R. R. Donnelley and Sons, Harrisonburg, Virginia.

Library of Congress Cataloging-in-Publication Data
Block, Geoffrey Holden, 1948–
Richard Rodgers / Geoffrey Block.
p. cm. — (Yale Broadway masters)
Includes bibliographical references (p.) and index.
ISBN 0-300-09747-6 (cloth : alk. paper)

1. Rodgers, Richard, 1902—Criticism and interpretation.   I. Title.   II. Series.
ML410.R6315B56 2003
782.1'4'092—dc21   2003002412

A catalogue record for this book is available from the British Library.
The paper in this book meets the guidelines for permanence and durability of the Committee on Production Guidelines for Book Longevity of the Council on Library Resources.

10   9   8   7   6   5   4   3   2   1

To my beloved parents

Ruth and Stanley Block

on their sixty-fifth wedding anniversary

with gratitude and love

Contents

Preface

THE YALE BROADWAY MASTERS series aims to introduce both general readers and students to major figures in Broadway theater. Each volume will be short, amply illustrated, and written in a lively, nontechnical manner—serious scholarly books that wear their scholarship lightly. Each will reflect the individuality of its subject and author, but certain elements will be consistent, including a biographical survey, at least one chapter devoted to a single show, an assessment of each subject's historical and artistic legacy, an authoritative work-list, and a selected discography.

While some may bristle at the word "master," we think the rubric Yale Broadway Masters well serves a series that focuses on the individual and collective accomplishments of American musical theater's greatest practitioners. Although most of the projected volumes single out composers, we hope to find room for a representative sample of masterful lyricists, librettists, directors, and choreographers who also richly deserve scholarly consideration commensurate with their popular acclaim and treasured places in our hearts and imaginations.

GEOFFREY BLOCK
General Editor

Acknowledgments

Richard Rodgers lived by the theory that the success or failure of a show can be traced to "the day somebody says, 'Let's do a show about . . .'" I think Rodgers's theory applies equally well to a book series. For this reason, my first acknowledgment goes to Harry Haskell, my imaginative, thoughtful, and invariably supportive editor at Yale University Press, for conceiving the idea of Yale Broadway Masters and inviting me to serve as general editor and to contribute a volume.

The Rodgers and Hammerstein Organization, under the visionary leadership of its president, Theodore S. Chapin, provided encouragement and assistance at every turn. Tom Briggs, director of the R&H Theater Library, allowed me to see unpublished librettos and scores and to photocopy indispensable materials in the Rodgers Collection at the Library of Congress. Robin Walton, director of legal affairs, helped me secure the rights to reprint libretto and book excerpts and photographs. Flora Griggs administered lyric permissions and Julie McDowell the musical examples on behalf of Williamson Music. Carol Cornicelli located many photos and in some cases discovered even better alternatives. Bruce Pomahac responded knowledgeably to my questions about orchestration and arrangement issues in *South Pacific*. Bert Fink was invariably a friendly source of useful information. Without the cooperation and encouragement of R&H, this project would not have been possible.

Special thanks go to Larry Starr, my University of Washington neighbor and friend, who took time away from his many projects to read a draft and offer insightful suggestions on the book's tone, structure, and substance.

Frederick Nolan's authoritative, eloquent, and generous reader's report corrected several errors that sooner or later would have proved embarrassing. Jeremy Briggs Roberts demonstrated his thoroughness as a proofreader. My new colleague, Robert Hutchinson, beautifully set the music examples on Finale. Yale's editorial and production staff was a joy to work with. In particular, Susan Laity offered useful advice on style and presentation, and Heidi Downey provided meticulous and helpful copyediting.

The University of Puget Sound generously funded my preliminary research at the Richard Rodgers, Oscar Hammerstein, and Joshua Logan collections at the Library of Congress and my visit to the theater and music divisions of the New York Public Library. Judy Reid and Carole Christensen provided and supervised music department assistance. The university library staff, especially Elin Gratton, Jada Pelger, and Sharon Seabrook, cheerfully and capably tracked down difficult-to-obtain materials. The following people and institutions shared their knowledge, time, or materials: Joy Abbott, Micheal F. Anders, Robin Boomer, Gwynne Kuhner Brown, Stephen Citron, Jeni Dahmus (Juilliard School), Albert I. Da Silva, Esq., William A. Everett, Rosemary Gawelko (Warner Bros. Publications), Mark Eden Horowitz (Library of Congress), William Hyland, Marty Jacobs and Marguerite Lavin (Museum of the City of New York), Jane Klain (Museum of Television & Radio), David Lombard (CBS Photo Archive), Ross Mulhausen, the State Historical Society of Wisconsin, Victoria Wilson, and Graham Wood.

Throughout the writing of this book, my wife, Jacqueline, and our daughters, Jessamyn and Eliza, provided emotional sustenance, perspective, and the daily sound of music. Family excursions to view local productions of both familiar favorites and unusual Rodgers shows as the centennial in 2002 drew closer was a highlight that will remain a cherished memory.

When my dad married his angel on July 3, 1938, Rodgers and Hart's *I Married an Angel* had been running a little less than two months. *Babes in Arms* had closed the previous December, and *I'd Rather Be Right* would close on July 9. Rodgers and Hart's next show, *The Boys from Syracuse*, made its debut before the year was over. By the time I arrived, the Rodgers and Hart era had given way to the age of Rodgers and Hammerstein. In my early childhood, my parents introduced me to their cast album of *South Pacific* (on seven 78 rpm records) and their 33 rpm album of *Carousel*, and took me to see the Rodgers and Hammerstein films that began to appear in the middle and late 1950s. When I was ten they presented me with a copy of *The*

Rodgers and Hammerstein Song Book (which then stopped at *Cinderella*). A few years later they took me to experience live productions of *The Sound of Music* and *No Strings* when their touring companies reached San Francisco. At the latter show I vividly recall my father explaining about the unusual practice of instrumentalists playing on the stage and Rodgers's decision to eschew strings in a musical called *No Strings*.

When Jacqueline and I were married nearly twenty years later, my dad surprised and delighted us all when he offered Rodgers and Hart's remarkably apropos "Where or When" as his wedding toast, a performance that returns to me wherever and whenever I hear this gorgeous song or remember this happy occasion. For the past sixty-five years, my mother, with a twinkle in her eye, rarely failed to recognize the tunes that her funny valentine, a man with many songs in his heart, played on the violin or piano. The interests they nurtured and encouraged in their son have led to a lifetime of emotional and intellectual fulfillment. And gratitude.

RICHARD RODGERS

Introduction: Rodgers, the Workaholic

I N HER INTRODUCTION TO THE SECOND EDITION OF RICHARD
Rodgers's autobiography *Musical Stages,* Mary Rodgers wrote about the
downside of her father's private emotional life.[1] Rodgers himself disclosed
in *Musical Stages* that shortly after the stunning success of the national
television broadcast of *Cinderella* in the spring of 1957 he "lost all interest" in his work and "simply didn't give a dam[n] about doing anything or
seeing anyone."[2] He also acknowledged a drinking problem as "one of the
most disturbing manifestations" of a prolonged and profound depression.
By June, Rodgers had checked himself into Payne Whitney, memorably described by Jean Stafford as a "high class booby hatch," a deluxe psychiatric
clinic frequented by celebrity patients, including Marilyn Monroe and Mary
McCarthy.[3] After twelve weeks of restful activities and psychiatric treatment,
Rodgers returned to his family "as if nothing had happened." An "extremely
baffling and frightening period" had passed and "never happened again."

Today the symptoms, causes, and treatment of clinical depression are
better understood and easier to talk about than when Rodgers wrote his
autobiography in the mid-1970s. Various collaborators (most vividly Arthur
Laurents) and Rodgers's daughters, Mary and Linda, publicly contend that
the drinking problems did not end with his release from treatment.[4] Nevertheless, Rodgers was soon able to work again on an exciting new project,
Flower Drum Song. In fact, work was Rodgers's therapy, sinecure, salvation,
and the simple secret to his well-being. According to Mary, "Theatre, and
theatre only, turned him on and cheered him up—all aspects of it, not just
the writing." Everyone who knew Rodgers agrees with Mary that he was hap-

piest when he was planning or working on a show. Fortunately for Rodgers, these activities accounted for most of his time. Even Dorothy Rodgers conceded that although she was the important *person* in her husband's life, *work* came first in the hierarchy of her husband's passions.[5] As Mary put it so well: "Theatre was his hobby. And his life." Not surprisingly, depression hit Rodgers hardest during his relatively inactive Hollywood years (the early 1930s) and again in 1957, when, for the first time in many years, no projects loomed on the horizon.

The more we get to know our artists (or our families and neighbors, for that matter), the more we become aware of dissonances between life and art, between public and private. And few humans emerge unscathed from biographical scrutiny. Until Dorothy's death in 1992, the general public knew little of Rodgers's personal demons. Now we know, as Frank Rich wrote in a *New York Times Magazine* centennial profile, that "far from whistling a happy tune and climbing every mountain, he feared bridges, tunnels, elevators and any kind of travel, among other crippling phobias."[6] Now we know that Rodgers "was an extremely complicated man and deeply unhappy much of the time."[7] But we have known much longer that this same unhappy and sometimes unresponsive man was able to express a wide range of feelings in hundreds of songs and dozens of musical stories that continue to move and delight millions of people. In this book I explore a sampling of these songs and musical stories—how they came into the world, what makes them work, how they have been interpreted and evaluated.

I will try to realize an elusive dream of the musical theater historian: to write a book that can reach neophytes suspicious of the occasional musical example while at the same time offering something new for specialists. My goal is a book for anyone who wants to learn more about what Rodgers himself focused on during most of his waking hours for nearly sixty years: his work. This emphasis does not preclude discussion of the intersection between Rodgers's life and his art. Readers will have many opportunities to meet the man who created the music to forty shows that appeared on Broadway between 1920 and 1979, twenty-six with Hart, nine with Hammerstein, and five after Hammerstein's death. Those who want to learn mainly about Rodgers the depressive, the alcoholic, the womanizer, and the difficult husband and father, however, will need to look elsewhere.[8] This book is the story of Rodgers the *workaholic*.

People who resist the natural urge to place a creative artist's work in three tidy compartments might make an exception for the neatly tripartite career of Richard Rodgers (1902–79): forty years of serial monogamy with two successive collaborators and a lonely third act that lasted nearly another twenty years. In the beginning was Lorenz Hart (1895–1943), a talented but troubled lyricist who for more than two decades (1919–43) set Rodgers's music and contributed his fair share to a parade of durable hit songs featured in fresh, innovative, and mostly hit shows now generally forgotten. Rodgers's second partnership, with the venerable, reliable, and equally if less pyro-technically talented Oscar Hammerstein 2nd (1895–1960), a librettist as well as lyricist, resulted in an impressive series of integrated and timeless musi-cals, beginning with *Oklahoma!* (1943) and ending with *The Sound of Music* (1959). Their partnership also resulted, not incidentally, in the creation of dozens of songs for which Rodgers is also remembered. Rodgers's remain-ing nineteen years after Hammerstein's death were marked by less compo-sitional activity, dwindling runs, and, according to most critics, historians, and theatrical producers, artistic decline.

The verdict of history goes something like this. Rodgers and Hart: great songs, but with one or two exceptions shows unworthy of revival without considerable revision of their books. Rodgers and Hammerstein: songs de-pendent on their dramatic contexts (and by implication less interesting as pure songs, either for jazz musicians or cabaret singers), and well crafted but perhaps overly optimistic, sentimental, and occasionally even "preachy" shows with more than a touch of condescension toward "people whose eyes are oddly made" and women who want more than to simply "enjoy being a girl." Rodgers without Hammerstein: less than a handful of memorable songs, and anachronistic musicals that fail to capture the imagination of the best shows by newcomers working in the Rodgers and Hammerstein tradi-tion—such as Jerry Bock and Sheldon Harnick's *Fiddler on the Roof* and Jerry Herman's *Hello, Dolly!* or the daring modernist musicals of Stephen Sondheim. Perhaps it is time to consider the possibility of reviving Rodgers and Hart shows without significant revision, to appreciate the autonomous musical delights of Rodgers's songs with Hammerstein, and even to chal-lenge the assumptions behind why most of Rodgers's final efforts have been doomed to obscurity.

It seems fair at the outset to reveal an agenda that seeks to partially re-dress critical judgments that almost invariably relegate the musicals Rodgers wrote with Hart to a Dark Age (1920s and 1930s) before the Enlightenment of the Rodgers and Hammerstein era (beginning with *Oklahoma!*). The evidence suggests instead that Rodgers, following the standard established by his model Jerome Kern, from the beginning sought opportunities to use his songs to tell a story. Whenever possible he made a conscious and often successful attempt to create a succession of integrated musicals that would break new ground, give audiences something nonformulaic, satisfy his own evolving tastes, and make money in the process. Throughout his long career Rodgers rarely abandoned this quest for theatrical innovation. At the same time, without giving up his theatrical vision, Rodgers almost until the end demonstrated remarkable consistency in his ability to anticipate what would work in front of live audiences.

The musicals of the Rodgers and Hart era, when revived at all, are rarely revived in their original form. In the most common scenario—albeit less with Rodgers and Hart than most of their contemporaries—revivalists restructure the books, rewrite what is perceived as stale and dated dialogue, and add, delete, and present songs in new contexts, more than occasionally for different characters. Consequently, the legacies of most musicals of the 1920s and 1930s have been noticeably altered, sometimes beyond recognition. Typically what remains is a repertory of song standards, in most cases at least one or two from even the most obscure and forgotten show. One of these "lost" musicals, *A Connecticut Yankee* (1927), was the longest running Rodgers and Hart musical of the 1920s and the only show that they themselves chose to revise and revive (in 1943), several months after Rodgers and Hammerstein had permanently altered the Broadway landscape with *Oklahoma!* Despite some arguable improvements, new songs (including another major hit, "To Keep My Love Alive"), and the presence of at least one certifiable star (Vivienne Segal) in an expanded role, the revived *Connecticut Yankee* failed to catch on. While it is instructive to learn why it failed in 1943, we also need to understand why it succeeded so well in 1927.

After a period of commercial setbacks and creative retrenchment in the years that followed *Yankee* (1928–31) and several relatively unproductive and unhappy years in Hollywood (1931–35), Rodgers and Hart returned to Broadway in 1935 to enjoy one of the greatest string of successes in Broadway history: nine hits and only one miss within an eight-year period (1935–42). *The Boys from Syracuse* (1938), perhaps their most frequently revived show, illustrates the ingenuity with which librettist George Abbott and Rodgers and Hart dramatically and musically transformed Shakespeare's underappreciated *Comedy of Errors* into Broadway's first important Shakespeare musical.

The legacy of Rodgers and Hart goes beyond an anthology of pretty songs, and several of these final shows, including *Syracuse*, deserve a place in the repertory and in their original form.

As changing values and evolving sensitivities to racial and gender issues continue to distance our own time from the bigotry and sexism explicitly or implicitly depicted in 1949, *South Pacific* continues to hold an exalted but uneasy position among the revered musicals of its time. It also demonstrates fascinating historical, cultural, and artistic issues in its departures from its literary source, James Michener's Pulitzer Prize–winning historical fiction, *Tales of the South Pacific* (1947). The commercially successful but artistically controversial film released in 1958 sheds considerable light on how an adaptation of a stage musical could respond to the Hollywood Production Code. Just as Rodgers and Hart musicals were subject to alteration, a revisionist telemusical broadcast in 2001 showed that Rodgers and Hammerstein were not immune from attempts to update and enhance their relevance for a new millennium.

Shortly before the release of the *South Pacific* film, Rodgers and Hammerstein created in *Cinderella* (1957) a milestone in the effort to bring the ideals of Broadway musical theater to a new medium: commercial television. Since the boffo theatrical success of *The King and I* six years earlier, the team that reinvented the Broadway musical with *Oklahoma!* and retained its hegemony with a string of popular and critically well-received musicals (notably *Carousel* and *South Pacific*) had suffered one near miss, *Me and Juliet* (1953), and even a box office failure, *Pipe Dream* (1955). In 1957, the biggest Broadway hit was Lerner and Loewe's *My Fair Lady* (1956), the latest in a long succession of musicals based on the Cinderella theme. Unfortunately, the televised *Cinderella* that featured *My Fair Lady* star Julie Andrews, live and in color in the title role, was preserved only on black and white kinescope, a format considered unacceptable for future showings. To remedy this problem, Rodgers, five years after the death of Hammerstein, supervised the creation of a revised libretto for a new color videotaped production that introduced several recycled Rodgers and Hammerstein songs and made other adjustments to the dramatic structure and tone of the earlier telecast. Nearly two decades after Rodgers's death, *Cinderella*, now in other hands, was transformed into yet another teleplay in 1997, a multicultural version that featured such contemporary stars as Whitney Houston and Brandy Norwood, three newly interpolated Rodgers songs (including one originally composed with Hart), and other musical and dramatic tinkering designed to please evolving dramatic tastes and cultural attitudes. Although these three versions share much of the same story and score, they are by no means the same show. In addition, just as directors often revise and rethink earlier plays and musicals, producers reinterpret our classic fairy tales for new generations of television viewers.

After the death of Hammerstein in 1960, Rodgers composed only five musicals in his remaining nineteen years: *No Strings* (1962), *Do I Hear a Waltz?* (1965), *Two By Two* (1970), *Rex* (1976), and *I Remember Mama* (1979). Two shows made money, *No Strings* and *Two By Two*, but only *No Strings*, the first and only complete show for which Rodgers wrote the words as well as the music, gained widespread critical acclaim. These five shows remain among the least known of any by Rodgers since the string of obscure Rodgers and Hart shows that followed *Connecticut Yankee* in the late 1920s. All were eventually recorded, but no commercial vocal scores were published for *Rex* or *I Remember Mama*. These infrequently performed shows, interesting in their own right as both curiosities and potential revivals, cause us to wonder about what happened to Rodgers after he lost his second longtime creative partner. They also raise a host of critical questions. To what extent should the creators of a show face sensitive social topics (*No Strings*)? Should authors learn to live with or should they minimize the defects of their characters when adapting a source (*Do I Hear a Waltz?*)? How do we gain perspective and understanding on the difficult collaborations and difficult stars that hampered the process and usually the results (all the shows after *No Strings*)? Does the absence of a creative cutting edge mean that a work forfeits its right to be reconsidered and perhaps even revived? Finally, to what extent should we hold Rodgers responsible for the problematic legacy of these troubled and neglected shows?

Rodgers's centennial in 2002 sparked a number of events, recordings, books, and a growing awareness of the composer's legacy. We have already noted the deconstructed pre-centennial version of *South Pacific* broadcast on primetime television and seen by millions in 2001. During the same year there was a Royal National Theatre production of *South Pacific* in London (directed by Trevor Nunn) and a two-hour *American Masters* documentary on Rodgers (PBS). The Royal National's highly regarded and longrunning *Oklahoma!* — also directed by Nunn and choreographed by Susan Stroman — opened at Broadway's Gershwin Theatre on March 21, 2002, almost exactly fifty-nine years after its first opening night. Two more New York productions would arrive before the centennial year was out. The Roundabout Theatre Company presented Rodgers and Hart's *The Boys from Syracuse* in August with a new book by Nicky Silver. One month later New York audiences witnessed the first major revival of Rodgers and Hammerstein's generally ignored and sometimes disdained *Flower Drum Song*, a widely discussed production that featured a radically altered book written from an Asian perspective by noted playwright David Henry Hwang.

A centennial provides an opportunity to take stock and to explore the largesse of an important historical figure. With 4,000 productions of his work annually, clearly Rodgers still means a lot to many of us. In addition to the usual suspects—*Oklahoma!*, *South Pacific*, and *The Sound of Music*—the centennial created a welcome excuse to revisit such forgotten early shows as *Dearest Enemy* with the Village Light Opera Group in New York City, and late shows such as *Two By Two* in a U.S. national tour with Tom Bosley, and a reconstructed *Rex* at the University of Findlay in Ohio. San Francisco's 42nd Street Moon theater company continued its comprehensive survey of Rodgers's shows with a season that presented such rarely seen works as *By Jupiter*, *Allegro*, *Peggy-Ann*, *A Connecticut Yankee*, and *Ever Green*.[9] Theaters everywhere presented the familiar and the esoteric, and just a glance at the Rodgers website (*www.rr2002.com*) reveals an enormous amount of activity. Even without a centennial to celebrate, one might speculate with some certainty that interest in Rodgers will continue to be "bustin' out all over."

CHAPTER 1

From Apprentice to Musical Dramatist

RICHARD RODGERS SHARED A GEOGRAPHICAL AND CULTURAL BACK-ground with his illustrious song- and show-writing contemporaries, most notably Jerome Kern (1885–1945), Irving Berlin (1888–1989), and George Gershwin (1898–1937). Like Kern and Gershwin, Rodgers grew up in New York City (Irving Berlin arrived in New York at age five from the Russian town of Temun). All four were the sons of Jewish immigrants from Central or Eastern Europe or Russia. Rodgers could trace his descent from the Levys on his mother's side and the Rogozinskys on his father's; both were Russian Jewish families who had immigrated to the United States in 1860.[1] William Rodgers and Mamie Levy married in 1896, two years before the birth of their first son, Mortimer. After settling in New York City, the Kern, Gershwin, Berlin, and Rodgers families worked diligently to, as Bianca's suitors would say in Cole Porter's "Tom, Dick or Harry," "attain the upper brackets," or at least the middle class. In the process, these assimilated sons of Jewish immigrants would retain social and cultural rather than religious ties to Judaism. However, at the urging of Grandpa Jacob Levy, who lived with his daughter and son-in-law until his death in 1928, Mortimer and perhaps also Richard Rodgers were bar mitzvahed.[2] Only Porter, a Protestant from Peru, Indiana, and heir to a timber, coal, and oil fortune, broke ranks from this ethnic, geographic, and economic profile. Perhaps for this reason he made a conscious effort to incorporate into his compositions what he felt were Jewish musical characteristics.[3] Among Rodgers's earliest, most vivid, and relatively few recollections were hearing his mother at the family piano playing and singing and his physician father joining her in the songs of

Victor Herbert's *Mlle. Modiste* (1905), Franz Lehár's *Merry Widow* (American debut in 1907), and Oscar Straus's *Chocolate Soldier* (1909), musical shows that his parents had attended when Richard was between the ages of three and seven. Late in life Rodgers recalled learning "Chopsticks," picking out melodies by ear at an early age, performing at home and at school assemblies, and associating his musical aptitude with approbation and love. A neighborhood production of *The Pied Piper* with De Wolf Hopper was the first stage performance that he could recall seeing. Rodgers learned every Herbert note and Henry B. Smith lyric of *Little Nemo* (1908), another score resting on the family piano and performed informally by his parents. Rodgers's memories of a Saturday matinee performance of *Nemo*, his first professional musical show, were so powerful that for the rest of his life he could recall his precise seat and two songs from Herbert's "exciting and tender score." Despite his powerful and lifelong connections to classical music, including opera (*Carmen*), ballet (Anna Pavlova and Vaslav Nijinsky in Sergei Diaghilev's *Ballets Russes*), and music for piano and orchestra (a stirring performance by Josef Hofmann of Tchaikovsky's Piano Concerto No. 1), Rodgers decided at an early age to devote his energies and passions—indeed, nearly his entire being—to popular musical theater.[4]

Within a few years of his exposure to professional musicals, Rodgers, at the age of fourteen, composed his first song: "Camp-Fire Days," written at Camp Wigwam in Harrison, Maine. Rodgers's handwritten manuscript for this song is preserved in a scrapbook and reproduced in *Musical Stages*.[5] The facsimile reveals that Rodgers had not yet mastered several basic elements of musical notation, including the proper placement of note stems. So rudimentary was his technique that Rodgers was even unable to consistently notate four beats (rather than more or less) in each bar of a 4/4 time signature. In common with many composers who quickly progress from uninspired juvenilia to early mastery ("Manhattan" would arrive only six years later), "Camp-Fire Days" suggests that "born" melodists might actually need time to develop their potential. Even Mozart did not hit his stride until he was nearly twenty.

Two days after his fifteenth birthday (June 30, 1917) Rodgers copyrighted a song for the first time. It was "Auto Show Girl." The song, with a lyric by an acquaintance, David Dyrenforth, described by Rodgers in *Musical Stages* as a "young would-be lyricist," resurfaced in *One Minute Please* before the end of the year (see example 1.1a). This was the first of Rodgers's fourteen amateur shows before *The Garrick Gaieties* rescued Rodgers and Hart from oblivion nearly eight years later. While the song does not necessarily suggest a brilliant future for the songwriter, "Auto Show Girl," reprinted in David Ewen's early biography, is a notable step up from "Camp-Fire Days" and demonstrates a high degree of competence and skill for a teenager.

The year before *One Minute Please* was staged Rodgers saw a production of *Very Good Eddie* (lyrics by Guy Bolton, music by Kern), the second in a group of shows that embodied a new intimate style of sophisticated American musicals. The productions came to be known as the Princess Theater shows, after the small theater in which several debuted. *Very Good Eddie* changed Rodgers's life. Kern immediately became Rodgers's first and lifelong model and inspiration. Although the Bolton-Kern collaboration, which Rodgers saw "at least a half dozen times," possessed neither ragtime nor the "Middle European inflections of Victor Herbert," from Rodgers's perspective it represented the "first truly American theatre music." This was the show that "pointed the way" Rodgers "wanted to be led." Like other Princess shows, *Very Good Eddie* was "intimate and uncluttered and tried to deal in a humorous way with modern, everyday characters," in refreshing contrast to "overblown operettas, mostly imported, that dominated the Broadway scene in the wake of *The Merry Widow* and *The Chocolate Soldier*," the European imports that formed Rodgers's happy childhood memories. In later years Rodgers attributed monumental significance to this early exposure to Kern, Bolton, and, soon, P. G. Wodehouse: "Actually, I was watching and listening to the beginning of a new form of musical theatre in this country. Somehow I knew it and wanted desperately to be a part of it."[6]

Armed with a musical theater ideal, Rodgers was primed for the most crucial event of his adolescence — indeed, of the next twenty-five years. On a historic afternoon, probably in the spring of 1919, Philip Leavitt, a Columbia classmate of Mortimer Rodgers, introduced the aspiring composer to his unusual and brilliant friend Lorenz Hart, a gifted lyricist who shared Rodgers's vision of a new American musical theater. Rodgers was captivated by Hart's artistic theories; by his disdain for most of contemporary musical theater, with its absence of adult subject matter in its stories; and by the contrasting literacy, technical virtuosity, and daring in Hart's then unpublished lyrics. As Rodgers first wrote in his "self interview" of 1939 and repeated in *Musical Stages*, he "left Hart's house having acquired in one afternoon a career, a partner, a best friend, and a source of permanent irritation."[7] At sixteen he had found a collaborator who shared his "conviction that the musical theatre, as demonstrated by the pioneering efforts of Bolton, P. G. Wodehouse

Portrait of the composer as a young man

and Kern, was capable of achieving a far greater degree of artistic merit in every area than was apparent at the time."[8]

Over the next six years Rodgers and Hart gained experience but suffered increasing frustration in a series of one- to three-night stands in social clubs and various school shows. The first show, the Akron Club's *One Minute Please* (1917), had provided the opportunity to stage "Auto Show Girl."[9] The second amateur effort, *Up Stage and Down* (1919), a show put on at the Waldorf-Astoria Hotel Grand Ballroom for the Infants Relief Society, carries an intriguing historical footnote: it marked an early appearance of Oscar Hammerstein 2nd in Rodgers's life, twenty-four years before *Oklahoma!* At the time, Hammerstein, seven years Rodgers's senior, was a Big Man on Campus, a Columbia University thespian and a friend of Richard's brother, Mortimer, who condescended to introduce his little brother to Hammerstein. Hammerstein recalled meeting the twelve-year-old Richard after an earlier Varsity Show matinee of a show that featured both Hammerstein and Hart, the latter playing Mary Pickford "like an electrified gnome."[10] In a touching *New York Times* tribute that appeared shortly before Hammerstein's death, Rodgers also recalled this first meeting, but he disputed Hammerstein's claim that he was wearing short pants.[11]

Those who think of the Rodgers and Hammerstein collaboration as beginning in the early 1940s will be surprised to learn that Hammerstein played a prominent role during Rodgers's early years. In fact, two of the four songs from this period known to have lyrics by Hammerstein were used on repeated occasions (with unaltered lyrics): "Weaknesses" (*Up Stage and Down, Fly with Me,* and *Say It with Jazz*) and "There's Always Room for One More" (*Up Stage and Down, Fly with Me,* and *Jazz à la Carte*). Another early Rodgers and Hammerstein song, "Can It," provided a third Hammerstein lyric in *Up Stage and Down,* and "That Boy of Mine" appeared in the second Akron Club show, *You'd Be Surprised.* In addition to supplying at least one song for six of Rodgers's amateur shows between 1919 and 1922, Hammerstein also served on the committee that selected Rodgers and Hart for the Varsity Show of 1920, *Fly with Me,* and he directed the Columbia University Varsity Show of 1921, *You'll Never Know.* In 1922, Hammerstein became the show doctor and de facto book writer for Rodgers and Hart's unproduced *Winkle Town.* The following year Hammerstein, in collaboration with Vincent Youmans on *Wildflower,* would inaugurate his long reign as one of the dominant lyricists and librettists on Broadway, scoring huge successes in shows like *Rose-Marie* (1924) with music by Rudolf Friml, *Sunny*

(1925) and *Show Boat* (1927) with Kern, and *The Desert Song* (1926) and *The New Moon* (1928) with Sigmund Romberg.

The list of Rodgers's amateur productions (see table 1.1) prompts a number of observations. It is perhaps most important to note that no theatrical venue was too lowly for Rodgers—nothing stood in the way of his desire to see his works performed on a stage. The Columbia Varsity Shows carried a certain amount of prestige, but in fact Rodgers was willing to stage his songs anywhere opportunity knocked. He gave fundraising performances at the Akron Club, the Infants Relief Society, the Evelyn Goldsmith Home for Crippled Children, the Park Avenue Synagogue, the Institute of Musical Art, where Rodgers was enrolled intermittently between 1920–24, and the Benjamin School for Girls, where Dorothy Fields, the sister of Herbert and Joseph and daughter of Lew Fields, was enrolled from 1922–24. Late in life Rodgers said in an interview that "if I were starting out and the Astor Hotel was still in existence, I would be satisfied to have my stuff shown in its men's room. Any place." [12]

The list of family, friends, and budding lyricists associated with these amateur shows reminds us that Rodgers and Hart were not creatively inseparable before their *Garrick Gaieties* breakthrough. Although Rodgers and Hart would work almost exclusively with each other between 1925 and 1942, the "amateur" years from 1919–25 were a period of transition during which Rodgers would set the music of a number of other lyricists—Engelsman, Bender, and Dyrenforth on *One Minute Please* (before meeting Hart); his brother Mortimer and Benjamin Kaye, a theatrical lawyer and family friend, on *Up Stage and Down* (March 1919, either shortly before or after he met Hart); and Hammerstein. Hart contributed no lyrics to *Up Stage and Down* (1919), *Jazz à la Carte* (1922), or *The Prisoner of Zenda* (1924). With the exception of a song here and there, Rodgers composed nearly all the music to the thirteen amateur shows and one play (sharing some composing duties in the Institute of Musical Art shows with Gerald Warburg and Sigmund Krumgold in *Jazz à la Carte* and Krumgold in *A Danish Yankee in King Tut's Court*). Rodgers also served in a variety of other creative roles: librettist for *Temple Belles*; co-librettist for *A Danish Yankee in King Tut's Court*; principal lyricist for *Up Stage and Down*; co-lyricist for *One Minute Please* and *A Danish Yankee*; and co-director (with Herbert Fields) for *Jazz à la Carte*.

Herbert Fields (1897–1958), the son of the prominent producer Lew Fields (1867–1941), would become Rodgers and Hart's principal librettist

Table 1.1. Richard Rodgers's Amateur Shows, 1917–1925

Akron Club
One Minute Please (December 29, 1917)
    Book by Ralph G. Engelsman
    Lyrics by Engelsman and Rodgers (additional lyrics by Milton G. Bender and
        David Dyrenforth)
    Directed by Bender
    Song Published: "Auto Show Girl" (Rodgers and Dyrenforth), David Ewen,
        Richard Rodgers, between pp. 158 and 159

You'd Be Surprised (1920, no specific dates available)
    Book by Milton G. Bender
    Lyrics by Hart and Bender (additional lyrics by Robert A. Simon, Oscar
        Hammerstein 2nd, and Herbert L. Fields)
    Directed by Bender

Say Mama (February 21, 1921)
    Lyrics by Hart
    Directed by H. Fields

Infants Relief Society
Up Stage and Down (March 8, 1919)
    Book by Myron D. Rosenthal
    Lyrics by Rodgers (additional lyrics by Mortimer W. Rodgers, Hammerstein, and
        Benjamin Kaye)
    Directed by Harry A. Goldberg
    Song published: "There's Always Room for One More" (lyrics by Hammerstein)
        [see also *Fly with Me* and *Jazz à la Carte*], *Rodgers and Hammerstein
        Rediscovered* (New York, n.d.)

Columbia University Players (Varsity Show)
Fly with Me (March 24–27, 1920)
    Book by Milton Kroopf and Philip Leavitt (adapted by Hart)
    Lyrics by Hart
    Directed by Ralph Bunker
    Song published: "A College on Broadway" (lyric by Hart), *Rodgers and Hart:
        A Musical Anthology*; "There's Always Room for One More" (lyric by
        Hammerstein) [see also *Up Stage and Down* and *Jazz à la Carte*], *Rodgers
        and Hammerstein Rediscovered* (New York, n.d.)

You'll Never Know (April 20–23, 1921)
    Book by Herman A. Axelrod and Henry William Hanemann
    Lyrics by Hart
    Directed by Hammerstein
    Song published: "When I Go on the Stage" (lyric by Hart), *Rediscovered
        Rodgers and Hart* (Secaucus, N.J., 1992)

Table 1.1. Continued

Institute of Musical Art
Say It with Jazz (June 1–2, 1921)
    Book by Dorothy Crowthers, Frank Hunter, and Maurice Lieberman
    Lyrics by Hart and Hunter (additional lyric by Hammerstein)
    Director not available

Jazz à la Carte (June 2–3, 1922)
    Book by Dorothy Crowthers
    Lyrics by Frank Hunter (additional lyrics by Hammerstein)
    Additional music by Gerald Warburg and Sigmund Krumgold
    Directed by H. Fields and Rodgers
    Song published: "There's Always Room for One More" (lyric by Hammerstein)
      [see also *Up Stage and Down* and *Fly with Me*], *Rodgers and Hammerstein*
      Rediscovered (New York, n.d.)

A Danish Yankee in King Tut's Court (May 31–June 1, 1923)
    Book and lyrics by Dorothy Crowthers, H. Fields, and Rodgers (additional lyrics
      by Hart and Robert A. Simon)
    Additional music by Sigmund Krumgold
    Directed by H. Fields

Benjamin School for Girls
The Chinese Lantern (May 7, 1922)
    Play by Laurence Housman
    Director not available
    Cast included Dorothy Fields

If I Were King (March 25, 1923)
    Lyrics by Hart
    Director not available

The Prisoner of Zenda (March 23, 1924)
    Lyrics by H. Fields
    Directed by H. Fields
    Cast included Dorothy Fields in the title role (wearing a beard)

Park Avenue Synagogue
Temple Belles (March 20, 1924)
    Book by Rodgers
    Lyrics by Hart (additional lyrics by Dorothy Crowthers)
    Directed by H. Fields

Evelyn Goldsmith Home for Crippled Children
Bad Habits of 1925 (February 8, 1925)
    Lyrics by Hart (additional lyrics by Robert A. Simon)
    Directed by Hart and Irving Strouse

between 1925 and 1928 (*Dearest Enemy, The Girl Friend, Peggy-Ann, A Connecticut Yankee, Present Arms*, and *Chee-Chee*, all but *Dearest Enemy* produced by his dad). He also played an early and prominent role during the amateur years, directing or (in the case of *Jazz à la Carte*) co-directing at least five Rodgers and Hart shows between 1921 and 1924, supplying the lyrics to *The Prisoner of Zenda* and choreography to several shows, including *The Garrick Gaieties*. In the title role of *Zenda* (and wearing a beard) was Herbert's sister Dorothy Fields (1905–74), the future lyricist of Kern's *Swing Time* and co-librettist of Berlin's *Annie Get Your Gun* (produced by Rodgers and Hammerstein). Surprisingly, Herbert Fields's sole contribution to book writing in these amateur shows was a minor role in the creation of *A Danish Yankee in King Tut's Court*, a burlesque of *A Connecticut Yankee in King Arthur's Court*. According to Ewen, Fields abandoned his acting aspirations for libretto writing at the suggestion of Rodgers, who was motivated in part by the hope that this switch would lead to opportunities writing shows produced by the old man.[13]

Within a few months of meeting Hart, Rodgers met Lew Fields, someone who would be almost as influential over the next decade as his new lyricist—and, for the next seven years, another source of irritation.[14] Lew Fields began his long career at the age of ten as the taller if not senior partner of the "Dutch" (that is, German-Jewish) dialect act with Joe Weber, also ten. Modern audiences can catch a glimpse of Lew Fields playing himself (without Weber) in the penultimate Fred Astaire and Ginger Rogers film, *The Story of Vernon and Irene Castle* (1939). The influence of Weber and Fields can be seen in the routines of Laurel and Hardy, Abbott and Costello, and Carney and Gleason (tall and thin versus short and fat), the Three Stooges, and Henny Youngman ("Take my wife . . . please!") (a variation on Weber and Fields's "Dat vas no lady, dat vas my wife"). Before their temporary rift in 1903, Weber and Fields had been, for more than a generation, one of the most popular acts on Broadway. Producers vied to be satirized in their burlesques of current plays, a practice popularized a half-century later on television's *Carol Burnett Show* and, since the early 1980s, Broadway's hysterical parodies of shows and stars, *Forbidden Broadway*. Although Weber and Fields would reunite in several comebacks over the years, including one during a vacuum between plays in the early 1920s, by the time Rodgers and Hart met him, Fields had for more than a decade been mainly producing and frequently acting in plays without his former partner. In the late 1920s Rodgers, Hart, and Herbert Fields (and Fields and Youmans in

Herbert Fields, Richard Rodgers, and Lorenz Hart, originally billed as Herbert Richard Lorenz

Lew Fields (1867–1941), the taller half of Weber and Fields, producer of
Rodgers and Hart shows in the 1920s, and father of Joseph, Herbert,
and Dorothy

Hit the Deck) would play major parts in Lew Fields's remarkable comeback
as the producer of *The Girl Friend, Peggy-Ann,* and *A Connecticut Yankee.*

Rodgers's first meeting with Lew Fields in early August 1919, like the
meeting with Hart earlier in the year, was arranged by Leavitt, who happened to be renting a summer cottage next door to Fields (Rodgers remembered that Hart was not present at the meeting, but Leavitt recalled that
he was). Lew was impressed with one Rodgers and Hart song, "Any Old
Place with You." Fields's idea was to interpolate this song in one of his own
shows, *A Lonely Romeo,* which had been running since June 10.[15] *A Lonely
Romeo* was co-authored by Fields (a first) and the prolific Harry B. Smith
(the author of *Little Nemo*); the lyrics were by Harry's brother Robert, and

the score was by Malvin Franklin and Robert Hood Bower. Fields starred in the title role. Herbert Fields, a longtime friend of both Leavitt and Hart, and the future choreographer and principal librettist for Rodgers and Hart for the next nine years, played Lew Fields's son on stage. "Any Old Place with You," purchased outright for a modest fee rather than an advance on a royalty, was scheduled to debut on August 26. But in a sign of the mixed luck (mostly bad) associated with Lew Fields over the next few years, an Actors' Equity strike closed down the thriving play three days before their big moment. By the time the strike was settled one month after it began on August 6, A Lonely Romeo had lost its momentum. It closed on October 10. Although it did well in Boston, Brooklyn, and Philadelphia for several months, Franklin and Bower sued Fields for failing to pay royalties, and the Shuberts were unwilling to take up the financial slack. It is unclear how many Broadway audiences heard "Any Old Place with You" between the aftermath of the strike and the show's move to Boston, but it could hardly have been much more than a third of the eighty-seven performances.

The next year Lew Fields offered his new songwriting team a chance to work on their first professional Broadway show, only a year after Gershwin had launched his first complete Broadway show, La La Lucille, at the age of twenty-one. The new show, Poor Little Ritz Girl, one of the numerous Cinderella shows to follow in the wake of Irene (1919) — Kern's Sally would appear a few months later — was to feature a score by Hart and Rodgers, who would turn seventeen less than a month before its premiere. After they completed their songs, Rodgers took a job as a camp counselor and staff composer at Camp Paradox in Maine (where Hart and Herb Fields had met a few years earlier) and had nothing else to do with the show until he showed up for the opening on July 28. Rodgers describes what happened next: "In the morning I rushed straight to the theatre — and received the bitterest blow of my life. Half of our songs had been cut and replaced by numbers written by the more experienced team of Romberg and Alex Gerber. Not only that; the story had been changed (Lew Fields was now crediting himself as co-author)." After noting that there had been significant casting changes and that a new musical director had been hired, Rodgers laments that "Fields simply obeyed the ancient show-business dictum that is still all too often followed today: If something is wrong, change everything!" Despite Fields's "at best inconsiderate and at worst deceitful" behavior, Rodgers, to his credit, "in fairness" concedes that "most of the changes were improvements."[16]

Rodgers and Hart themselves had replaced another team that Lew Fields had found lacking: Alfred Bryan, the composer of "Who Paid the Rent for Mrs. Rip Van Winkle?" which, according to Broadway historian Gerald Bordman, was a showstopper that stopped *The Honeymoon Express* when sung by Al Jolson in 1913, and George W. Meyer, the lyricist for another Jolson vehicle, "Where Did Robinson Crusoe Go with Friday on Saturday Night?" from *Robinson Crusoe, Jr.* in 1916. Despite favorable local reviews and excellent attendance at the Boston tryout of *Poor Little Ritz Girl*, Fields panicked when he read the following notice: "It is said that both are close friends of Fields' son, Herbert [the original stage manager], and whether 'Daddy' dug down and put on the show to give his son's friends an opportunity and to put Herbert into the producing business in this manner is a question."[17]

Although Rodgers and Hart were devastated by the removal of half their score, audiences and critics responded favorably to the new version. The *New York Post* lauded "an intelligent plot, well worked out," and the *New York World* found the various elements "so dexterously blended that the farce did not interfere with the musical comedy and the musical numbers are never allowed to interfere with the progress of the plot." If Rodgers found any vindication in critic Heywood Broun's conclusion that Romberg's "more serious songs" were "pleasing, but hardly as striking as the lighter numbers" [by Rodgers], he remained silent, although he does quote from Broun's favorable assessment of the show as a whole. Despite a strong box office showing well into October, Fields's landlord, Lee Shubert, closed down the show prematurely after 119 performances to make way for a higher bidder: a film company willing to pay a premium to use the Central Theatre to screen a motion picture.

The next professional opportunity arrived in November 1921, when Fields hired Rodgers, then enrolled at the Institute of Musical Art, to rehearse and conduct local pit orchestras on a vaudeville tour. Upon Rodgers's return in the spring, Rodgers, Hart, and Herbert Fields began work on *Winkle Town*, a show they felt possessed professional potential. Perhaps Rodgers's preoccupation with this work kept him from enrolling at the institute during the 1922–23 academic year. The show, their pride and joy, was about the eventually fruitful efforts of an enterprising protagonist to persuade Winkle Town that an "'electronic' system that obviates the use of electric wires for communication and electric power" would be "both practical and beneficial."[18] One year later, Hammerstein, flush with his first major success with

Wildflower, found enough in the concept and the score to try to solve the daunting libretto problems. In the end these proved insurmountable, and Rodgers was persuaded to abandon *Winkle Town*, although he was encouraged by the producer, Laurence Schwab, to use its excellent songs to audition a new show.[19]

It was Schwab who set up this audition with the powerful and usually prescient music publisher Max Dreyfus, who infamously concluded that Rodgers's music, including "Manhattan," contained "nothing of value." Dreyfus may have also heard four other *Winkle Town* songs that later became part of Rodgers and Hart's early professional successes: "The Three Musketeers" from the *Garrick Gaieties* of 1925; "Old Enough to Love" and "The Hermits" in Rodgers, Hart, and Fields's first book show, *Dearest Enemy*, also in 1925; and "I Want a Man," which would appear in their early London success *Lido Lady* in 1926.[20] Armond and L. Marc Fields offer the irony that family connections may have hindered more than aided the ambitious trio: "When Herbert, Rodgers, and Hart tried to peddle their work [*Winkle Town*], other producers would inevitably ask, 'If you guys are as good as you think you are, how come Mr. Fields isn't interested in producing your show?'"[21]

One year before *The Garrick Gaieties*, Lew Fields offered Rodgers and Hart the third and last professional Broadway opportunity of their amateur years. This time Lew contracted the pair to compose two songs, "Moonlight Mama" and "I'd Like to Poison Ivy," for what would become the short-lived play *Melody Man*. Herbert wrote the book, the story of a classical composer who must endure the transformation of his lofty Dresden Sonata into a cheap Tin Pan Alley tune before regaining his creative liberty when his daughter marries the song's publisher. According to Armond and L. Marc Fields, the show offered timely social commentary and a satire of the world of Tin Pan Alley and received such "generally favorable notices and a large outlay for advertising" that *Variety* was left wondering why it closed after only seven weeks and fifty-six performances.[22] One happy consequence of the show for all concerned was the idea to cast the talented team of Eva Puck and Sam White, who sang both of Rodgers and Hart's *Melody Man* songs, as leads in *The Girl Friend* two years later. In another positive legacy, Rodgers and Hart—with some help from co-librettist George Abbott—would rework the conflict between jazz and classical music in their 1936 hit *On Your Toes*.

"Which Comes First—the Words or the Music?"

Critics, historians, and amateur listeners alike have long appreciated the variety and complex psychological makeup of individual Rodgers and Hart songs. Examples range from the young woman simultaneously wary of and enjoying emerging powerful feelings in "I'd Like to Hide It" (*Dearest Enemy*) and the bittersweet loneliness of another young woman relishing as well as suffering unrequited love in "Glad to Be Unhappy" (*On Your Toes*) to the self-awareness of an older married woman about to embark on an adulterous affair in "Bewitched" (*Pal Joey*). In what may be the first extended article on either Rodgers or Hart, Ted Goldsmith, writing on Hart in *Theatre Magazine* in 1931, took it as a given that "it was the lyrics that first drew popular attention to the two bright young lads," though he concedes in the next sentence that "the success of the lyrics is in no small measure due to the musical background whereupon they glitter so brilliantly."[23] By the end of the decade, an article about Hart without Rodgers or Rodgers without Hart was unthinkable. At least no one thought to write one.

In the words of a *Time* cover story from 1938, "nobody ever fused words and music more effectively than Rodgers & Hart."[24] At first, commentators were struck by the complementary qualities of music and text—see, for example, the following description in *Time*: "When Rodgers's melodic line expresses gaiety, sadness, humor, Hart's lyrical line invariably complements and fulfills it," resulting in "the power of a single musical expression" greater than even Wodehouse and Kern.[25] Later critical responses emphasize the *contrast* between Hart's worldly and sardonic view of the world (for example, "It's Got to Be Love") and occasionally even wicked lyrics ("To Keep My Love Alive"), and Rodgers's jazzy and seemingly straightforward, nonironic musical lines. This has become the reigning view. Few writers in recent decades neglect to observe Rodgers and Hart's harmonious clash of approaches to love and loss.

Before offering a response to the perennial question of "Which comes first—the words or the music?" it might be beneficial to briefly review the form that Rodgers and Hart inherited and, for the most part, embraced. I'm referring to what is widely known as thirty-two-bar song form. By the time Rodgers and Hart launched their professional career in the mid-1920s, a variety of song forms had, over the past decade or so, evolved into a few variations on a single form. The main portion of a song (the chorus or refrain) usually consisted of thirty-two measures organized in four units of eight measures each and arranged in one of the following patterns: A-A-B [the release or bridge]-A ("My Heart Stood Still"), A-B-A-C ("My Romance"), or A-B-A-B ("Thou Swell"). In these and other examples the almost invariably recurring A section contains the most recognizable portion of the tune, the B section forms the main melodic and often harmonic and rhythmic contrast to the A section, and the relatively infrequently used C section serves as a varied climax (but usually recognizably related to A) to conclude the chorus instead of a B, or, more commonly, an A. Although the minor mode and the interweaving of major and minor were options and were occasionally favored by Gershwin and Porter to capture Jewish musical signifiers (for example, the Gershwins' "The Man I Love" and "My One and Only," Porter's "Night and Day" and "My Heart Belongs to Daddy"), major was overwhelmingly the preferred mode.[26] When Rodgers composed a song in the minor, most famously in "My Funny Valentine," the lyrics often suggested and in fact led to an ending in major.[27] In most cases a verse—a musical introduction analogous to recitative in opera and typically a less memorable tuneful link between spoken dialogue and soaring melody—preceded the chorus. In performances outside the shows themselves, especially jazz performances, verses were often viewed as expendable. Recordings of Astaire, who popularized many of these songs for Kern, Berlin, the Gershwins, Porter, and Arthur Schwartz and Howard Dietz, if not Rodgers, typically include the verse, but only after a full statement of the chorus.

Song composers infrequently tampered with phrase lengths, though there are some exceptions—for example, Gershwin's later film songs or "I Got Rhythm," with its slightly extended final phrase, A [8]-A [8]-B[8]-A [10], or the seven-measure A sections in Rodgers's "Better Be Good to Me" from *Chee-Chee*. When they do adjust phrase lengths, these departures rarely alter the familiar four-phrase pattern that songwriters (and musical dramatists) found satisfying for forty or more years. Again, with some exceptions— or, in the case of Rodgers and Hammerstein, altered musical surroundings (for example, portions of sung dialogue or extended or returning verses) —the thirty-two-bar song form, or modest variants, would serve Rodgers throughout his career. In reference to his Hart songs, Rodgers expressed acceptance of this "traditional form of song construction at the time": "Though occasionally I did play around with the formula—'Manhattan,' for example, has no release, or 'B' theme, at all—Larry and I never felt restricted but rather enjoyed the challenge of coming up with something fresh within the prescribed regulations."[28]

Perhaps the most famous formal exception among Rodgers and Hart songs is "A Ship Without a Sail" from *Heads Up!* In *Musical Stages* Rodgers describes the form and sense of fun he found in this modest departure from a usually welcome formal straightjacket: "For this ballad I divided the refrain into twelve-, eight- and twelve-bar sections, thereby achieving a mild break-through with an 'ABA' form. It was still thirty-two bars, of course, and I don't suppose many people noticed it, but I enjoyed getting away even slightly from the accepted strictures of songwriting. When I first played the melody for Larry, he said it sounded like a barcarole. Since the show had a nautical setting, the idea of comparing one's lovesick emotions to a ship without a sail was a particularly felicitous notion and Larry developed it into one of his most beautifully crafted lyrics."[29]

What Rodgers does not mention is less easy to describe than a formal departure but probably more significant. If we assume that a title preceded the composition of this song, Rodgers captured the idea of being "all alone, all at sea!" by avoiding a clear tonic triad until the last possible moment (the end of the first phrase twelve measures later). The absence of a tonal ground-ing succeeds as a musical metaphor for the idea of a ship without a sail and is viscerally more powerful than the unusual twelve-bar phrases. Of course, the eventual appearance of the clear tonic provides a touch of irony, since the punch line "like a ship without a sail" is associated with the first sign of tonal stability in the song. But by then the point has been made. The lyrical depiction of loneliness and the absence of tonal mooring went on as long as formally possible (four measures longer than expected), and it would be un-grateful to reject the need for a musical sail to guide the end of this phrase toward a musical harbor.

Rodgers himself offers evolving responses on the perennial question of which comes first. This is what he said in the "self interview" published in 1939:

Actually, there is no set procedure whatsoever. My favorite blight and part-ner, Mr. Lorenz Hart, often hands me a completed lyric to be set to music. More often I have a tune ready for him to work on, the tune being what it is because it seems to fit a given situation in a musical play and not because the composer was the victim of a rush of hot inspiration, brought on by a beautiful girl or a breath-taking sunset. (I guess you can see I'm pretty sen-sitive about inspiration.) Sometimes we sit in a room and hate each other until we get a title: then I throw Larry out of the house and fool around until

I get a satisfactory melody, inspired entirely by the title and not by nostalgia for Venice in the spring.[30]

Rodgers's self interview, the first in a series of many articles and reviews over the next four decades, appeared at a time when he was increasingly faced with an absent partner. The same year the article appeared, necessity prompted Rodgers to write the lyrics for "Heroes in the Fall," the opening number of *Too Many Girls*, without his "favorite blight and partner." The team would complete only three more new musicals, *Higher and Higher*, *Pal Joey*, and *By Jupiter*, and several new songs for the *Connecticut Yankee* revival.

By the time he got around to writing *Musical Stages*, Rodgers had modified the ratio of "lyrics first" from "often" to a qualified "seldom," but the importance of a title and a dramatic situation rather than an amorphous inspiration would remain key components in the creation of a song:

> One of the questions I'm most frequently asked is about our working method. This cannot be answered simply, because there were many methods. Larry seldom gave me a completed lyric; at best it would be no more than a verse or opening chorus [the latter is what Rodgers wrote for *Too Many Girls* when Hart was indisposed and unavailable]. Occasionally he would give me a title that would suggest a melody. Most of the time I would play a completed melody for him and we'd sit around tossing titles and lyric ideas at each other. Once we agreed on the general theme, Larry would write the words and we'd have a finished song.[31]

In an interview published in 1925, Hart reveals something about his methods.

> If I am trying to write a melodic song hit I let my composer, Richard Rodgers in this instance, get his tune first. Then I take the most distinctive melodic phrase in his tune and work on that. What I choose is not necessarily the theme or first line, but the phrase that stands out. Next I try to find the meaning of that phrase and to develop a euphonic set of words to fit it. For example, in one of my songs just published the first line runs like this: "Here in my arms it's adorable." The distinct melodic phrase came on the word "adorable," and the word "adorable" is the first word that occurred to me, so I used it as my pivotal musical idea. And as the melodic phrase recurs often in the chorus it determined my rhyme scheme [for example, "adorable/deplorable," "kissable/permissable," and "affable/laughable"]. Of

course, in a song of this sort, the melody and the euphonics of the words themselves are really more important than the sense."[32]

Since no source convincingly documents a single specific instance in which a Hart lyric (other than a verse) preceded a Rodgers melody, the assumption will remain that the creation of a Rodgers and Hart song, like nearly all of the songs by Kern and Hammerstein and the Gershwins, began with the music. Such a conclusion needs further refinement, however, since on many occasions a title, whether offered by Rodgers or Hart, is known to have preceded the words (exhibit A: "My Heart Stood Still"). Since titles typically appear in prominent places within a song, such as the opening or closing, the presence of a title also means that, at least in one important sense, the lyrics do in fact come first.

Finding a Musical Voice

Of the more than one hundred songs Rodgers and Hart composed during their amateur years, few would be recycled in their professional shows, either before or after *The Garrick Gaieties*. Exceptions include four *Poor Little Ritz Girl* songs, previously introduced in amateur shows and now outfitted with new lyrics. "Don't Love Me Like Othello" from *You'd Be Surprised* was transformed into the Freudian-inspired "You Can't Fool Your Dreams," and three songs from *Fly with Me*, "Dreaming True," "Inspiration," and "Peek in Pekin," metamorphosed, respectively, into "Love Will Call," "All You Need to Be a Star," and "Love's Intense in Tents." Also recycled in *Ritz Girl* was "Mary, Queen of Scots," introduced in *You'd Be Surprised* with a rare lyric by Herbert Fields. Interestingly, in nearly every case the retooled amateur songs rather than the songs conceived for *Ritz Girl* were the ones that survived the cut after Fields added Romberg and Gerber's score. On the other hand, although Robert Kimball's figure of "more than half" is somewhat exaggerated, five songs from the unproduced *Winkle Town* did reappear in the early professional productions, most spectacularly "Manhattan," but also several other songs that Rodgers had composed by the time of his audition with Max Dreyfus.

The fate of nearly all the songs that Rodgers and Hart composed before 1925, professional and amateur, was sealed by their relative absence from the published anthologies that followed in the decades after Hart's and later Rodgers's death. In fact, as of this writing only four amateur songs are readily accessible—two Hart songs from *Fly with Me*, "A College on Broadway" and "Peek in Pekin" (with its later title and lyric, "Love's Intense in Tents"); "There's Always Room for One More" with lyrics by Hammerstein from the same Columbia University Varsity Show in 1920; and "When I Go on the Stage," a Hart lyric from *You'll Never Know* in 1922, another Columbia show.

As his first professional song, "Any Old Place with You" carried special meaning for Rodgers. Although he conceded that the song "will seem pretty sophomoric," he quipped that "perhaps this can be excused on the grounds that I wasn't to be a sophomore for another three years." In addition, Rodgers chose to include it as the opening song in *The Rodgers and Hart Song Book* published in 1951.[33] The lyric, perhaps a slight caricature of Hart's pyrotechnics in the 1920s, in this case is a series of clever rhymes based on places where the song's protagonist intends to romance his girl—Portugal and "court you, gal" and "I'll go to hell for ya / or Philadelphia." The music of the seventeen-year-old Rodgers is melodically and rhythmically repetitive (half of its sixteen bars contain the same melodic and rhythmic figure), and harmonically competent but unadventurous (mostly C major triads).[34] Three years before "Manhattan" Rodgers is producing somewhat impersonal work analogous to Gershwin's first published song in 1916 at about the same age, "When You Want 'Em, You Can't Get 'Em, When You've Got 'Em, You Don't Want 'Em," but with a more romantic theme and a shorter title.

Poor Little Ritz Girl contained "Love's Intense in Tents" (as we have noted, with the same music as "Peek in Pekin" from *Fly with Me*), which joins long since discovered songs such as "Thou Swell," "There's a Small Hotel," and "Any Old Place with You" in the anthology *Rediscovered Rodgers and Hart*.[35] The chorus of this early professional song, like that of "Any Old Place with You," with only sixteen measures, exudes the simple grace that evokes Kern's Princess songs. Its verse displays an imaginative increase in harmonic intensity (Gb major in the key of D) on the words "rents increase," and when the melody returns to D major four measures later, the harmony refuses to comply until the chorus begins four measures later. The verse and chorus also contain some subtle intervallic connections (for example, the prolonged fifth, D to A, on the word "camping" that also introduces the chorus). It might also be noted that the lyric, with one lonely internal rhyme "Not a cent of rent in our tent," contains an infelicitous Hart rhyme, the imperfect "paradise" and "skies," an imperfection that would become

Example 1.1. Four Early Songs (a) "Auto Show Girl" (chorus, first 4 measures) (b) "Any Old Place with You" (chorus, first 2 measures) (c) "Love's Intense in Tents" (verse, first 2 measures) (d) "Manhattan" (chorus, first 3 measures)

increasingly rare in future years. As shown in example 1.1b and 1.1c, both "Any Old Place with You" and "Love's Intense in Tents" open their choruses and verse, respectively, with an oscillation between a primary note of a triad and a half step below followed by leaps, an idea also used in "Auto Show Girl" (see example 1.1a).[36]

The ascending note varies, ranging from a minor third ("Loves's Intense"), a fourth ("Any Old Place with You"), and a fifth ("Auto Show Girl"). Rodgers would transform this simple idea into gold in "Manhattan" (example 1.1d), which again begins with the same oscillation on the fifth before ascending to a major third. This time Rodgers harmonizes his melody with a striking and imaginative diminished seventh on the tonic (F-G#-B-D).[37]

Although the songs mentioned so far, including "Manhattan," were then unknown and virtually unheard, Rodgers had, by the age of twenty, unknowingly composed his first hit, "Manhattan." Two other songs, "Old Enough to Love" and "The Hermits," would enhance *Dearest Enemy*, Rodgers and Hart's first professionally staged musical comedy, three years later. The presence of one bona fide hit composed at the age of twenty (or perhaps twenty-one) and heard to great acclaim before one's twenty-third birthday compares well with the career trajectories of Kern, Berlin, Gershwin, and Porter. All four songwriters spent a valuable hazing period interpolating songs in shows composed by others. This was Kern's central professional activity before he got the opportunity to compose a show of his own, *The Red Petticoat* in 1912. Although Kern had largely graduated from revues by 1920, during the time of Rodgers's long apprenticeship in amateur shows, Berlin, Gershwin, and Porter were busy composing music for Broadway revues. By the time Rodgers and Hart succeeded with *The Garrick Gaieties*, only Kern was regularly composing complete scores for musical comedies.

Our quintet of songwriters also shares the phenomenon of the breakthrough song. In each case, after years of composing dozens, even scores, of songs, one particular song connected with the public and rocketed these songwriters to instant and prolonged fame. For Berlin, the song was "Alexander's Ragtime Band" (no. 60 in Charles Hamm's collected edition of Berlin's first 190 songs), published in 1911, when Berlin was twenty-one.[38] Berlin's next major hit, "When I Lost You," appeared about a year (or sixty-seven songs) later, but only a handful of Berlin's first 190 songs became perennials in Berlin songbooks and movie retrospectives and calvacades.[39] After Berlin's "Alexander's Ragtime Band" and "When I Lost You" came Kern's "They Didn't Believe Me" in *The Girl from Utah* (1914). By then, Kern had reached the relatively advanced age of twenty-nine. Gershwin was twenty-one when "Swanee," enthusiastically promoted by the superstar Jolson, became a hit in *Sinbad* (1919). After entertaining his sophisticated friends for years, Porter was a late blooming thirty-seven when his first major sensation, "Let's Do It," appeared in the musical revue *Paris* in 1928. In most cases future hits would closely follow the breakthrough song. After the debut of "Manhattan" in 1925, a Rodgers hit would emerge almost without fail at the rate of one to six songs in nearly every show, at least until "The Sweetest Sounds" and the title song in *No Strings* in 1962.

Before the 1920s, Kern was already well established, but Berlin, Porter, Gershwin, and Rodgers and Hart had managed to get at least some of their work on Broadway. Berlin composed *Watch Your Step* (1914) and the *Ziegfeld Follies of 1919*, and Gershwin received an early opportunity to compose a book musical with *La, La, Lucille* in 1919. Porter suffered a short-lived professional production of a musical in 1916, *See America First* (fifteen performances), before embarking on a twelve-year European sojourn. As noted earlier, Rodgers, the youngest member of this coterie, got early breaks from Lew Fields. Only Kern was associated with a truly successful book musical in the early 1920s: *Sally* (1920). Before *Lady, Be Good!* in 1924 and *The Cocoanuts* in 1925, Gershwin and Berlin focused exclusively on the revue format.

Having composed the music for two successive Varsity Shows, Rodgers had, by April 1921, accomplished his central purpose at Columbia. In fact, it is unlikely that Rodgers took part in any academic activities this second year, since by spring of 1921 he was completing his first year at the Institute of Musical Art (renamed the Juilliard School of Music in 1946). Biographers from Stanley Green to Meryle Secrest note that the first of Rodgers's three institute shows, *Say It with Jazz*, was performed in June, but they invariably and incorrectly assign his matriculation to the spring of 1921 rather than the fall of 1920.[40] *Jazz à la Carte* and *A Danish Yankee in King Tut's Court* (two performances each) would follow over the next two springs. *Say It with Jazz* was a parody of Rimsky-Korsakov's opera *The Golden Cockerel*; it addressed the artistic conflicts between jazz and classical music, a theme that would reappear in *The Melody Man* and in his ballet parody of Rimsky-Korsakov's *Scheherazade* (a ballet Rodgers recalled hearing on Hart's phonograph) in *On Your Toes*. The third institute show presented a prototype of another dramatic subject that would be adapted into a successful musical based on Twain's *Connecticut Yankee in King Arthur's Court* six years later.

Although he did not graduate from the institute with either a degree or a certificate, Rodgers, who majored in theory and secondary piano, seriously pursued his musical education. Here is a summary of the classes he took:

> *1920–21, October 11–May 31*
> Secondary piano (Mr. Conrad C. Held)
> Theory (Mr. A. Mandeley Richardson, Mr. George A. Wedge)
> Ear-training (Mr. Wedge, Miss Helen W. Whiley)
> *1921–22, October 10–January 4*
> ["withdrawn on account of leaving New York for several months to direct a musical enterprise"]
> Secondary piano (Mr. Held)
> Theory (Mr. Wedge)
> Ear-training (Mr. Wedge)
> Lectures (Mr. William J. Henderson)
> *1922–23*
> Not enrolled

1923–24, *October 11–May 30*
    Secondary Piano (Miss Edna Fearn)
    Theory (Mr. Percy Goetschius)
    Ear-training (Mr. Wedge, Mr. Franklin W. Robinson)

A high point of Rodgers's study at the institute was the opportunity to enroll in Percy Goetschius's special class in harmony his last year there — a class limited to five students. Goetschius, a fixture at the institute since 1905, would retire at the end of the following year. He wrote numerous books on music theory, including multiple editions of *The Theory and Practice of Tone-Relations: An Elementary Course of Harmony with Emphasis upon the Element of Melody* (seventeen editions between 1892 and 1917) and *Exercises in Melody-Writing* (nine editions between 1900 and 1923) and was arguably the most influential pedagogue of his era.[41] Although Nicholas Slonimsky in *Baker's Biographical Dictionary of Musicians* characterizes Goetschius as a "fossilized" German theorist who "stood in horror before any vestige of unresolved dissonances," Rodgers found his teaching and advice fascinating and useful.

Goetschius's texts are filled with homilies and rules on how to construct pleasing melodies, suggestions on how to harmonize these melodies, and the principles of modulation and the creation of larger forms. A look at one representative passage from *The Theory and Practice of Tone-Relations*, "completely re-written and slightly enlarged" several years before he taught Rodgers, provides a glimpse of what Rodgers may have picked up in Goetschius's class.[42] The chapter on melody immediately makes several important points (all in paragraph 41 followed by Ex. 25): 1) that the "quality" of a melody "depends upon the *choice* of the tone, and their *rhythm* or time-values"; 2) that unlike those of harmony, melodic principles are "far more vague"; 3) that, again, in contrast to harmony, the laws of melody "can hardly be reduced to a system, but must be left largely to the individual talent, native sagacity, or acquired skill of the composer."[43] In the next paragraph Goetschius steps where angels fear to tread and offers a cardinal rule of good melody:

RULE I. The general requirements of *good* melody are: *a.* smooth and natural undulation (to the exclusion of awkward interval-successions); *b.* rhythmic variety; *c.* definite and symmetrical delineation — including frequent confirmation of the melodic figures, either upon the *same* steps (as direct

Example 1.2. Percy Goetschius on Good and Bad Melody (1) "An example of bad melody" (2) "A good melody" [Beethoven's "Ode to Joy"]

repetition), or upon other, *higher or lower steps* (as sequence—par. 128 *b*). For illustration:
  *1) An example of bad melody, in which all the above-named requirements are wanting.
  *2) A good melody, fulfilling all the given conditions.

In *Musical Stages*, Rodgers fondly remembers his classes in music theory, harmony, and ear training, and the mesmerizing lectures on Beethoven delivered by Henry Krehbiel, the eminent critic of the *New York Tribune*.[44] He also acknowledges that, throughout his study at the institute, faculty and fellow students alike displayed support and respect for the kind of music Rodgers wanted to compose. Shortly before Rodgers enrolled, Roy Webb, a Columbia Varsity songwriter, gave him some informal instruction on conducting, and guidance on how to prepare his own piano-vocal scores.[45] The anthologized songs, especially the verse of "Peek in Pekin"/ "Love's Intense in Tents," attest to Rodgers's competence and occasional harmonic daring by the time he began his formal musical studies.[46] Rodgers remains somewhat uninformative about what he actually learned, but it seems, both from what he recalled in *Musical Stages* and from the melodic language of his songs soon after he left, that Rodgers's time at the institute may have helped him learn how tones behave in a musical line ("musical magnetics"), for example, that the "fourth step of the scale was pulled down to the third, and that the seventh was pulled up to the eighth" (RULE II).[47]

Rodgers specifically mentions that he learned from Goetschius why it was a good idea to avoid "ending a phrase with a straight-out tonic chord"— that is, a chord in which the root, third, and fifth appear in stacked thirds. Unfortunately, this is the only example Rodgers gives of the kind of obvious devices Goetschius referred to as "pigs," easy and predictable solutions that should be avoided at all costs. One is tempted to conclude that Rodgers's subsequent predilection for surprise notes at the end of his musical phrases somehow can be traced to Goetschius's advice. In any event, the advice matched the predilection, and until the end of his life such surprises became a prominent, even ubiquitous, feature of Rodgers's melodies.

The Rodgers literature so far has been silent on which of Goetschius's many texts, if any, Rodgers actually used in his harmony class. Rodgers himself offers only the few recollections noted here. Perhaps it would be prudent to refrain from making too much of Rodgers's study at the institute. After all, Rodgers arrived with several years of experience and acquired competence and might have found other ways to cultivate his melodic (and harmonic) muse had he not enrolled. It is instructive to compare Goetschius's anonymous "bad melody" with the beginning of Beethoven's "Ode to Joy." The bad melody exhibits unnatural and awkward intervals, and an absence of rhythmic variety, while Beethoven's melody fulfills Goetschius's conditions to the letter. The melodic parallels between many of Rodgers's compositions and Beethoven's even allow one to imagine that under different circumstances Rodgers might have composed something like "Ode to Joy" and Beethoven could have composed a melody not unlike "My Heart Stood Still" (see example 1.2). In any event, Goetschius's classical principles applied more to the musical language of Kern, Gershwin, and Rodgers than to future American modernists. Charles Hamm in *Yesterdays* notes a number of salient features that the popular music of the era shared with its classical predecessors from whom Goetschius derived his rules.[48]

Although it is difficult to establish a direct link between Goetschius's rules and the melodies of his famous pupil, the fact remains that several of Rodgers's most distinguishing melodic characteristics are both similar to and compatible with Goetschius's principles of melody as well as nineteenth-century harmonic language from Beethoven to Brahms and Rachmaninoff. But attempts to generalize about Rodgers's melodic and harmonic language falter in the face of his versatility. In his classic study *American Popular Song* Alec Wilder offers the following observations of Rodgers's style circa 1933:

> Up to this point in Rodgers's career, twelve years, he has written many fine songs. And, during this time, certain characteristics of style have emerged: great facility in step-wise writing, the adroit use of successive fourths, opulent but unobtrusive harmonic progression, special talent for writing verses (which are almost always in the musical character of the chorus), a great gift for writing waltzes, a preference for the A-A-B-A form. Yet were I to choose from among the songs written up to this point, let's say "Mimi," "Manhattan," "Lover," and "A Ship Without a Sail," would I find within them sufficient stylistic qualities to be able to identify them as Rodgers's songs? Even

Example 1.3. "Blue Room" (chorus, first 8 measures)

though I like and highly respect every one of them, if I didn't already know that they were his songs, I doubt I could tell it from the content.

    This conclusion in no way affects my estimation of the songs. What it does do, on the other hand, is make me less concerned with recognizability and accept the multi-faceted nature of Rodgers's writing, and thus search only for manifestations of good taste, musicality, inventiveness, wit, and sophistication.[49]

One point of agreement among those who know Rodgers's songs centers on his proclivity for stepwise and scalar melodies. Gerald Mast offers a list that ranges from the verse of "Manhattan" and the chorus of "Mountain Greenery" in his first song hits with Hart to his "hymn to the musical scale itself, 'Do Re Mi,'" in his final musical with Hammerstein.[50] The Rodgers and Hart song "I Like to Recognize the Tune" shifts easily between scales during the first half of each A section and during an answering sequence of fourths in the second. Rodgers also frequently imbeds the scale within a melodic line—for example, in "Blue Room" (see example 1.3), where an ascending scale from F to D in the first six measures of the chorus (one note added in each measure) alternates with the wedge note C (invariably preceded by an upper D) that serves as a resting point for the rhymes "blue," "new," and "two" in the first A section (and in later A sections "ball," "small," and "hall," and "you sew," "trousseau," and "Robinson Crusoe").[51]

    The B section of "Blue Room" offers a more extended scale, from E up to F, a ninth above. In addition to exploiting the possibilities of scales, the other central aspect of Rodgers's melodic language as a songwriter is his ability to offer unexpected notes that take the idea of avoiding the pig at the ends of phrases to a new creative level. As Wilder writes, "Rodgers achieved his amazing innovations without resorting to more than an unexpected note

Example 1.4. "Dancing on the Ceiling" (chorus, first 8 measures)

here and there, completely startling at first hearing, and ever after a part of one's musical memory."[52]

These two features, ubiquitous scales and surprise notes, can be found in a number of Rodgers songs. The familiar "Dancing on the Ceiling" will stand for many (see example 1.4).

The song begins with a scale that ascends from C to A before descending to D. Then, instead of continuing downward one note further to C, Rodgers has the tune *leap* a seventh to the upper C. The next note descends one step to a non-chord tone, B-natural, which is supported by an unexpected harmony in the key of F (E minor).

Only rarely does a melodic "surprise" border on a cliché, but in these cases Rodgers himself can claim a large share of ownership. One frequent Rodgers melodic figure might be called the "Rodgers leap," a sudden leap to the third of the tonic chord, a personal marker that appears with striking regularity after 1930, usually toward the end of a chorus. Example 1.5a–c offers three examples of this feature. In "Falling in Love with Love" Rodgers leaps to the third of the tonic on the word "fool," in "Ev'rything I've Got" on the word "do," and in "If I Loved You" on the word "know."

Even this brief melodic description should be enough to suggest that it is virtually impossible—and probably undesirable, if harmony were not so formidable to discuss in prose—to separate Rodgers's surprising melodic turns from his endless *harmonic* surprises. Nearly every song offers evidence of this inextricable bond. For example, at the ends of phrases in "Bewitched" he combines unexpected harmonies with anticipated melody notes (or conversely, expected harmonies and unanticipated melody notes).[53] The twelve-measure metaphoric delay of the tonic triad in "A Ship Without a Sail" has already been noted. In "I Didn't Know What Time It Was" Rodgers

Example 1.5. The "Rodgers Leap" (a) "Falling in Love with Love" (chorus, mm. 9–16) (b) "Ev'rything I've Got" (chorus, mm. 8–12) (c) "If I Loved You" (chorus, mm. 29–32)

takes Hart's metaphor of a character unaware of the time and does not allow her a harmonic resolution of G major until the end of the song (on the words "wise" and "now"). Coming on the unexpected note A, the diminished seventh on the words "loved you" in Rodgers's setting of Hammerstein's title "If I Loved You" has the power to surprise, bewitch, and even chill us, no matter how often we hear it.

One song set to words by Hart, "My Heart Stood Still," was one of *Variety*'s Golden 100 Tin Pan Alley Songs between 1918 and 1935, and thus one of the most popular songs of its era (see example 1.6).[54] "My Heart Stood Still" loomed large in the success of Rodgers and Hart's London revue *One Dam Thing After Another* and later that season in their New York musical comedy *A Connecticut Yankee*, the longest running Rodgers and Hart show of the 1920s. Not only does "My Heart Stood Still" demonstrate both direct and disguised scales and some melodic and harmonic surprises, the music also serves the text and the dramatic situation of a young couple recalling their overpowering feelings of love at first sight. Incidentally, the expression "my heart stood still" was not a phrase invented on the spot when Rita Kempner, a friend of Hart's, expressed relief that their taxi narrowly missed being hit by another taxi in Paris.[55] Documented use of the expression can be found as early as 1915 in D. H. Lawrence's *Women in Love* and Wodehouse's 1919 novel *A Damsel in Distress*.

The answer to the question "Which came first?" is complicated here and in numerous other instances by the fact that the *title* probably preceded the first musical ideas, as well as the other words in the lyric. It has already been suggested that because titles can comprise some of the words, often the key words, of a song, we should not take the music first (Hart) versus lyrics first (Hammerstein) dichotomy too literally. In "My Heart Stood Still" variations on the title phrase occur three times, once in each A section of the A-A-B-A chorus ("And then my heart stood still," in future A sections altered to "And yet my heart stood still" and "when my heart stood still"), roughly half of the words allotted to these sections. In each case, Rodgers's decision to end the phrase on long held notes on the word "still" simply and effectively captures the idea of stillness. The rest was up to Hart. Somewhat defensively, Hart explained in an interview that he wasn't interested in exploiting every available rhyming opportunity. On this occasion he followed "I *took* one *look* at you" with "That's all I meant to do" rather than with "I threw the *book* at you."[56]

Hart also captures the directness and simplicity of the emotion with a preponderance of monosyllables. In the release (the B section) Hart restrained himself from matching "tell" and "well" on the second accented A-flat and offered the word "clasp" instead (though preceded by the subtle "el" sound in the word "un*felt*"). Hart nevertheless could not resist rhyming "took" and "look" in the opening line and eventually gets around to the word "well" in the B section. He also exhibits characteristic sensitivity to declamation throughout, by matching the most important words to Rodgers's half notes: "look" and "meant" in the first A section and "step" and "move" in the second. In the final A section, Hart matches Rodgers's thrilling climactic apex note on D with the word "thrill" within a climactic internal rhyme "Un*til* the *thrill* of that moment when my heart stood *still*." The musical thrill on the word "thrill" is no doubt due in large part to its role as the most prominent high note. But the surprising and culminating harmonic move to a welcome subdominant chord (the IV chord) is equally dramatic, especially

Example 1.6. "My Heart Stood Still" (chorus, complete)

after all the prominent G minor seventh chords (ii7 chords) in the A sections ("look," "meant," "heart" [two times], "step," "move," and "lived") and the four harmonizations of the melodic note A-flat in the B section (F minor, C augmented, F minor sixth, and a C seventh with an augmented fifth on measures 17, 19, 21, and 23, respectively).

The scales of "My Heart Stood Still" are both hidden and overt. In the A sections, the microcosm of successive three-note descending patterns appears within a larger ascending scalar context that moves from F-G-A-Bb-C in the first two A sections, one note below the culminating D ("thrill"); in the final A section Rodgers breaks up the ascending scale after F-G-A and goes directly to the thrilling D on the subdominant, following the climactic D with the longest descent of the song (six notes), which moves down anticlimactically to the F that started it all. The direct ascending scale in the B section also moves from F to D, but with some surprises. Although Rodgers moves to the minor mode when he replaces the A-natural with an A-flat, he substitutes a D-natural on the word "was" and the following syllable "spo-" for the now expected D-flat, anticipating the melodic apex of the tune. Although in the end unrealized, the ascent and descent of four successive whole notes (Ab-Bb-C-D), suggest the *possibility* of a six-note whole-tone scale starting on A-flat, a scale popularized by Debussy but unusual in a Broadway song in 1927 (or later).[57]

The Songwriter as Musical Dramatist

The idea that Rodgers and Hart were dramatists and not merely songwriters appears as early as the first critical writings on Rodgers and Hart that go beyond brief newspaper critiques. Most conspicuous of these articles are a *Time* magazine cover story and Margaret Harriman's two-part profile in the *New Yorker*, both published in 1938.[58] In Rodgers's first important published essay—virtually the last for more than a decade—the "self interview" of 1939, the composer tellingly writes that he composed "scores and not isolated song numbers; therefore the particular song in question must bear a family resemblance to the other musical material in the piece."[59] Harriman, dismissing such innovative 1920s shows as *Dearest Enemy*, *Peggy-Ann*, *A Connecticut Yankee*, and *Chee-Chee*, most likely draws on interviews with her subject when she espouses the view that commercial restrictions were the main obstacles to Rodgers and Hart achieving their ideals before the late 1930s: that "a musical comedy should be as well constructed as a straight drama" and that songs should be "centerd [*sic*] around a situation in the plot."

According to Harriman and prominent critics like Brooks Atkinson of the *New York Times*, who represent prevailing critical assumptions, unfortunately still rarely challenged, the history of modern American musical comedy starts with Kern, Bolton, and Wodehouse in the 1910s, moves on to an ever-improving Rodgers and Hart in the 1920s and 1930s, and attains perfection with Rodgers and Hammerstein in the 1940s. Clearly this widespread historical interpretation retrospectively and unfairly diminishes the achievements of Rodgers and Hart. For Harriman, *Dearest Enemy* and *A Connecticut Yankee* appear in the same category as *The Girl Friend* and *Spring Is Here*, 1920s musicals whose principal function was to pave the way for 1930s shows like *On Your Toes*, which "came nearer to a reasonable combination of plot and song." Unaware of the Rodgers and Hammerstein revolution to follow shortly, Harriman suggests that with Rodgers and Hart's *Babes in Arms*, their first show in which "every number was a 'plot' number, including the hit song, 'The Lady Is a Tramp,'" Rodgers had already realized his vision.

Rodgers's letters to his future wife, Dorothy, reveal that the balance between art and commerce may have uncharacteristically tipped in the former direction during the creation of *Chee-Chee* in 1928. During the Philadelphia tryouts Rodgers wrote with pride that "no matter what happens to us commercially we've accomplished what we've been after for years" (September 7) and offered the opinion that his innovative show was "the best musical thing I've ever seen" (September 12). Years later in *Musical Stages* Rodgers offers a glimpse of why he felt that way at the time:

> From a strictly creative standpoint it offered the challenge of introducing an entirely new concept within the framework of musical theatre. Larry and I had long been firm believers in the close unity of song and story, but we were not always in a position to put our theories into practice. *Chee-Chee* gave us that chance. To avoid the eternal problem of the story coming to a halt as the songs take over, we decided to use a number of short pieces of from four to sixteen bars each, with no more than six songs of traditional form and length in the entire score. In this way the music would be an essential part of the structure of the story rather than an appendage to the action. The concept was so unusual, in fact, that we even called attention to it with the following notice in the program: "NOTE: The musical numbers, some of them very short, are so interwoven with the story that it would be confusing for the audiences to peruse a complete list."[60]

Had *Chee-Chee* been received more kindly in the marketplace, especially one not soon to be threatened by a Depression economy, Rodgers and
Hart might have been able to further cultivate and develop their vision of a
well-constructed, innovative musical comedy filled with plot songs. In any
event, *Chee-Chee* was followed by both artistic retrenchment and financial
setbacks that affected Rodgers and Hart and virtually everyone connected
with Broadway. Further realization of the vision would have to wait until
their return from Hollywood seven years later (see Chapter 3).

Rodgers's remarks help dispel the impression that the 1920s constituted a
primitive dramatic phase. In fact, Rodgers and Hart's attempt to create shows
that made dramatic sense and sold tickets was evident from the beginning.
Especially in comparison to their contemporaries, Rodgers and Hart's shows
readily met prevailing dramatic standards. Atkinson, who would review (generally favorably) nearly every Rodgers show until he retired from the *New
York Times* in 1960, concluded his review of *The Girl Friend* (1926)—a show
remembered more for its trendiness than for its innovations—with a short
but crucial list of a successful show's attributes: "Puck [Eva Puck, starring as
the "girl friend"], a first-rate chorus, diverting songs and a collection of generally capable principals is what the theatergoer may expect to find among
the assets of *The Girl Friend*."[61] For Atkinson and presumably his *Times*
readers, these qualities, which did not include more than a serviceable plot,
was nevertheless sufficient—"more than enough, the musical comedy situation being what it is." In the 1920s, "enough" consisted of plausible, coher-
ent, and well-crafted plots, including the bizarre but delightful dreams in
Peggy-Ann. The chief requirement, however, was a series of opportunities to
feature songs, dances, and stars, which, unlike the librettos (at least before
the Princess shows), had to sparkle memorably for a show to succeed. In the
context of all these virtues, a merely serviceable plot could be viewed as a
noteworthy fringe benefit.

It may come as a surprise then that a critical mass of reviews in the New
York dailies suggest that critics, who had praised the freshness and originality
of Rodgers and Hart's *songs*—from *Poor Little Ritz Girl* (1920) to *By Jupiter*
(1942)—managed to find positive things to say about the "richly colored design of the plot" as well, as early as *Dearest Enemy*.[62] Since critics and audiences were aware but more benignly tolerant of weak books and plots than
future critics and audiences, it is significant that the plots of Rodgers and
Hart shows were regularly praised in their day. Reviewer after reviewer expressed delight with the captivating freshness of *Peggy-Ann*, and Atkinson

complimented Herbert Fields's libretto for its "frequent flights of imagination." Contemporary critics and most musical theater historians share the
view that Rodgers became less artistically ambitious after *Chee-Chee*'s devastatingly brief thirty-one-performance run and that a musical like *Spring
Is Here* (1929) reflects some creative backtracking. Nevertheless, a writer as
sensitive to innovation as Ethan Mordden can describe *Heads Up!*, also from
1929 and known today almost exclusively as the source of "A Ship Without a
Sail," as a show in which "the inventions simply tumble over themselves."[63]
Although conventional plots were tolerated, innovation combined with the
integrated plot narratives of the best contemporary American plays were welcome and appreciated decades before the Rodgers and Hammerstein era.

In his introduction to the *Rodgers and Hart Song Book*, Rodgers singles
out "You Can't Fool Your Dreams" from their earliest professional score,
Poor Little Ritz Girl, to show his and Hart's "willingness to employ subject matter hitherto ignored by the songwriting profession."[64] Significantly,
Rodgers then moves directly from the song to the show: "This desire to explore did not stop with the individual songs. It extended to the shows themselves. Looking at the table of contents of this book, it is clear that there must
have been an almost continual search for diversification of subject matter."

When *Time* magazine decided to devote a cover story to the boys from
Columbia (September 26, 1938), Rodgers and Hart were on the verge of
revealing yet another hit musical, *The Boys from Syracuse* (adapted from
Shakespeare's *A Comedy of Errors*). The team, known to the public for more
than a dozen years, had recently been playing a significant role in keeping
Broadway afloat. *Time* notes that aside from one week, the "U.S. Gilbert &
Sullivan" had had a "smash hit" for three years running, as well as road shows
and innumerable hit songs. In its attempt to explain the phenomenon of
Rodgers and Hart, *Time* offers what might be termed the Rodgers and Hart
Credo, which I have summarized as "Know Thy Audience" and "Fear Not
Innovation," two powerful principles that would be appropriated by Rodgers
and Hammerstein.

No. 1: Know thy Audience

According to *Time*, the success of Rodgers and Hart "rests on a commercial instinct that most of their rivals have apparently ignored." Even though
Rodgers did not embrace commercial success as a goal in itself and always
aimed to please his own tastes and interests, the fact remains that Rodgers,

with both Hart and Hammerstein, possessed an enviably reliable if not in-fallible radar for what audiences wanted, a sensitivity that allowed him to feel audience approval "on the back of his neck."[65] Rodgers's early letters to the future Dorothy Rodgers between 1926 and 1928 reveal the acquired nature of this instinct. The man who later had unshakable faith in *Oklahoma!* when many worried that its daring qualities would go unappreciated, in his early Broadway years had expressed considerable anxiety about how his shows would fare with audiences. On one hand he could be surprised when a show he viewed as mediocre, like *Lido Lady*, thrived (albeit in London, in a foreign country with foreign tastes). Conversely, if he liked a show, he feared that audiences would not. For this reason Rodgers feared that audiences might reject the artistic daring of *Chee-Chee*, "the best musical thing I've ever seen." Ten years later, at the premiere of *I Married an Angel*, Rodgers thought they had a flop for sure, but this time it was Hart who knew that audiences would accept the non sequitur that inexplicably led them from heaven to Radio City Music Hall.[66] With a few exceptions Rodgers stayed attuned to what audiences wanted until he faltered at the end of his career.

No. 2: Fear Not Innovation

The *Time* profile also emphasized the spirit of adventure, another Rodgers and Hart ideal frequently attained. "As Rodgers & Hart see it, what was killing musicomedy was its sameness, its tameness, its eternal rhyming of June with moon. They decided it was not enough just to be good at the job; they had to be constantly different also. The one possible formula was: *Don't have a formula*; the one rule for success: *Don't follow it up*." The first part of this quote might have been transcribed verbatim from that conversation in the spring of 1919 when Rodgers and Hart met. In numerous interviews, articles, and his autobiography Rodgers expressed tremendous pride in the innovations that tumbled over themselves, decades before *Oklahoma!*

I offer here two examples from the 1920s; others appear in Chapter 3.

Dearest Enemy (1925): The first important musical comedy to be based on a historical subject (an incident that occurred in the American Revolution). This idea was so unconventional that Lew Fields, the father of the show's librettist, Herbert Fields, declined to produce the show, despite the success of *The Garrick Gaieties*. The show gained attention at the time with its opening: the female lead, Helen Ford, was introduced swimming in the nude (although the audience and the British Captain Sir John Copeland first see her discreetly, if still somewhat provocatively, wearing a barrel).

Peggy-Ann (1926): Rodgers writes, "By 1926 Freud's theories, though much discussed, had not yet found expression in the theatre, and the time seemed ripe for a musical comedy to make the breakthrough by dealing with subconscious fears and fantasies. That's exactly what we did in *Peggy-Ann*."[67] Fourteen years before *Lady in the Dark* (book by Moss Hart, lyrics by Ira Gershwin, music by Kurt Weill), *Peggy-Ann* displayed no music for the first fifteen minutes—not even an overture—and the sets and costumes were changed without a backdrop. The dream sequences were fantastic and memorable, featuring talking fish, pills the size of golf balls, policemen sporting pink mustaches, and a race horse submitting to an interview. Small wonder that Rodgers considered *Peggy-Ann* his favorite among his 1920s shows.[68]

Rodgers and Hart's amateur years corresponded to a period on Broadway that favored plays (comedies, satires, and serious dramas), and, on the musical stage, revues and operettas. Among the latter, however, only *Blossom Time* and *Rose-Marie* could boast successful road tours as well as long Broadway runs. In discussing why Lew Fields spent most of the time between *Poor Little Ritz Girl* and *The Melody Man* on the road, far from Broadway, Armond and L. Marc Fields offer an explanation that may shed light on why Rodgers and Hart were similarly kept away from their chosen venue: "Fields's self-imposed exile coincided with a serious slump in the quality and profitability of the Broadway musical. A combination of factors—the financial downturn, rising production costs, the onset of Prohibition, the growth of motion pictures—explained Broadway's economic problems, but not the artistic poverty of the Broadway musical."[69] On December 1, 1924, one day before the premiere of the future smash hit of the decade, *The Student Prince*, a jazzy musical comedy partially stemmed the operetta tide and paved the way for some parity between the musical genres: George and Ira Gershwin's *Lady, Be Good!* Within a year Rodgers and Hart would be able to join in some of this fun.

By the late spring of 1925, Rodgers had composed and recycled more than a hundred songs in fourteen amateur productions, had seen at least some of his work on the professional stage, and had been paid at least nominally for one of his amateur productions. He had also written at least one libretto and a number of song lyrics, directed at least one show, and toured with a vaudeville company under the auspices of the Shuberts and Lew

Fields. For more than six years Rodgers had been working with a lyricist who shared his vision of a sophisticated and dramatically driven musical theater pioneered by Kern a decade earlier. On his own and as a student at the Institute of Musical Art, Rodgers had learned basic musicianship and the craft of composition. Even though Lew Fields had not shown enough faith in Rodgers and Hart's talents to produce a complete show, he did provide several compensatory professional opportunities. By 1925, Herbert Fields, Rodgers, and Hart had formed an artistically stable triumvirate, listed on the bill of *The Melody Man* (1924) for the first and only time as "Herbert Richard Lorenz." In Herbert Fields, Rodgers had found a librettist who would serve him well for the next three years. In Hart, Rodgers had discovered a lyricist of enormous theatrical knowledge, talent, and promise with whom he would work for seventeen years. Two partners, two best friends, and two amiable sources of irritation. From childhood on Rodgers had been blessed with parents who supported his dreams emotionally and to some extent financially. He also received a useful education and moral support from teachers and fellow students at the Institute of Musical Art. By 1925 Rodgers had craft, experience, some connections, and a musical theater ideology. He had also enjoyed a few favorable critical reviews and had experienced mostly favorable audience responses to his work.

Although still not quite twenty-three, Rodgers had been playing the amateur game for nearly eight years, the last six with Hart. He was also becoming discouraged, and by 1924 he was plagued with insomnia. His parents were becoming less inclined to finance his amateur habit. The years of amateurism, the problematic book of the unfinished and unproducible *Winkle Town*, and the failure to turn his best songs into professional opportunities were taking its toll. The absence of hit musical comedies between 1921 and 1924 in favor of operettas like *Blossom Time, Wildflower, Rose-Marie,* and *The Student Prince* and several successful annual revues was one thing, but so far Rodgers and Hart had also been unable to capitalize on the return of musical comedy inaugurated by *Lady, Be Good!* By the end of the 1924–25 season both Rodgers and Hart were considering abandoning amateur theater.

As any survey of Rodgers and Hart will inform us, in the spring of 1925, on the eve of throwing in the towel on the world of musical theater for a secure position selling children's underwear, Rodgers got a call from Benjamin Kaye—one of several lyricists in Rodgers's second amateur show in 1919 and a contributor of sketches to the forthcoming Theatre Guild fundraiser—

who convinced Rodgers that a benefit performance to raise money for curtains under the auspices of the prestigious Guild was more than just another amateur hour. The result, described by Robert Benchley as "by miles the cleverest and most civilized show in town," was *The Garrick Gaieties*.[70] Favorable reviews and audience response prompted the Theatre Guild to close its successful but waning show, *The Guardsman*, and to use the space for a longer run of the new revue. *The Garrick Gaieties* of 1925, with its hit, "Manhattan," one of the songs that Max Dreyfus had dismissed as possessing "nothing of value," had created a sensation and would run an impressive 211 performances. It also launched a three-year period of astonishing productivity, innovation, and commercial success before the dismal failure of *Chee-Chee* in 1928. The onset of the Depression led to artistic retrenchment and disappointing runs, and it prompted Rodgers and Hart (without Lew or Herbert Fields) to seek their fortune in Hollywood. For the time being, however, after six years of wandering in the amateur desert, Rodgers and Hart could savor their 42nd Street moment, which arrived not a moment too soon.

CHAPTER 2

A Tale of Two *Connecticut Yankees*

FOR RODGERS AND HART, THE BRIEF PERIOD FROM *THE GARRICK Gaieties* (May 17, 1925) to *Betsy* (December 28, 1926) was marked by a frenzy of activity and a nearly unbroken string of successes in New York City and London. It encompassed three New York revues, the "schmaltzy and smart" *Garrick Gaieties* of 1925 and 1926 on Broadway and a nightclub revue at the Fifth Avenue Club (*The Fifth Avenue Follies*). It featured a musical comedy that successfully catered to London tastes, *Lido Lady* (1926), equipped with a surefire hit from Broadway's *Dearest Enemy*, "Here in My Arms." At the end of these busy months came the first failure, *Betsy*.[1]

The central theatrical legacies of this productive time are three sometimes topical, often original and innovative, but nonetheless generally ignored musical comedies: the Revolutionary War romance-comedy *Dearest Enemy* (1925), the trendy show about a bicycle race, *The Girl Friend* (1926), and the comically Freudian dreamy fantasy-romance, *Peggy-Ann* (1926). All three musicals offered hip, smart-alecky, sometimes funny, and sometimes punny librettos by Herbert Fields. The last two shows were produced by Herbert's father, Lew.[2] Among the many songs to appear during these twenty months, several, including "Manhattan" (actually composed in 1922 during the "amateur" years), "Sentimental Me," "Mountain Greenery," "Here in My Arms," "Blue Room" (see example 1.3), "The Girl Friend," "Sleepyhead," "Where's That Rainbow?" and "A Tree in the Park" scored hits in their own time, "This Funny World" (see example 2.1b) belatedly in ours. The stylistic mixture displayed in these shows—from ballads suitable for operetta to songs composed in a popular American vernacular with more than a trace of jazz—would continue in *A Connecticut Yankee*, embodied in "My Heart Stood Still" (see example 1.6) and "Thou Swell."

Connecticut Yankee in 1927

A Connecticut Yankee, which opened on November 3, 1927, was Rodgers and Hart's greatest Broadway success of the 1920s, and the only show the partners ever revived (November 17, 1943). The original *Yankee* has so far resisted attempts to be fully reconstructed. In any event, the 1943 revival made such attempts ultimately unnecessary, fool's errands for the historically curious. The more important question is this: Who can explain the success of the 1927 *Yankee* and the relative failure of an (arguably) improved version sixteen years later? (See table 2.1 for a comparative list of musical numbers in each version.)

Four days into the *Yankee* revival and two days before the death of Larry Hart, Rodgers's "blight and partner" for twenty-four years, Rodgers reminisced in the *New York Times* about the show's roots:

> Back in 1921, Herb Fields and I wandered into the Capitol Theatre to see a silent picture called *A Connecticut Yankee*, with Harry C. Myers in the lead [Douglas Fairbanks had declined the honor]. We laughed for nearly two hours and walking home decided that there, by cracky, was the perfect idea for a musical comedy. Mr. Hart thought so too, so a couple of days later I walked into the office of the lawyer for the Mark Twain estate to try to get the necessary permission to make a musical version of the novel. The lawyer was Mr. Charles Tressler Lark. I was 19. One hour later I walked out of Mr. Lark's office with a six months' option—for free![3]

Two years after securing the rights from Lark, Rodgers and Hart joined Fields and several other writers—and a now forgotten composer, Sigmund Krumgold, for one song—to present Rodgers's second annual musical at the Institute of Musical Art, *A Danish Yankee in King Tut's Court,* a show inspired both by Mark Twain's novel *A Connecticut Yankee in King Arthur's Court* (1889) and the recent discovery of Egyptian King Tutankhamen's tomb. *A Danish Yankee* ran two nights, May 31 and June 1, 1923, and no sources are listed in the Library of Congress guide to its Richard Rodgers Collection.[4] In 1927, the now successful Rodgers-Hart-Fields trio was ready to return to Twain's *Yankee* (back home in Connecticut) as the source for a

Table 2.1. *A Connecticut Yankee,* 1927 and 1943

1927	1943
Prologue—Grand Ballroom of a Hotel in Hartford, Conn., 1927	Prologue—Grand Ballroom of a Hotel in Hartford, Conn., 1943
"*A Ladies' Home Companion*"[1] (*Fay, Principals, and Ensemble*) [Music missing. Dropped from *Betsy* before its New York opening.]	**"Here's Martin the Groom" (Martin, Judge Thurston Merrill, and Ensemble)**
	"This Is My Night to Howl" [#1A] (Fay and Ensemble)[2]
"My Heart Stood Still" (Martin, Sandy, and Ensemble)	**"My Heart Stood Still" [#2]** (Martin and Sandy) [Lyric updated.]
ACT I SCENE 1—The Road to Camelot, 528 A.D. Untitled: "An opening number done by factory hands, etc." [No music or lyrics extant.]	ACT I SCENE 1—The Road to Camelot, 528 A.D. **"Tree Opening" [#3] (Instrumental with Dialogue)**
"Thou Swell" (Martin and Sandy)	"Thou Swell" [#4] (Martin and Sandy)
Reprise: "My Heart Stood Still" (Sandy and Martin)	
SCENE 2—Courtyard of King Arthur's Castle	SCENE 2—Courtyard of King Arthur's Castle
"Knight's Opening" (Arthur, Merlin, Lancelot, Galahad, Knights, and Ladies) [Designated "At the Round Table" in *Complete Lyrics.*]	"Knight's Opening" [#5] (Company)
"On a Desert Island with Thee" (Galahad, Evelyn, Knights and Ladies)	"On a Desert Island with Thee" [#6] (Galahad, Evelyn, Gawain, and Ensemble)
	"To Keep My Love Alive" [#7] (Morgan Le Fay) (segue #8)
	"Knight's Exit" [#8] (Instrumental)
	Finale ACT I [#9]

Table 2.1. Continued

1927	1943
Reprise, "My Heart Stood Still" (Martin and Sandy)	Reprise, "My Heart Stood Still" (Martin and Sandy)
Finale (Company)	Finale (Company) [Alternate lyrics used.]
ACT II	ACT II
SCENE 1—Corridor of a Factory Opening (Ensemble)	SCENE 1—Corridor of a Factory **Opening Act II [#10] (Instrumental) (segue #10A)**
	"[Ye] Lunchtime Follies" [#10A] (Galahad and Ensemble)
Reprise: "Thou Swell" (Martin and Sandy)	
"Nothing's Wrong" (Sandy) [Lyric missing. Replaced "I Blush" in Philadelphia.]	**"Can't You Do a Friend a Favor?" [#11] (Morgan Le Fay and Martin)**
"I Feel at Home with You" (Galahad, Evelyn, and Ensemble)	"I Feel at Home with You" [#12] (Galahad, Evelyn, Gawain, and Ensemble)
Dance (Sandy and Galahad)	Dance [#12A] (Sandy and Galahad) "N.B. There is no No. 13." [Note in Piano-Vocal Score.]
	Cue: "The galloping Jeep" [#14] (Segue AS ONE)
SCENE 2—The Road from Camelot	SCENE 2—The Road from Camelot
	[#14 Cont.] "We've been working on the railroad" (Martin and Arthur)
"The Sandwich Men" (Knights) [Music missing.]	**"You Always Love the Same Girl" [#15] (Arthur and Martin)**
"Volga Boatman" (Martin and Arthur)	"Anchors Aweigh" [#16]

Table 2.1. Continued

1927	1943
SCENE 3—Palace of Morgan Le Fay	SCENE 3—Palace of Queen Morgan Le Fay
"Evelyn, What Do You Say?" *(Evelyn and Knights)* [Music missing.]	**"The Camelot Samba"** [#17][3] [Preceded by "Thou Swell" and "Desert Island."]
	Reprise: "Can't You Do a Friend a Favor?" [#18] **(Morgan Le Fay and Martin)**
	Montage [#19]
SCENE 4—Gardens of the Hotel in Hartford, 1927	SCENE 4—Gardens of the Hotel in Hartford, 1943
Finale (Company)	Finale (Company) [#20] ["My Heart Stood Still" and "Thou Swell."]

1. Deletions from 1927 *Yankee* in *italic type*; additions to 1943 *Yankee* in **boldface** type.
2. Probably a late addition. After Martin's line "To the bride. Long may she wave!" the 1943 working libretto offers a return of "A Ladies' Home Companion" (listed simply as "NUMBER (FAY AND ENSEMBLE)") followed a few lines of dialogue later with a "CHORUS (TO BE WRITTEN)." The performance libretto, which removed "Ladies' Home Companion" in favor of "Here's Martin the Groom" two pages earlier, follows Martin's line with the designation "NUMBER #1A, 'MY NIGHT TO HOWL,'" but without the lyrics.
3. Lyrics to "Camelot Samba" are absent from the working and performing librettos of 1943, and from the first edition of *The Complete Lyrics*. The appendix to the revised *Lyrics* contains partial lyrics, but the most complete lyrics are found in the Tams-Witmark Vocal Score, formerly rented to interested production venues.

new musical. Before the triumph of *Garrick Gaieties*, free rights were worthless since no one would take a risk on unknowns for such a project. After a string of hits on one or both sides of the Atlantic (*The Garrick Gaieties, Dearest Enemy, The Girl Friend, Lido Lady*), however, the trio was eventually able to interest Lew Fields in their *Yankee*. As the cost of fame, a new arrangement with Mr. Lark and the Twain estate required "both a high fee and a whopping royalty arrangement."[5]

The team's most recent triumph, *Peggy-Ann*, had been thriving on Broadway since its opening at the end of the previous year, and a London opening was scheduled for late July. On May 19, producer Charles B. Cochran's London revue *One Dam Thing After Another*, starring Jessie Matthews and Sonnie Hale, opened to favorable reviews. In *Musical Stages* Rodgers gives the Prince of Wales credit for the revue's seven-month run.[6] The prince, who had distracted audiences on opening night by his royal presence, became intimately familiar with the song "My Heart Stood Still" when Rodgers and the prince's friend Edyth Baker personally played it for him a number of times. Shortly thereafter, the prince made headlines when he taught the song by rote to Teddy Brown's orchestra at the Royal Western Yacht Club. Just as a recommendation from talk show hostess Oprah Winfrey would send millions scurrying to read a novel, an endorsement from a prince— "THE SONG THE PRINCE LIKED," a newspaper headline read—generated enormous sheet music and record sales for "My Heart Stood Still." And audiences flocked to hear Matthews and Baker (who also played the song in the show on a white piano) sing the song one damn time after another (see *Yankee* recordings in table 3.5).

For the first scene of their new Broadway show Rodgers and Hart composed a new love song, "You're What I Need." Although resuscitated in the 1992 piano-vocal anthology *Rediscovered Rodgers and Hart*, the song remains virtually unknown, perhaps even unrecorded.[7] Even the five volumes of Ben Bagley's *Rodgers and Hart Revisited*, which offer recorded renditions of other *Connecticut Yankee* songs abandoned in the Philadelphia tryouts, among them "I Blush" and "Someone Should Tell Them," did not record this song. Unlike "I Blush," which formed the basis of a future classic, "This Funny World," and unlike "Someone Should Tell Them," which was recycled in *America's Sweetheart* (1931) with a new set of lyrics, "You're What I Need" would briefly rise again as itself. It was introduced and reprised on several occasions by Irene Dunne, Jack Whiting, and the Nightingale Quartette in Rodgers and Hart's next show, *She's My Baby* (1928), with lyrics and title unchanged. Despite this return, the catchy song unfortunately remains one of the relatively few featured jazzy love ballads by Rodgers and Hart that did not regain a life of its own outside its original home. Although it falls short of "My Heart Stood Still" as a central romantic love ballad for *Connecticut Yankee*, "You're What I Need" is a simple but engaging song that deserves to be better known.

The documentary record is silent concerning why Rodgers and Hart decided to drop the song. Perhaps its deletion in 1927 can be attributed to a lyric that is less than Hart's best ("You're what *I* need / I mean, *my* need").

Perhaps its pervasive syncopations were considered too similar to those in "Thou Swell," which came next in the show. At some point, Rodgers and Hart realized that what they needed was a romantic ballad like "My Heart Stood Still." Why not use the real thing? Surely "My Heart Stood Still" had a good chance of duplicating its London success, and *One Dam Thing After Another* would definitely not be traveling to New York. Only two obstacles stood in the way. First, Rodgers and Hart had to inform producer Charles Dillingham that the song would be used in *Connecticut Yankee* and would therefore be unavailable for Beatrice Lillie to use in Dillingham's latest New York show. As Rodgers wrote in *Musical Stages*, Lillie was an outstanding comedian but unable to do vocal justice to a lyrical ballad like "My Heart Stood Still" with all those sustained tones at the ends of phrases. Having made this excuse, Rodgers and Hart "had to make sure that the song really was in the show."[8] This led to the second obstacle, the need for Cochran to relinquish the song. For a cut of the royalties (amounting to the then very grand sum of $5,000), Cochran agreed to return the song to its rightful owners.

From the beginning, "My Heart Stood Still" was recognized as a central song of *Connecticut Yankee*. Some critics, however, found other songs — usually unnamed — equally appealing. *Variety* reviewer Sid Silverman preferred "Thou Swell" over "My Heart Stood Still," and suggested that it would make a "better bet for the first act finale."[9] Charles Brackett of the *New Yorker* thought that several other songs "may well rival 'My Heart Stood Still' in popularity."[10] *Time* reviewer Wells Root found Rodgers's music on the whole "immensely better (in at least three songs) than is most music in most musical comedies," but he felt that in the end, "the master song, 'My Heart Stood Still,' becomes a nuisance."[11] Writing in the *New York Herald*, Percy Hammond concluded that the chorus, the costumes, "and four or five alluring songs from the harmonium of Mr. Rodgers were the nicest things in 'The Connecticut Yankee.'"[12] Only *Life*'s Robert Benchley, who perhaps not incidentally designed the amusing pseudo-medieval map of Camelot as a drop curtain, found "My Heart Stood Still" to be "perhaps the loveliest musical comedy song in recent years."[13] Whatever their conclusions, if a critic mentioned even one song by name, that song would be "My Heart Stood Still."

The 1927 *Connecticut Yankee* premiered on November 3 at the Vanderbilt Theatre, several months into a season that would offer at least 264 Broadway productions (some accounts go as high as 270), more than any season before or since. Within just one month of *Yankee's* debut audiences could see Helen Hayes in *Coquette*, Fred and Adele Astaire in George and Ira Gershwin's *Funny Face*, Edward G. Robinson as a Chicago gangster in *The Racket*, and the Irish Players in Sean O'Casey's succès d'estime, *The Plough and the Stars*. By the end of the year *Yankee* would also be competing with *Show Boat*, the third musical of 1927 (after *Rio Rita* and *Good News!*) that would eventually surpass *Yankee's* 418-performance run. For Rodgers and Hart, however, *Yankee's* record would stand as their personal best until the 427 performances of their final collaboration, *By Jupiter*, in 1942.

In reporting the failure of *Connecticut Yankee's* 1943 revival, Ethan Mordden expresses incredulity over why the work had *succeeded* in 1927, especially since, in Mordden's view, "Fields's book reduces Twain to the one-joke culture shock of anachronism."[14] Mordden's question merits at least an attempt at an answer. First, several opening-night reviewers in 1927 shared Mordden's posthumous judgment and found the one-joke anachronisms too much of a good thing. Hammond, for example, found lines such as "The hell thou sayest!" amusing but the "constant reiteration of the burlesque lingo of King Arthur's court" tedious.[15] Without placing himself among their number, Root reported that for "keener critics" the "device of mixing current slang with Arthurian bombast ('Varlet, thou are full of the juice of the prune') palled somewhat before the evening ended."[16] Brackett devoted the longest of his five paragraphs to the wearing use of anachronistic language by the second act. Silverman, who attributed the "main fault" of the show to the fact it played its entire hand — the two major songs, "My Heart Stood Still" and "Thou Swell" — within its first thirty minutes, thought that some places in the book were "slow." Nevertheless, alone among the 1927 reviewers, Silverman praised Fields's book for its "deft twists in applying the abbreviated and expressive tongue to stock situations in a knightly setting."[17] Overall, despite some complaints, including overuse of the hybrid of medieval and hip language, encapsulated so famously in the song title, "Thou Swell," Fields's adaptation of a well-known novel was generally appreciated and welcomed.

Fields's tale begins on the evening before Martin (William Gaxton) is to be married to Fay Morgan (Nana Bryant). It soon becomes evident that he is marrying for mercenary reasons and still loves Alice (Constance Carpenter). When Alice arrives unexpectedly at his bachelor party, Martin finds her irresistible. Soon Fay discovers Alice on Martin's lap; Fay bops him on the head with a champagne bottle, knocking him into a dream world set in Arthurian

England in A.D. 528. Not surprisingly, the characters and situations he en-
counters parallel people and events in Connecticut. Shortly after his arrival
in Camelot, Martin meets and falls in love with Alice's counterpart, the
Demoiselle Alisande Le Carteloise, or Sandy (Carpenter), and rejects the
aggressive advances of Fay's doppelgänger, the often-married Queen Morgan Le Fay (Bryant), sister of the king. At the end of his Camelot adventure
Martin awakens from his stupor in the arms of Alice, the woman he loves
in real life as well as in his dreams.

After the party that forms the prologue, invented by Fields, the entire
first act relies almost exclusively on the first six chapters of Twain's novel.
This section of the book begins with Martin's capture and imprisonment and
concludes when he demonstrates his magical powers by predicting a solar
eclipse; he wins his freedom and becomes second in command after the
king. In act II, Martin, now The Boss, rapidly introduces new technologies
and ideologies to the medieval world. In the novel, Alisande was a talka-
tive pest who only gradually metamorphoses into a loyal wife and mother;
her daughter, Hello Central, is born in later chapters. The musical con-
verts Twain's anti-romanticism into a conventional love story only partially
counteracted by Sandy's proto-feminist advocacy of women's suffrage. After
singing their song of first love, "Thou Swell," Alisande and Martin unite
the two worlds—Connecticut (operetta) and Camelot (musical comedy)—
when they adopt "My Heart Stood Still," the song Alice and Martin sang in
Connecticut, as a culminating love song shortly before the first-act finale.
The central plot machination in act II is the kidnapping of Alisande by Morgan Le Fay, Morgan's capture of her brother, King Arthur, who is traveling
incognito with Martin, and their rescue by motor trucks.[18]

Among the relatively few remaining specific uses by Rodgers, Hart, and
Fields of Twain's novel, widely but by no means unanimously interpreted by
scholars as an indictment of a primitive and unenlightened feudal past in the
light of a progressive American nineteenth-century present, one brief comic
episode from act II, scene 3, deserves special mention, despite its minor role
in the drama:[19]

> LE FAY: Sit ye down here, and I will make my minstrels to play for thee. (She
> rings. THREE PLAYERS enter with banjo and mandolins. THEY sit at
> the foot of the divan.)
> BOSS: Nifty band you've got . . .
> LE FAY: Jazz Band No. 1 . . . PLAY! (They play very badly) They are really
> finished musicians . . .

BOSS: They will be if they don't quit that. (The BANJO PLAYER hits one
terrific chord. LE FAY rises furiously and motions a slave forward)
LE FAY: Have that man hung . . . (The PLAYER rises in disgrace and goes
toward slave)
BOSS: Wait, Goldwyn . . . Hang the rest of them. (The OTHER TWO rise
and exit with SLAVE) Gosh! That's a system that never should have been
abolished.[20]

While this dialogue seems tailor-made for musical comedy, the inspiration
is actually clearly derived from Chapter 17, "A Royal Banquet," in Twain's
novel: "In a gallery a band with cymbals, horns, harps and other horrors,
opened the proceedings with what seemed to be the crude first-draft or original agony of the wail known to later centuries as 'In the Sweet Bye and Bye.'
It was new, and ought to have been rehearsed a little more. For some reason or other the queen had the composer hanged, after dinner."[21] Before
the hanging, Twain's Boss, a reasonable man, asked the musicians to play
the tune again, "saw that she was right, and gave her permission to hang the
whole band."[22]

The problems that face theater historians who wish to understand why
a particular 1920s musical succeeded or failed can be attributed not only
to historical distance but to the unavailability of surviving artifacts such as
librettos, scores, cast albums, and films. The problems are compounded with
A Connecticut Yankee because some music and lyrics are missing from the
original 1927 version, and in some cases the placement of several known
songs is unclear from the extant libretto. To assess the success of a show, contemporary scholars and audiences must take into account that the era was
one in which an entertaining musical comedy adaptation of a famous novel
was an event, and in which the presence of two consecutive hit songs could
go a long way toward satisfying an audience eager for an excuse to visit a new
musical comedy (even at the steep top price of $5.50). In addition to its two
immensely appealing songs, *A Connecticut Yankee* had a great working idea,
a more than serviceable book, and some impressive stagecraft—for example,
the creation of a Ford car in an Arthurian assembly line. Some critics found
the show less imaginative and "neither a sequel nor equal" to *Peggy-Ann*, and
most concurred that the combination of old English and modern slang grew
wearing. Nonetheless, *Yankee* was widely praised, not only for the quality of
the book and the score, but for its cast, sets, costumes, and choreography.
The production was also greatly enhanced by two relative newcomers, the

William Gaxton (Martin/Yankee) and Constance Carpenter (Alice/Alisande) in the original *Connecticut Yankee* (1927)

leading man, William Gaxton (born Don Arturo Antonio Gaxiola), and the choreographer, William Berkeley Enos, forever known as Busby Berkeley.

Gaxton, a former vaudevillian who was widely praised in the double central roles of Martin and The Boss, had appeared in Irving Berlin's *Music Box Revue* of 1922 but not yet in a musical comedy. Unlike his future comic partner, Victor Moore, who is in the Berlin-Astaire-Rogers film classic *Top Hat* (1935), Gaxton and his films are now forgotten (including the 1931 *Fifty Million Frenchmen*). Gaxton's vocal qualities are not so much scorned as simply unknown, and his time on the stage has failed to generate the kind of fond memories reserved for a contemporary star such as Gertrude Lawrence, whose stage persona more than compensated for her vocal inadequa-

Gordon Burby (Sir Kay, the seneschal) and William Gaxton in the original *Connecticut Yankee*

cies. Mordden dismisses Gaxton as an "overweight clunker" who "threaded his way through the Third-Age musical [i.e., the Golden Age musical from about 1920–1970] on nerve more than entitlement, and no one, apparently, objected."[23]

If Gaxton possessed a captivating stage persona, the qualities that made him such have been long buried. We can, however, note that critics of the 1943 *Yankee* revival who remembered (or imagined) him in the 1927 version, lamented Gaxton's absence. We might also consider that although he lacked charisma when compared with the sensational Ethel Merman or the master comedian Moore (the latter in six shows with Gaxton, nearly all hits), Gaxton possessed a knack for picking the right horses. Should we believe that as a romantic-comic lead Gaxton did not contribute to the success of the string of musical comedy hits that included Cole Porter's *Fifty Million Frenchmen* (1929), *Anything Goes* (1934) with Merman and Moore, and *Leave It to Me* (1938); the Gershwins' *Of Thee I Sing* (1931); and Berlin's *Louisiana Purchase* (1940) (also with Moore)? In *A Connecticut Yankee*, Broadway audiences saw Gaxton in his first starring role, in which he introduced "My Heart Stood Still" and "Thou Swell," both in the first half hour of the evening.

The 1927 *Yankee* also marked the debut of Busby Berkeley as a choreographer for a major Broadway book show. With the arrival of sound films Berkeley would soon gain notoriety for his kaleidoscopic dance formations —still instantly recognizable as Berkeley's work or as parodies—captured in aerial or underground photography in many Hollywood films (most famously in *42nd Street* and *Gold Diggers of 1933*).[24] Although with *Yankee* he had not yet developed this striking visual signature, he was already exhibiting an imaginative personal touch that did not go unnoticed. Percy Hammond, for example, wrote that Berkeley's "many lovely dancing girls" were, along with "the costumes and four or five alluring songs," highlights of the show. As far as Hammond was concerned, Berkeley's dancers "did things" that had "not yet been done by any of the Weyburn, the Tiller, the Rasch or the Foster girls."[25] According to Gerald Bordman, "Busby Berkeley's dancers won their share of accolades as their routines sent them prancing over tables, over sofas, over anything between them and the other side of the stage."[26]

The following year Berkeley was featured in another Rodgers-Hart-Fields production, *Present Arms,* which included a number—"You Took Advantage of Me," with Berkeley and Joyce Barbour—that would become the hit of the show. As the choreographer of this show, Berkeley would receive serious critical attention from dance critic John Martin.[27] Martin, whose influential career at the *New York Times* (1927–62) corresponds closely to that of theater critic Brooks Atkinson (1924–41 and 1946–60), focused over the years mainly on modern dance and ballet. His exploration of Berkeley may be the first serious treatment by anyone of a Broadway choreographer. After acknowledging the artistry of popular theater music and the nonartistry of musical theater books, Martin writes that "the cognoscenti are beginning to be aware of 'qualities' in stage dancing, and this not because of any lowering of the critical eyeline, but rather because of the prodigious raising of the level of the dancing." Martin offers the following explanation of Berkeley's accomplishment:

What Berkeley actually did in *A Connecticut Yankee,* and to an even greater
extent in *Present Arms,* was to discover a new and sound basis upon which
to build for novelty. Though he has thus far relied to a certain extent upon
external devices in the conventional way, he has also delved into the actual
rhythmic structure of jazz to a degree that has not before been attempted,
and the results he has achieved in this direction are not only novel but un-
wontedly artistic in their manner of utilizing to the fullest extent the actual
material which author and composer have provided for him.

In short, before moving on to objectifying the human body and creating his
kaleidoscopic dance formations in Hollywood musicals, and before George
Balanchine, Agnes de Mille, and Jerome Robbins further revolutionized
musical theater dance, Busby Berkeley was successfully integrating dance
into a Broadway show.

Relatively few 1920s musicals are still revived or remain in our consciousness, and not even the best known among these, *No, No, Nanette, Good
News!* and *Show Boat* have survived with their original books and scores intact. If it is difficult to determine why a 1920s musical succeeded in its time,
it is also a challenge to reconstruct the work as it existed in its own time.
But it is not impossible. Thanks to the painstaking efforts of Miles Kreuger
and John McGlinn we now know, for example, much about what the 1927
Show Boat was like, and modern directors and conductors may choose to
stage and record either the 1927 or 1946 versions or a hybrid of stage and
film versions.[28] This has not yet happened with *A Connecticut Yankee.* What
makes the reconstruction of the show unusually problematic is the ironic
fact that its *pre*-Broadway history is well documented, but its Broadway history contains significant gaps. Thus, while three of the five songs dropped
along the road have survived and are even available in an accessible vocal
score selection—a fourth song is probably an earlier version of the song it
replaced—in several cases the songs that audiences actually heard during
the Broadway run are now lost.[29]

The five deleted songs are "You're What I Need" (replaced by "My Heart
Stood Still"), "I Blush," "Morgan Le Fay," "Someone Should Tell Them,"
and "Britain's Own Ambassadors." The worst case is "Britain's Own Ambassadors." Neither lyrics nor music are extant, and no one seems to know
who sang it or where it was placed. Tommy Krasker and Robert Kimball in
their indispensable *Catalog of the American Musical* identify a lyric sheet
for "Morgan, Morgan, Morgan Le Fay" in the Rodgers and Hammerstein
Theatre Library; this song served as the basis for "Evelyn, Evelyn, What Do

You Say?" From this they credibly conclude that the songs share "virtually the same lyric" and are "probably set to the same music."[30] It is not known where "Someone Should Tell Them," sung by Martin and Morgan Le Fay, was placed in the tryouts.[31] Most likely this unusual song, with its frequent alternations between triple and duple meter, occurred in the spot reserved sixteen years later for "Can't You Do a Friend a Favor?" As he did with many unused songs with both Hart and Hammerstein, Rodgers recycled "Someone Should Tell Them," and three years later it resurfaced with new lyrics and a new title, "There's So Much More," in *America's Sweetheart.*[32]

Hart's lyrics to the final deleted song, "I Blush," revolve around various medieval scandals, including the sordid tales of Guinevere and Lancelot and Tristan and Isolde, which are enough to make one blush. But the real object of Hart's satirical jabs is the perceived excess of Wagner's operatic depiction of these legendary medieval characters:

> Tristan told his heart to Isolde [Iseult in the published sheet music]
> in song . . . I blush!
> Oh dear, but the song was six hours long . . . I blush!
> What they did was wrong beyond a doubt
> If it took so long to sing about,
> And the thought can make my lily
> Cheek to flush . . . I blush!
> Oh dear, how they yodeled of love and death . . . I blush!
> They died not from love but from lack of breath . . . I blush![33]

Although the lyrics hardly apply to whatever Florenz Ziegfeld was cooking up, the tone and style of this song would have suited the comic talents of Beatrice Lillie, the vocally challenged comedian denied the opportunity to ruin the lyrical "My Heart Stood Still." The following year Lillie would get to sing an appropriately tongue-in-cheek comic Rodgers and Hart song in *She's My Baby,* "A Baby's Best Friend," a song about the bond between a baby and her mother.

The compositional origins of the final cut song, "I Blush," are instructive.[34] Eventually the song, introduced by Constance Carpenter (Alisande), a bit player and Lawrence's understudy in *Oh, Kay!* the previous year, would give way to another waltz in act II, scene 1, "Nothing's Wrong," during the Philadelphia tryouts. A letter from Rodgers to Dorothy on October 13 suggests that the substitution happened between October 5 and 12: "Connie [Carpenter] has a new number replacing 'I Blush.' It's a cute one and goes

very well."[35] The immediate dramatic context for the new song most likely
was the exit of The Boss and the entrance of Galahad with the direction
"MUSIC STARTS!":

> GALAHAD: How now, maid Alisande, art meditating with thyself?
> SANDY: Galahad, I am perplexed. Just now the Boss and I sat on the bench.
>   He held my hand and kissed my lips, and held me close! Now, did I do
>   anything wrong?
> GALAHAD: I don't know. I wasn't with you.
> (INTO WALTZ, GALAHAD AND ALISANDE)

Since the waltz song is not given a title in the 1927 libretto (act II, scene 1,
p. 10), it is not possible to be certain of its whereabouts in the show. Nevertheless, a song called "Nothing's Wrong" would make a logical response to
Sandy's questions about whether she did anything wrong. Following the decision to expand the role of Fay at the expense of Sandy for the revival,
"Nothing's Wrong" was replaced by a new duet for Fay and Martin, "Can't
You Do a Friend a Favor?" As partial compensation, Sandy is allowed a reprise of "Thou Swell" with Martin in the same scene.

A textless piano-vocal score holograph in 4/4 time in the Rodgers collection at the Library of Congress offers additional clues on the placement
of "Nothing's Wrong," as well as some insight into Rodgers's compositional
reworking. Although other numbered manuscripts are unavailable, the number "10a" on this holograph would correspond to a song that appeared early
in the second act. On a separate page Rodgers jotted down a melody (labeled
"Refrain") in which the tune of the 4/4 chorus of the "Nothing's Wrong"
piano-vocal score is transformed into a single-line melodic draft in 3/4 time
—that is, a waltz.[36]

Some questions remain unanswered, including the extent to which Galahad participated vocally in the song. The evidence is also unclear about
whether Hart's text corresponded to the duple version, the triple version, or
both. Another possibility is that the duple version was sung and the waltz
version simply danced as indicated in the description "waltz Galahad and
Alisande." The waltz "Nothing's Wrong" was included in the piano selections sold in the lobby during the original Broadway run.[37] Steven Suskin
singles out "Nothing's Wrong" for special praise: "Hidden in *Connecticut
Yankee* is a truly luscious waltz. Rodgers was to write a whole bouquet of
exquisite waltzes, but this first one is a neglected orphan. It's called 'Noth-

ing's Wrong,' and if anybody can find the lyric and/or verse, please do send it along!"[38]

An earlier stage in the evolution of "I Blush" takes us back to Ziegfeld's *Betsy* (1926), a hastily assembled starring vehicle for Belle Baker that staggered through thirty-nine performances.[39] In *Musical Stages* Rodgers shares his unhappy experiences with this show, including the stressful rehearsal schedule, which overlapped with rehearsals for *Peggy-Ann* (*Peggy Ann* opened on December 27, *Betsy* on December 28. *Betsy* is best remembered for two songs, both introduced by Baker, Berlin's perennial "Blue Skies," a last-minute interpolation inserted without Rodgers and Hart's knowledge, and Rodgers and Hart's lesser known sleeper "This Funny World." Berlin's ballad was the hit of the show, and it gained additional recognition when it was featured by Al Jolson in the first talking picture, *The Jazz Singer* (released the following October), and by Bing Crosby in the film *Blue Skies* (1946). Compared to Berlin's ballad and Borrah Minnevitch and his Harmonica Orchestra, the latter, according to Atkinson, "the unquestioned hit of the evening," Rodgers and Hart, "two of the brighter and more sophisticated song and dance tunesmiths," were on this occasion simply "not up to standard."[40] With the exception of "This Funny World," history has so far endorsed this contemporary view and neglected all the other *Betsy* songs. Even "This Funny World" went underground for several decades until Matt Dennis "rescued it from oblivion and included it in his popular nightclub act."[41]

We have already observed Rodgers's ability to recycle an unused early song for an appropriate new dramatic context, with or without a change of lyrics. The practice would continue for the rest of his career. Two conspicuous examples are "Dancing on the Ceiling" (see example 1.4), a hit in the 1930 London production *Ever Green*, famously rejected by Ziegfeld in *Simple Simon* earlier that year, and "There's a Small Hotel" from *On Your Toes*, a refugee from *Jumbo*. When Rodgers gave up on a show (for example, *Betsy, She's My Baby, Chee-Chee*) he felt no compunction about reusing songs from these shows, with or without new titles and lyrics. The discarded "I Blush" offers an unusual twist on this standard practice. To the best of my knowledge it has so far gone unreported that "I Blush," the most likely suspect for the waltz that preceded "Nothing's Wrong" (another waltz), can be traced to a melody in duple meter (4/4 time) for an earlier show, "This Funny World" from *Betsy*. The derivation of "I Blush" from "This Funny

Example 2.1. Creating a Funny World (a) "I Blush" (chorus, first 8 measures) (b) "This Funny World" (chorus, first 3 measures)

World," shown in example 2.1, is unusual. Although Rodgers retains nearly all the pitches of its predecessor (and the same key, G), the transformation in tempo from slow to fast combined with the transformation from duple to triple serves to make the melody seem new. But the only major added melodic feature is a phrase necessitated by the need to accommodate the words "I blush," the new musical and lyrical punchline that now concludes most phrases of the tune.

Almost exactly one year after it closed in New York, *A Connecticut Yankee* moved across the Atlantic, where, retitled *A Yankee at the Court of King Arthur,* it played for forty-three performances (October 10–November 16).[42] The October Stock Exchange crash may have played a role in its rapid close, but other reasons are possible. Although the London production retained Constance Carpenter in the role of Alice/Alisande, William Gaxton was about to open *Fifty Million Frenchmen* in New York and was therefore unavailable, and the show was also without the services of Busby Berkeley.[43] Perhaps the most significant omission, however, was "My Heart Stood Still," which had captivated London audiences two years earlier in *One Dam Thing After Another.*[44]

A Connecticut Yankee *in 1943*

Although revivals are now a crucial component of any Broadway season, and even have their own competitive award category, revivals of musical shows were rare before the 1950s. Perhaps unprecedentedly, *Show Boat* was re-engaged for a revival only three years after it closed in 1929. And it would return again with significant revisions by Hammerstein and Kern in 1946 —the version that would form the basis for most future productions until McGlinn's reconstruction in the 1980s. In 1942, seven years after its premiere and five years after the death of George Gershwin, *Porgy and Bess*, shorn of its controversial recitative, was successfully revived in Cheryl Crawford's Off-Broadway production.

The 1943 production of *A Connecticut Yankee*, which opened on November 17 at the Martin Beck Theatre, was much more than a simple revival. It represented a serious new look at an earlier musical, with a revised and updated book and a score that added seven new songs and subtracted four. Why a new production? Although not a crime, the simple answer can be boiled down to motive and opportunity. First the opportunity. After taking the world by storm in March, *Oklahoma!* was running inexorably along its record-shattering path. Its success allowed Oscar Hammerstein to indulge his long-term interest in setting Georges Bizet's *Carmen* with an updated book and new lyrics. Since he was setting lyrics to a preexisting score, he did not need Rodgers's music. The result was *Carmen Jones*, which opened a few weeks after the revised *Yankee* and ran well over a year. Temporarily without the services of his new lyricist, Rodgers was also free to work on another project. Just as the seeds of the original *Yankee* were planted after seeing a silent film, the catalyst for mounting a second *Yankee* was an advance screening of a moving new sound film based on the life of Mark Twain starring Fredric March.[45]

Enter the motive: Rodgers's desire to give Hart a project less taxing than the creation of a completely new show. Hart had demonstrated a gracious response to the phenomenal success of *Oklahoma!* in March, but he never recovered from the death of his mother in April. Rodgers thought the *Yankee* revival would help his despairing lyricist. According to Meryle Secrest, Rodgers possessed "a sense of loyalty and obligation" and "put up $100,000 of his own money to produce a revival of *A Connecticut Yankee* because he felt he owed it to Larry."[46]

In the Columbia University interviews Rodgers recalls positive memories of the last months working with Hart on the six new *Yankee* songs: "[H]e was in absolutely wonderful shape. Wrote some of the best lyrics he ever wrote. Easy to work with. He used to come out to the country and work with me. And everything was fine, until the opening night in Philadelphia of *Connecticut Yankee*. And he fell apart and never came together again."[47] After being forcibly removed from the theater on opening night, Hart was found the next day in a drunken stupor and died in a hospital from a combination of pneumonia and heart failure on November 22.[48]

In recognition that the show was a wartime revival, the time of the new *Yankee* Prologue (labeled first scene in both the working and performance scripts) was updated from 1927 to 1943. The Hartford characters were uniformed military officers, and in the Arthurian portions Fords and trucks were replaced by military jeeps. No other structural changes were necessary to accommodate the desired topicality. "A Ladies' Home Companion" was replaced by a new opening number, "Here's Martin the Groom"; "Nothing's Wrong," "The Sandwich Men," and "Evelyn, What Do You Say?" completed the list of discarded songs.[49]

Herbert Fields also made a considerable number of changes to make the show funnier and more accessible for a new generation needing momentary distraction from the war overseas. It is striking how an evolving cultural literacy can render phrases and topical references incomprehensible after only sixteen years. Gone were references to Lucy Stone, the nineteenth-century pioneer of women's rights, far better remembered seven years after women got the right to vote than she was during World War II. Instead of the League of Lucy Stone, the "modern" Alisande now joins the League of C.I.O., an abbreviation for the Camelot International Objectors rather than the expected Congress of Industrial Organizations (the labor organization that would merge with the American Federation of Labor in 1955). Also vanished are the formerly famous Scottish baritone Harry Lauder—"Louder, Harry—louder"—and the trio of servants named after the directors Ernst Lubitsch, Cecil B. de Mille, and Samuel Goldwyn, even though all were probably equally well known in 1943.

In both the new working and performing librettos were references to Tyrone Power, Deanna Durbin, Tommy Manville, Don Ameche, the Ballet Russe de Monte Carlo (the latter replacing Vassar), Haig and Haig, Bernard Shaw, and Santa Claus. Martin's 1927 incantation "Martinelli . . . Mussolini / Keller, Thurston and Houdini" is replaced in 1943 by the less political (and less magical) "Gypsy Rose and Cleopatra / Rudy, Bing and Frank

Sinatra." A by no means exhaustive list of topical (and presumably funnier) references includes the following: low down (replacing dope) [although the latest dirt is now the latest dope], unicorn (replacing giant), pip (replacing dish), Rexy (replacing King), kibitzer (replacing applesauce, a slang word for nonsense), thou art wacky (replacing thou sap head), the Loewe circuit is replaced by a U.S.O. tour, Jolson's Mammy is replaced by Porgy and Bess, "Anchors Aweigh" by "Volga Boatman," and ham sandwiches by Benzedrine. Some libretto references, such as one to Tommy Manville, did not make the cut to the performing libretto, but most were retained. In contrast to current motives for changing words and phrases, Fields's changes did not serve the interest of political correctness. Thus in 1943 as well as 1927 (and in Twain's novel) Sandy remains "a sweet kid, dumb as hell, but sweet."

In 1927 Arthur asks Martin, "Do ye dare to mock a king?" Sixteen years later Martin's silly response, "I'd mock a turtle," is absent. Perhaps fewer people in 1943 would be expected to know about mock turtle soup, defined by the *American Heritage Dictionary* as "soup made from calf's head, veal, or other meat and spiced to taste like green turtle soup." The 1927 libretto also contained the following play on the words ween/wean and a corny pun:

GALAHAD: Flattering things I ween.
MARTIN: You ween! How old are you? You just try to get into Boston!
GALAHAD: What's this thou art telling me?
MARTIN: I'm not telling you, I'm ERSKINE you.

Although wartime audiences would not be asked to ponder the references to Boston blue laws or the once popular writer Erskine Caldwell, Fields does, however, retain his faith in the amusing play on the words ween and wean. As spelled in the libretto, ween is an archaic term that means to think or suppose, but of course Martin, unaware of medieval English, jumps to the conclusion that Galahad has not yet abandoned his mother's breast.

In 1943, Fields removed the pun "Say, you're the roughest knight I have had." Is it possible that Martin's comment to Sir Kay could be construed with a gay subtext analogous to the dancer involved in a "queer romance" with her boyfriend in Hart's "Ten Cents a Dance"?[50] If so, why would Fields *add* this passage of dialogue in 1943?

MERLIN: The knights will joist without shields and armor—wearing nothing but their plumes.
ARTHUR: This day will be known as the Queen's Day. And at night—

Can this be construed as a reference to men in drag (that is, drag queens), or is it simply an innocuous and innocent reference to Queen Guinevere, who in her tryst with Lancelot is undoubtedly wearing less than plumes. Another example of a possible gay reading can be found in the character of Galahad. Both the 1927 and 1943 books suggest that this young knight may have unspoken reasons for his obliviousness to Evelyn's advances. In any event, although Galahad's brain remains appealingly "embryonic," he will in the end happily join the sexually aggressive Evelyn on their metaphorical desert island.

The major change in both the book and the score was the expansion of the role of Queen Morgan Le Fay, a decision that noticeably and certainly deliberately skewed the drama away from Alisande, now also deprived of "Nothing's Wrong." Cast as the new Fay was Vivienne Segal, a starring alumna of two Rodgers and Hart shows, Countess Peggy Palaffi in *I Married an Angel* and Vera Simpson in *Pal Joey,* and a close personal friend of Hart's. After the opening number, "A Ladies' Home Companion," Nana Bryant, the original Morgan Le Fay, had little to sing about in 1927. In fact, during tryouts the song "Morgan Le Fay" was retitled "Evelyn, What Do You Say?" and given to June Cochrane (Mistress Evelyn La Belle-ans), and "Someone Should Tell Them," a duet for Gaxton and Bryant, was summarily dropped.

In the 1943 *Yankee,* Segal has three songs to sing, all new: "This Is My Night to Howl" and "To Keep My Love Alive" in act I, and, with Martin, "Can't You Do a Friend a Favor?" in act II. Although Fields added several pages of dialogue in 1943 to set up "To Keep My Love Alive," jokes about Fay's many husbands and the inherent risks of marrying her already loomed large in 1927. The song title and basic idea of "Can't You Do a Friend a Favor?" is anticipated in the first scene of the 1927 script when Alice asks Martin, "Please marry me, can't you do a person a favor?" (act I, scene 1, p. 12). Also in 1943 the singing roles of Galahad and Gawain are expanded, the former taking the lead in "Ye Lunchtime Follies" and the latter in "The Camelot Samba," both new production numbers in act II.[51]

King Arthur, songless in 1927, is given a newly composed duet with Martin, "You Always Love the Same Girl." Presumably audiences would recognize that the idea of the song reflects the greater dramatic reality that Martin, if not Arthur, does in fact really love the same girl who simultaneously resides in modern-day Connecticut and medieval England in the sixth century.[52] The musical component suggests a "post-Hartian song," a song that in contrast to other newly composed *Yankee* songs bears the signature of the new era. This raises the larger issue of the extent to which the two Rodgerses are one, a topic rich in nuance and broad implications that warrants further study. The short answer is that a fair amount of Rodgers and Hammerstein can be found in Rodgers and Hart, and vice versa. More remarkable, however, are the subtle connections and the elusive nature of the transformation from Richard I to Richard II. We return to these connections in future chapters.

Throughout their collaboration Rodgers and Hart considered a deleted song or a song taken from a show with no realistic possibility of a tour, a London production, or a film fair game for reuse. We have already seen that they recycled several discarded songs from *A Connecticut Yankee*. "You're What I Need" returned unchanged in *She's My Baby*, "Someone Should Tell Them" resurfaced with a new lyric in *America's Sweetheart*, and "I Blush" emerged out of the ashes of *Betsy*'s "This Funny World." "I Must Love You" and "Singing a Love Song," two of the principal songs from *Chee-Chee*, would return with new lyrics two years later in *Simple Simon* as "Send for Me" and "I Still Believe in You." Occasionally, direct fragments from abandoned songs reappear in new contexts. Alec Wilder noticed (and notated) eleven consecutive notes buried in measures 4–6 of "You're the Mother Type," from *Betsy*, that provided "a few seeds that sprouted a short time later in 'You Took Advantage of Me.'"[53]

More surprising are the fragments that anticipate Rodgers's work with Hammerstein. The chorus of *Chee-Chee*'s "Singing a Love Song" foreshadows the release of "Happy Talk," and the opening of "Don't Tell Your Folks" from *Simple Simon* suggests "Honey Bun," both from *South Pacific*. At least two passages from "You're the Cats" (from the film *The Hot Heiress*), subtly in the case of "You're such a tasty meal, you're very genteel" and blatantly in the frequently repeated and from a modern perspective sexually suggestive punchline "Gee, but I am awfully glad I came," return respectively in the release of *South Pacific*'s "Younger Than Springtime" ("And when your youth and joy invade my arms") and the final phrase of "Oh, What a Beautiful Mornin'" ("Oh, what a beautiful day") in *Oklahoma!*

When in "You Always Love the Same Girl" Arthur sings "The moment that you meet her / you know you've met before," his words recall a sentiment expressed in Rodgers and Hart's "Where or When" ("It seems we stood and talked like this before"). The music, however, looks *forward* to Rodgers and Hammerstein. The climactic phrase "More pow'r to you!" di-

Example 2.2. A Touch of Rodgers and Hammerstein in Rodgers and Hart (a) "You Always Love the Same Girl" (chorus, mm. 40–48) (b) "Impossible" (chorus, mm. 20–22)

rectly anticipates the elongated version of the phrase "impossible" in the song "Impossible" from *Cinderella* (see example 2.2).

A more pervasive parallel can be found in the distinctive accompaniment figure that supports "You Always Love the Same Girl," reminiscent of *Oklahoma!*'s "I Cain't Say No" or anticipatory of many future Rodgers and Hammerstein songs. The opening rhythm of "You Always Love the Same Girl" also shares the rhythmic scansion of the opening of *Flower Drum Song*'s "I Enjoy Being a Girl." Just this handful of examples are enough to suggest that before Rodgers began to set Hammerstein's words his musical language was beginning to evolve to a new style. In fact, a case could be made that "You Always Love the Same Girl" would not be out of place in any number of Rodgers and Hammerstein shows.

Even if it were possible to resurrect the lost songs and lyrics from 1927 and to argue that the expansion of Morgan Le Fay's role overcompensated for her silence in 1927, the 1943 version, Rodgers and Hart's last word on the subject, would remain the one and only definitive performing version of *A Connecticut Yankee* available. Just as it would be unthinkable for modern productions of *Annie Get Your Gun* to omit "An Old Fashioned Wedding," Berlin's stunning double melody added to the show twenty years after the fact, Fay's "To Keep My Love Alive" joined "My Heart Stood Still" and "Thou Swell" among the trio of *Connecticut Yankee* hits.[54]

Reviews of the 1943 production in eight New York daily papers were favorable but fell considerably short of ecstatic. According to Steven Suskin's "Broadway Scorecard," the new *Yankee's* score consisted of five favorable and three mixed reviews, with no raves (but also no unfavorables or pans). Only Alan Jay Lerner and Frederick Loewe's *What's Up?*, which opened six days before the first of *Connecticut Yankee's* 135 performances, however, received lower marks and closed more rapidly.[55] To gain perspective on the relative meaning of these judgments, here is a comparative score sheet from 1943:

January 7: *Something for the Boys* (book by Herbert and Dorothy Fields; music and lyrics by Porter) 422 total performances
    Scorecard: six raves, two favorables
March 31: *Oklahoma!* (book and lyrics by Hammerstein; music by Rodgers) 2,248 total performances
    Scorecard: five raves, two favorables, one mixed
October 7: *One Touch of Venus* (book by S. J. Perelman and Ogden Nash; lyrics by Nash; music by Kurt Weill) 567 total performances
    Scorecard: three raves, four favorables, one unfavorable
November 11: *What's Up?* (book by Arthur Pierson and Lerner; lyrics by Lerner; music by Loewe) 63 total performances
    Scorecard: one rave, one favorable, two mixed, four unfavorable
December 2: *Carmen Jones* (book and lyrics by Hammerstein; music by Bizet) 502 total performances
    Scorecard: seven raves, one unfavorable

The perceived strengths of the revised show start with Vivienne Segal, specifically her rendition of the new song "To Keep My Love Alive," widely believed to be the final Hart lyric used in a show.[56] In discussing this song, most reviewers devoted attention and praise to Hart's lyrics rather than to Rodgers's music. Louis Kronenberger thought the song contained the "wittiest and funniest lyrics in years," and John Chapman considered it "not a melody, but a hilarious ditty of many verses sung by Vivienne Segal."[57] On the downside, *New York Post* critic Willela Waldorf wrote that the reliance on Segal was so great "that it often seems in danger of falling into a light slumber when she isn't on hand to give it a sly poke in the ribs to wake things up."[58] Nearly every review singled out Vera-Ellen (Evelyn), both for her looks ("the brightest and cutest young thing that the season has so far popped into a musical," wrote Kronenberger) and for her dances with

Galahad, played by Jere Mahon.[59] For one reviewer, the pair who sang and danced "Desert Island" and "I Feel at Home with You" (both from 1927) "took the show away from the entire cast (including the featured Miss Segal and Mr. Foran)."[60] At least they offered "some welcome zip at times when the thee-thou stuff threatens to bog everything down."[61] A number of reviewers commented on and appreciated the incongruous parody of then teen heartthrob Frank Sinatra in "Ye Lunchtime Follies."

Unfortunately, neither Dick Foran nor Julie Warren, two Broadway newcomers who would never return, were received with much critical enthusiasm. When you are playing Martin and are described as "immediately afflicted with wax-works gestures" as soon as you try to use your "pleasant if hardly spectacular singing voice" (Waldorf), or if you're playing Alisande/Alice and are dismissed as a "pleasant though not entirely adequate ingenue" (Kronenberger), it is evident the production has a problem that Vivienne Segal alone can't fully correct. For Waldorf, the two big songs sung by Foran and Warren ("My Heart Stood Still" and "Thou Swell") displayed "all the vitality and zip of lukewarm soda pop." Chapman *imagined* that Foran lacked the "brashness" and "unctuousness" of William Gaxton in the original *Yankee*, and lamented that the Foran and Warren duo could actually ruin "My Heart Stood Still," which for Chapman and probably many others remained "of course, the best song in any show on Broadway."

What is perhaps most surprising about these contemporary assessments is the absence of any reference to the elephant in the critic's cubicle: *Oklahoma!* Like Jimmy Durante, when confronted stealing a real elephant in *Jumbo*, the 1943 reviewers seemed to be saying, "What elephant?" Although some critics compared the new *Yankee* to other work by Rodgers and Hart, they all avoided any direct comparisons with Rodgers and Hammerstein. Perhaps a charismatic Alisande/Alice such as Mary Martin, then shining brightly as Venus in *One Touch of Venus* a block away, might have helped balance Segal's star power. Perhaps a star like Gaxton could have helped enliven Fields's dialogue and Rodgers and Hart's songs. Then again, perhaps not. Although Porter had one more fair-sized old-fashioned hit on the way in January 1944, *Mexican Hayride* (four raves, three favorables, one mixed), by 1943 even a carefully reworked version of Rodgers and Hart's most popular musical of the 1920s might be considered a casualty of the as yet unacknowledged *Oklahoma!* era.

By the next decade reviewers were speaking more openly about the effects of Rodgers and Hammerstein. Not even Elaine Stritch singing an in-

Vera-Ellen (Mistress Evelyn La Rondelle) and Jere McMahon (Sir Gawain),
dance sensations in the revised *Connecticut Yankee* (1943)

terpolated hit song from *Present Arms* could rescue the 1954 revival of *On Your Toes* (one mixed, five unfavorables, and one pan, ouch), although thirty years later a more faithful revival—albeit with an updated book—was impervious to a lonely indictment from supposedly influential *New York Times* critic Frank Rich and became a hit both in New York and London. Sometimes it is difficult to know what to blame—a production, evolving standards of excellence, the audience, or the work itself. Whatever the reasons, even the dramatic improvements, the new songs, the new topical references, the star quality of Segal in an expanded role, and all the knights of the Round Table could not rescue *A Connecticut Yankee*.

The 1943 *Connecticut Yankee*, thanks to a few new jokes by Neil Simon and three other show doctors, was chosen as one of two "1920s" Rodgers and Hart musicals presented in reasonably complete versions on national television (March 12, 1955).[62] (The other show was *Dearest Enemy*.) On July 16, 1964, *Yankee* was revived for one performance, and during the summer of 1989 it had a run at the Goodspeed Opera House in East Haddam, Connecticut, not too far from the Yankee's (and Twain's) Hartford. The show has faded away to the point that Tams-Witmark no longer rents it for performance, and neither a libretto nor a complete vocal score are commercially available. A concert performance for the popular *Encores!* Series at City Center in February 2001 failed to generate the kind of buzz accorded earlier performances of *The Boys from Syracuse* and *Babes in Arms*, and plans for a recording were shelved. As they had in 1927 and 1943, critics once again found the anachronistic language overdone and tiresome. In the words of *New York Times* critic Ben Brantley, "A little of this, frankly, goeth a long way." Despite praise for the "ravishing interpretation of Rodgers's score (from Don Walker's 1943 orchestrations)" and the "terrific" Coffee Club Orchestra that played it, Brantley blithely and categorically dismissed the show as "quaint."[63]

As we now know, it is no longer possible to fully construct what Broadway audiences heard when they saw *A Connecticut Yankee* in 1927, and for sixty years the 1943 *Yankee* has seemed as anachronistic as Arthurian romance itself. Taken together, the two versions yielded three bona fide classics and a number of other songs still heard and remembered. Nevertheless, like all but a handful of 1920s musicals—a truly lost musical theater generation— a future on the stage for this Broadway blockbuster seems as likely as the return of armor, sandwich men, and chivalry.

CHAPTER 3

Hits, Long Runs, and a
Musical Comedy of Errors

B
Y 1935, RODGERS AND HART HAD BEEN AWAY FROM BROADWAY FOR
a little more than four years. It was at least some consolation that,
during this economically bleak period on the New York stage, Hollywood was willing to support the life to which the partners had grown ac-
customed. Despite relative inactivity in their temporary home, Rodgers and
Hart managed to create the lyrics and music for a film masterpiece, *Love Me
Tonight* (1932), starring Maurice Chevalier and Jeanette MacDonald and
produced and directed by Rouben Mamoulian (the future director of *Porgy
and Bess, Oklahoma!,* and *Carousel*). They also wrote the words and music
to two musical films that allow modern-day audiences to see and hear the
stars George M. Cohan in *The Phantom President* (1932) and Al Jolson in
Hallelujah, I'm a Bum (1933). Neither actor was in his prime.

Rodgers took considerable pride in a number of technical achievements
in these films, especially in *Love Me Tonight*. As filmed by Mamoulian, the
song "Isn't It Romantic?" moves from Chevalier's tailor shop to a passing taxi
driver to his fare (who happens to be the composer) to a group of soldiers on
a train to a gypsy boy to MacDonald in her princess's chateau in the French
countryside.[1] Another innovative scene in the film was the deer hunt staged
as a "zoological ballet." Rodgers "had to create two contrasting and inter-
cutting themes, one—on the brass—for the pursuing dogs and horses, the
other—on the strings—for the frightened deer." The "rhythmic" or "musical
dialogue" in *Hallelujah* would return prominently in the opening scene of
Carousel.

Despite these satisfactions, in *Musical Stages* Rodgers would join others in asking, "What on earth could have compelled me to devote so long a period of time to what was, for the most part, the most unproductive period of my professional life?"[2] The short answer: money. All Rodgers and Hart had to show for themselves the year after *Love Me Tonight* was "one score for a film that wasn't made," "one score, mostly unused for a film no one can recall," and isolated songs for Samuel Goldwyn and David Selznick.[3] By the spring of 1934 money was no longer a consolation, and Rodgers was ready to "repair" his "damaged career." One frustrating year later, Rodgers and his partner got the call from producer Billy Rose to compose a score for a "grandiose scheme to mount a production that would be part circus and part musical comedy"—*Jumbo*.[4]

In terms of sheer productivity, the final Broadway phase of Rodgers and Hart's partnership (1935–43)—ten new shows and one revival—fell somewhat short of the pre-Hollywood years (1925–31), during which they produced fourteen Broadway shows, one New York nightclub musical, three new London productions, and three exports. In terms of contemporary popularity and their legacy, however, the last period might be seen as the Rodgers and Hart era, much as the next period, from 1943 to 1951, would be dominated by Rodgers and Hammerstein (table 3.1). In Hollywood, Jerome Kern, with lyricist Dorothy Fields, created the music for one of the finest Fred Astaire–Ginger Rodgers films, *Swing Time* (1936), but three years later his collaboration with Hammerstein, *Very Warm for May*, was a dismal failure on the New York stage, a sad ending to a glorious Broadway career that had lasted nearly three decades. George Gershwin (with Ira) completed some of his greatest songs for two excellent Hollywood films in 1937, *Shall We Dance* and *Damsel in Distress*, but his death that July ended the promise of a return to his Broadway roots. Although Irving Berlin was similarly focusing on Hollywood musicals, he managed to produce two well-received Broadway shows during these years, the loosely historical book musical *Louisiana Purchase*, which was a hit in 1940, and the patriotic revue *This Is the Army*, in 1942.

Other than Rodgers and Hart, the most prolific Broadway composers during the late 1930s and early 1940s were Cole Porter (eight shows) and Kurt Weill (four shows), and only later did they truly give Rodgers and Hart real competition.[5] By most any criteria, Rodgers and Hart, rich, successful, and innovative, indeed loomed large during these years. Even though *Jumbo*, staged in the refurbished Hippodrome, lost money on its considerable investment, Rodgers and Hart's first post-Hollywood diaspora show

Table 3.1. Broadway Productions by Rodgers and Hart, Porter, and Weill, 1934–1943

	Rodgers and Hart	Porter	Weill
1934		*Anything Goes* (420)	
1935	*Jumbo* (233)	*Jubilee* (169)	
1936	*On Your Toes* (315)	*Red, Hot and Blue!* (183)	*Johnny Johnson* (68)
1937	*Babes in Arms* (289) *I'd Rather Be Right* (290)		
1938	*I Married an Angel* (338) *The Boys from Syracuse* (235)	*You'll Never Know* (78) *Leave It to Me* (291)	*Knickerbocker Holiday* (168)
1939	*Too Many Girls* (249)	*DuBarry Was a Lady* (408)	
1940	*Higher and Higher* (108) *Pal Joey* (374)	*Panama Hattie* (501)	
1941		*Let's Face It!* (547)	*Lady in the Dark* (467)
1942	*By Jupiter* (427)		
1943	*A Connecticut Yankee* (135)	*Something for the Boys* (422)	*One Touch of Venus* (567)

Note: Numbers in parentheses refer to first-run Broadway performances.

would nonetheless emerge as the longest running musical of 1935.[6] *On Your Toes* was, by a long shot, the hit musical of 1936. *Babes in Arms* and *I'd Rather Be Right* were by far the two longest running book shows of 1937. For nearly everyone not associated with Rodgers and Hart, however, the lot was not a happy one. Those who lament the dearth of new Broadway shows in the modern era might take solace in recalling the still darker times of the Depression. The nadir arrived in the summer of 1937; at one point *Babes in Arms* was the *only* book show running on Broadway. In 1938, Rodgers and Hart surpassed these successes with their biggest hit of the decade, *I Married an Angel*, which was the top book show of the year. Their other musical from 1938, *The Boys from Syracuse*, ended up as the third longest run of the year after Porter's *Leave It to Me*. In another sign of their New York pres-

Rodgers and Hart

ence, Rodgers and Hart were the subjects in 1938 of a two-part profile in *The New Yorker* and of a *Time* cover story (discussed in Chapter 1).[7]

After creating the top box office draw each year and several runners-up from 1935 to 1938, the Broadway hegemony of Rodgers and Hart entered a three-year gradual decline. The big show of 1939, Porter's *DuBarry Was a Lady*, left the more modest Rodgers and Hart hit, *Too Many Girls*, a distant second. In 1940, both Porter's *Panama Hattie* and Berlin's *Louisiana Purchase* would surpass the first run of *Pal Joey*, Rodgers and Hart's longest run since their first version of *A Connecticut Yankee* in 1927. *Pal Joey*, which opened on Christmas, continued its run during most of the following year, but 1941 would be the first year since 1934 without a new show by Rodgers and Hart.[8] Their longest first run, *By Jupiter*, opened in June 1942 after all the hits of the previous year—Ira Gershwin and Weill's *Lady in the Dark*, Hugh Martin and Ralph Blane's *Best Foot Forward*, and Porter's *Let's Face It*—had either completed or entered the waning months of their runs.[9] With the exception of *Rosalinda*, an updated English translation of Johann Strauss Jr.'s *Die Fledermaus*, no show that year would come close to challenging Rodgers and Hart's final collaboration.

All this would change in 1943 when five shows, in chronological order, Porter's *Something for the Boys*, Rodgers and Hammerstein's *Oklahoma!*, Franz Lehár's *Merry Widow*, Weill's *One Touch of Venus*, and Hammerstein's *Carmen Jones*, an updated version of Bizet's opera classic, surpassed the return engagement of *A Connecticut Yankee* on November 17. But before the end of their long run, with the exception of a few gaps, most extensively between the closing of *Pal Joey* (November 29, 1941) and the premiere of *By Jupiter* (June 3, 1942), the Broadway sun had rarely set on Rodgers and Hart. Few months went by without the opportunity to see at least one, and usually two, Rodgers and Hart shows on a Broadway stage. Such sustained activity and success were unprecedented and would not be challenged until Rodgers teamed with Hammerstein. The charmed nature of these years was not lost on Rodgers, who remembered this period fondly in *Musical Stages:* "From the fall of 1935 through 1942 was a period of almost unbelievable productivity for Larry and me. We had ten shows in those seven years, all but one a success. It seemed as if nothing we touched could go wrong. We had the freedom to do what we wanted and the satisfaction that what we wanted to do, others wanted to see. We could experiment with form and content not only in our songs but also in the shows themselves."[10]

Most of these once-upon-a-time hit shows are today remembered primarily as the storage facilities for songs still savored for their sophistication, style, and memorability. But in their own day, songs were by no means the whole show. Audiences arrived expecting novel stories, stageworthy dramatic constructions, good jokes and lots of laughs, imaginative dances, beautiful set designs, and funny, talented, and often beautiful stars—the whole package.

Despite Rodgers and Hart's predilection for innovation and artistic change, most aspects of these shows exhibited a remarkable continuity of vision, sound, movement, and words provided by an impressive talent pool. On the visual side of things was Jo Mielziner (1901–76) and his consistently striking, realistic sets. Mielziner's name turns up from the 1920s to the late 1960s in the credits for some of the most successful, highly praised, and lasting plays of these years.[11] Mielziner would eventually design the sets for about four hundred plays and musicals, including seven of Rodgers and Hart's final ten shows (all but *Jumbo*, *I'd Rather Be Right*, and *Babes in Arms*). In two of these, *Too Many Girls* and *By Jupiter*, Mielziner was also responsible for the lighting, a dual role that would continue throughout the Rodgers and Hammerstein years.[12]

The sound of these Rodgers and Hart musicals was even more the product of a consistent "vision." In fact, after sharing the work on *Jumbo*, Hans Spialek (1894–1983) orchestrated every Rodgers and Hart show until Don Walker took over for *By Jupiter* and the *Connecticut Yankee* revival. For the past few decades classic CD collectors have sought the good listening seal, "played on original [i.e., historical] instruments." In fact, in recent years collectors are frequently challenged to find recordings of works such as Bach's *Brandenburg* Concertos played on modern instruments. In an analogous development, Spialek's original orchestrations survived forty years of neglect to emerge in the 1980s as a major selling point in new recordings of *On Your Toes*, *Babes in Arms* (two recordings), *The Boys from Syracuse*, and *Pal Joey*.

Working on the premise that one chart, in this case table 3.2, is worth a thousand words, only a few comments need be added to reinforce what can be gleaned by a perusal of Rodgers and Hart's team of librettists, producers, directors, choreographers, music directors, orchestrators, set, lighting and costume designers, and casts. One statistic that might be a candidate for the *Guinness Book of Records* is the fact that three pairs of men choreographed, directed, and produced eight of the final ten Rodgers and Hart shows: Robert Alton and George Balanchine (choreographers), George Abbott and Joshua Logan (directors), and Abbott and Dwight Deere Wiman

Table 3.2. The Rodgers and Hart Repertory Company, 1935–1943
Based on two or more shows

Librettists

George Abbott: *On Your Toes* [with Rodgers and Hart], *The Boys from Syracuse* [with Rodgers and Hammerstein: *Me and Juliet*]

Rodgers and Hart: *On Your Toes* [with Abbott], *Babes in Arms, I Married an Angel, By Jupiter*

Producers

George Abbott: *The Boys from Syracuse, Too Many Girls, Pal Joey*

Dwight Deere Wiman: *On Your Toes, Babes in Arms, I Married an Angel, Higher and Higher, By Jupiter* [with Rodgers]

Directors

George Abbott: *Jumbo, On Your Toes* [uncredited], *The Boys from Syracuse, Too Many Girls, Pal Joey* [with Rodgers and Hammerstein: *Me and Juliet*]

Joshua Logan: *I Married an Angel, Higher and Higher* [also libretto], *By Jupiter* [with Rodgers and Hammerstein: *South Pacific* (also libretto with Hammerstein)]

Choreographers

Robert Alton: *Too Many Girls, Higher and Higher, Pal Joey, By Jupiter*

George Balanchine: *On Your Toes, Babes in Arms, I Married an Angel, The Boys from Syracuse*

Music Directors

Harry Levant: *I'd Rather Be Right, The Boys from Syracuse, Too Many Girls, Pal Joey*

Gene Salzer: *On Your Toes, Babes in Arms, I Married an Angel*

Orchestrations

Hans Spialek: *Jumbo* [with others], *On Your Toes, Babes in Arms, I'd Rather Be Right, I Married an Angel, The Boys from Syracuse, Too Many Girls, Ghost Town* [ballet], *Higher and Higher, Pal Joey*

Don Walker: *By Jupiter, A Connecticut Yankee* [revival]

Settings

Jo Mielziner: *On Your Toes, I Married an Angel, The Boys from Syracuse, Too Many Girls, Higher and Higher, Pal Joey, By Jupiter* [with Rodgers and Hammerstein: *Carousel*]

Lighting

Jo Mielziner: *The Boys from Syracuse, Too Many Girls, Pal Joey, By Jupiter* [with Rodgers and Hammerstein: *Allegro, South Pacific, The King and I, Me and Juliet, Pipe Dream*]

Table 3.2. Continued

Costumes

Raoul Pène Du Bois: *Jumbo, Too Many Girls, Ghost Town* [ballet]
Irene Sharaff: *On Your Toes, I'd Rather Be Right* [with John Hambleton], *The Boys from Syracuse, By Jupiter* [with Rodgers and Hammerstein: *The King and I, Me and Juliet*]

Casts

Ray Bolger: Junior in *On Your Toes*, Sapiens in *By Jupiter*
Leila Ernst: Tallulah Lou in *Too Many Girls*, Linda English in *Pal Joey*
Ronald Graham: Antipholus of Ephesus in *The Boys from Syracuse*, Theseus in *By Jupiter*
Wynn Murray: Baby Rose in *Babes in Arms*, Luce in *The Boys from Syracuse*
Vera-Ellen: Minerva in *By Jupiter*, Evelyn in *A Connecticut Yankee* [revival]
Vivienne Segal: Countess Palaffi in *I Married an Angel*, Vera Simpson in *Pal Joey*, Queen Morgan Le Fay in *A Connecticut Yankee* [revival]
Mary Jane Walsh: Judge's Girl in *I'd Rather Be Right*, Eileen Eilers in *Too Many Girls*
Marcy Wescott: Luciana in *The Boys from Syracuse*, Consuelo in *Too Many Girls*

(producers). Eight actors and actresses played prominent roles in at least two of these shows.

Throughout his long career, Rodgers's financial success gave him and his collaborators freedom to follow their artistic inclinations and desire for growth. In contrast to their cautious Broadway work after the fiasco of *Chee-Chee* in 1928, the post-Hollywood years bestowed on Rodgers and Hart the luxury of knowing that they could select and develop new and occasionally daring material. From 1935 to 1943 Rodgers and Hart created ten new and mostly imaginative shows and significantly revised an eleventh. Their impulses to create original and stageworthy work rarely led them astray, either artistically or financially, in the Depression and World War II marketplace. Only one new show, *Higher and Higher*, and the revival of another, *A Connecticut Yankee*, fell short of what was then a respectable and profit-making run of 230 performances.[13] *Yankee* marked the end of Hart's magnificent career, but Rodgers, now with Hammerstein, would dominate the remaining years of the forties with *Oklahoma!, Carousel*, and *South Pacific* on Broadway; a successful film, *State Fair*; major productions of two musicals not by Rodgers (the extensive revival of Hammerstein's and Kern's *Show Boat* and a new hit, Berlin's *Annie Get Your Gun*); and several hit plays with Rodgers and Hammerstein as producers.[14] Against all this success came one relative failure, *Allegro*, and even that made some money on the strength of advance sales.

During the years of Rodgers and Hammerstein (and their progeny), some of the later shows by Rodgers and Hart began to make a comeback. The starting point was a successful studio recording of *Pal Joey* in 1950 that helped create an appetite and a market for a stage revival two years later—at 542 performances, it surpassed all previous *original* runs for a Rodgers and Hart show. Soon, however, the taste for Rodgers and Hart dissipated. *New York Times* theater critic Brooks Atkinson, for example, who had nothing but praise for *On Your Toes* in 1936, concurred with most ticket buyers when he concluded that by 1954 the Rodgers and Hammerstein musical had passed Rodgers and Hart by.[15]

In 1955, commercial television presented reasonably faithful versions of *A Connecticut Yankee* (the 1943 version) and of Rodgers and Hart's first book show, *Dearest Enemy*.[16] The Hollywood Production Code's prohibition of depictions of adultery (one of the original dubious virtues of the Broadway *Pal Joey*) led to a comically distorted film starring Frank Sinatra, Kim Novak, and Rita Hayworth, released in 1957. The 1960s saw a slightly more faithful *Jumbo*, the last of several dozen films adapted from the stage, with a score that included five of the original eleven songs in addition to Rodgers and Hart songs from other shows. After these films, two shows returned with Off-Broadway runs, each leading to reasonably complete recordings for the first time: a well-received return of *The Boys from Syracuse* (1963) and a lesser run of *By Jupiter* (1967). Over the next two decades the Goodspeed Opera House offered somewhat doctored and unrecorded revivals of *Dearest Enemy* (1976), *Babes in Arms* (1979), and *A Connecticut Yankee* (1989). For several years rumors have been circulating in theatrical circles that a revised *Pal Joey* with a new and improved book will appear in a major Broadway revival sometime soon. Perhaps such a production would partially vindicate the work after its last disappointing Broadway production in 1976.

After a thirty-year hiatus, in 1983 mainstream Broadway produced a spectacularly successful revival of Rodgers and Hart's *On Your Toes* (505 performances). The production resurrected the original director and writer George Abbott (then a spry ninety-seven) and made a point of restoring all the songs in the original order, usually sung by their rightful owners, and featuring the original orchestrations by Spialek, who was also alive to help supervise.[17] Beginning in the late 1980s, *On Your Toes* would be joined by another three nearly complete recordings, *Babes in Arms, The Boys from Syracuse,* and *Pal Joey,* all of which similarly displayed and prominently marketed Spialek's original period sounds. The latter two were byproducts of the successful and critically acclaimed New York revival series, City Center *Encores!* Great American Musicals in Concert. In the 1998–99 season this noble enterprise added a third Rodgers and Hart show to its list, another *Babes in Arms,* along with a recording still more complete. Another staged revival of *Syracuse,* with a new book by Nicky Silver (billed as "based on the original book by George Abbott"), was presented by the Roundabout Theatre Company to celebrate the Rodgers centennial in the summer of 2002.

A summary of what historians have chosen to highlight and a synthesis of critical opinion should help those who want to grapple with the historical legacy of these final Rodgers and Hart shows, especially for readers who may have heard the soundtracks or isolated songs but are unfamiliar with the dramatic contexts for most of the shows. Below I discuss the sporadic and often problematic documentary remnants of these shows. For details, organized by show, see table 3.5.

First, a few generalizations about the source material. Although Hart's lyrics are accessible, reliable, and nearly complete in *The Complete Lyrics of Lorenz Hart,* librettos and scores (especially reliable ones) are often difficult to obtain. Unfortunately, in nearly every case the films adapted from these shows offer rewritten and distorted versions of the original books and stories. The films also invariably removed many of the songs that made the original shows memorable and added other songs by Rodgers and Hart or occasionally by others. One may, of course, judge the results on their own terms, but viewers and listeners should not expect to see and hear these works in anything approaching their original form. Since comprehensive cast albums were not produced during the Rodgers and Hart years, original cast recordings are incomplete or nonexistent.[18] Modern listeners instead must rely on reconstructions, modern productions, studio recordings, or miscellaneous recorded song anthologies, such as Ben Bagley's *Rodgers and Hart Revisited* series, to hear these songs.[19] I encourage readers to consider these shows as dramatic entities, and to imagine—or better, see—how they work on the stage (which they usually do) when they come to town.

Legacies and Epiphanies

Musicals that are not widely known are especially susceptible to repeated (and untested) historical anecdotes and facile critical encapsulations. Perhaps the central critical verdict concerning Rodgers and Hart's final flurry of shows is, as we have noted, that an endless parade of clever lyrics and memorable tunes is buried in unrevivable shows. This is not strictly true, of course. We have also noted successful Broadway revivals of *On Your Toes* and *Pal Joey* and other resuscitations. *The Boys from Syracuse* and *Babes in Arms* are frequently revived in various states of dramatic and musical revision in regional and amateur theater. And we now have reliable recorded facsimiles of the four above-named shows and rereleased period recordings of others. But even the best-known Rodgers and Hart musicals remain far less known today than the popular works Rodgers wrote with Hammerstein.

In the innovation-conscious years prior to the postmodern era, historians and Rodgers himself emphasized the original aspects of these shows with Hart (as he would later do with his Hammerstein shows). However conventional, tame, and dated they may seem to us now, and regardless how out of context their songs and lyrics may have become, we should remember that Rodgers and Hart viewed their works as dramatic entities, with each show adding something new in the way of form and content. Below is a survey of the innovations in the final shows, as well as the most commonly repeated anecdotal remarks and critical epiphanies attached to each show:

Jumbo: The first—and so far the last—attempt to combine a musical with a real circus, in the refurbished Hippodrome, exhibited an astounding total of five hundred live animals (including more than one elephant). Other historical distinctions were the then astonishing production cost of $340,000 and what may have been a record-shattering imbalance between rehearsal time and length of actual run. *Jumbo* also marked the musical directing debut of George Abbott, the first of his five collaborations with Rodgers and Hart. Unless someone has ready access to circus animals, the musical will probably remain dormant.

On Your Toes: In Rodgers's words, "For the first time ballet was being incorporated in a musical-comedy book."[20] Although this historical assessment has not gone unchallenged, the fact remains that *On Your Toes* introduced the classical (and popular) choreography of George Balanchine to the American book musical.[21] In addition to a lengthy number on taps and toe shoes set to the title tune in act II, each act culminated in a full-length ballet, even though these ballets formed somewhat less than an "integral part of the action." A number of songs from this show, including "There's a Small Hotel" (originally intended for *Jumbo*) have become standards, and the second act ballet, the jazzy "Slaughter on Tenth Avenue" has experienced a rich life of its own outside the show. *On Your Toes* also marked the first star billing of dancer-comedian Ray Bolger, three years before he would portray the Scarecrow in the Hollywood film *The Wizard of Oz*.[22]

Babes in Arms: Read a dozen critical commentaries—or several dozen— and the verdict is nearly unanimous: almost everyone thinks *Babes in Arms* has the best Rodgers and Hart score ever. Indeed, to the six songs anthologized in Rodgers and Hart songbooks one could easily add another four (or more). It is also more than a historical footnote that this quintessential "let's put on a show" musical took the somewhat daring step of casting actual "kids," ages sixteen to twenty-five, in all the leading roles. As we have noted, Rodgers took pride in the fact that perhaps for the first time not only the ballets but all the songs were part of the plot.[23] *Babes in Arms* also marked the theatrical debuts of twenty-three-year-old Alfred Drake (who six years later would star as Curly in *Oklahoma!*), the Nicholas Brothers, Dan Dailey, and Robert Rounseville. Equally striking, especially from today's economic vantage point—but even in its own era in comparison with *Jumbo*—was the low production cost. At $55,000 it was one of the biggest bargains in musical theater history.

I'd Rather Be Right: Along with Weill's *Johnny Johnson*, *I'd Rather Be Right* was probably the most significant political book musical since the Gershwin trilogy earlier in the decade, *Strike Up the Band* (1930), *Of Thee I Sing* (1931), and *Let 'Em Eat Cake* (1933). Much has been made of the fact that real contemporary historical figures are portrayed, most notably President Roosevelt and his on-stage butler Alf Landon, who in real life ran unsuccessfully against Roosevelt in 1936. The show marked the much-anticipated return of Cohan after a long absence from Broadway (four years after playing a fictional film president in Rodgers and Hart's *The Phantom President*). The show's topicality and the absence of a strong score—"Have You Met Miss Jones?" is the only unequivocal hit—has left this show a historical footnote, a musical often mentioned but neither heard nor seen (though it could be *read* since its libretto was published).

I Married an Angel: Rodgers and Hart's biggest hit of the 1930s with the longest run of any of their shows since *A Connecticut Yankee* in 1927. *Angel* was arguably the first important show of its time in which the female lead dances rather than sings. It is also remembered as the musical source of the film that dismally concluded the successful operetta film career of Nelson Eddy and Jeanette MacDonald (the latter a singing rather than a dancing angel). In contrast to the Broadway version, Count Palaffi (Eddy) in the film dreams of marrying an angel before marrying her counterpart in real life. In fact, in *Musical Stages* Rodgers pointed with pride to the decision to *avoid* the dream worlds of *Peggy-Ann* and *Yankee* and have a waking Count marry a "real angel."[24]

The Boys from Syracuse: Although *Jumbo* has been interpreted as a loosely updated version of *Romeo and Juliet*, *The Boys from Syracuse* was the first musical in the modern era (that is, after 1920) directly based on a Shakespeare play. Just as *I'd Rather Be Right* used real contemporary political figures, *The Boys from Syracuse* used Shakespeare's actual characters and closely followed his characterization and dramatic structure. Surveys more often than not inform readers that only one line is borrowed from Shakespeare (see below for some revisionism on this point). Nearly everyone also notes that the selection of *The Comedy of Errors* stemmed in part from the fact that Larry Hart's actor brother Teddy bore an uncanny physical resemblance to Jimmy Savo, a resemblance that could be exploited for comedic purposes in the roles of the servant twins, Dromio of Ephesus and Dromio of Syracuse (see page 94).[25] No less an authority than Lehman Engel places *The Boys from Syracuse* along with *Pal Joey* and *Porgy and Bess* as one of a trio of revivable shows from before the Rodgers and Hammerstein era.[26]

Too Many Girls: A 1930s collegiate musical in the tradition of Kern, Guy Bolton, and P. G. Wodehouse's *Leave It to Jane* (1917) and Ray Henderson, B. G. DeSylva, and Lew Brown's *Good News!* (1927). A central historical footnote to this now arcane but once successful musical is the introduction of Desi Arnaz as a conga drum–playing fullback featured in "All Dressed Up (Spic and Spanish)." It was unfortunate that this once popular film was for the most part invisible before its release on videocassette in 2001, since it offered the most faithful contemporary example of a Rodgers and Hart score, with seven songs retained from the show and a new gem, "You're Nearer," expressly written for the new medium. Unlike most film adaptations, the movie, directed by its original stage director, Abbott, also featured many from the original stage cast. It marked the first film pairing of Lucille Ball (Consuelo) and Arnaz (Manuelito), who were introduced on the set and married the following year. The show also marked the beginning of Hart's serious decline and incapacitation to such an extent that Rodgers was forced to create the lyrics to the opening number, "Heroes in the Fall." Any show in which a character named Pepe ("Peppy") sings a song called "Spic and Spanish" or, joined by Manuelito, "She Could Shake the Maracas," might have trouble finding a modern audience. Another politically incorrect song, "Give It Back to the Indians," seems destined to permanently offend yet another group of Americans. On the other hand, a show with songs like "Love Never Went to College," "I Like to Recognize the Tune," and "I Didn't Know What Time It Was" has something going for it.

Higher and Higher: The only flop of this last glorious phase in the long and fruitful career of Rodgers and Hart, *Higher and Higher* provides excellent examples that support two pet theories of the composer: 1) "It's impossible to redesign a show once the basic concept proves unworkable"; and 2) "If a trained seal steals your show, you don't have a show."[27]

Pal Joey: The show that marked the stage debut of imminent film star Gene Kelly in the title role, *Pal Joey* is widely heralded as the greatest Rodgers and Hart show. Most historians and critics join Rodgers in noting the significance and sophistication of a heel as the central protagonist, and the presence of unsavory aspects of life, including adultery and blackmail. Because of such widely quoted remarks as those by Atkinson—who found the subject matter odious and asked at the end of his *New York Times* review, "Can you draw sweet water from a foul well?"—*Pal Joey's* success in its own time is frequently overlooked.[28] Nevertheless, the 1952 return was one of the few times a revival has outlasted its original. Although unseen on Broadway for decades, the show remains a staple of regional theater and a historical and artistic milestone of the musical theater.[29]

By Jupiter: Perhaps largely due to the star status of Bolger as Sapiens, three years after playing the Scarecrow in *The Wizard of Oz*, *By Jupiter* completed the Broadway reign of Rodgers and Hart with a show that surpassed all others in its initial run. Bolger was likely the principal audience attraction. In any event, when he left the show to entertain the troops, the show quickly folded. After an unsuccessful Off-Broadway revival in 1967, all that remains are the songs. The best known of these, Rodgers's final waltz with Hart, "Wait Till You See Her," was cut from the show and restored only near the end of the run. In the original play, *The Warrior's Husband*, the playwright, Julian F. Thompson, describes Sapiens as "feminine by training but in no sense effeminate." Despite this disclaimer, gay and misogynist subtexts inherent in the male-female role reversals, especially as portrayed by Ernest Truex in the 1933 film, might preclude (or perhaps inspire) future revivals.[30]

The Sources

Lyrics: Fortunately, the lyrics for all the songs in all these shows, and nearly every other Rodgers and Hart song, can be easily located in *The Complete Lyrics of Lorenz Hart*, edited by Dorothy Hart and Robert Kimball. Despite an omission here and there—some rectified in an appendix added to a second edition—this source is a model of scholarship and indispensable for any study of Rodgers and Hart shows, scholarly or casual.

Librettos: Few librettos were published before the Rodgers and Hammerstein era. Consequently, as indicated in table 3.5, librettos (sometimes with incomplete lyrics) for five of the eleven shows surveyed in this chapter are obtainable only from the Rodgers and Hammerstein Theatre Library, which until recently would rent revised rather than original scripts. Four librettos can be found in the New York Public Library. Only three were published in their time or since: *I'd Rather Be Right, Too Many Girls,* and *Pal Joey*. It is not easy to get to know the dramatic contexts of Rodgers and Hart's songs.

Recordings: Compared with the libretto shortage, recordings of Broadway, Off-Broadway, and concert performances, historic recordings, studio recordings, film soundtracks, and television productions are plentiful and more or less accessible. In many cases, especially in the absence of published vocal scores, these recordings are the most reliable way to discover the musical content of these shows.

Films: For those born too late to see the original stage productions, film versions present a potentially valuable source for how these shows might have held together. However, as we have noted, the stage and film versions typically depart significantly from their sources. Even in later years, when Rodgers and Hammerstein were in a position to exercise control over what went on in their films, only rarely did they try to follow their stage creations with absolute fidelity. Even with such "integrated" shows as *Oklahoma!* and *Carousel* they deleted songs: *Oklahoma!* ("It's a Scandal! It's an Outrage!" and "Lonely Room"); and *Carousel* ("Geraniums in the Window" and "The Highest Judge of All"). From *The King and I* they removed four songs, "My Lord and Master," "Shall I Tell You What I Think of You?" "I Have Dreamed," and "Western People Funny." With *South Pacific* however, they restored a song, "My Girl Back Home" (dropped during the tryouts) to the film. The practice of adding songs, and deleting others, would continue in the three films that Rodgers partially supervised after Hammerstein's death (*Flower Drum Song*, the remake of *State Fair*, and *The Sound of Music*), as well as the second (and after Rodgers's death the third) televised broadcast of *Cinderella* (see Chapter 5).

Between 1939 and 1962 no fewer than eight of Rodgers and Hart's final eleven shows were executed (double entendre intended) on the screen: *On Your Toes* and *Babes in Arms* (1939); *The Boys from Syracuse* and *Too Many Girls* (1940); *I Married an Angel* (1942); *Higher and Higher* (1944); *Pal Joey* (1957); and *Jumbo* (1962). Not one of the films presents a show with all the songs intact. Most tamper with the story, sometimes beyond recognition. Here is a mercifully brief rundown.

To its credit, the film version of *On Your Toes* shows the ballets and gives viewers a glimpse of Vera Zorina, the original stage angel from *I Married an Angel*, now dancing with Rodgers and Hart's nondancing stage regular Eddie Albert (the original Antipholus of Syracuse). Aside from the ballets, however, the film retained only three songs, and these were used to underscore dialogue rather than sung. Notoriously, from the rich *Babes in Arms* score only the title song and "Where or When" remain. On the plus side, this film has been credited with preserving the spirit of the Rodgers and Hart book (albeit with new dialogue and songs by other composers and lyricists). *The Boys from Syracuse* presented the original story with new dialogue but without outside song interference and a relatively faithful adherence to the original structure. Nonetheless, it scrapped all but four songs of the original score and added two new ones, "The Greeks Have No Word for It" and "Who Are You?"[31] *Too Many Girls* offers a screenplay relatively faithful to the original problematic script, seven actors from the original stage version, sung versions of five of the original fourteen songs, no interpolations by others, and a new song classic expressly written for the film, "You're Nearer." *I Married an Angel*, the last of the eight-film partnership with MacDonald and Eddy, featured MacDonald as a singing rather than a dancing angel and kept only four songs. Viewers of *Higher and Higher* heard only one song from the original show. *Pal Joey* included five songs from the stage version, but expurgated perhaps in response to the Hollywood Production Code, and four songs from other Rodgers and Hart shows. In *Jumbo*, five original songs joined two other Rodgers and Hart songs.

Scores: Vocal scores are currently available for four Rodgers and Hart musicals: *Babes in Arms* (Chappell, 1960), *Pal Joey* (Chappell, 1962), *The Boys from Syracuse* (Chappell, 1965), and *On Your Toes* (Chappell, 1985). All were generated by revivals. The publication of *On Your Toes* followed the 1983 revival and includes some of the changes in song order used in that stage production. The *Babes in Arms* score is based on the 1959 revival directed and with a new book by George Oppenheimer. Consequently, it contains neither the original overture nor the ballets, and gone entirely is the racially controversial "All Dark People." The score for *The Boys from Syracuse* reflects a number of musical changes that were adopted in the 1963 Off-Broadway production (including the overture and ballets, thus removing the quotation from Debussy's *Prelude to the Afternoon of a Faun*, and everything else, from the latter). Even the *Pal Joey* score reflects a number of modest changes from the 1952 revival.

Other shows have been issued as song selections. These include the selections from *Jumbo* (based on the movie but including all the recorded numbers listed in the soundtrack above) and A *Connecticut Yankee*, a hybrid that offers the four hits of 1927 ("My Heart Stood Still," "Thou Swell," "On a Desert Island With Thee!" and "I Feel at Home with You"), three new songs from the 1943 revival ("To Keep My Love Alive," "Can't You Do a Friend a Favor?" and "You Always Love the Same Girl"), and two songs dropped during the Philadelphia tryouts ("I Blush" and "Someone Should Tell Them").

The songs have long since become more familiar artifacts than the scores, and even those unfamiliar with these Rodgers and Hart shows might know many of them by sound if not by title—for example, when they hear them accompanying perfume ads on television ("My Romance" for Ralph Lauren, sung by Carly Simon), in hotel lobbies, or in department stores. To take *only* the forty-eight songs that are included in the major published anthologies, the song legacy is extraordinarily fecund, and no show is represented by fewer than three songs. In the case of *Babes in Arms*, *The Boys from Syracuse*, *On Your Toes*, and *Pal Joey*, many more equally fine songs, not included in the published song anthologies, can be enjoyed in the vocal scores and selections mentioned above.

Babes in Arms offers a good test case for measuring the joys and tribulations of reconstructing a 1930s hit. Like several other shows, *Babes* exists in various forms: the original 1937 Broadway show, a 1939 film, a 1959 revival in Palm Beach, and two reconstructed recordings (1989 and 1999). The only published vocal score to date follows the short-lived Palm Beach production (March 30–April 4)which was also shown in Miami Beach (April 6–18), with a new book by Oppenheimer. A number of songs appear in new positions, but only a few musical numbers were deleted ("All Dark People," "You Are So Fair," and "Peter's Journey Ballet," the latter revolving around the song "Imagine"). The score also recycled two songs from other shows, Rodgers and Hart's "You're Nearer," previously added to the film adaptation of *Too Many Girls*, and a snippet of "A Wonderful Guy," from Rodgers and Hammerstein's *South Pacific*. The latter appears early in the show, replacing (for the moment) "Where or When," which was moved to later in the first act, and follows some orchestral underscoring for the title song. The score indicates a Press Agent cue, "She can be another Mary Martin," after which are heard the final measures of "A Wonderful Guy" (six statements of "I'm in love"). Taking even a fragment from a song hit, with a Hammerstein lyric no less, contradicts Rodgers's own limits on recycling to songs that were either unused or from shows unlikely to be revived.[32] Although the idea of interpolating these songs probably did not come from Rodgers, he not only agreed to allow their use but to allow the 1959 version to stand as the definitive musical version of his show. Until recently (the 1937 *Babes* is now a rental option), this was the only version that the Rodgers & Hammerstein Organization rented to producers and directors who wanted to perform this work.

In his notes to the first reconstructed recording of *Babes in Arms* (1989), musical theater reconstructionist Tommy Krasker explains why the concert performance at Avery Fisher Hall conducted by Evans Haile and the resulting recording on New World Records was incomplete: "The authors' estates felt that the lyric to the DeQuincy Brothers' song, 'All Dark People,' might be misinterpreted out of context and asked that the number be omitted."[33] (Krasker and Robert Kimball have written the one and only guide to manuscript sources, *Catalog of the American Musical: Musicals of Irving Berlin, George & Ira Gershwin, Cole Porter, Richard Rodgers & Lorenz Hart.*) In 1999 audiences who attended the City Center *Encores!* concert performances finally got a chance to hear the *music* of "All Dark People," retitled "Light on Their Feet," a title derived from the opening lyric of the main chorus, "Play that music for me and my sweet / All dark people is light on their feet." Theodore S. Chapin, president of the Rodgers & Hammerstein Organization, writes in his notes to the DRG recording that "the song on this album entitled 'Light On Their Feet' is a cut down version of the original 'All Dark People,' a song for the black characters whose lyric feels potentially offensive to modern ears."[34] Constance Valis Hill reports that Viola Nicholas (the mother of Fayard and Harold) was most offended by the "grammatical construction of the line, 'All dark people is,' because it fed the conception of blacks as ignorant and unable to speak proper English."[35] The solution on the recording was to make the song a dance rehearsal number.

Those who have seen only the 1939 movie musical with Judy Garland

and Mickey Rooney or the 1959 rental stage version would have no idea how indispensable the African American DeQuincy brothers were to the original plot. In the 1937 Broadway version, the bigoted southerner, Lee Calhoun, refuses to fund the babes' show unless the DeQuincys' act is removed. As Ivor DeQuincy phrases it, "We is a little too brunette for his taste." [36] At first, Val (the funny valentine) agrees to compromise his values, thinking that the Calhoun funding will lead to a future production. After Val explains to Ivor that he and his brother are not going on because he's too young, Lee tells the hurtful truth that they are not going on because they're "too *black!*" Val responds by socking Lee on the jaw and allowing Ivor to go on with the show as the act ends.

There is no question that the song "All Dark People" reinforces stereotypes that are not alleviated by good intentions—assigning a positive but essentialist quality to African Americans as a whole. [37] But racially integrated shows were unusual in the 1930s. It is often reported that Helen Broderick refused to take bows with Ethel Waters in As Thousands Cheer. Waters brought down the house with Berlin's "Heat Wave" and broke audiences' hearts with "Supper Time," a lament sung by a woman wondering how to tell her children that her husband has been lynched and will not be coming home for supper. The decision to integrate a Broadway show and the show-within-the-show was a courageous one in its time, not unlike Benny Goodman's decision to hire Teddy Wilson and Lionel Hampton a few years earlier. Unfortunately, the song the DeQuincys are asked to sing takes a step backward in a musical that also preaches racial tolerance and understanding more than a decade before South Pacific's "Carefully Taught." By making the song an instrumental dance rehearsal number that features the 1920s sound of two pianos, the Encores! reconstruction at least allows "All Dark People" and the two black characters that perform it to stay in the show, without the potentially offensive title and lyrics.

The Boys from Syracuse

As Rodgers tells the story, the idea of adapting Shakespeare into what would become their best known and most frequently revived Broadway show was born on a train ride to Atlantic City early in 1938. Rodgers credits Hart with the idea. In fact, sixteen years earlier Hart had collaborated with Morrie Ryskind on "Shakespeares of 1922," a vaudeville sketch that brought several Shakespeare plays "up to date" so that "five acts you won't have to wait." The

Jimmy Savo and Teddy Hart (Larry's brother), the original twin Dromios in
The Boys from Syracuse

sketches consisted of send-ups of famous speeches interspersed with songs.
Here is most of the *Hamlet* parody, the perfect tonic for an audience recently
subjected to the vicissitudes of Prohibition: "To be or not to be, that is the
question! Whether 'tis nobler to buy your Gordon's gin, and pay the prices
of outrageous bootleggers, or to take arms against this sea of highwaymen,
and make your own home brew! To drink, to die (to dream, perchance).
Alcohol, aye, there's the rub! Home brew does make cowards of us all."[38]
For the Broadway stage, Hart wanted to set a comedy rather than to burlesque a tragedy. We have noted that nearly every source reports that *The
Comedy of Errors* was chosen over more likely Shakespeare plays in order to
take advantage of the resemblance between Larry's brother Teddy and the
actor Jimmy Savo. Since Teddy and Jimmy Savo were frequently confused,
casting them as the twin Dromios would make comic art out of real life.

Since Rodgers and Hart did not begin to plan their *Errors* adaptation until 1938, it is possible also that their Shakespearean choice was influenced by Russian director Theodore Komisarjevsky's 1938 production at Stratford-on-Avon. Chances are good that news from Stratford had spread to New York during the creation of *Syracuse*.[39] Komisarjevsky offered one of the first attempts to deconstruct Shakespeare. Ephesian burghers sported bowler hats à la Charlie Chaplin, the Courtesan was cast as a Mae West impersonator, and viewers and critics were struck by such bold modernity and absurdist touches as a clock invariably striking the wrong hour. Among the many ideas that may have crossed the Atlantic, the decision to convey Aegeon's opening narrative through choral unison and pantomime—the latter technique adopted in the 1984 BBC filmed production—may have given Rodgers, Hart, and Abbott some food for thought in their own un-Shakespearean introduction.

George Abbott (1887–1995), credited as the "book director" on *Jumbo* and the director and co-librettist (with Rodgers and Hart) for *On Your Toes*, was the first choice to direct this Shakespearean venture. Rodgers tells how Abbott took over the book writing as well: "Moreover, George was so enthusiastic that he decided to produce the show himself. At first Larry and I were supposed to collaborate on the script with him, but he had it all finished before we could get started. The book was so sharp, witty, fast-moving and, in an odd way, so very much in keeping with the bawdy Shakespearean tradition that neither Larry nor I wanted to change a line."[40]

Considering the Bard's enormous popularity with American audiences, it is remarkable that *The Boys from Syracuse* was the first attempt to bring Shakespeare to Broadway.[41] As with so many "firsts," this one also was not, at least technically. *La Marjolaine*, "based loosely" on the Shakespeare play *Cymbeline*, appeared on Broadway only months after its composition and Parisian debut in 1877.[42] In any event, by 1938 the first Shakespeare musical had happened a long time ago, and its composer, the long-forgotten Charles Lecoq, Jacques Offenbach's closest rival in operetta in their day, was French, not American.

Those who have observed strong parallels between the plot machinations of *The Comedy of Errors* or *The Boys from Syracuse* and Mozart's *Marriage of Figaro* and *Così fan tutte* will not be surprised to learn that Mozart's librettist for these operas, Lorenzo Da Ponte, once set Shakespeare's *Comedy* to music by Mozart's friend Stephen Storace. The work was titled *Gli equivoci* (translated roughly as *The Misunderstandings*). Storace was the brother (but not an identical twin) of Nancy Storace, the first Susanna in *Figaro*, which premiered only a few months before the Da Ponte–Storace Shakespearean comedy. Winton Dean, in praising Da Ponte's adaptation for its fidelity "to the spirit of the play," sees parallels between Shakespeare's source, Plautian farce, and Mozartean opera, since in his view such farce "was almost an archetype of the *opera buffa* at which Da Ponte was so adept."[43]

Shakespeare's Plautian sources were the *Menaechmi* (or *Two Menaechmuses*), a Greek play of unknown origin, and to a much lesser extent *Amphitruo*. The addition of Aegeon (father to the two Antipholi) was adapted from another allegedly Greek source, *Apollonius of Tyre*.[44] The farces of the Roman dramatist Plautus (c. 254–184), misplaced in the Middle Ages and rediscovered in the fifteenth century, formed a part of Shakespeare's education and were considered, along with the work of the Roman poet Terence, as the "best models for English comedies" in Shakespeare's day.[45] Scholars have conjectured that Shakespeare probably taught these texts during his early days as a schoolteacher.

Plautus has enough to occupy himself with one set of twins, the two Antipholi. Shakespeare compounds the farcical confusion by creating a second set of twins, the two Dromios, their servants since birth. At the same time, through the addition of Aegeon and his poignant story and the insertion of romance, especially between Antipholus of Syracuse and Luciana, the sister of Adriana (the wife of Antipholus of Ephesus, where the play now takes place), Shakespeare also transforms farce into romantic comedy.

Shakespeare scholar Kenneth Muir offers an informative précis of Shakespeare's alterations to Plautus and their dramatic effects:

> Shakespeare's play is much more complicated than Plautus's. The invention of the two Dromios leads to many additional "errors." The invention of Luciana provides a bride for Antipholus of Syracuse and a confidante for Adriana. The wife becomes a central figure in the play, instead of a peripheral one, and the courtezan [sic] becomes a minor figure, her relationship with Antipholus being comparatively innocent. The wife gives the invitation to dinner to the wrong Antipholus, not by the courtezan, as in Plautus. The change to a Christian setting enables Adriana to plead for the sanctity of marriage. Although Shakespeare adds more farcical elements to Plautus's plot—Dromio's wife, Dr. Pinch and others—he also added elements that are not farcical at all. The doomed Aegeon opens the play on a serious note, and his discovery of his wife is a moving scene. The study of Adriana's jealous love, the lyrical proposal of Antipholus of Syracuse to Luciana, and his sense of bewilderment and horror lift the play above the farcical.[46]

Abbott, like Hart no stranger to Shakespeare, writes in his autobiography, "*Mr. Abbott*," that several years before embarking on his transformation of *The Comedy of Errors* he had created abridged versions of *The Merchant of Venice, All's Well That Ends Well*, and *King John* in the early 1930s.[47] When converting *The Comedy of Errors* into a Rodgers and Hart show, Abbott would adopt a similar attitude and approach: "I had always felt that Shakespeare was a practical playwright—that he wrote shows, not dramas, that he was trying to create excitement in the theatre with no thought of posterity, and that while he certainly hoped that his sonnets would bring him fame, he had never for a moment suspected that anyone would ever publish his plays."[48]

From Abbott's perspective, Shakespeare was a prototypical librettist for Rodgers and Hart, and no play was intrinsically more like a musical comedy than *The Comedy of Errors*. For Abbott, the plot was the thing, and the plot was the play. Thus Abbott explains the rationale behind the most radical component of his adaptation, the cavalier abandonment of Shakespeare's beautiful language, both prose and poetry. Abbott even ignores Shakespearean puns such as the one about Nell's [Luce's] receding forehead, which, like France's, stands "armed and reverted making war against her heir [pronounced "hair"]" (III, ii, 126), a pun not unlike those found in Herbert Fields's *Connecticut Yankee* ("You're the roughest knight I've ever had"). Abbott explains what motivated his heretical approach: "Most of the actors of today who consider themselves Shakespearean actors believe that the verse is most important. I cannot believe this. I am confident that Shakespeare wanted to move his audience—to carry them away, to make things real. To our modern ears his language is contrived and stylized, but so was all the language of that day."[49]

Since 1938 the conventional wisdom has invariably instructed us that Abbott "pitched out every line of Shakespeare's dialogue, because he likes his own better."[50] Rodgers and every commentator to follow offer one lonely exception to the rule of plot over poetry, two lines uttered by the Abbess (a Seeress in Abbott's adaptation) toward the end of the final scene: "The venom clamor of a jealous woman poisons more deadly than a mad dog's tooth."[51] In the odd event that someone would mistake this ostentatiously exquisite phrase for Abbott, Dromio of Syracuse immediately emerges from the temple and calls out "Shakespeare!" Although the point remains that Abbott borrowed few actual words from his source, it has so far gone undisclosed that a little later in this closing scene Abbott raided Shakespeare more than previously thought:

Shakespeare	*Abbott*
ABBESS: Most mighty Duke, behold a man much wronged. *All gather to see them.*	SEERESS: Most mighty Duke— behold a man much wronged. (*ANTIPHOLUS S. and Dromio S. behind him enter on temple steps*) (*Astonished reaction from ALL.*)
ADRIANA: I see two husbands, or mine eyes deceive me.	ADRIANA: What! I see two husbands.
DUKE: One of these men is genius to the other; And so of these, which is the natural man, And which the spirit? Who deciphers them?	DUKE: Which of you is real and which the imitation?
S. DROMIO: I, sir, am Dromio; command him away.	DROMIO S: I'm Dromio. Make him go away (*Pointing to Dromio S.*)
E. DROMIO: I, sir, am Dromio; pray let me stay.	DROMIO E: No, I'm Dromio. Let me stay.
V, i, 332–337	Act II, scene 5, pp. 36–37

Interestingly, most Shakespeare scholars have responded charitably to Abbott's sacrilege. In his notes to the Signet edition, Harry Levin considered *The Boys from Syracuse* "one of the happiest collaborations between the vibrant scores of Richard Rodgers and the colloquial lyrics of Lorenz Hart" and a production "paced by the assured direction of George Abbott and enhanced by the brilliant choreography of George Balanchine."[52] Without acknowledging Abbott's contribution, Maureen Grice concludes her stage history of the play by mentioning the "hilarious and impudent musical version of the comedy by Richard Rodgers and Lorenz Hart," which "delighted New York audiences during the 1938/39 season at the Alvin Theatre and was successfully revised in 1963/64 for a long run."[53] Also without mentioning Abbott by name, Harold Bloom in *Shakespeare: The Invention of the Human* succinctly notes that "Shakespeare himself was adapted splendidly by Rodgers and Hart."[54]

Once (and if) we can get beyond Abbott's substitution of Shakespeare's elegant verse for prosaic American vernacular speech—something different from the anachronistic hipness of Fields's *Connecticut* libretto—it may be possible to appreciate the brilliance of selecting this particular play and how Abbott was able to adapt Shakespeare's plot machinations and characters.

The wacky nature of *The Comedy of Errors*, including a liberal amount of abusive physical humor of the Three Stooges or Laurel and Hardy variety, makes it probably the closest Shakespeare came to capturing the qualities that would be prized in well-made television situation comedies. One episode from the sitcom classic of the 1990s, *Seinfeld*, comes to mind. In "Bizarro Jerry," characters nearly identical in appearance to Jerry Seinfeld and his male friends, but opposite in nature, temporarily occupy a parallel universe in another part of New York City with Seinfeld's female cohort, Elaine. While sitcoms are not the same thing as musical comedies, both genres need well-crafted silliness to succeed, and both lend themselves to comedies of errors.

As with their counterparts in American popular culture, Shakespeare's error-prone comedic characters invariably fail to consider what is most logical, even when their blindness leads to an absurdity that borders on madness. In both *Errors* and *Syracuse*, Antipholus of Syracuse and his Ephesian counterpart both know they have a twin. In fact, the Syracusan Antipholus has been relentlessly searching for his twin for the past five years (seven years in Abbott's adaptation), and the sole purpose of his visit to Ephesus was to find his brother. Despite this, it is not until the end of the play, when the brothers meet face to face, that either Antipholus considers the other's presence as a way to explain the craziness of the four previous acts. Today, when someone forgets a conversation they had with us a few minutes earlier, we might be inclined to blame Alzheimer's rather than magic, but most of us remain susceptible to comical misinterpretation and misunderstandings. Both Shakespeare and Abbott capture an essence of human folly: the inability to make sense of events that are out of the ordinary.

The opening of *Syracuse* especially demonstrates Abbott's underappreciated art of letting the composer and lyricist take over. After a fanfare, characters in traditional Comedy and Tragedy masks do a tap dance and explain the bare essentials: "This is a drama of Ancient Greece. It is a story of mistaken identity. If it's good enough for Shakespeare, it's good enough for us."[55] The musical has officially begun, or as Stephen Sondheim would say later in his own adaptation of Plautus, *A Funny Thing Happened on the Way to the Forum*, "Tragedy tomorrow—comedy tonight!" Abbott next turns to Shakespeare's opening scene in "I Had Twins," in which we meet the long-winded Aegeon (Egeon in Shakespeare). As Aegeon tells his tale of woe, serio-comic in its tragic improbabilities, he sings no words and is reduced instrumentally to a "plaintive E-flat clarinet." The Duke, also silent, is represented by a bass clarinet with a predilection for ending phrases on ominous descending tritones (or diminished fifths, such as C–F#). What the instruments are saying—and they always get to speak first—is translated into words by the Sergeant of Police as he repeats each musical line. The Sergeant can do this because he (and only he) is able to see and hear a court proceeding through a window. This theatrical device allows the audience to hear Aegeon's message, which gets the play going, but by depriving Aegeon the opportunity to kvetch directly, Abbott and Co. are now better able to keep a musical comedy tone.

The Sergeant speaks for both Aegeon and the Duke, and the Crowd responds directly and without translation:

> SERGEANT: Our rigid laws of Ephesus most rightfully refuse a
> Visa to any citizen of uncivilized Syracuse
> [pronounced "kyooz a" as in Shakespeare]
> If any one of us would dare to go to that barbaric city
> He'd get the axe the same as he—
> That's why he gets no pity.
> CROWD: Give him the axe—the axe—the axe!
> Give him the axe—the axe!
> (DUKE—bass clarinet)
> SERGEANT: Unless he can pay a thousand marks
> Or borrow it from the local sharks.
> [1938 Libretto, Act I, scene 1, p. 3]

The Crowd wants justice and, better, blood ("Give him the axe—the axe—the axe!") but will accept bribes. Throughout the scene Rodgers and Hart not only convey Aegeon's story with the minimum of words but with musical simplicity (tritones excepted, we hear lots of straightforward ascending and descending scales and uncomplicated rhythms and harmonies). The Crowd explains that "There'll be an execution" since "the law makes retribution." A citizen asks, "What did he do?" The Sergeant answers, "He came from Syracuse!" Through this terse exposition, it takes only a few stanzas for the audience to find out what it needs to know. Viewers quickly learn how a shipwreck parted Aegeon from his wife, his son Antipholus, and his son's servant, Dromio. They hear how the son and slave who remained, improbably also named Antipholus and Dromio, went to search for the missing Antipholus seventeen years later. They also learn about Aegeon's own fruitless search for both sets of twins and his growing realization that the execution awaiting him at the end of the day (unless he can pay the 1,000 marks or borrow it from the local sharks) would be a welcome resolution to his travails.

In future scenes, Shakespeare frequently adopts rhymed verse similar to that used by Hart in the Prologue. Among Shakespeare's comedies, only *A Midsummer Night's Dream* and *Love's Labour's Lost* contain a higher percentage of rhyme.[56] Scenes between Adriana and Luciana, and Luciana and Antipholus of Syracuse, contain the most rhymed couplets, but considerable rhyming also appears in less lyrical scenes, such as between the master and slave of Ephesus in act III, scene 1 (lines 11–85). When Antipholus of Syracuse courts his "sweet mistress" Luciana, he even occasionally speaks in interior rhymes such "I *know* not" and "you *show* not," a device that would not be out of place in a Hart lyric (for example, "Lovely *witches*, let the *stitches*" in "Falling in Love with Love").[57]

In the process of plotting Rodgers and Hart's songs, Abbott's libretto takes a number of additional liberties in his efforts to transform Shakespearean farce into musical comedy, some of which will be examined here. For an overview of the ways Shakespeare found his way into the songs of *The Boys from Syracuse*, see table 3.3.

After "I Had Twins," which pithily pares a long speech, one is continually struck by the looseness with which Abbott treats his source. This freedom is perhaps the most striking aspect of the adaptation. With few exceptions ("Falling in Love with Love," "This Can't Be Love," "Let Antipholus In," and "Come with Me") it is difficult to pinpoint specific lyrical Shakespearean counterparts. By the time act II arrives, correspondences are rough at best and in some cases nonexistent. Some songs are loosely based on a scene or a portion of a scene in the play ("He and She"), others capture a hypothetical off-stage moment ("You Have Cast Your Shadow on the Sea"), and some, like Dromio of Ephesus's lament at the loss of his brother ("Big Brother"), are freely invented. The framing characters of Egeon (Aegeon) and the Abbess (Seeress) now have little to say and sing no songs. On the other hand, Abbott's Luce (Shakespeare's Nell) causes considerably more traffic on Shakespeare's stage. In *Comedy*, Nell, the wife of the Ephesian Dromio, appears in a virtually nonspeaking role, although she gains attention as the object of tasteless locker room talk regarding parallels between the shape of her body and various countries. In *Syracuse*, Luce is featured in one trio, two duets, and one solo turn, more singing than any other character (see table 3.4).

In Shakespeare's play, not only are the two Antipholi identical in physical appearance, they are improbably and inexplicably dressed in identical

Table 3.3. *The Boys from Syracuse* and Its Shakespearean Counterparts

The Boys from Syracuse	A Comedy of Errors
Act I	*Act I*
"I Had Twins"	I, i (all)
(Sergeant and Crowd)	(Egeon and Duke)
"Dear Old Syracuse"	I, ii, 33–40
(Dromio and Antipholus of Syracuse)	(Dromio and Antipholus of Syracuse)
	Act II
"What Can You Do with a Man?"	II, i, 58–69
(Dromio of Ephesus and Luce)	(Dromio of Ephesus)
"Falling in Love with Love"	II, i, 103–15 (Adriana and Luciana)
(Adriana and Ladies)	II, ii, 204–05 (Adriana and Antipholus of Syracuse)
	Act III
"The Shortest Day of the Year"	III, i, 1–10
(Antipholus of Ephesus; reprised by Adriana)	(Antipholus of Ephesus)
"This Can't Be Love"	III, i, 1–70
(Antipholus of Syracuse and Luciana)	(Luciana and Antipholus of Syracuse)
"Let Antipholus In" (Ensemble)	III, i, 27–123 (Antipholus of Ephesus, Dromio of Ephesus, Dromio of Syracuse, Luce, Angelo, Balthasar)
Act II	
"Ladies of the Evening"	Off-stage after III, i
(Courtesans and Sergeant)	
"He and She"	Freely based on III, ii, 77–160
(Luce and Dromio of Syracuse)	(Dromio of Syracuse, Antipholus of Syracuse; Luce appears briefly III, i, 47–60)
"You Have Cast Your Shadow on the Sea" (Antipholus of Syracuse and Luciana)	No counterpart, occurs after III, ii, 169–90
	Act IV
"Come with Me"	IV, i, 70–71, 80
(Sergeant, Angelo, and Crowd)	
"Big Brother" (Dromio of Ephesus)	No counterpart

Table 3.3. Continued

The Boys from Syracuse	A Comedy of Errors
Ballet [Twins's Dance]	No counterpart
"Sing for Your Supper" (Adriana, Luciana, Luce, and Ladies)	Corresponds very roughly to IV, ii, 1–28 (Adriana and Luciana)
"Oh, Diogenes!" (Luce)	Adapted from IV, iii, 70–80
	Act V
Finale ["This Can't Be Love"] (Ensemble)	No counterpart

clothes. In a new touch, Abbott makes the coincidence in dress credible by having Antipholus of Syracuse unknowingly acquire his brother's suit from the tailor early in the story. The larger point, however, is that, despite the physical resemblance, the two Antipholi in both the Shakespeare and the Abbott-Rodgers-Hart versions possess significant personality *differences,* so much so that they could provide a good counterargument to those who favor nature in the nature-nurture debate. Both the play and musical also highlight their differences by establishing a dramatic disparity in their time on the stage. In the play, Antipholus of Syracuse speaks far more lines and, in the musical, sings many more songs than his brother.

Antipholus of Ephesus figures prominently in the act I finale ("Let Antipholus In!") but is allowed only one song, "The Shortest Day of the Year." In this poetic song audiences learn that, despite difficulties communicating his feelings, Antipholus of Ephesus loves his wife, Adriana, and much prefers her company to that of a Courtesan. To convey these feelings, however, the tongue-tied Antipholus uses Adriana's words ("You know what she said to me the other night") rather than his own to express his love. Perhaps more significantly, his lyrics and melody exhibit little of the verbal wit, musical humor, and jazzy fun displayed by his brother. Rodgers's successful attempt to build the longest possible melodic phrase out of the shortest possible phrase—achieved by concluding each phrase with an unresolved, open-ended pitch—has not gone unnoticed. In his enthusiastic, nostalgic review of Hart's lyrics and Rodgers's music in his *New York Herald Tribune* review of the revival, Walter Kerr concluded that "I've decided that I never *will* expect the modulations in 'The Shortest Day of the Year,' and I'm not going to try."[58] Chapin, in his notes to the 1997 *Encores!* recording, discusses the

Table 3.4. Who Sings What for Their Supper in *The Boys from Syracuse*

Antipholus of Syracuse
  "Dear Old Syracuse" (3)*
  "This Can't Be Love" (with Luciana) (7)
  "You Have Cast Your Shadow on the Sea" (12)

Antipholus of Ephesus
  "The Shortest Day of the Year" (6)

Luciana (sister of Adriana)
  "This Can't Be Love" (with Antipholus of Syracuse) (7)
  "Sing for Your Supper" (with Adriana and Luce) (16)

Adriana (wife of Antipholus of Ephesus)
  "Falling in Love with Love" (5)
  "Sing for Your Supper" (with Luciana and Luce) (16)

Dromio of Syracuse
  "He and She" (11) (with Luce)

Dromio of Ephesus
  "What Can You Do with a Man?" (4) (with Luce)

Luce (Nell, kitchen maid to Adriana in Shakespeare; wife of Dromio of Ephesus
    in the musical)
  "What Can You Do with a Man?" (with Dromio of Ephesus) (4)
  "He and She" (with Dromio of Syracuse) (11)
  "Sing for Your Supper" (with Adriana and Luciana) (16)

Courtesan
  "Oh, Diogenes!" (17)

---

*Numbers in parentheses refer to song numbers in the Vocal Score (Chappell & Co., 1965).

bond between Hart's lyrics and Rodgers's melody in this song: "The lyrics for the first four lines of the refrain form one complete thought—which needs your attention all the way through to make sense. So Rodgers tricks you by taking the melody where you don't feel it will go. The notes he chose for the end of each of the first two lines—'The shortest day of the *year*, Has the longest night of the *year*'—are not the notes for which the preceding phrase has prepared you. Both notes have an unexpected and 'blue' quality that Rodgers used so cleverly ('Oh, what a beautiful *mornin'*' for example) throughout his career."[59]

After "I Had Twins" the audience meets Antipholus of Syracuse, who, like "a drop of water / that in the ocean seeks another drop," has begun to search for his brother and finds himself in Ephesus. The Syracusan Antipholus's first song, "Dear Old Syracuse," follows the scene with the entrance of a tailor who seems to know him and his servant by name and miraculously supplies them with suits that fit perfectly. Much earlier than in Shakespeare, Rodgers and Hart's Antipholus of Syracuse already has had enough of Ephesus and wants to return to his dear old small, old-fashioned Syracuse with its "quorum of cuties in the forum," a place where a married gander can philander. By the end of act I, however, the alien Antipholus meets and falls in love with his sister-in-law Luciana, who, mistaking Antipholus of Syracuse for Adriana's husband, tries to hide her feelings and to remain faithful to her sister. In an interesting detail, Abbott's Luciana, unlike Shakespeare's counterpart, actually notices something different about the foreign Antipholus.

In her song lyrics, however, Adriana interprets the absence of dizzy spells as a sign that it "can't be love" and attributes such thoughts to lightheadedness brought about by hunger. "This Can't Be Love," the first duet in *Syracuse*, constitutes one of the relatively few opportunities after "I Had Twins" where it is possible to directly compare the play with the musical. Although Shakespeare offers passionate and suggestive poetry, nothing can break down Luciana's resolve or loyalty to her sister's marriage vow. Besides, she considers Antipholus mad. In contrast, Abbott's dialogue and Rodgers and Hart's song reveal a Luciana who, while remaining faithful to her sister, tries to explain that the wonderful feelings she feels demonstrate the absence rather than the presence of love.

Antipholus of Syracuse's final song, the lyrical but somewhat lugubrious "You Have Cast Your Shadow on the Sea" (act II, scene 1), with a verse that suggests Debussy's musical seascape *La Mer* in the orchestral accompaniment, is also a duet with Luciana. It follows an exchange, not in Shakespeare, in which Antipholus of Syracuse assures his newly beloved sister-in-law that "nothing happened" when he spent the night with his alleged wife, Adriana. In contrast to Shakespeare's ambiguity on this point, Abbott's Antipholus of Syracuse informs Luciana that, although he was upstairs with her sister, he claimed to have a "sick headache" and "lay there thinking of you." After he tries to kiss Luciana and she breaks away, he recaptures his earlier resolve to return to Syracuse and sings his song.

We have noted that despite their identical appearance, Shakespeare's two Antipholi are quite different people at the outset of the play. One of the joys of the play is the transformation of Antipholus of Syracuse when he discovers love. Rodgers and Hart capture these differences through contrasting lyrical and musical styles, and "Shadow on the Sea" in particular persuasively shows how love has transformed the Syracusan Antipholus. Before our eyes and ears he literally changes his tune (and musical style). Gone are Hart's witty rhymes and Rodgers's jazzy syncopations. Instead, we have a touch of a shadowy descending chromaticism in the first measure of each A section (A-G-G♭-F), lots of even notes and held notes, and generally fewer signs of his earlier rhythmic life. In the B section he briefly returns to the B section rhythm of "This Can't Be Love," in which three quarter-notes begin on the second beat of a phrase, but this is clearly a different Antipholus than the man who wanted to go back to Syracuse when the musical began. Now he sings: "My heart's no longer free. / When you cast your shadow from the sea / You'll be with me." Two scenes later the nonduplicitous Luciana gives Adriana a full report on what has happened and confesses that her future husband will "be like Antipholus, only nicer." It might be love after all.

The final song, "Oh, Diogenes!" stands apart from the others by its delightful extraneousness in the tradition of Porter's "Blow, Gabriel, Blow" from *Anything Goes*. Abbott's songs may not always follow Shakespeare, but at least the other songs in the show relate to some aspect of the original plot. The showstopping "Oh, Diogenes!" serves as an excuse to give Wynn Murray, who literally blew audiences away with "Johnny One Note" the year before in *Babes in Arms*, another non-sequitur musical story about a character who does not belong to the show. Antipholus of Syracuse denies taking a ring from the Courtesan. This prompts the Courtesan to lament that, like her fellow Athenian Diogenes, who does not have even a walk-on part in either Shakespeare's or Abbott's play, she will continue her futile search for an honest man. When the Courtesan says, "If you find an honest one, save him for me," Luce replies, "Yeah? I'll save him for myself" and bursts into song, "Oh, Diogenes!"[60] In a potentially meaningful parallel, the song returns to the repeated descending minor thirds associated with "Give him the axe, the axe, the axe!" in the opening song, "I Had Twins."

My discussion up to this point has been based almost entirely on Abbott's original 1938 libretto, the source for what audiences and critics first enjoyed at the Alvin Theatre on November 23. Speaking again for the *New York Times* and perhaps for many New Yorkers, Atkinson, while perhaps a little embarrassed by the "ribald complications" and other "bawdries," gave the

Rodgers and Hart repertory company and their "exuberant comedy" high marks across the board.[61] Atkinson praised Abbott as director for living up to his reputation for "freshness, spontaneity and spinning pace" and approved of Abbott's decision as author "to pilfer Shakespeare's idea and leave his text alone, which is valuable for costumes and settings" (which also earned lavish praise). Atkinson's assessment of Balanchine's choreography (his fourth and last Rodgers and Hart show) reflects growing critical awareness of the dramatic potential inherent in dance: "Particularly at the close of the first act ["Let Antipholus In"] Mr. Balanchine has found a way of turning the dancing into the theme of the comedy and orchestrating it in the composition of the scene." Writing for the opposition, Alan Brien, reviewing the unsuccessful London importation of the 1963 New York revival, wrote that "Mr. Abbott's glittering mausoleum of fossilised vulgarity reveals itself as a monumental folly, marooned miles off the track of modern entertainment."[62]

The 1963 *Boys from Syracuse* followed *A Connecticut Yankee, Pal Joey,* and *On Your Toes* (1943, 1952, 1954) as the fourth major New York revival of a Rodgers and Hart show. It had a successful Off-Broadway production at the Theatre Four. If one overlooks the smaller scale of Off-Broadway, in absolute numbers this *Syracuse,* with 502 performances, falls not far behind the Broadway revivals of *Pal Joey* in 1952 (542) and close on the heels of the future *On Your Toes* in 1983 (505). The legacy of the 1963 revival is also considerable. In particular it formed the foundation for the one and only published vocal score and the first complete (or nearly complete) cast recording, which aside from changes in the instrumental and ballet music follows the original version quite closely. The Off-Broadway *Syracuse* also produced the libretto that has since then been circulated to professional and amateur theater companies wishing to perform the show. Earlier I remarked that the libretto to *The Boys from Syracuse* was arguably the only musical comedy from the pre-*Oklahoma!* era that *could* be performed in its original state. Unfortunately, this remains a hypothetical, for although the changes from 1938 to 1963 do not constitute an overhaul, they do considerably alter the tone and the impact of Abbott's original.

In contrast to the radically revised book of *On Your Toes* in 1954 and even in the historically conscious 1983 reconstruction, changes in the libretto for *The Boys from Syracuse* are superficially modest ones. The main changes are the additions of several dozen new attempts at comedy scattered throughout the new script. Abbott alerts us to these "improvements" when he complains of being criticized for the "old-fashioned jokes in the book." Abbott continues: "But I was puzzled when one of the reviewers cited one of these jokes, a corny pun: 'Dozens of men are at my feet.' 'Yes, I know, chiropodists.' This kind of humor is so alien to me that I knew I could never have written it; and when I got back to New York I found that the 'old jokes' in the revival were new jokes inserted by Mr. York to 'modernize' the script. I took out some of these gags, but because the production as a whole was so delightful, I couldn't get very angry."[63]

Although the chiropodist joke was removed from the 1963 script now rented by the Rodgers and Hammerstein Theatre Library, many others remained. Presumably these jokes can be attributed not to director Richard York himself (as Abbott concluded), but to lyricist Fred Ebb, who is acknowledged "for his additional dialogue."[64] Here are eight samples of new chiropodist-type jokes from the 1963 libretto that Abbott was unable to remove:

DROMIO E.: Don't you miss home cooking?
ANTIPHOLUS E.: Yes, whenever possible. (p. 5)

DROMIO E.: Your wife?
ANTIPHOLUS E.: My what?
DROMIO E.: Not your "what," your wife, my mistress.
ANTIPHOLUS E.: My wife is your mistress? (p. 10)

DROMIO E.: He kicks me to here and then you kick me back again. Boy, you sure get a kick out of me.[65] (p. 15)

ANTIPHOLUS S.: This is very peculiar. What do you know about Ephesus women?
DROMIO S.: Just what I've been able to pick up. (p. 17)

LUCE: What are you, a man or a mouse? Well, don't just stand there, squeak up! (p. 18)

LUCE: Did you bring your harp?
DROMIO S.: No.
LUCE: Good, then you can pick on me. (p. 19)

DROMIO E.: We have our quarrels, but we patch everything up—my nose, my lips, my ears, my jaw. (p. 28)

COURTESAN: To think I gave you the best weekends of my life. (p. 53)

Most of the other changes consist of small additions, deletions, or modifications, generally less obtrusive than the above. For example, in 1938, Luciana and Luce compare notes about what they're looking for in a man (act II, scene 3). Luce, who had sung "What Can You Do with a Man?" in act I—and she would know—wants something more than a man "like Dromio, only nicer," a phrase that echoes Luciana's desire for a man "like Antipholus, only nicer." In 1963, Luce wants someone "like Dromio, only alive."[66] Just as contemporary radio censors refused Reno Sweeney the option that she might "get" a "kick from cocaine" in the lyrics to "I Get a Kick Out of You," in 1963 Antipholus of Syracuse no longer says "My God—I wonder if I've been taking dope," after Adriana invites him to dine alone with her upstairs.

Major additions are rare: a few lines of added dialogue between Adriana and the Maid at the end of act I, scene 2, and some new dialogue between Antipholus of Ephesus and the expanded role of the Courtesan in the reworked ballet that now concludes act I. Occasionally, the 1963 version adopts a political incorrectness not present in 1938. For example, in 1938 Dromio of Syracuse voices the following appreciation of the maid's outfit: "Very attractive. Very nice combination you've got there." Twenty-five years later he puts it this way: "Such a pretty apron you're wearing . . . (*Looks at bosom.*) . . . aren't they?"

In *Shakespeare, The Movie* Diana E. Henderson considers *The Comedy of Errors* a play "less likely to capture the imagination of modern audiences and producers," one destined "to be filmed infrequently and almost obligatorily as part of canonical projects such as the BBC-TV Shakespeare series."[67] Douglas Brode in *Shakespeare in the Movies* notes a silent film version of *Comedy* from 1908 and the 1940 adaptation of Rodgers and Hart's *Syracuse* as being "as appealingly stilted as its Broadway predecessor and, for that matter, Shakespeare's own agreeable forced farce," and points out the absence of either a major Hollywood or a European adaptation.[68]

Harry Levin mentions a 1987 television version by the Flying Karamazovs, who staged a vaudeville-circus take on the play at the Goodman Theater in 1983, and emphasizes its "worldwide diffusion" rather than the absence of large-scale movie productions. For Levin, Shakespeare, Plautus, and, by extension, Abbott, Rodgers, and Hart, "had hit upon an important archetype: the question of identity and otherness, the self and the *alter ego*, the haunting apparition of the Double."[69] Readers are also invited to substitute the musical for the play (and add a few great tunes) when reading

Levin's concluding thoughts: "It has been a long time now since critics objected to the play on grounds of improbability; doubtless their afterthoughts reflect a shift from presumptions of stability and rationalism toward a state of mind where confusion comes closer to social norms. . . . At all events it is heartening that Shakespeare can still speak to an age of existential absurdity, and that his comedy of errors can vie with those of Beckett and Ionesco for distinction in the Theater of the Absurd."[70]

The same can be said for Rodgers, Hart, and Abbott. In contrast to most shows before *Oklahoma!*, *The Boys from Syracuse* has to a considerable extent survived the ravages of time, evolving tastes, and a barrage of non-Abbott jokes that were never excised from the 1963 revival. Nevertheless, like its Shakespearean counterpart, the show remains underappreciated. The musical comedy of errors given pride of place in this chapter has so far escaped the serious critical and analytical attention it deserves. It has been my goal to partially remedy this oversight. Rodgers, Hart, and Abbott in *The Boys from Syracuse* accomplished more than the creation of the first important Shakespeare musical. In their inspired version of Shakespeare's *Comedy of Errors*, a musical comedy trio in 1938 created a masterful musical adaptation of a Shakespeare play worthy of Spewack-Porter, Robbins-Laurents-Sondheim-Bernstein, and even Boito-Verdi.

Table 3.5. Sources for Rodgers and Hart Shows, 1935–1943

Jumbo

November 16, 1935–April 18, 1936 (Hippodrome) [233 performances]

LYRICS: *Complete Lyrics of Rodgers and Hart*, 214–19
LIBRETTO: Ben Hecht and Charles MacArthur
  Publication: None
  Libraries: Rodgers and Hammerstein Theatre Library (few lyrics)
SCORES:
  Vocal Score: None
  Vocal Selections: T. B. Harms/Belwin Mills
    Contents: "My Romance," "Over and Over Again," "The Circus Is on
    Parade," "Little Girl Blue," "The Most Beautiful Girl in the World,"
    "This Can't Be Love" [from *The Boys from Syracuse*]
  Selections in Song Anthologies: "The Most Beautiful Girl in the World,"
  "My Romance," "Little Girl Blue" (*Song Book, Anthology*)
RECORDINGS:
  a) Original 1935 Cast, *The Ultimate Rodgers and Hart, Vol. II* (Pearl GEM
    0114)
  Songs: "Little Girl Blue" (Gloria Grafton with Paul Whiteman and his
    Orchestra), "My Romance" (Grafton and Donald Novis with Whiteman)
    [also on *The Hits of Rodgers & Hart* (PAST CD 9794]
  b) 1962 MGM Film Soundtrack (Columbia OS-2260)
  Songs: "Over and Over Again," "The Circus Is on Parade," "The Most Beautiful
    Girl in the World," "My Romance," and "Little Girl Blue" [added Rodgers
    and Hart songs: "This Can't Be Love" (*The Boys from Syracuse*) and "Why
    Can't I?" (*Spring Is Here*)]
FILM: *Billy Rose's Jumbo*, MGM (1962), directed by Charles Walters (with Busby
  Berkeley)
  Songs: Same as recording

On Your Toes

April 11–November 29, 1936 (Imperial); November 30, 1936–January 23, 1937
  (Majestic) [315 performances]

LYRICS: *Complete Lyrics of Rodgers and Hart*, 220–25
LIBRETTO: Richard Rodgers, Lorenz Hart, and George Abbott
  Publication: None
  Libraries: New York Public Library (all lyrics); Rodgers and Hammerstein
    Theatre Library (all lyrics)
SCORES:
  Vocal Score: Chappell & Co., 1985 (Broadway 1983)
  Selections in Song Anthologies: "It's Got to Be Love" (*Anthology*); "Too Good
    for the Average Man" (*Rediscovered*); "There's a Small Hotel" (*Song Book,
    Anthology, Rediscovered*); "Quiet Night" (*Anthology*); "Glad to Be Unhappy"
    (*Anthology*); "On Your Toes" (*Rediscovered*)

Table 3.5. Continued

RECORDINGS:

    a)   Original 1936 Broadway Cast, *The Ultimate Rodgers and Hart, Vol. II* (Pearl GEM 0114)

Songs: "On Your Toes/The Heart Is Quicker Than the Eye," "Glad to Be Unhappy," "There's a Small Hotel/It's Got to Be Love" (Edgar Fairchild & Adam Carroll, pianos)

    b)   1936 Studio Recording, *The Hits of Rodgers & Hart* (PAST CD 9794)

Ballet: "Slaughter on Tenth Avenue" (Paul Whiteman and his Orchestra)

    c)   1937 London Cast, *The Ultimate Rodgers and Hart, Vol. II* (Pearl GEM 0114)

Songs: "On Your Toes," "Quiet Night," "There's a Small Hotel/It's Got to Be Love" (Jack Whiting with Carroll Gibbons & the Savoy Hotel Orpheans); "On Your Toes/The Heart Is Quicker Than the Eye" (Whiting), "There's a Small Hotel" (Whiting), "Slaughter on Tenth Avenue" (orchestra, edited) ["There's a Small Hotel" and "On Your Toes" (Whiting) also on *The Hits of Rodgers & Hart* (PAST CD 9794]

    d)   1954 Original Broadway Cast Revival (Decca MCAD-11575)

Songs: "Two a Day for Keith," "The 3 B's," "It's Got to Be Love," "Too Good for the Average Man," "There's a Small Hotel," "The Heart Is Quicker Than the Eye," "Quiet Night," "Glad to Be Unhappy," "On Your Toes," "You Took Advantage of Me" [from *Present Arms*], "Slaughter on Tenth Avenue"

    e)   1983 Original Broadway Cast Revival (TER CDTER 1063; rereleased on Jay Records CDJAY 1361)

Songs: Complete, including the ballets, "Princess Zenobia" and "Slaughter on Tenth Avenue"

FILM: Warner Brothers (1939), directed by Ray Enright

Songs: "Slaughter on Tenth Avenue," "Princess Zenobia"; "There's a Small Hotel," "On Your Toes," "Quiet Night" [instrumental background]

Babes in Arms

April 14–October 23, 1937 (Shubert); October 25–December 18, 1937 (Majestic) [289 performances]

LYRICS: *Complete Lyrics of Rodgers and Hart*, 227–31
LIBRETTO: Richard Rodgers and Lorenz Hart
    Publication: None
    Libraries: Rodgers and Hammerstein Theatre Library (all lyrics)
SCORES:
    Vocal Score: Chappell Music Company, 1960 (Miami Beach 1959)
    Selections in Song Anthologies: "Where or When" (*Song Book, Anthology, Rediscovered*); "I Wish I Were in Love Again" (*Anthology, Rediscovered*); "Way Out West" (*Rediscovered*); "My Funny Valentine," "Johnny One Note," "The Lady Is a Tramp" (*Song Book, Anthology, Rediscovered*)

Table 3.5. Continued

RECORDINGS:
   a)   Original 1937 Broadway Cast, *The Ultimate Rodgers and Hart, Vol. II*
        (Pearl GEM 0114)
   Songs: "Babes in Arms/I Wish I Were in Love Again," "All at Once," "My Funny
        Valentine (Fairchild & Carroll), "Johnny One Note" (Wyn Murray), "Where
        or When" (Ray Heatherton) ["Where or When" (Heatherton) also on
        The Hits of Rodgers & Hart (PAST CD 9794)]
   b)   1939 Film Cast, *The Ultimate Rodgers and Hart, Vol. II* (Pearl GEM 0114)
   Song: "I Wish I Were in Love Again" (Judy Garland)
   c)   1990 Studio Recording (New World Records NW 386-2)
   Songs: All except "All Dark People" and "Calhoun's Follies"; includes the
        ballets, "Johnny One-Note" and "Peter's Journey"
   d)   1999 New York Cast Recording, City Center's *Encores!* (DRG 94769)
   Songs: All, including "All Dark People" [renamed "Light on Their Feet"] and
        "Calhoun's Follies" (Intro)
FILM: MGM (1939), directed by Busby Berkeley
   Songs: "Babes in Arms," "Where or When"

I'd Rather Be Right

November 2, 1937–May 21, 1938 (Alvin); May 23–July 9, 1938 (Music Box)
   [290 performances]

LYRICS: *Complete Lyrics of Rodgers and Hart*, 232–39
LIBRETTO: George S. Kaufman and Moss Hart
   Publication: Random House, 1937
   Libraries: Rodgers and Hammerstein Theatre Library (some lyrics)
SCORES:
   Vocal Score: None
   Selections in Song Anthologies: "Have You Met Miss Jones?" (*Song Book,
        Anthology, Revisited*); "I'd Rather Be Right" (*Anthology*); "Everybody Loves
        You" [cut] (*Anthology*)
RECORDINGS:
   a)   *Ben Bagley's Rodgers and Hart Revisited* (Painted Smiles PSCD-116 [1990];
        PSCD-126 [1991]); "Take and Take and Take," "Sweet Sixty-Five," "I'd Rather
        Be Right" (two versions) (PSCD-116); "Everybody Loves You" [cut] (PSCD-
        126) [the one widely known song from the show, "Have You Met Miss Jones?"
        has been recorded frequently]
FILM: None

I Married an Angel

May 11, 1938–February 25, 1939 (Shubert) [338 performances]

LYRICS: *Complete Lyrics of Rodgers and Hart*, 191–95, 244–49

Table 3.5. Continued

LIBRETTO: Richard Rodgers and Lorenz Hart, adapted from the play by John
  Vaszary
  Publication: None
  Libraries: Rodgers and Hammerstein Theatre Library (most lyrics)
SCORES:
  Vocal Score: None
  Selections in Song Anthologies: "I Married an Angel," "Spring Is Here"
    Song Book, Anthology); "At the Roxy Music Hall" (Anthology)
RECORDINGS:
  a)   Liberty Music Shop Studio Recording 1938 (AEI-CD 002) [1985]
  Songs: "Did You Ever Get Stung?," "I Married an Angel," "I'll Tell the Man in
    the Street," "How to Win Friends and Influence People," "Finale Act I,"
    "Spring Is Here," "Angel Without Wings," "A Twinkle in Your Eye," "At the
    Roxy Music Hall"
  b)   Original 1938 Broadway Cast, The Ultimate Rodgers and Hart, Vol. II
    (Pearl GEM 0114)
  Songs: "At the Roxy Music Hall," "How to Win Friends and Influence People"
    (Audrey Christie)
  c)   1942 Film Cast, The Ultimate Rodgers and Hart, Vol. II (Pearl GEM 0114)
  Songs: "I Married an Angel," "Little Word-a-Day World," "Spring Is Here,"
    "I'll Tell the Man in the Street" (Nelson Eddy)
  d)   Ben Bagley's Rodgers and Hart Revisited (Painted Smiles (PSCD-116
    [1990]; PSCD-126 [1991]; PSCD-139 [1992]); "Did You Ever Get Stung?"
    "How to Win Friends and Influence People" (PSCD-126); "Angel Without
    Wings" (PSCD-139); "A Twinkle in Your Eye" (PSCD-126); "At the Roxy
    Music Hall" (PSCD-116); "Tell Me I Know How to Love" [cut] (PSCD-140)
    ["Spring Is Here" and title song have been recorded frequently]
FILM: MGM (1942), directed by W. S. Van Dyke II
  Songs: "I Married an Angel," "Spring Is Here," "A Twinkle in Your Eye,"
    "I'll Tell the Man in the Street," "At the Roxy Music Hall" [with a new title,
    "Tira Lira La" and new lyrics by Robert Wright and George Forrest],
    "Did You Ever Get Stung?" [with a new title, "Little Workaday World," and
    new lyrics by Wright and Forrest]

The Boys from Syracuse

November 23, 1938–June 10, 1939 (Alvin) [235 performances]

LYRICS: Complete Lyrics of Rodgers and Hart, 250–56
LIBRETTO: George Abbott, based on the play The Comedy of Errors by William
  Shakespeare
  Publication: None
  Libraries: Rodgers and Hammerstein Theatre Library (most lyrics)
SCORES:
  Vocal Score: Chappell & Co., 1965 (Off-Broadway 1963)

Table 3.5. Continued

Selections in Song Anthologies: "Falling in Love with Love," "This Can't Be Love" (*Song Book, Anthology, Rediscovered*); "Sing for Your Supper" (*Anthology, Rediscovered*); "Who Are You?" [film] (*Anthology*)

RECORDINGS:

a) 1938 Studio Recording, *The Hits of Rodgers & Hart* (PAST CD 9794)
Song: "Sing For Your Supper" (Rudy Vallee with orchestra conducted by Victor Young)

b) 1963 Original Off-Broadway Cast Revival (Capitol TAO-1933)
"I Had Twins," "Dear Old Syracuse," "What Can You Do with a Man?" "Falling in Love with Love," "The Shortest Day of the Year," "This Can't Be Love," "Ladies of the Evening," "He and She," "You Have Cast Your Shadow on the Sea," "Come with Me," "Sing for Your Supper," "Oh, Diogenes!"

c) 1963 London Cast (Decca 882 281) [includes six bonus tracks with recordings by Rudy Vallee and Frances Langford]

d) 1997 Original New York Recording, City Center's *Encores!* (DRG 94767)
Songs: Complete, including the "Prologue," "Let Antipholus In," "Big Brother," and "Twins Ballet"

FILM: Universal (1940), directed by A. Edward Sutherland
Songs: "Sing for Your Supper," "He and She," "This Can't Be Love," "Falling in Love with Love" [added for film: "Who Are You?" and "The Greeks Have No Word for It"]

Too Many Girls

October 18, 1939–May 18, 1940 (Shubert) [249 performances]

LYRICS: *Complete Lyrics of Rodgers and Hart*, 257–63
LIBRETTO: George Marion, Jr.
Publication: Dramatists Play Service, 1940
Libraries: Rodgers and Hammerstein Theatre Library (all lyrics)
SCORES:
Vocal Score: None
Selections in Song Anthologies: "'Cause We Got Cake" (*Anthology*); "I Like to Recognize the Tune" (*Anthology, Rediscovered*); "I Didn't Know What Time It Was" (*Song Book, Anthology, Rediscovered*); "Give It Back to the Indians" (*Song Book, Anthology*); "You're Nearer" (*Anthology, Rediscovered*)
RECORDINGS:

a) 1940 Film Cast, *The Ultimate Rodgers and Hart, Vol. II* (Pearl GEM 0114)
Song: "You're Nearer" (Frances Langford)

b) 1989 Studio Recording (Ben Bagley) (Painted Smiles PSCD-104)
Songs: Complete, including "You're Nearer" [film]

FILM: RKO Radio (1940), directed by George Abbott
Songs: "Heroes in the Fall," "Pottawatomie," "'Cause We Got Cake," "Spic and Spanish," "Love Never Went to College," "Look Out," "I Didn't Know What Time It Was" [added for film: "You're Nearer"]

Table 3.5. Continued

Higher and Higher

April 4–June 15, 1940; August 5–24, 1940 (Shubert) [108 performances]

LYRICS: *Complete Lyrics of Rodgers and Hart*, 264–69
LIBRETTO: Gladys Hurlbut and Joshua Logan, based on an idea by Irving Pincus
    Publication: None
    Libraries: New York Public Library (all lyrics); Rodgers and Hammerstein
        Theatre Library (all lyrics)
SCORES:
    Vocal Score: None
    Selections in Song Anthologies: "Disgustingly Rich," "Lovely Day for a Murder"
        (*Anthology, Rediscovered*); "It Never Entered My Mind" (*Song Book,
        Anthology, Rediscovered*)
RECORDINGS:
    a)   1940 Studio Recording, bonus recordings on 1943 Original Cast Revival of
          A *Connecticut Yankee* (Decca 440013 560-2)
    Songs: "Nothing But You," "Ev'ry Sunday Afternoon," "From Another World,"
          "In Never Entered My Mind" (Shirley Ross with orchstra conducted by Ray
          Sinatra) ["It Never Entered My Mind" also on *The Hits of Rodgers & Hart*
          (PAST CD 9794)]
    b)   *Ben Bagley's Rodgers and Hart Revisited* (Painted Smiles PSCD-106 [1989];
          PSCD-116 [1990], PSCD-139 [1992])
    Songs: "A Barking Baby Never Bites" (PSCD-139); "From Another World"
          (PSCD-139); "Mornings at Seven" (PSCD-106); "Nothing But You" (PSCD-
          116); "Disgustingly Rich" (PSCD-139); "Blue Monday," "Ev'ry Sunday
          Afternoon" (PSCD-116); "Lovely Day for a Murder," "How's Your Health?"
          (PSCD-106); "It Never Entered My Mind," "I'm Afraid," "It's Pretty in the
          City" [cut], "Life! Liberty!" [cut] (PSCD-116)
FILM: RKO Radio, directed by Tim Whelan
    Songs: "Disgustingly Rich" [other songs by Harold Adamson (lyrics) and Jimmy
        McHugh (music)]

Pal Joey

December 25, 1940–August 16, 1941 (Ethel Barrymore); September 1–October 18,
    1941 (Shubert); October 21–November 29, 1941 (St. James) [374 performances]

LYRICS: *Complete Lyrics of Rodgers and Hart*, 270–75
LIBRETTO: John O'Hara, based on a series of short stories in the *New Yorker* by
    O'Hara
    Publication: New York: Duel, Sloane, and Pearce, 1941; *Pal Joey: The Novel and
        the Libretto and Lyrics* (New York: Vintage, 1983)
    Libraries: Rodgers and Hammerstein Theatre Library (all lyrics)
SCORES:
    Vocal Score: Chappell & Co., 1962

Table 3.5. Continued

Selections in Song Anthologies: "You Mustn't Kick It Around" (Anthology);
  "I Could Write a Book" (*Song Book, Anthology, Rediscovered*); "Happy
  Hunting Horn" (*Anthology*); "Bewitched" (*Song Book, Anthology,
  Rediscovered*)

RECORDINGS:
  a)   1950 Studio Recording (Columbia Chart Busters JST 4364 [1988 reissue])
  Songs: All except "Chicago" and "The Flower Garden of My Heart"
  b)   1952 Original revival, Studio Cast (Angel ZDM 0777-7-646962-2-1)
  Songs: All except Ballet ("Chez Joey")
  c)   1957 Film (Capitol W-912)
  Songs: "There's a Small Hotel" (from *On Your Toes*), "Bewitched," "Do It the
    Hard Way," "Plant You Now, Dig You Later," "You Mustn't Kick It Around,"
    "That Terrific Rainbow," "I Didn't Know What Time It Was" (from *Too
    Many Girls*), "The Lady Is a Tramp" (from *Babes in Arms*), "Dream
    Sequence," "My Funny Valentine" (from *Babes in Arms*), "I Could Write a
    Book," "Great Big Town [Chicago]," "Zip"
  c)   1995 Original New York Recording, City Center's *Encores!* (DRG 94763A)
  Songs: All except "The Flower Garden of My Heart"; also includes the ballet,
    "Joey Looks into the Future" and "I'm Talking to My Pal," the latter dropped
    from the 1940 original
FILM: Columbia (1957), directed by George Sidney
  Songs: Same as recording

By Jupiter

June 3, 1942–June 12, 1943 (Shubert) [427 performances]

LYRICS: *Complete Lyrics of Rodgers and Hart*, 280–88
LIBRETTO: Richard Rodgers and Lorenz Hart, based on the play *The Warrior's
    Husband* by Julian F. Thompson
  Publication: None of the libretto; the play was published by Samuel French,
    1933
  Libraries: New York Public Library (all lyrics); Rodgers and Hammerstein
    Theatre Library (all lyrics)
SCORES:
  Vocal Score: None
  Selections in Song Anthologies: "Jupiter Forbid" (*Anthology*); "Nobody's Heart"
    (*Song Book, Anthology, Rediscovered*); "Ev'rything I've Got" (*Anthology,
    Rediscovered*); "Wait Till You See Her" [dropped during original run]
    (*Song Book, Anthology, Rediscovered*)
RECORDINGS:
  a)   1940 Studio Recording, bonus recordings on 1943 Original Cast Revival of
    A Connecticut Yankee (Decca 440013 560-2)
  Songs: "Careless Rhapsody," "Jupiter Forbid," "Ev'rything I've Got," and
    "Nobody's Heart" (Hildegarde with orchestra directed by Harry Sosnik)

Table 3.5. Continued

---

b)   1967 Original Off-Broadway Cast (RCA LSO (S)-1137
Songs: Complete
c)   *Ben Bagley's Rodgers and Hart Revisited* (PSCD-106 [1989]; PSCD-126
[1991])
Songs: "Life Was Monotonous" [cut] (PSCD-106); "Fool Meets Fool" [cut]
(PSCD-126); "Nothing to Do But Relax" [cut] (PSCD-106)
FILM: None

A Connecticut Yankee [Revival]

November 17, 1943–March 11, 1944 (Martin Beck) [135 performances]

LYRICS: *Complete Lyrics of Rodgers and Hart*, 107–111, 294–96
LIBRETTO: Herbert Fields, adapted from the novel *A Connecticut Yankee in King
Arthur's Court* by Mark Twain
Publication: None
Libraries: 1927: New York Public Library (most lyrics); Rodgers and
Hammerstein Theatre Library (most lyrics); 1943: Tams-Witmark Music
Library (some lyrics)
SCORES:
Vocal Selections: (1927) "My Heart Stood Still," "Thou Swell," "On a Desert
Island with Thee!" "I Blush" [cut], "Someone Should Tell Them" [cut];
(1943) "To Keep My Love Alive," "Can't You Do a Friend a Favor?" "You
Always Love the Same Girl"
Selections in *Song Anthologies:* (1927) "My Heart Stood Still," "Thou Swell"
(*Song Book, Anthology, Rediscovered*); "On a Desert Island with Thee" (*Song
Book, Anthology*); "I Feel at Home with You" (*Song Book*); "You're What I
Need" [cut] (*Rediscovered*); (1943) "To Keep My Love Alive" (*Song Book,
Anthology, Rediscovered*); "Can't You Do a Friend a Favor?" (*Anthology*)
RECORDINGS:
a)   1927 London Cast, *One Dam Thing After Another*
The Ultimate Rodgers and Hart Vol I (Pearl GEM 0110) and *The Song Is . . .
Rodgers and Hart* (Living Era CD AJA 5041).
Song: "My Heart Stood Still" (Jessie Matthews with Leslie Hutchinson at the
piano) [also with Edythe Baker, vocal and piano, on *The Hits of Rodgers &
Hart* (PAST CD 9794)]
b)   1928 Studio Recording, *The Song Is . . . Richard Rodgers and Lorenz Hart*
(Living Era CD AJA 5041)
Song: "Thou Swell" (Bix Beiderbecke [cornet] and His Gang)
c)   1943 Original Broadway Revival (Decca 440013 560-2)
Songs: "My Heart Stood Still," "Thou Swell," "On a Desert Island with Thee,"
"To Keep My Love Alive," "Can't You Do a Friend a Favor?" "I Feel at Home
with You," "You Always Love the Same Girl"
d)   1955 Original Television Broadcast Recording (AEI-CD 043)

Table 3.5. Continued

Songs: "My Heart Stood Still," "Thou Swell," "At the Round Table," "On a
    Desert Island with Thee," "Finale ACT I," "I Feel at Home with You," "This
    Is My Night to Howl," "To Keep My Love Alive," "Ye Lunchtime Follies,"
    "Can't You Do a Friend a Favor?" "You Always Love the Same Girl," and
    "The Camelot Samba"
FILM: NBC Network, March 12, 1955
    Songs: Same as above

CHAPTER 4

World War II, the Musical: *South Pacific*

One of the finest musical plays in the history of American theatre.
—RICHARD WATTS, JR., *New York Post*

Set on a small island in the early days of WW II, it [*South Pacific*] tells of two sets of lovers, French exile planter Emile de Becque and Navy nurse Nellie Forbush, and Navy Lieutenant Joe Cable and the Tonkinese girl Liat. Racial prejudice figures in both plots: Nellie is finally able to overcome her aversion to de Becque's two children by a native woman, but Cable cannot bring himself to marry the Asian girl he loves. These two stories unfold against the backdrop of American sailors trying to cope with the exotic island world into which they have been plunged.
—MARGARET M. KNAPP, in *Cambridge Guide to American Theatre*

PRIOR TO *SOUTH PACIFIC*, RODGERS AND HAMMERSTEIN'S MUSICALS inhabited earlier eras and remote American locales. *Oklahoma!* takes place in the Indian Territory of the future state "just after the turn of the century." *Carousel* is set in a New England fishing village over a fifteen-year period, between 1873 and 1888. *Allegro* (1947) eventually makes its way to 1940, but much of it transpires in the Midwest between 1905 and the 1920s. *South Pacific* is the first Rodgers and Hammerstein (henceforth R&H) show to present a dramatic story in an exotic, contemporary setting: the South Pacific islands during the recently concluded World War II. Although in the post–Vietnam War era the ideological perspective of the show seems out of touch with evolving cultural and even artistic values, in 1949 critics and audiences alike were ready for a musical about sex and race set against the backdrop of a recent victorious war: World War II, the Musical.

    South Pacific made its much-awaited debut at the Majestic Theatre on April 7, 1949. Nearly five years and 1,925 performances later, R&H's phenomenal hit closed, on January 16, 1954, as the second-longest-running musi-

Rodgers and Hammerstein

cal to open in the 1940s—No. 1, *Oklahoma!*, had closed at 2,212 performances in 1948—and came within three months of outlasting its popular
1951 successor, *The King and I*. The later stages of *South Pacific*'s Broadway
run corresponded with an impressive two-year, 802-performance engagement in London, as well as briefer engagements in Melbourne (1952), Stock-
holm (1953), and Madrid (1955).[1] Several months after it opened, *South Pacific* launched a five-year tour that visited 118 U.S. cities (1950–55).[2] Enough
people purchased the original cast album, released first on seven shellac
records (followed soon thereafter by a still more popular vinyl 33 rpm disk),
that sales went beyond a million copies, Gold Record status.[3] Following in
the illustrious footsteps of *Carousel* and *Brigadoon*, *South Pacific* became
the third musical to receive the New York Drama Critics Circle Award. It
also won several Tony Awards in 1950, one year after *Kiss Me, Kate*.[4] In 1950,
R&H's fourth Broadway musical became only the second musical to win
the Pulitzer Prize for Drama (eighteen years after *Of Thee I Sing*).[5]

   South Pacific was unambiguously adored, not only for its exceptionally
fine R&H score, but also for its book by Hammerstein and Joshua Logan,
Logan's direction, the settings and lighting by Jo Mielziner, and a stellar cast
headed by Mary Martin and Ezio Pinza. Several critics, including Howard
Barnes, praised the work as an embodiment of the "integrated musical," high
praise indeed in the heyday of the integrated musical. For Barnes, the "numbers are beautifully integrated" and "the lyrics are part and parcel of a captivating musical unity."[6] Most reviewers mentioned the extraordinary advance
notices the show received (which translated into a huge advance sale) and
made a point to remark that the show lived up to or exceeded its formidable
expectations. A number of reviewers commented on the absence of dancing (either ballet or "hot hoofing"), but after what seemed an overreliance
on dance and movement in R&H's *Allegro*, conceived by choreographer-
director Agnes de Mille, and the rash of obligatory dream ballets by R&H
and their epigones, the omission of dance was perceived more as a positive
than a negative. Barnes also noted Logan's successful incorporation of the
lap dissolve, a technique borrowed from film that would be frequently mentioned in discussions of the show.[7]

   The score, especially Rodgers's music, was invariably highlighted for
praise—in contrast with the scores for subsequent Pulitzer Prize winners or
new millennium phenomena such as Mel Brooks's *The Producers* (2001).
Brooks Atkinson singled out "Some Enchanted Evening" (a "masterly love
song" that "ought to become reasonably immortal") and "Bali Ha'i" ("one of

Mr. Rodgers's finest songs").[8] In Barnes's view, the island Bali Ha'i "is celebrated in one of the loveliest of the Rodgers-Hammerstein songs."[9] Robert
Coleman considered the score a worthy rival to the score for *Oklahoma!* —
"without a bit of filler" and with songs "so outstanding that it is difficult to
decide which will be the most popular" (under these circumstances Cole-
man exercised considerable restraint in limiting his song picks to five: "Some
Enchanted Evening," "There Is Nothin' Like a Dame," "Bali Ha'i," "I'm
Gonna Wash That Man Right Outa My Hair," and "A Wonderful Guy").[10]
Ward Morehouse named four "exhilarating song hits" ("Wonderful Guy,"
"Wash That Man," "Some Enchanted Evening," and "Honey Bun"), and
John Chapman added "Happy Talk" to this growing list, considering it "the
sweetest, fetchingest number of the evening."[11] Richard Watts Jr., whose
personal favorite was "Some Enchanted Evening," added yet another title,
"Younger Than Springtime," to his quintet of memorable songs.[12] In all,
the above lists offer eight different contenders for popularity, an impressive
number even when compared with *Babes in Arms*.

For younger viewers, such a combination of critical and popular acclaim may seem almost beyond belief. In the age of Stephen Sondheim and
Andrew Lloyd Webber, it has not been easy to have it both ways. When considering, for example, the reception of three later Pulitzer Prize–winning
musicals, one can observe a comparatively sharp division among contemporary audiences and critics. Despite initially positive reviews, even supportive reviewers of *A Chorus Line* (1975) remained less than ecstatic, even dismissive, about Marvin Hamlisch's score. *Sunday in the Park with George*
(1984) was more a critical than a popular success, and in some circles Sondheim's score was unfairly accused of capturing the intellectuality and lack
of warmth attributed to its artist subject, Georges Seurat. The most recent
Pulitzer recipient, *Rent* (1996), generated harsh criticism from many quarters, and some critics branded Jonathan Larson's score as derivative (as well
as excessively loud).

Criticism of *South Pacific* was in short supply in the eight daily New York
papers competing for readers in 1949.[13] Perhaps the sharpest barb was Atkinson's remark that "Miss Martin's attack on a song" came perhaps a little too
close to her depiction of her Annie Oakley role and that "perhaps this should
be exorcised by slow degrees." By the standards of effusiveness established in
other reviews, Morehouse's directive to "let Broadway enjoy it for a couple
of years" seems understated. Some might raise their eyebrows when they
read that Barnes praised Pinza's performance of "This Nearly Was Mine"

rather than the song itself. Barnes, who cited only "Bali Ha'i" among R&H's "loveliest," did not care that "the Rodgers music is not his finest" but considered it a positive attribute that the music "fits the mood and pace of *South Pacific* so felicitously that one does not miss a series of hit tunes." One of the most laudatory reviews came from Watts. After beginning, like other reviewers, by noting that the show was able to withstand the burden of its "out-of-town superlatives" and informing his readers about how R&H and Logan adapted James A. Michener's novel, Watts made the following unreserved pronouncement: "I do not think it is first-night excess which causes me to hail it as one of the finest musical plays in the history of American theatre." All this in the first paragraph.

From a later perspective, opening-night critics got the point but missed a few things too. Apparently "Some Enchanted Evening" loomed so large in the opening scene that no critic found space to mention "Dites-Moi," "A Cockeyed Optimist," or the innovative and unusual "Twin Soliloquies." "Bloody Mary" went unnoticed, and with the exception of Coleman's review, comments about "There Is Nothin' Like a Dame" refer to its characterization rather than its merits as a song. "This Nearly Was Mine" was virtually ignored. More surprisingly, when considering how the media and historians have since placed race in the foreground in discussions of musicals and other representations of American culture, contemporary reviewers were silent on the issue of racial prejudice that for many forms the core and larger meaning of the show. In particular, not one first-night reviewer remarked on the powerful lyrics of "Carefully Taught," which espouse the view that prejudice is taught rather "born in you." In fact, no one mentioned this song at all.[14]

Within a year of its closing, *South Pacific* appeared in a steady stream of limited engagement revivals in New York, St. Louis, San Francisco, Los Angeles, Kansas City, and Dallas.[15] Four years after the show closed the lucrative but artistically controversial film version was released. In 1967 the Music Theater of Lincoln Center, of which Rodgers was then president and producing director, presented *South Pacific* in a series of performances between June 12 and September 9 that starred Florence Henderson and Giorgio Tozzi (the latter the voice of Rossano Brazzi in the 1958 film). When reviewing the 1987 New York City Opera production, *New York Times* critic John Rockwell recalled that already by 1967 "the show struck many as dated."[16] For Rockwell, the musicals of Sondheim have "long since transcended its formal innovations," and the popular television program

M*A*S*H had "contemporized this same setting." In short, since "the magical transformation from the awkwardly archaic to the sweetly nostalgic hasn't taken place," Rockwell viewed *South Pacific* as old enough to be dated but not old enough to be enjoyed as a nostalgic anachronism. Further exemplifying *South Pacific*'s decline from topical masterpiece to an embodiment of artistic decay, Manuela Hoelterhoff of the *Wall Street Journal*, who placed this musical at "the top of my list of things to shun," concluded that "unlike Bloody Mary's shrunken heads, this 1949 musical by Rodgers and Hammerstein isn't improving with age."[17] To counteract this revisionism, we can turn to the counter-revisionism of Broadway historian Ethan Mordden, an articulate and perceptive advocate of R&H in general and *South Pacific* in particular. In *Rodgers & Hammerstein*, Mordden attributes revival difficulties to the problem of casting two principals of the stature and exceptional qualities of the original Nellie Forbush and Emile de Becque.[18] In the more recent *Beautiful Mornin'*, Mordden, still perceptively persuasive about the show's artistic and social significance, seems to have changed his mind about casting problems, however, when he concludes that "it doesn't matter who plays these parts."[19]

The Novel

When Rodgers and Hammerstein first read it, Michener's *Tales of the South Pacific* (1947) was a new commodity and its author a new face—albeit a forty-year-old new face—who had based the novel on experiences similar to those of the book's occasional narrator.[20] Not only did Michener's promising first novel win a Pulitzer Prize for fiction, the financial windfall gained from its adaptation to the stage allowed Michener to retire as an editor for Macmillan. In his new profession as an independent full-time author, Michener (1907–1997) went on to enjoy a staggeringly productive and lucrative fifty-year career.[21] Although R&H originally offered Michener 1 percent of the gross—lower than the 1.5 percent they had offered Lynn Riggs for the right to adapt *Green Grow the Lilacs* into *Oklahoma!* but higher than the 0.8 percent they paid Ferenc Molnár for the privilege of turning *Liliom* into *Carousel*—in an act of generosity they allowed Michener to purchase a second share, and even lent him the $4,500 to do so.

Although considered a novel by the Pulitzer committee and by Michener himself, *Tales of the South Pacific* does not fit neatly into the novel genre. Perhaps one might more accurately describe the work as a collection of nineteen occasionally connected short stories. Short story collections by Damon Runyon, Shalom Aleichem, and Kathryn Forbes would later inspire, respectively, Frank Loesser's *Guys and Dolls*, Jerry Bock and Sheldon Harnick's *Fiddler on the Roof*, and Rodgers's own last effort, *I Remember Mama*. More unusual than Michener's idea of developing a frequently discontinuous novel was the sheer topicality of his story. The war was very much in the current memory, even if the exotic South Pacific islands were remote from most Americans' wartime (or peacetime) experience.

As with Hammerstein's adaptation of Edna Ferber's novel *Show Boat*, and the plays on which *Oklahoma!* and *Carousel* were based, the R&H and Logan adaptation was faithful to the spirit of Michener's *Tales* but took many liberties in organization, structure, and interpretation. Like most adaptations from a novel to the musical stage (then and now), *South Pacific* softens some of the less savory aspects of plot and character. Although the musical *South Pacific* did not shy away from such daring themes as miscegenation, racial prejudice, war, and death, a musical war needed to be less bloody than either a real war or a war described on the printed page. In most cases, a musical play requires a more streamlined plot and fewer characters than would be customarily welcome in a novel. It also helps if the characters on stage are more likable than their novel counterparts. Despite its boldness, the *South Pacific* adaptation observed these general rules. Consequently, the war it depicts is dramatic rather than messy, and the characters, while credible and three-dimensional, are more in keeping with what a Broadway audience might have been able to appreciate in 1949.

In a *New York Times* article that appeared two months after the Broadway opening, Michener shared his thoughts about the adaptation from his novel to the stage. He describes what stayed the same, what was new, and his assessment of what was gained and lost in translation. At the outset Michener lays his cards on the table: "I find to my deep pleasure that Messrs. Oscar Hammerstein 2d, Richard Rodgers, and Joshua Logan have improved my work at almost every point. I cannot imagine a writer who could be more satisfied with a stage translation than I am with 'South Pacific.'"[22] From Michener's perspective, the creators of *South Pacific* remained faithful to each of his principal romantic characters, Nellie Forbush and Emile de Becque from the story "Our Heroine," Liat and Joe Cable from "Fo' Dolla'" ("four dollars" in Bloody Mary's dialect). But in contrast to his own *Tales*, the central characters in *South Pacific* are now intertwined. For Michener, "the manner in which the loves of this strange quartet cross and become involved and lead on to tragedy and triumph is the exclusive work of Hammerstein and Logan."

Michener also sets the record straight when he describes Captain Brackett and Stewpot as new creations and notes that "Lieutenant Harbison is cleaned up and promoted to a commander." Even Bloody Mary, less profane and less bloody with betel juice, "stands somewhat improved because of the tremendous impact of her two songs." Michener is also "bitterly envious" that it was not his idea to have Luther Billis fall out of the PBY [a military plane] and create the $600,000 of diversionary havoc, for "that is precisely what he would have done." Although Michener expresses regret that Hammerstein and Logan were unable to use the touching last story, "A Cemetery at Hoga Point," he feels that the presence of "You've Got to Be Carefully Taught" captures the plea for brotherhood inherent in that story. His only criticism is that instead of having four daughters de Becque has a boy and girl, but even here he is willing to concede that "for stage purposes the scenes are more effective with a little boy thrown in."

Conflation of character and event is a useful and usually effective way to streamline a novel "for stage purposes," most of which Michener does not mention in his short essay. For example, de Becque's decision to join Cable on his treacherous mission after being rejected by Nellie, a major development in the musical, is absent in *Tales*. In fact, de Becque and Cable do not meet in Michener (neither, for that matter, do Nellie and Cable nor Nellie and Liat). An individual known as the Remittance Man, who like Cable will ultimately be killed, accomplishes Cable and de Becque's undercover mission to collect intelligence on Japanese movements. The pilot Bus Adams, a minor character in the show, carries out Billis's unintentionally diversionary exodus from the PBY in the novel. A list of relatively inconsequential but revealing changes like these could go on for several more paragraphs.

The emphasis on "Our Heroine" and "Fo' Dolla'" should not obscure the presence of plot elements from other stories in the collection, in particular "The Boar's Tooth." In some cases information from the other stories helps to explain important plot details. For example, commentators usually report that R&H and Logan kill off Cable to spare him having to live up to his newfound racial tolerance and his admission of love for Liat. In "Fo' Dolla'," Michener leaves this point and even whether Cable lives or dies unclear, but in "A Cemetery at Hoga Point" readers learn not only that Cable died, but that he died a hero. Readers of Michener's *Tales* also learn that Cable had gotten into two fights over his attachment to Liat. In the second

fight he hit an officer and was locked up in the brig. But Cable's command-
ing officer gave him another chance, so instead of rotting in a military jail,
Cable died fighting the Japanese.

In the late 1940s, novels generally had a higher tolerance for ambiguous
(as well as less likable) characters than did Broadway musicals. Michener's
Nellie is not only less complex but less desirable. Readers of *Tales* meet her
in the ironically titled "An Officer and a Gentleman," several stories before
"Our Heroine." The earlier story features Ensign Bill Harbison (a minor role
in the Broadway show), a married man who leads a cushy and idle existence
waiting for a commission and a transfer. After his "mother-complex" relationship with the nurse Dinah Culbert (another minor but named character
in the show) runs its course, Harbison condescends to date Nellie, a "common little girl from some hick town," who throws herself at him. Late in the
story Michener describes Nellie as the "silly girl [who] was obviously in love
with him," whom Harbison could have had "for a whistle" but "turned her
down." In the final paragraph the blithely indifferent Harbison attends to his
primary concern, the first detectable "thin line of fat attacking him" in the
stomach. By the time Nellie meets Emile, she has been seduced and abandoned—damaged goods. Clearly the musical *South Pacific* left a few things
out.[23]

Michener's Nellie would have still more to overcome in her staged reincarnation were the truth of her recent past known. Before being cast out by
Harbison in the first Nellie Forbush story, our heroine manages to save her
virtue by bopping the "gentleman" on the head with a coconut. As Michener
describes the scene, Harbison "ripped her dress and brassiere" and "paid no
attention to her entreaties but kept clawing at her underwear." After returning Nellie to the nurses' quarters, Harbison offers a "stiff goodnight" and
a perfunctory apology. Nellie confides to Dinah but is unable to discover
whether the man she loves is married. Twelve hours later Nellie finds out.
After learning about Nellie's boy back home (soon to be Emile's rival at the
beginning of their romance), Harbison responds by drawing her close and
whispering terms of endearment. Michener continues: "Then, in a delir-
ium of love, he calmly proceeded to do what twelve short hours before she
had hit him over the head with a coconut for doing."[24] Harbison then says
(to himself) "after all I am an officer!" and (to Nellie) "I'm married" and
"I thought you knew." It doesn't quite happen this way in *South Pacific*, the
musical.

If Michener's Nellie is no longer virginal, Emile, too, is somewhat less of a catch than he might have been. On stage, Nellie readily accepts that Emile murdered a man in self-defense, although for most of act II she has to struggle to accept his former marriage to a Polynesian woman (interestingly, Nellie has no problem embracing their young daughter and son). Michener's Emile has a few more wives and progeny to contend with. For starters, Emile of the *Tales* actually did not marry any of these women, a detail that makes his adorable children illegitimate, something else for Nellie to worry about. He also slept with at least several others who did not produce children. The grand total in the novel was eight illegitimate daughters with four different women, who represent no fewer than three ethnic types: two Javanese (four daughters), one Tonkinese (two daughters), and one Polynesian (two daughters). Of these non-wives, the most difficult to accept was the last: "To Nellie's tutored mind any person living or dead who was not white or yellow was nigger." Thus in Michener's novel Nellie has more to overcome than her own prejudiced background. Perhaps this burden would have been too much for a woman from Little Rock to conquer in act II of a musical play in 1949.

Although *South Pacific* presents a reasonably gritty picture of military and island life, *Tales* confronts its readers with several more unpleasant elements—for example, an attempted rape of Nellie (who is rescued by Emile). Michener's story of Cable and Liat describes naked bodies and a bloody blouse that provided "incarnadine proof that he was the first who had loved her."[25] One of Emile's grown daughters, Latouche, had an affair with Bus Adams, murdered her husband in an action planned to look like self-defense, and then married Tony Fry, another important character in several *Tales* who shares some of Luther Billis's character traits.[26] We have already noted that *South Pacific*, the musical, in contrast to the novel or the war, stops short of the bloody "Landing of Kuralei" and the touching epilogue of "A Cemetery at Hoga Point."

Michener is unduly modest when he discounts his own special influence on the dramatic trajectory of the show. In addition to providing the basic story lines and characters, and the magical island of "Bali-ha'i" (his spelling), Hammerstein is also clearly in Michener's debt. In "Dry Rot," in which Billis and another GI discuss girls with Billis's Jewish friend Weinstein (the Professor in the novel and the show), Michener writes of "moonlight upon tropic waters," an image that may have inspired Hammerstein to open "There is Nothin' Like a Dame" with "We got sunlight on the sand, / We got moonlight on the sea" and perhaps the idea of the song as well.[27] Readers of *Tales* also learn that Cable was "carefully taught" in Philadelphia society, teachings he ignores for a time in the throes of first love.[28] In at least one case, "Twin Soliloquies," the idea and images of a song can be directly traced to the novel. In Michener's words, "To himself De Becque said, 'This is what I have been waiting for. All the long years. Who ever thought a fresh, smiling girl like this would climb up my hill?'" Compare this description with Hammerstein's lyrics: "This is what I need, / This is what I've longed for, / Someone young and smiling / Climbing up my hill!"

Genesis

Rodgers

According to Rodgers, the genesis of the musical *South Pacific* began when he found a cryptic reference to "Fo' Dolla'" in his black notebook.[29] Several days later Logan refreshed Rodgers's memory of a party in which he told the composer about a story from Michener's *Tales of the South Pacific*. Soon R&H had both read Michener's entire collection of stories and had the foresight to secure the rights to all of them. Further discussions with Hammerstein brought the pair to the conclusion that "Fo' Dolla'" contained too many similarities to Puccini's *Madama Butterfly* (1904). After considering other stories, R&H decided that "Our Heroine," the tale of the love affair between Emile and Nellie, "had to be the main story." For "comic leavening" they decided to bring in Luther Billis from a third story.[30] In Rodgers's opinion, the presence of two serious love stories worked "against the accepted rules of musical-play construction" established in *Oklahoma!* and *Carousel*, in which the secondary stories provide "comic relief." Mordden contradicts this claim when he interprets Nellie as a "fundamentally comic character who is put through a serious test" and notes the interplay of seriousness and levity in both sets of romantic partners.[31] In Mordden's view, "what R&H did to tradition was less to vary it than to naturalize it, finding the humor in the deep people and the tragedy in the light."[32]

Casting established stars was a departure from R&H's usual practice, and another hedge against failure after the disappointment of *Allegro*. Rodgers relates that he found Ezio Pinza when producer Edwin Lester called to find out whether R&H had any use for the famous Metropolitan Opera bass to spare Lester from having to pay a $25,000 penalty clause for not putting Pinza to use. After making history by signing up the first opera superstar for a Broadway musical, R&H hired Mary Martin, the musical-comedy star of *One Touch of Venus* and of a touring production of *Annie Get Your Gun*. To assuage her fears of being overshadowed, and perhaps even drowned out by Pinza's powerful operatic basso, Rodgers "assured her that we'd write the score without a single duet for her."[33] This turned out to be a slight exaggeration, since in the second act Nellie and Emile sing an abbreviated reprise of "A Cockeyed Optimist" in "Sweet Adeline fashion." In July 1948, Martin and her husband-manager, Richard Halliday, heard five songs and promised to make a decision the next morning. The memoirs of both Rodgers and Martin report that Mary, worried that R&H might offer someone else the part, could not wait that long. Rodgers remembered that she called at dinner, and Martin's memoirs place the time at 3 A.M., but like Honoré and Grandmama in Lerner and Loewe's *Gigi*, both "remember it well."[34] Rodgers goes on to explain how he and Hammerstein averted the potential financial disaster that would result if they paid two high-priced stars full market value (their first three shows featured lesser known and less expensive, albeit talented, casts). They persuaded Pinza and Martin to work at half pay, one of several examples of the power and prestige that R&H wielded at this stage of their career.

Even before the New Haven and Boston tryouts Rodgers considered the show "failure-proof": "The story was honest and appealing, the songs were closely interwoven but still had individuality, the staging was masterly, and it certainly didn't hurt to have the leading roles played by two such luminaries."[35] The casting of Pinza, however, created a few headaches and tensions. In fact, Rodgers reported that Pinza's problems with English diction "precipitated the only major fight that Oscar and I had with Josh Logan and Leland Hayward." Logan and Hayward, co-producers at 49 percent, wanted to replace Pinza, but R&H, who owned 51 percent, "managed to prevail upon them to give Pinza a little more time." Pinza stayed and R&H again showed that might could also equal right. After defending the decision to retain Pinza, Rodgers concludes his published reminiscences by expressing his displeasure with Pinza's frequent and, from Rodgers's perspective, unjustified absences. In his own memoirs Pinza admits that he "gave the reporters no explanation for my repeated absence from the show" and somewhat lamely attributes this dereliction of duty to a punctured eardrum that led to pushing his voice to the point where dreaded nodes were beginning to

Rodgers, Joshua Logan, Hammerstein, and Leland Hayward, the creative and production team of *South Pacific*

form on his vocal cords.[36] Because opera singers do not sing the eight performances per week required of Broadway singers, Pinza had insisted from the beginning that his contract spare him from singing, beyond "Twin Soliloquies," one solo number in each act ("Some Enchanted Evening" in act I and "This Nearly Was Mine" in act II) and fragments of "Cockeyed Optimist" and "I'm Gonna Wash That Man." The many unexcused absences suggest that Pinza never quite adjusted to the rigorous Broadway schedule.

In *Reminiscences* Rodgers goes to greater lengths than he would in *Musical Stages* to address the issues of his compositional speed and of musical theater as social commentary. Concerning the former, he emphasizes the hard work and thought (rather than the inspiration) that preceded the five minutes that went into the composition of "Bali Ha'i." As Rodgers explains it, a song is not composed effortlessly in five minutes any more than a woman has a baby in a half-hour.[37] Also in *Reminiscences* Rodgers acknowledges that "Carefully Taught" reflected his and Hammerstein's feelings on the subject and that "it was wise to keep it in," despite some opposition. In *Musical*

Stages, Rodgers changes his tune when he denies that "Carefully Taught" was intended to bear a message of any kind. Instead, Rodgers interpreted this song less politically and more simply as a song designed to satisfy the dramatic need "in a particular spot for a Princeton-educated young WASP who, despite his background and upbringing, had fallen in love with a Polynesian girl."[38]

Logan

In *Josh: My Up and Down, In and Out Life* (1976), Joshua Logan (1908–88) offers a personal narrative of *South Pacific*'s genesis and the mixture of humiliation and triumph he suffered and enjoyed as its director and co-author.[39] His story begins when Rodgers called to ask him to help Hammerstein, who was experiencing writer's block. Logan called Hammerstein, and the librettist acknowledged his difficulties with capturing military matters in dialogue and invited Logan and his wife, Nedda, to come to his Connecticut country home that afternoon. Logan's father was an officer at a military academy, and Logan himself had served with the Air Force Combat Intelligence and recently co-authored a popular play about Navy life, *Mister Roberts* (1948). His understanding of the military was potentially invaluable to the struggling Hammerstein. Although Logan was under contract to serve only as director and co-producer for *South Pacific*, he agreed to help Hammerstein with the embryonic libretto.

According to Logan, at the time of their first conversation Hammerstein had completed only the opening scene between Emile and Nellie, a portion of the scene in which Cable and Liat meet, and the lyrics for one song, "A Wonderful Guy." After two days collaboratively planning the sequence of scenes, Hammerstein asked Logan to spend a third day to help him on the second scene, which introduces Bloody Mary and American Seabees, sailors, and Marines. In the end Logan stayed ten days to help Hammerstein grind out the rest of the libretto. Hammerstein devoted the mornings to the lyrics, and the two spent the afternoons and evenings reading dialogue into a Dictaphone. Before they returned to work the next day their words would be transcribed by their secretaries and collated by their wives. Like Nellie, Logan was from the South (raised in Louisiana) and he "spontaneously spoke all of Nellie's lines"; Hammerstein countered as a "very suave Emile de Becque." Logan describes how they became stymied when they reached Emile's party at the end of act I. Whatever they tried, the entertainment at the party dissipated the emotional tension. Logan generously credits Hammerstein with devising the ingenious solution: "to begin *after* the party, with the guests calling good-bye in French offstage."

Gradually, Logan reached an uncomfortable realization: "After three-fourths of the first act, I realized that Oscar was throwing me lines for Emile de Becque, Bloody Mary, and sometimes for Captain Brackett, and I was doing all the rest." Although the creative process was exhilarating, Logan became increasingly troubled that they had not discussed how or even whether under these new circumstances R&H would modify the author's credits. In the original plan Hammerstein was to receive sole credit, but he was also expected to write the libretto unaided. Conversations with Nedda convinced Logan that he was being used. Despite these feelings, the desire to avoid a confrontation and his own excitement in the work kept him from bringing up the delicate matter of compensation for his ideas.

After an intense ten days in which Hammerstein and Logan had completed most of the *South Pacific* libretto, the Logans returned to New York. Immediately Logan became obsessed by the absence of provisions to give him an author's credit. His frustration was exacerbated by Rodgers's characteristically understated response to the script he read on the train to Boston. All Rodgers would say about the libretto when he called Logan was that he "had a very pleasant trip." Logan considered taking legal action, then decided against it. The following day Hammerstein noticed that something was wrong, and Logan managed to request half credit for the book. Hammerstein immediately acquiesced and expressed regret that he himself had not suggested this compensation.

The Logans' celebration was short-lived. One day later, "speaking lines he had been instructed to say—whether by Dick [Rodgers] or their lawyer," Hammerstein informed Logan that, although Logan would share "equal credit" for the book, he would be deprived of any share of the author's royalties. Logan's director's credit was also diminished to 60 percent, and he would not be able to move any part of his director's royalties (which ended when the show closed) to the continuing author's royalties. Later Logan learned that his lawyer, who feared the consequences of his client's response, had signed the director's contract for him, a contract that not only made the severe financial terms explicit but forced Logan to sign within hours or be dismissed as director. We have previously noted that Martin and Pinza were also asked to accept a similar ultimatum, although it was couched in friendly terms. The message was simple and powerful: you can be replaced.

Logan mainly blamed Rodgers. At the same time he was indebted to Rodgers for past kindnesses. Perhaps this passage gives a better idea of the complexity of Logan's response to Rodgers, former crony and fun guy:

> Surely, Dick Rodgers did more for me, more to solidify my career in musical comedy, than any other person. He scowlingly (which means warmly) approved of me initially to direct my first musical, *I Married an Angel*. He liked my work on that in spite of the fact that I didn't. He insisted on having me for his next, *Higher and Higher* [Logan served as co-librettist as well as director for this show, the only Rodgers and Hart failure after their return from Hollywood], and after I had had my well-publicized nervous breakdown, Dick was the first person to offer me another show, *By Jupiter*. After the war, he offered me *Annie Get Your Gun* while I was still overseas. And show after show till *South Pacific*.[40]

In addition to its personal testimony, Logan's memoir offers invaluable information concerning what happened at rehearsals and out-of-town tryouts, during which Rodgers, Hammerstein, and Logan became aware of staging infelicities and problems with the dramatic material. Here are the thorniest rehearsal snags and the often-simple means by which they were overcome:

> "Twin Soliloquies"
> Problem and Solution: "This was the moment when for me the show became great. But the song stopped too quickly; the music had to continue to strengthen the passionate, almost sexual, feeling. Trude [Rittmann] provided the thrilling continuation later."[41]
> "Some Enchanted Evening"
> Problem: With Pinza's Italian accent the song sounded like "Enshonted Evening."
> Solution: "He [Pinza] worked hard, and before long his diction was both understandable and attractive."[42]
> "There Is Nothin' Like a Dame"
> Problem: How to move sex-starved military men to act like the natural caged animals they are.
> Solution: Not a problem. "Within fifteen or twenty minutes" Logan had created an "*acted* musical scene" and "one of the things most remembered" about his staged work.
> "I'm Gonna Wash That Man Right Outa My Hair"
> Problem: Nellie needed a song "to help her decide to break it off with Emile."
> Solution: Since Mary's short hair dried in three minutes, why not wash it

on stage? Everyone, including Logan, credits the shower idea to Martin shortly before rehearsals.

"Younger Than Springtime"

Problem: Cable needed a suitable love song to sing to Liat in act I.

Solution 1: "My friend, my friend, / Is coming around the bend."

Solution 2: "Suddenly Lovely" (later transformed into "Getting to Know You" and placed in *The King and I*).[43]

Solution 3: "Younger Than Springtime" (new words adapted to "My Wife," an unused song originally intended for *Allegro*).

"Happy Talk"

Problem: Hammerstein "couldn't imagine how it could be staged."

Solution: Using Betta St. John's (Liat's) expressive finger and hand gestures to illustrate Hammerstein's lyrics.

"Now Is the Time"

Problem: The words, "Now is the time to act, no other time will do," were belied by the absence of action.

Solution: Replacing "Now Is the Time" with a new reflective song, "This Nearly Was Mine"—in Rodgers's words, a "big bass waltz."

So much for the rehearsals. Next Logan discusses how he and his collaborators solved additional staging problems and responded to audience reactions during the out-of-town tryouts. In New Haven Logan discovered that when Nellie took the shower *before* singing "Wash That Man," audiences became disconcerted and distracted. When Nellie took a shower *after* the song, the number became a huge success. The second week in Boston Logan concluded that "A Wonderful Guy" should be a "soliloquy with Mary's intimate feelings revealed." To solve this perceived flaw, Hammerstein removed the nurses (at least at the outset) and changed the "yous" to "theys." Tryout audiences responded with a new alacrity. Logan's readers also learn that Martin's familiar high vocal note that ends "A Wonderful Guy" replaced a cartwheel after the heroine fell into the orchestra pit, injuring rehearsal pianist Rittmann.

Logan suffered further humiliation when both the *New York Times* review and the Pulitzer Prize notices initially omitted his name. The error was corrected, but much of the damage had already been done. Additional problems with R&H developed when Logan tried to make staging changes in the second company production. Hammerstein wrote Logan that "second companies should be staged by croquet players—stage managers who can keep their feet on the ground," to which Logan replied, "If it's staged by croquet players, it will be almost as exciting as croquet." Rodgers does not

Ezio Pinza (Emile de Becque) and Mary Martin (Nellie Forbush) with de Becque's children Barbara Luna (Ngana) and Michael DeLeon (Jerome) in the final scene of the original *South Pacific*

mention the second company production in his *Reminiscences* or in *Musical Stages*, but he does recall in the latter his response to Logan's projected staging for the first London production, which starred Martin: "Expecting to see a reasonable facsimile of our New York production, I was shocked at what I saw at the dress rehearsal."[44] The recollection includes a scene with Hammerstein, Logan, Martin, and Rodgers in a crowded London dressing room. As Rodgers tells it, the tearful star threatened to leave the show unless Logan agreed to return to the original staging (he did, of course). Rodgers concludes by noting that from where he was positioned he could see Martin winking at him in her mirror.

Logan's work on *South Pacific* earned him a shared Pulitzer Prize for

Drama, Tony and Donaldson awards for best direction, and even the mixed pleasures of seeing his staging become sacrosanct in the eyes of Rodgers and Hammerstein. Despite these triumphs, the experience, as we have observed, bore its share of negatives for Logan. Before agreeing to write the show, R&H first insisted on acquiring 51 percent of the rights. And after Logan bailed out Hammerstein when he was unable to produce credible military and southern dialogue, R&H deprived him of his fair share of copyright royalties as co-author and refused to transfer his director's royalties to author's royalties. To add injury to insult, during the intermission of the first New Haven tryout performance, Logan learned that R&H had given him an ultimatum to either sign their contract within hours or be dismissed from his directorial duties. In the end, the negative feelings overwhelmed the positive, and Logan turned down R&H's offer of full co-authorship and direction of their next project, *The King and I*. Logan would regret this decision for the rest of his life. Before the end of the next decade, however, Logan did agree to direct the *South Pacific* film. The effects of this decision are examined later in this chapter.

Although Logan felt that Hammerstein did not quite have the backbone to defend Logan's right to receive copyright credit, he seemed to have felt more pity than anger toward his co-author. Logan was particularly sympathetic to the fact that Hammerstein was beholden to Rodgers. After all, Rodgers rescued his older partner after eleven years of failure. Logan concludes his memories of working with this duo with a conversation he had with Hammerstein during the creation of *The King and I*. Rodgers's understated response to the *South Pacific* libretto had disturbed Logan, and it seems that Hammerstein suffered similar feelings over Rodgers's cavalier and diffident response to "Hello, Young Lovers." After four days of torment waiting for Rodgers to react to this lyric (which Hammerstein felt was his very best work), Rodgers called him about a mundane business matter. Only as an afterthought did Rodgers even acknowledge that he had received the lyric, with a positive but dismissive remark, "it works fine." Logan knew just how Hammerstein felt.

What the Manuscripts Say

Musical and literary manuscript sources complement Logan's recollection of how *South Pacific* took its initial shape and evolved during the final months before rehearsals began. In addition, the manuscripts have much that is new to tell us. With the exceptions of "Dites-Moi," "Happy Talk," and "Honey Bun," at least some musical sketches are extant for all of the songs.[45] Lyrics as well as music have been preserved for most of the songs that were left on the road. A libretto dated January 21, 1949, shortly before rehearsals started, is also invaluable because it consolidates ideas developed during the latter months of 1948 and early weeks of 1949. This libretto makes it possible to note a number of changes made during the two months of rehearsals and tryouts leading up to the New York premiere on April 7.[46] Table 4.1 compares the songs contained in the two librettos

A comparison between the two columns of the table reveals that between the completion of the Logan-Hammerstein libretto of January 21 and the libretto published later that year by Random House (the version that closely approximates what transpired on opening night in New York) several significant deletions and replacements occurred in the song scenario. Unfortunately, writers who have addressed these changes, including those responsible for writing, performing, and producing the show, occasionally omit one song or another in their published accounts or make statements that inadvertently contribute to the confusion or ambiguity about *South Pacific*'s compositional history. In my survey I take advantage of these accounts and statements but rely on the documentary sources to help set the record straight.

The changes begin in the opening scene. The original plan called for a song, untitled in the January libretto and in the published lyrics of Hammerstein, but designated "Canary Yellow" in the sketches and "A Bright Canary Yellow" in Rodgers's piano-vocal holograph.[47] Those familiar with "A Cockeyed Optimist," which directly follows, will notice that Hammerstein reuses the opening line, "The sky is a bright canary yellow," adding only an introductory "when."[48] "A Bright Canary Yellow" is a short and simple song that consists of two identical eight-bar periods, less a song than a verse to a song, "A Cockeyed Optimist."

The January draft also indicates that "A Bright Canary Yellow" was reprised by Emile as "Loneliness of Evening" (act II, scene 2). The new words begin, "I wake in the loneliness of sunrise" (first stanza) and "I lie in the loneliness of evening" (second stanza). Both stanzas would be dropped prior to the first Broadway performance. Just as it reinstates "My Girl Back Home" two scenes later, the film finds a way to bring back this song. As in the January draft, the words were the words that Emile wrote on a card with the flowers he gave Nellie after the Thanksgiving show. Also in the January draft

Table 4.1. *South Pacific*, January to April 1949

January 21, 1949, Libretto	Published Libretto
ACT I	

SCENE 1: EMILE DE BECQUE'S PLANTATION HOME

"Dites-Moi" (Ngana and Jerome)	"Dites-Moi" (Ngana and Jerome)
"Bright Canary Yellow" (Nellie and Emile)	
"A Cockeyed Optimist" (Nellie)	"A Cockeyed Optimist" (Nellie)
"Twin Soliloquies" (Nellie and Emile)	"Twin Soliloquies" (Nellie and Emile)
"Some Enchanted Evening" (Emile)	"Some Enchanted Evening" (Emile)
Reprise, "Dites-Moi" (Ngana and Jerome)	Reprise, "Dites-Moi" (Ngana and Jerome)

SCENE 2: ANOTHER PART OF THE ISLAND

"Bloody Mary" (Sailors, Seabees, Marines)	"Bloody Mary" (Sailors, Seabees, Marines)

SCENE 3: THE EDGE OF A PALM GROVE NEAR THE BEACH

Reprise "Bloody Mary" (Sailors, Seabees, Marines)	
"There Is Nothin' Like a Dame" (Billis, Sailors, Seabees, Marines)	"There Is Nothin' Like a Dame" (Billis, Professor, Stewpot, Sailors, Seabees, Marines)
"Bali Ha'i" (Bloody Mary, Billis, Cable [whistles])	"Bali Ha'i" (Bloody Mary, Billis, Cable [sings])

SCENE 4: THE COMPANY STREET

No songs.	No songs.

SCENE 5: INSIDE THE ISLAND COMMANDER'S OFFICE

No songs.	No songs.

SCENE 6: THE COMPANY STREET

No songs.	No songs.

SCENE 7: THE BEACH

"I'm Gonna Wash That Man Right Outa My Hair" (Nellie and Nurses)	"I'm Gonna Wash That Man Right Outa My Hair" (Nellie and Nurses)

Table 4.1. Continued

January 21, 1949, Libretto	Published Libretto
"Now Is the Time" (Emile)	**"Will You Marry Me?"** (Emile) [March 24, 1949] **Reprise, "Some Enchanted Evening" (Emile and Nellie) [replaced "Will You Marry Me?" March 29, 1949]**
"A Wonderful Guy" (Nellie and Nurses)	"A Wonderful Guy" (Nellie and Nurses)

SCENE 8: INSIDE THE ISLAND COMMANDER'S OFFICE

[Scene 8 and 9: Company Street]	
No songs.	No songs.

SCENE 9: ANOTHER PART OF THE ISLAND

[Scenes 10 and 11]	
Reprise, "Bali Ha'i" (Native girls)	Reprise, "Bali Ha'i" (French girls)

SCENE 10: INTERIOR OF NATIVE HUT ON BALI HA'I

Scene 12	
"Suddenly Lovely" (Cable)	**"Younger Than Springtime"** (Cable)

SCENE 11: NEAR THE BEACH OF BALI HA'I

Scene 13	
Reprise, "Bali Ha'i" (French girls)	Reprise, "Bali Ha'i" (French girls)

SCENE 12: EMILE'S TERRACE

Scene 14	
Reprise, "A Wonderful Guy" (Nellie and Emile)	Reprise, "A Wonderful Guy" (Nellie and Emile)
Reprise, "Twin Soliloquies" (Nellie and Emile)	Reprise, "Twin Soliloquies" (Nellie and Emile)
Reprise, "A Cockeyed Optimist" (Nellie and Emile)	Reprise, "A Cockeyed Optimist" (Nellie and Emile)
Reprise, "I'm Gonna Wash That Man Right Outa My Hair" (Emile)	Reprise, "I'm Gonna Wash That Man Right Outa My Hair" (Emile)
Reprise, "Some Enchanted Evening" (Emile)	Reprise, "Some Enchanted Evening" (Emile)

Table 4.1. Continued

January 21, 1949, Libretto	Published Libretto

ACT II

SCENE 1: THE STAGE DURING A PERFORMANCE OF
"THE THANKSGIVING FOLLIES"

Soft-shoe dance.	Soft-shoe dance.

SCENE 2: IN BACK OF THE STAGE

"Loneliness of Evening" (Nellie and Emile)	
[same music as "Bright Canary Yellow"]	
"Happy Talk" (Bloody Mary)	"Happy Talk" (Bloody Mary)
	Reprise, "Younger Than Springtime"(Cable)

SCENE 3: THE STAGE

"Lyric coming later."	**"Honey Bun" (Nellie and Girls)**

SCENE 4: IN BACK OF THE STAGE

"My Girl Back Home" (Cable)	
"You've Got to Be Carefully Taught" (Cable and Emile)	"You've Got to Be Carefully Taught" (Cable)
Reprise, "Now Is the Time" (Emile and Cable)	**"This Nearly Was Mine" (Emile)**

SCENE 5: ANOTHER PART OF THE ISLAND

No songs.	No songs.

SCENE 6: THE COMMUNICATIONS OFFICE

No songs.	No songs.

SCENE 7: THE COMMUNICATIONS OFFICE

No songs.	No songs.

SCENE 8: THE RADIO SHACK

No songs.	No songs.

SCENE 9: THE COMPANY STREET

Reprise, "A Wonderful Guy" (Nurses)	Reprise, "A Wonderful Guy" (Nurses)

Table 4.1. Continued

January 21, 1949, Libretto	Published Libretto
SCENE 10: THE BEACH	
Reprise, "Some Enchanted Evening" (Nellie)	Reprise, "Some Enchanted Evening" (Nellie)
SCENE 11: THE COMPANY STREET	
No songs.	**Reprise, "Honey Bun" (Sailors, Seabees, Marines)**
SCENE 12: EMILE'S TERRACE	
Reprise, "Dites-Moi" (Nellie, Ngana, Jerome, and Emile)	Reprise, "Dites-Moi" (Nellie, Ngana, Jerome, and Emile)

Note: Deletions from January 21, 1949, libretto in *italic type*; additions to published libretto in **bold-face type**.

Nellie sings the card in Emile's presence; in the film he speaks the words in a voice-over with the music providing a subtle underscoring of the song. Several years after Hammerstein's death Rodgers found a suitable place for the song in the 1965 remake of *Cinderella*, which adopted the second stanza of this song for its new title, "Loneliness of Evening."[49]

In a scene containing no fewer than four memorable songs ("Dites-Moi," "A Cockeyed Optimist," "Twin Soliloquies," and "Some Enchanted Evening"), the removal of "A Bright Canary Yellow" can hardly be considered a major loss. The omission also makes good dramatic sense. By introducing Nellie with "A Cockeyed Optimist" she is allowed to sing about her own nature in her own musical character rather than utter the generic mood painting that characterizes "A Bright Canary Yellow." In particular, the chromatic line on "robin's egg blue" (and perhaps also its somewhat precious poetic imagery) does not seem to suit Nellie's character. Ten years later its absence gave the cinematographer one less color to coordinate with a lyric, all things considered probably a good thing.

The next major change between the January draft and the Broadway libretto occurs in act I, scene 7, "On the Beach," a scene framed by two perennial song favorites performed by Nellie and the nurses: "I'm Gonna Wash That Man Right Outa My Hair" and its rebuttal, "A Wonderful Guy." According to Logan, "Wash That Man" was created about a week before rehearsals, while the lyrics to "A Wonderful Guy" constitute the sum total of what Hammerstein had completed before he asked for Logan's help with the dialogue.[50] Between January and April, Hammerstein let Emile make an additional appearance to reprise "Some Enchanted Evening" (with Nellie interjecting and modifying the concluding phrases, "Who can explain it? / Who can tell you why?" and "Once you have found *him* / Never let *him* go"). Rodgers introduces this "Enchanted Evening" reprise by introducing new material that relates harmonically and melodically to "Dites-Moi."

In the dialogue that leads to this introduction, Emile summarizes his "political philosophy," describes the circumstances which led to the accidental murder of the town bully (not unlike the accidental death of *Oklahoma!*'s villain Jud Frye) that brought Emile to the islands, and asks Nellie to marry him. In the January draft the bully provokes the young Emile. In collusion with a corrupt police force, he even burns down Emile's father's house. The bully's murder is literally hands on, since Emile seeks out the bully and strangles him with his bare hands. In the Broadway version the bully, more like Jud, falls on a rock in the process of attacking Emile.[51]

Instead of the gentle introduction and "Enchanted Evening" reprise known today, the January version presented a martial and march-like song in 6/8 meter, "Now Is the Time." The lyrics of this song were reprinted in Hammerstein's *Lyrics*; the music was reused as instrumental underscoring in No. 43, "The Take Off, Scene 5" and No. 44, "Communication Established," in the published vocal score.[52] Also extant in the *South Pacific* boxes of the Hammerstein Collection in the Library of Congress is a lyrical sketch with a March 24 date and a lyric nearly identical to "Will You Marry Me?"—a song that would find its permanent home in *Pipe Dream* in 1955. Assuming that March 24 belongs in the year 1949, one can conclude that before deciding on a reprise of "Some Enchanted Evening" with a new verse, R&H had considered "Will You Marry Me?" as a replacement for "Now Is the Time." The next stage was the creation of a new "Enchanted Evening" verse. Nellie sings "born on the opposite sides of the sea"; Hammerstein drafts the new verse on the opposite page and dates it March 29, about a week before opening night. Small wonder that Pinza complained so much about receiving new material as rapidly as he learned the old.[53]

Without placing the song's original conception in connection with a particular show, Rodgers recalled in *Musical Stages* the spontaneous creation of a tune "some years before *South Pacific* went into production."[54] Since Rodgers during his years with Hammerstein rarely wrote music without a lyric, dramatic situation, or at the very least a title in mind, it was an unusual circumstance that prompted him to play an impromptu melody for Dorothy and his girls. He credits his daughters Mary and Linda for remembering the melody and for suggesting that "it had exactly the qualities of romantic inno- cence for the song Cable sings to Liat."[55] According to Stephen Citron and Hugh Fordin, it was Hammerstein who recalled this tune and suggested its use in *South Pacific*.[56] All agree that when Hammerstein added new lyrics to this tune, the result was "Younger Than Springtime."[57] Citron confirms *Alle- gro* as the originally intended show for "My Wife," presumably the title of the song that Dorothy, Mary, and Linda and/or Hammerstein heard, and prints a musical example which juxtaposes its opening lyrics ("You are so lovely, my wife / You are the light of my life") to the opening lines of "Younger Than Springtime" ("Younger than springtime are you, / Softer than starlight are you").[58]

Logan in his memoirs noted that previous attempts to create a song for Cable and Liat were considered either uninspired or inappropriate for the dramatic occasion. The first, the prosaic "My friend, my friend" falls into the former category. No one seems to recall what "My Friend" sounded like, and if a manuscript ever existed, it is now unknown. All that remains are the opening lyrics that Logan included in *Josh*, which have the unformed and even improvised flavor of "dummy" lyrics, "My friend, my friend, / Is coming around the bend," which, according to Logan, reflected Hammerstein's fas- cination with Liat waiting for Cable's boat to come around the bend. In any event, even without hearing the melody, it is possible to imagine Logan's emotional dismissal of this first attempt at a song that captured Cable's feel- ings after making love to Liat: "That's awful! That's the worst song I ever heard. Good God, that's terrible!"[59]

The second attempt, "Suddenly Lovely" (the song Logan referred to as "Suddenly Lucky"), is well known in its future reincarnation as "Getting to Know You" in R&H's next show, *The King and I*. Sketches, a piano-vocal score holograph, the January libretto, and contemporary recollections con- firm that "Suddenly Lovely" was conceived for *South Pacific* and remained a part of the show until it was replaced in rehearsals. Rodgers and Hammer- stein understood Logan's original reaction: "I love the tune, but isn't that song a bit lightweight for a hot, lusty boy to sing right after making love to a girl who will change his life?"[60] Interestingly, the decision to reprise "Younger Than Springtime" occurred after the January libretto and provides an excellent example of how the change of even one word ("younger than springtime *were* you") can transform the meaning of a song and help it respond to evolving dramatic circumstances.[61]

The last major song changes between January and April occur in act II, scene 4.[62] The January draft opens the scene musically with a scene between Cable and Nellie, and Cable's song, "My Girl Back Home." For undisclosed reasons, perhaps simply to save time in a show that was running a little long, the song was deleted. In contrast to "Suddenly Lovely," "My Girl Back Home" would not be replaced (although it would be reinstated in the film and in the Royal National Theatre London revival in 2001). In the January draft, "You've Got to Be Carefully Taught" included material for Emile that was subsequently dropped. Also gone was the simple reprise of "Now Is the Time," a song that had already been replaced by a reprise of "Some Enchanted Evening" and preceded by a new verse (act I, scene 7). Instead, Pinza was finally given a major new song, "This Nearly Was Mine," a pessimistic romantic waltz ballad that captured Emile de Becque's sorrow for a paradise lost.

The Movie

I hated them and will always hate them, but since I instigated them, I found myself powerless to do anything about them in the end but suffer. What am I talking about? Those garish color changes that upset the whole chemistry of the movie of *South Pacific.*—Joshua Logan, "Inglorious Technicolor," in *Movie Stars, Real People, and Me*

Despite such changes as the belated reversal of scenes 1 and 2–3, the film version of *South Pacific*, released on March 19, 1958, was in most respects a remarkably faithful adaptation of the original stage production.[63] Portions of some songs were shortened, and Cable's poignant reprise of "Younger Than Springtime" was eliminated, but no original songs were cut, in marked contrast to the other five films adapted from R&H's shows between 1955 and 1965 — including *Oklahoma!*, *Carousel*, and *The King and I* from 1955 and 1956. One song, "My Girl Back Home," deleted during the tryouts, got a second chance. Filmed on location on Kauai, Hawaii, with backgrounds shot in the Fiji Islands, the movie version of *South Pacific* offered gorgeous scenery and lush vegetation. Film audiences were also able to see real water and real airplanes as the film realistically opened up what could only be suggested on a stage. In addition to retaining the stage director, Logan, the film production included the original Bloody Mary, Juanita Hall (dubbed by the London Mary, Muriel Smith), and everyone's favorite Martian and *Damn Yankee* Devil, Ray Walston, who had replaced Billis in both the 1950 touring and London companies.

But something went wrong, and today the film is an object of disdain, derision, and ridicule. When asked how he liked the film in his *Reminiscences*, Rodgers's response is similar to what the Marine told the sailor when asked how he liked the Thanksgiving show: "It stunk." Only marginally more tactfully but more specifically, Rodgers "thought it was awful" and "overproduced," and that "the use of color was atrocious." After criticizing the bigness of this amateur show and its excessively large military audience, Rodgers complained about the loss of "personal contact" throughout the film. He especially could not resist additional comment about the use of color: "[It] didn't do much good to see the girl's face turn from natural color to yellow when she started to sing." Finally, Rodgers expresses skepticism about Logan's disavowal of his use of color and the promise that the filters could be cheaply recast.[64]

Although some found fault with the casting and the dubbing of several leading characters, the use of color was and remains the most frequently criticized attribute of the film. Who can explain it? Logan tries. Before hearing from Logan, however, we will backtrack to a memorandum dated July 29, 1957, addressed to Logan from David Zeitlin of Time, Incorporated.[65] Zeitlin wrote that he and his colleagues wanted to showcase the familiar songs by creating visual images that responded to the key lyrical lines. Zeitlin and Co. wanted "to instill a kind of fairy tale air into our story" with a visual effect that was "atmospheric to the point of being surrealistic." After these general remarks, Zeitlin's memo offers specific images for nine of the songs, some of which Logan adopted, including Zeitlin's description of the visual image to accompany "A Cockeyed Optimist": "The yellow sky here should really be a really insane yellow. We see this as an impressionistic scene full of light and sparkle." Logan succeeded all too well in realizing this vision. Not all of Zeitlin's suggestions were followed. The idea of showing the words and the music of "My Girl Back Home" directly on the screen, for example, was one such idea that Logan cut even before it arrived in the cutting room.[66]

In the "Inglorious Technicolor" chapter of *Movie Stars, Real People, and Me* (1978), Logan takes great pains to explain that he went along with the idea of the color filters with the understanding that they could be easily altered if proved unsatisfactory. Assured by photographer Leon Shamroy that the color changes would be subtle, Logan was shocked at their blatancy.

Rossano Brazzi (de Becque) and Mitzi Gaynor (Forbush) at the conclusion of "Twin Soliloquies" in the film *South Pacific*

Since previews were already paid for and the film was over budget, studio executives were unwilling to spend "three months in the lab to make the colors come out right." Logan does not place the blame on Shamroy, who "had not been allowed into the lab to check" on how the color changes were realized. He does find fault with George Skouras, president of the Magna Theatre Corporation, which produced the film, for placing financial considerations over technical quality. He also accuses R&H—as controlling partners they had authority to overrule Skouras—of capitulating to time and financial pressures. Near the end of "Inglorious Technicolor" Logan expresses the following wish: "I wanted (and still want) to carry a sandwich board in front of every line at the box office, saying, I DIRECTED IT AND I DON'T LIKE THE COLOR EITHER!"[67]

Logan goes on point out the "ghastly" irony that the movie was more lucrative than all of his other plays and movies "put together." The profits from one theater in London's West End, where the film ran for more than five years, could have paid *"the entire production* cost" (emphasis Logan's). In his *Reminiscences* Rodgers conceded that the film made money, then quoted the title of a song from *Allegro*, "Money Isn't Everything." Money was no consolation to Logan either. Nor was the irony that Alan Jay Lerner and Frederick Loewe loved the garish and unsubtle colors of *South Pacific* and sought out Logan to direct the film version of *Camelot*. For Lerner and Loewe's money, the only film musical they had seen "done with flair and imagination was *South Pacific.*" Sure enough, Logan's film version of *Camelot* in 1967 came equipped with bizarre and unnatural colors. Extending the irony, Lerner and Loewe were pleased enough with *Camelot* to hire Logan to direct his last major film work, *Paint Your Wagon*, two years later, a film devastatingly described by Mordden as the "first all-talking, no-singing, no-dancing musical [film]."[68]

Despite its essential fidelity to the letter of the original show, the *South Pacific* film departs from the Broadway show in countless details. We might start with the opening musical gesture. The stage overture familiar to the many who had heard the show on recordings began with the opening three notes of "Bali Ha'i." The Hollywood soundtrack overture begins with "Some Enchanted Evening," the song most beloved or at least most familiar. More substantive was the decision to begin the film story portion by introducing a new scene showing Cable flying over various South Pacific islands on Bus Adams's PBY. This change allowed film audiences to immediately obtain a bird's-eye view of the beautiful terrain in a manner impossible to capture on a stage. Also through this change film audiences learn something about Emile de Becque before we meet him, and like Adams, infer that Cable's presence was inspired by a mission. The scene then shifts to a beach where the Seabees are singing "Bloody Mary Is the Girl I Love."[69]

Missing in this new scenario is the intimate stage opening, which began with two children, Ngana and Jerome, singing a chorus of "Dites-Moi" before they are chased away by Henry, Emile de Becque's servant. When the film finally gets to this scene, it skips over "Dites-Moi" and instead opens with Emile and Nellie in conversation. The film will, however, use "Dites-Moi" to close the scene after Nellie leaves. On Broadway, R&H use Emile's plantation as a frame to mark the beginning and the end of the show, and in the opening scene, "Dites-Moi" serves as a frame within a frame. The film's opening emphasizes the military over the romance. The opening scene in the PBY was part of the initial conception in the screenplay, but the more radical decision to follow the PBY with Seabees on the beach rather than de

Becque's plantation occurred during filming, perhaps as late as the editing process.[70]

We will now take a look at some of the more telling departures in the transfer from stage to film. After the reversal of military and domestic scenes we turn to the removal of the following dialogue in scene 1, a passage that marked the transition from Nellie's "Want to know anything else about me?" to Emile's abrupt non sequitur in lieu of a response, "Would you like some cognac?":

> EMILE: Yes. You say you are a fugitive. When you joined the Navy, what were you running away from? (*He returns the clipping to her*)
> NELLIE: Gosh, I don't know. It was more like running *to* something. I wanted to see what the world was like—outside Little Rock, I mean. And I wanted to meet different kinds of people and find out if I like them better. And I'm finding out. (*She suddenly becomes self-conscious*) (*Six Plays*, 276)

Significantly, the above exchange contained the most direct reference to Little Rock, which had in the years since the show's Broadway debut become a city marked by racial conflict. The reference to "different kinds of people" was ambiguous, but it could be obliquely interpreted to encompass people who have practiced miscegenation. Although later in the film Nellie informs Cable about her prejudiced mother in Little Rock, film audiences are deprived of a text that might help prepare them for her eventual acceptance of Emile's world.

In scene 3 of the stage version Brackett learns that Billis and his fellow Seabees have been making grass skirts. His response is characteristically macho: "Dressmakers! (*Starting to blow up*) Do you mean to tell me the Seabees of the United States Navy are now a lot of—."[71] Stage audiences can fill in the blank depending on the term they use to describe men who make dresses. In the film, Brackett replaces "Dressmakers" with "Seabees!" and gets the point across without a fill-in-the-blank name-calling: "Do you mean to tell me the Construction Battalions of the United States Navy are now sitting around in sewing circles—."[72] The exchange between Cable and Mary a few lines later in which Mary thanks Cable for kicking her off Navy property is absent from the final film script. Someone must have reinserted it into the film when no one was looking.[73]

Two exchanges from the end of act I, scene 5, were omitted in the film.[74] In the first, Brackett, somewhat angered by Cable's suggestion that a young nurse like Nellie would not be attracted to a middle-aged man, informs

Cable that he will take Cable's money when they play bridge. At the end of the scene, Harbison and Broadway audiences catch Brackett about to send a grass skirt to a woman who lives in Cleveland. Since the film was made with the cooperation of the U.S. Navy, it might have been considered prudent to remove the appearance of hypocrisy, however comical, of an officer banning a product and then purchasing one as a gift.

The final conversation between Cable and Nellie in act I, scene 6, is revised in the film. On stage, Cable tells Nellie that her mother's advice to leave an older man alone might be sound.[75] Nellie's response is to crumple her mother's letter and throw it away. Cable says, "Well, don't say I didn't warn you" and leaves, and *"NELLIE comes back and picks up the letter and starts reading as she walks off."* Cable's final advice in the film (added after the June 1957 script) is more direct:

NELLIE: Suppose you had a sister and she was in love with a man like . . .
CABLE: De Becque.
NELLIE: Yeah.
CABLE: I'd tell her to lay off.[76]

With such definitive guidance Nellie is prepared to wash Emile out of her hair.

In act I, scene 7, a portion of "Wash That Man" (from "You can't light a fire when the wood's all wet" to "And drum him outa your dreams! Oh-ho! Oh-ho!") has vanished in the film.[77] Also absent is the ensuing dialogue in which Emile comments on the strange subject matter of American songs ("Wash That Man") and his preference for unabashed love songs ("Some Enchanted Evening"). One page later in the scene the film deletes nearly all of the "Some Enchanted Evening" reprise, retaining only the new verse, Emile's musical questions, "Who can explain it? / Who can tell you why?" to which Nellie responds with "Fools give you reasons" and a kiss.

The film version of the crucial final scene in act I (scene 12) departs significantly from the stage version in the manner in which Emile shares his second secret—the first disclosure that he killed a man in self-defense had been remarkably easy for Nellie to accept.[78] On the stage and in the final film script Emile first gives her an abbreviated concert of "Wash That Man." Then he says, "Nellie, I have a surprise for you. You sit over there— something that I have been preparing for two days. Close your eyes. No peeking."[79] Emile's playful imitation of Nellie creates a humorous moment before he reveals an unwelcome surprise. In the final film script Emile was to sing two lines of the song ("I'm going to wash that man right out of my hair / And send him on his way! . . ."), considerably less of the song than he sang on stage where he continued to sing from "Don't try to patch it up" to "Yea, Sister!"[80] But at least he sang something. In the final cut of the film, however, Emile says only, "Nellie, I have a surprise for you" (adding a "Stay there" not in the Broadway libretto) before surprising her with a son and daughter from a previous marriage to a Polynesian woman. Not one line of "Wash That Man" remains, and no semblance of humor survives to blunt the shock.

Changes between the original act II on stage and its adaptation to film are less frequent and less pronounced. In addition to some reordering of material in scene 2, film audiences now actually see Nellie's tearful and moving breakdown at the Thanksgiving rehearsal rather than learn about her feelings in a secondhand exchange between Billis and Emile. An effective touch. A telling omission in the film is Cable's reprise of the conclusion of "Younger Than Springtime." In the stage version the past tense, "Younger than springtime *were* you," created a moment of poignancy in its juxtaposition against the applause that follows act I of the Thanksgiving show. All this is missing in the film. The film also omitted the final punch line (when the Marine expresses his considered opinion that the show "stunk").

A few additional small departures from act II complete this survey of changes from stage to film. In adapting scene 6 the film removed the opening exchange between the Enlisted Man who is awaiting messages from Emile and Cable and Brackett and begins with a discussion of the aftermath of Billis's $600,000 rescue mission. The film also considerably abbreviated the original stage dialogue in scene 11. On stage, Billis learns that Nellie will probably be serving in a local military hospital; film audiences actually see Nellie in the hospital where she hears the fighter pilots discussing the heroics of the "Frenchman"—her Frenchman.[81] Gone from the stage version is the shortened martial reprise of "Honey Bun" sung by the Marines as they embark on their mission.

Bloody Mary, already toned down in the adaptation from novel to stage, becomes further sanitized in the film. Now instead of the epitaph "stingy bastard" she utters the less salty "stingy stinker." Even Billis, a Navy man, softens his language for the film. Instead of saying "You're *damn* well right, not enough," in the film he now says, "You're *tooting* well right it's not enough." That "*damn* Bali Ha'i" becomes that "*darn* Bali Ha'i." Captain Brackett asks Cable what makes him *so* sure rather than *damn* sure. But audiences should "be thankful for the things they got." At least the Hollywood Production Code allowed Hammerstein's "damn" lyrics to stay in the songs "Bloody Mary" and "There Is Nothin' Like a Dame."

R&H themselves either initiated (or agreed to) a lyric change that may reflect a shift in cultural literacy between 1949 and 1958. In the published libretto and the final film script, the second stanza of "Bloody Mary Is the Girl I Love" begins with the line, "Her skin is as tender as DiMaggio's glove." The great New York Yankee center fielder Joe DiMaggio was not only extraordinarily famous, he also lost three precious seasons at the peak of his career in order to serve in World War II. When a song lyric had his name in it, people could be expected to get it. After retiring from baseball in 1951, DiMaggio remained in the public limelight when he married actress and sex symbol Marilyn Monroe. Perhaps in the mindset of the Production Code this last action was reason enough to omit his name from a film lyric. In any event, Mary's skin in the film is as tender as a nameless, generic baseball glove. Less than ten years after being excised from the *South Pacific* film, DiMaggio's name again figured prominently on screen and soundtrack when Paul Simon and Art Garfunkel asked, "Where have you gone, Joe DiMaggio?" in the song "Mrs. Robinson" from the popular film *The Graduate* (1967), a lyric perhaps inspired by the Yankee Clipper's demotion to television pitchman for the Mr. Coffee coffeemaker. Shortly before his death in 1999, the private DiMaggio became the subject of public revelations about his sad personal life. In 2001 the television *South Pacific* restored DiMaggio and his glove.

In the film version, seldom, if ever, is heard another word that Broadway audiences (and perhaps most Americans) heard and spoke frequently in the 1940s. The derogatory word "Jap" is now replaced by the more respectful "Japanese" and the "enemy" or is circumvented entirely. In World War II the use of "Jap" expressed contempt for a formidable enemy and seemed appropriate in the wake of Pearl Harbor. By the time *South Pacific* was filmed, however, the Japanese were U.S. allies and trading partners. Even if the word substitution led to less authentic military speech, it did respond decisively to new sensitivities brought about by the aftermath of the war.

One final change. In act I, scene 8, Emile, deeply in love with Nellie and with much to lose, refuses Brackett's and Cable's request to help the United States on a dangerous mission in Japanese-held territory. In the course of the conversation Emile is asked "to help us lick the Japs" (the Japanese in the film). After Emile leaves, the film offers another revealing departure from the stage original. In 1949, Harbison comments that although the armed forces can't guarantee Emile "a better world if we win," he knows "it'll be worse if we lose." When Harbison asks, "Can't we . . . (*Hotly*) Well, can't we?" Brackett replies "Of course." Nine years later in the film, Brackett responds with less certainty. Now he simply says, "I don't know." In the intervening years the world had seen not only another bloody war (the Korean War) but also two world powers in perpetual confrontation and the distinct possibility of a nuclear war. If any single revision can stand for the changes between the confidence of the world at the time of the stage version and the cautious optimism of the late 1950s, it might be found in Brackett's altered response between 1949 and 1958.

South Pacific and the Hollywood Production Code

In the years immediately preceding Stanley Kubrick's 1962 film adaptation of Vladimir Nabokov's *Lolita* (banned for years in its original form as a novel) and the filmed adaptation of Edward Albee's *Who's Afraid of Virginia Woolf?* (1966), which further challenged sexual and language restrictions, the Motion Picture Association of America Production Code Administration had begun to lighten up. Leonard J. Leff and Jerold L. Simmons in their informative history of the Production Code, *The Dame in the Kimono*, note that one year before the film version of *South Pacific* went into production the Code revisions "lifted all remaining taboos except nudity, sexual perversion, and venereal disease."[82] When "'treated within the careful limits of good taste,' drug addiction, prostitution, and childbirth were suddenly acceptable subjects." Even so, previous taboos, including mild profanity, if deemed gratuitous, and provocative clothing or gestures were still subject to Code objections and required removal—the gestures, not the clothing. If they followed the Code, a movie would be rewarded with the coveted seal of approval essential to a family picture, especially a family musical like *South Pacific*, and would gain admittance to theaters, nearly all of which were controlled by the film industry.

In adapting Michener's novel to the stage, Hammerstein and Logan had faced the problem of how to let audiences know beyond a shadow of a doubt, without direct graphic representation, that Cable and Liat have sexual intercourse. A blackout would allow for some ambiguity on this point, but Hammerstein and Logan were not seeking ambiguity. Twenty years before the musical *Hair* (1968) softened the rules, Logan came up with the

A shirtless John Kerr (Lt. Joseph Cable) and France Nuyen (Liat) in the film

idea to have Cable remove *his* shirt before moonlight turned to morning light.[83] The scene would create new problems for a film adaptation, since the Code's contradictory goal from Twentieth Century-Fox was to ensure that film audiences did *not* get the impression that sexual activity had taken place, especially between two people of different races.[84] Logan's solution for the film was, like the stage version, to again have Cable take off his shirt, but now he would do this daring deed while still on the boat as it sailed for Bali Ha'i. The earlier removal made it at least feasible that he took off his shirt to get a good suntan (and probably a burn) and perhaps even to show off his physique, but not necessarily to facilitate lovemaking.

In the scene where Bloody Mary introduces Cable and Liat the film adds "Liat nice daughter—No?" and "Make nice wife—yes," to her opinion that the Tonkinese "are ver' pretty people—No?"[85] On Broadway (and again

in the recent television version), Mary delays delivering the shocking information that Liat is her daughter until the following morning. This is by no
means a trivial detail, because if Cable did not think Liat was Mary's daughter, he would assume that she was a prostitute procured by Mary. The stage
Mary also waits a little to plant the idea of marriage. Shortly after Cable and
Liat have established that they speak *un peu français,* Mary comments, "You
talk lots French now, *oui?*" This verbal innuendo—the amount of French
that Cable and Liat will actually speak to one another will probably be inconsequential—is replaced by Mary's devilish, wordless laugh. When we see
Cable and Liat the next morning the Production Code wanted audiences
to believe that nothing happened.[86] Cable's shirt may be off, but didn't he
take it off on the boat the day before? Anyway, he still has his pants on and
Liat is fully clothed. Perhaps they were discussing the finer points of Marcel
Proust or Anatole France.

Included among the Joshua Logan Papers in the Manuscript Division of
the Library of Congress are five memos dated between May 28 and July 17,
1957, that shed some light on how Twentieth Century-Fox and the Motion
Picture Production Code Administration perceived and responded to potential and real concerns about the degree to which *South Pacific* conformed
to the Code guidelines.[87] The first was an internal memo from corporate
executive Frank McCarthy to producer Buddy Adler (with a carbon copy
to Logan). McCarthy, who recently read the Revised Temporary Script of
May 22, concluded that "an excellent job has been done of bringing this
story into line with the Code and the Legion of Decency [the Catholic
code]" and was going to send the script for approval.[88] In the rest of the
memo he goes on to mention "one or two items hanging over from the last
script" (he actually lists four) but suggests "doing nothing about these until
we hear from them." McCarthy notes the possible confusion of Cable's line,
"How did that Bloody Mary get a kid like you to come here—I don't get
it" in light of the fact that she was introduced on the previous page as her
daughter. He predicts that the Code might question the implication that
Liat is a prostitute. McCarthy also notes five remaining uses of the word
"Japs" and without reference to the Code points to specific places where
substitute words "should be used." He suspects the Code will ask that the
word "hell" be removed from the dialogue—yet allow it to remain in the
lyrics—and notes that "in the female impersonation scene, we are asked to
eliminate the skirt thrust."

On June 4, Geoffrey M. Shurlock, vice president and director of the Production Code Administration, responded to the Revised Temporary Script. On the plus side he notes that two previous "principal problems," "the relationship of Emile with the Polynesian woman" and "the problem of Bloody Mary's introduction of Cable to Liat" have been "corrected." On the other hand, "the one other major problem, namely that of Cable's relationship with Liat, still seems to us to remain." Either McCarthy had an exceptionally good ear for perceived Code violations or he knew more than he disclosed in his memo to Adler. In any event, Shurlock continues: "In our opinion, the manner in which the scenes are played beginning on Page 71 and continuing through 73 inescapably suggests that the two have indulged in an affair. We point out to you Cable's horrified reaction on Page 72 when he finds out that Bloody Mary is Liat's mother; as well as the immediate foregoing dialogue, 'How did Bloody Mary get a kid like you to come here and—I don't get it.' Furthermore, the stage directions that indicate that Cable has taken off his shirt (Page 73) further heighten the impression. Lastly, even though these details were to be changed, it would be necessary to handle the kiss and embrace at the end of Scene 90 Cont. with great delicacy and taste so as to avoid the impression that an affair takes place."

In addition, Shurlock cites seven "details" that should be resolved, including two of the remaining three passages predicted by McCarthy, the use of the word "hell" in Brackett's speech and the "business of the boy reaching his hand up under Billis's skirt." Somehow Shurlock overlooked or did not care about the use of the word "Japs." He was, however, concerned that Nellie's robe "not be suggestively short," that "the nakedness referred to in Scene 70 [also Scene 91] is not meant literally," that Twentieth Century-Fox heed their "previous admonition regarding scenes in which animals are used," and that "the line, 'Yah, let's go walk down Broadway and pick up a couple of—,' would be unacceptable."

In the next memo, June 21, Shurlock responds to the Final Film Script of June 10. Some objectionable elements were easily remedied. For example, instead of a "skirt thrust" Billis is simply whacked by a passing hand. Only three of the original problematic areas required further comment. The reference to a "short robe" when Nellie gets out of the shower caused the Code to "recall our previous caution," and the line about picking up "a couple of—" needed to be removed. The most important matter, the nature of the relationship between Cable and Liat, remained unresolved: "As we have pointed out several times before, a picture that would contain the suggestion that Cable and Liat were having a sex affair would be unacceptable under the

Code. We feel that this suggestion is clearly present in this version of the story. For details we refer you to our previous letter of 4 June 1957."

Within the next two weeks McCarthy, along with Hammerstein and Logan, conferred with Shurlock and informed Adler in a memo dated July 8 that they agreed to two additional changes to the final film script, "neither of which is of any importance." The second Marine now suggests that that they "pick up a couple of *dames*," as in "There Is Nothin' Like a Dame," a term that encompasses a wide range of females, including the girls back home. In a final concession on the Cable and Liat affair, McCarthy offered to follow "But you're just a kid" with "How did an innocent kid like you get mixed up with Bloody Mary?" rather than the line, "How did that Bloody Mary get a kid like you to come here and—I don't get it." The new question allows audiences to consider the notion that Liat is sexually innocent. In any event, the new line allowed Shurlock to respond in his memo to McCarthy on July 17 "that this material seems to meet the provisions of the Production Code." Despite this happy ending, Shurlock nonetheless inserted the proviso that "final judgment will be based on the finished picture."

On at least one occasion—for example, Billis's suggestive description of the boar's tooth ceremonial—lines deleted from the final film script mysteriously appeared in the actual film. The ceremony itself is also captured in greater detail on the screen than on stage. Here is one banned passage that made it past the "final judgment":

> BILLIS: But, another thing goes on over there—the ceremonial of the boar's tooth. After they kill the boar they pass around some of that coconut liquor and women dance with just skirts on . . . (*His voice becoming evil*) and everybody gets to know everybody pretty well. . . . (*He sings*) Bali Ha'i will whisper—(*BILLIS starts [to] dance as he hums the melody seductively. Then he stops and talks*) It's just a little tribal ceremonial and I thought you being up in the shooting war for such a long time without getting any—recreation—I thought you might be interested. (*Six Plays*, p. 296)

In his memo of June 4, Shurlock wrote McCarthy for some assurance: "We presume that the nakedness referred to in Scene 70 is not meant literally since this would be unacceptable under the Code." In compliance with this presumption, no such reference appears in the script of June 10 (either in Scene 70 or the other offending moment in Scene 29). Nevertheless, although the final film script excised both Billis's suggestive description and "evil" tone, both managed to find their way into the film. Logan may have

failed in his efforts to fix the color filters, but it seems that he managed to
put one or two over on the Production Code.

South Pacific 2001: The Television Broadcast

> An all-new, television production of Rodgers & Hammerstein's South Pacific
> premiered on ABC-TV on March 26, [2001], giving the network an en-
> chanted evening as 16,000,000 viewers tuned in, and made it the most-
> watched event of the night. Four years in the planning, this South Pacific
> marked a major achievement for contemporary television programming:
> three hours of prime-time devoted to a serious adaptation of a classic Broad-
> way musical.[89]

The above report introduced an article in the Summer 2001 issue of
the Rodgers & Hammerstein Organization newsletter Happy Talk. The ambitious project received the full cooperation of the Organization, but the
driving force behind its realization was the prestige and popularity of Glenn
Close, who both produced and starred as Nellie Forbush. In response to
one of the central criticisms of the 1958 film, none of the cast members
was dubbed, and in the gorgeous scenes filmed on location on the island
of Moorea and northeastern Australia the camera work studiously avoids
eccentric and blatant color filters.[90] In the post–Saving Private Ryan era, executive producer and script writer Lawrence Cohen perhaps felt obliged to
insert World War II more directly and more realistically. In keeping with
this greater realism, the Japanese can again be called "Japs." The people responsible for this new version were for the most part respectful of the original Broadway show and spared no expense—some published estimates are
placed at $15 million, others as high as $20 million—to create a production worthy of the name South Pacific. Nevertheless, the new creative team
also felt that some things could be altered, even improved, to better reach
a modern audience.

In terms of its structure, the television version matches the film more
closely than the stage version. Most noticeably, in the opening scene viewers see Cable flying in a plane followed by the Seabees singing "There Is
Nothing Like a Dame" rather than Nellie and Emile sipping cognac on a
terrace. Both the movie and the television versions "open up" the story to
take advantage of their respective media. Both are mostly faithful to the score
(although not its order), and both adopt the Hammerstein-Logan libretto as
the principal source, retaining substantial amounts of original language. In

contrast to the film, which kept everything from the stage version and even
added a previously cut song, "My Girl Back Home," the television broadcast
removed one song, "Happy Talk."[91] According to *TV Guide,* the song was
dropped because "producers found the 52-year-old tune offensive to Asians."
Happy Talk, the R&H Organization newsletter, offers the more likely explanation that "Happy Talk" "was cut due to time constraints and not, as erroneously reported, because of PC censorship."[92] As shown below, the television version took numerous liberties with song order that go beyond the
simple transfer of Seabee beach songs and the songs on Emile's plantation
terrace.[93]

Television	Broadway
There Is Nothin' Like a Dame	Dites-Moi
A Cockeyed Optimist	A Cockeyed Optimist
Bloody Mary	Twin Soliloquies
Bali Ha'i	Some Enchanted Evening
Twin Soliloquies	Dites-Moi (reprise)
Some Enchanted Evening	Bloody Mary
Dites-Moi	There Is Nothin' Like a Dame
Younger Than Springtime	Bali Ha'i
I'm Gonna Wash That Man Right Outa My Hair	I'm Gonna Wash That Man Right Outa My Hair
Some Enchanted Evening (reprise)	Some Enchanted Evening (reprise)
A Wonderful Guy	A Wonderful Guy
Carefully Taught	Younger Than Springtime
This Nearly Was Mine	Happy Talk
Honey Bun	Younger Than Springtime(reprise)
Dites-Moi (reprise)	Carefully Taught
This Nearly Was Mine	Dites-Moi (reprise)

In addition to changes in song order, contexts and "staging" have been
considerably altered. For example, in the new version we actually see the
romantic principals the moment they meet as strangers "across a crowded
room" (the Officer's Club). Nellie also sings "A Cockeyed Optimist" to
Emile not long after this initial eye contact rather than a few weeks later
on his terrace. Perhaps to remove lingering charges of preachiness and sentimentality, "Carefully Taught" and "This Nearly Was Mine" are sung as solos
by Cable and Emile, respectively, and reflect their private thoughts. Cable's
"Carefully Taught" is also slower and far less rhythmically active than previous versions. More in sorrow than in anger—more "Ol' Man River." During
the course of the song the camera moves away from Cable to single out the

black workers in this integrated military unit ("people whose skin is a differ-ent shade") rather than Tonkinese islanders like Liat ("people whose eyes are oddly made").

Theater historians and critics seem to have reached a consensus that Cable is killed—off-stage and off-camera in the stage and film versions, graphically and in plain sight in the television version—so that audiences would not have to confront the unpleasant reality that this Princeton man could never bring Liat home to Philadelphia, Pa. This may be a good place to challenge this assumption. In the few lines of dialogue separating "Care-fully Taught" from "This Nearly Was Mine" Cable reaches at least a mo-mentary epiphany that de Becque has "the right idea" about living on an island: "Yes, sir, if I get out of this thing alive, I'm not going back there! I'm coming here. All I care about is right here. To hell with the rest."[94]

In the television version, Cable adds a more sensitive clarification: "I'll stay here with Liat, if she'll have me." For several decades after World War II, students of *South Pacific* were incredulous that a man on the verge of death would make such a statement about his priorities in life, especially since his future bride speaks virtually no English and only "un peu français." Without acknowledging the extent to which a possible subtext of World War II was the racial as well as political antagonism toward the "yellow peril," one might also question the extent to which the show's racial tolerance and intermar-riage obscure another issue applicable to audiences then and now: class. Per-haps a new television version of *South Pacific* could have confronted a topic studiously avoided in artistic representations of America's allegedly "class-less society." Would Cable, a Philadelphia blueblood, have brought *Nellie*, a middle-class woman from the South without papers, home to meet his mother, especially now that she is old enough to *be* his mother?

This last question introduces another delicate issue: age. The original R&H Nellie is an ingenue whose cockeyed optimism has not been tested, at least not before her arrival in the South Pacific. In the musical, both on stage and film, she fell in love with an attractive middle-age man old enough to be her father. Mary Martin was thirty-five when she played the first Nellie on the stage, and by all accounts she managed to convey youthful exuberance and appearance. Although she convincingly portrayed the youthful Maria in the stage version of *Sound of Music* ten years later, Martin was bypassed for the film version of *South Pacific*. From Jeanne Crain to Shirley Jones to Julie Andrews to Mitzi Gaynor to Lesley Ann Warren, a glimpse at film credits supports the hypothesis that R&H would not have hired a fifty-three-year-old woman—nearly the same age as Emile, played by Rade Sherbedgia, a tenor instead of a bass (another cause for possible complaint)—to portray Nellie Forbush.[95] One need turn only to her persuasive portrayal of the aging actress Norma Desmond in the musical version of *Sunset Boulevard* in the early 1990s to appreciate Glenn Close as a truly magnificent actress and singer. Nevertheless, her physical appearance significantly alters the dynamics in this new *South Pacific*. No longer is this the story of an older man's last chance to find love and happiness with "someone young and smiling." Listeners tuned in to the lyrics might also reasonably wonder about the verisimilitude of these lines: "Younger men than I, / Officers and doctors, / Probably pursue her— / She could have her pick." In the words of *New York Times* critic Julie Salamon, "'I'm stuck like a dope with a thing called hope' means one thing where you are in your 20's, something else when you are not."[96]

Compared with the stage and film versions, if not the life of an officer stationed on a remote island in the South Pacific during World War II, the treatment of Cable's initial encounter with Liat in the television version reveals a modern perspective. Within seconds after Cable meets this beautiful Tonkinese younger-than-springtime woman, who had appeared fleetingly in a white and virginal vision when Bloody Mary sang "Bali Ha'i," Liat removes all her clothes, an action that might create a credible opportunity to sing a song called "Suddenly Lovely," and perhaps from Cable's perspective a song set to Logan's title, "Suddenly Lucky." In the absence of the Production Code, Bloody Mary can serve as a madame for an exotic brothel and delay informing Cable that Liat is her daughter rather than an ordinary prostitute. In the 2001 *South Pacific* only the most soporific viewers will be left wondering what was happening between Cable and Liat when the camera moved on to the next scene.

Despite this modern presentation, the message of the television movie remains an old-fashioned message that made sense to many in the 1940s and for several decades beyond: that romantic sexual love can overcome all linguistic, class, cultural, and racial barriers, spoken and unspoken. After an internal struggle with his own prejudices ("Carefully Taught") and the possibility of death on a dangerous mission, Cable decides he will return to Liat. Perhaps it is now time to take Cable at his word and accept the notion that R&H did not kill off a bigot.

Musical Family Resemblances

Music historians have cause to lament that Rodgers, like most composers, wrote precious little about what he was doing musically. Rodgers's lack of technical specificity on what he learned at the Institute of Musical Art has been noted in Chapter 1. Occasionally, as in *Musical Stages* or in his introduction to the *Rodgers and Hammerstein Song Book*, he would include a few comments and a musical illustration about how his music expressed a text. From these examples we can learn that Rodgers was trying to musically depict scurrying chicks and ducks in "Surrey with the Fringe on Top" (with sudden leaps getting out of the way of repeated notes) and that the "restless and jumpy" music (leaps and dotted notes) in "It Might as Well Be Spring" from *State Fair* was an attempt to portray a singer with spring fever. This last disclosure allows us to assume that Emile and Nellie's shared "jittery and jumpy" musical lines in "Twin Soliloquies" tell us that they have contracted the same pleasant disease.[97]

When Rodgers discussed music, he mainly spoke in terms of its success or failure and its ability to communicate a dramatic situation. Perhaps like the centipede he didn't want to risk thinking too much about how he managed to compose so many hits. On the other hand, silence does not necessarily indicate obliviousness. In an occasionally quoted conversation with Stephen Sondheim designed to contrast Rodgers's intuitive approach with Sondheim's articulate self-consciousness, Rodgers comes across as unaware that the B section of "People Will Say We're in Love" "was an exact musical inversion of the beginning."[98] But it is equally likely that Rodgers was confused by the assumption, since after the inverted fifth (rising in the A section, falling in the B section), the inversion is not at all exact. In fact, it disappears.[99]

In the early "self-interview" that appeared in *Theatre Arts* in 1939, Rodgers first explained that "no tunes have ever come to me anywhere. I've had to go to them."[100] Only when he knew the dramatic context of a song was he "ready to start searching for a melody that will conform to a number of arbitrary conditions." Rodgers continues by stating a major creative objective: "To begin with, I write scores and not isolated song numbers; therefore the particular song in question must bear a family resemblance to the other musical material in the piece." Unfortunately, although Rodgers goes on to discuss the importance of creating a "sharp contrast" from one song to another, he offers no further explanation of what he means by "family resemblance."

Sometimes, as in the case of Billy's "Soliloquy," the first song Rodgers composed for *Carousel,* we can point knowledgeably to a song hub out of which other musical spokes radiate.[101] With *South Pacific* we have Rodgers's recollection that he had composed five songs at the time he asked Mary Martin and her husband-manager Richard Halliday to come over to his Connecticut home, and Logan's memoirs suggesting that the first of these was "A Wonderful Guy." In recalling the evening with Rodgers, Martin vividly remembers hearing "Twin Soliloquies" and Emile's "glorious 'Some Enchanted Evening,'" which would never be hers.[102] We have noted in the first chapter that fragments of three songs composed with Hart eventually—and almost certainly arbitrarily—made their way into *South Pacific* and that "My Wife" from *Allegro* (one of the songs precociously anticipated in a song with lyrics by Hart, "You're the Cats") was adapted to fit "Younger Than Springtime," Rodgers's third attempt at a song for Cable to sing to Liat. Because the decision to use "My Wife" occurred during the later stages in its evolution, one cannot speak of "My Wife" as a starting point for *South Pacific,* even though Rodgers composed at least the main chorus of the song two years earlier. Nevertheless, it may be more than coincidental that "My Wife" most definitely resembles its new companions.

One can easily discover arbitrary connections between and among songs of a given score. But how do we know which connections are generic or accidental and which are musically or dramatically meaningful? Further, the absence of connections between one song and another does not preclude a sense of belonging any more than the absence of physical resemblance negates the relationship between a parent and a child in biological families.

We have previously quoted Rodgers's remark that in *South Pacific* "the songs were closely interwoven but still had individuality." At the forefront of this interweaving are three dramatically meaningful musical family resemblances. All are conventional devices presumably audible to or subliminally understood even by listeners who do not customarily perceive music in technical terms: leading tones, sequential melody supported by identical harmonies, and the period return of distinctive rhythmic figures. A few words of clarification may help some readers grapple with these concepts. In a major scale (for example, C major, C-D-E-F-G-A-B-C) the seventh note (in this case B) "leads" by a half-step and presses toward a return of the tonal center (C), one octave higher. The psychological impact of a leading tone can be

Example 4.1. "A Wonderful Guy" (chorus, last 12 measures)

Example 4.2. "Bali Ha'i" (chorus, first 6 measures)

powerful and readily perceived. In "Bewitched" from *Pal Joey* the frequent presence of leading tones and their resolution (B-C) effectively demonstrates Vera Simpson's obsession with Joey.[103] When Nellie tells us eighteen times at the conclusion of "A Wonderful Guy" (a fast waltz, the music of love) that she's in love with her wonderful guy, she expresses her music still more exuberantly with one leading tone to tonic move after another (B-C-C B-C-C B-C-C), eighteen times in all (see example 4.1).

In "Bali Ha'i," the idea of leading tones moving up to their tonics has become broadened to include half-steps on various tones of the scale, in each case preceded by an ascent to the octave (see example 4.2). The main distinction is not which note of the scale Rodgers uses but the emphasis on the ascending half-step. "Bali Ha'i" calls Cable via a leading tone, but the emphasis remains on the leading tone itself (or other lowered half-steps) rather than its upward resolution. At this stage in the drama Cable has not yet succumbed to the siren song.

Although it comes only on the last long-held note on the word "heart," Nellie's first song, "A Cockeyed Optimist" briefly anticipates the movement

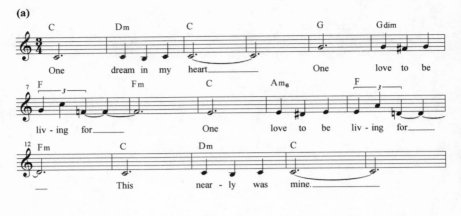

Example 4.3. Strange Bedfellows (a) "This Nearly Was Mine" (chorus, first 16 measures) (b) "Plant You Now, Dig You Later" (chorus, first 8 measures)

from leading-tone to tonic that will break out several songs later at the end of "A Wonderful Guy." In the song that follows "A Cockeyed Optimist," "Twin Soliloquies," Nellie and Emile demonstrate their compatibility as Rodgers has them express their similar privately expressed feelings of excitement, anticipation, anxiety, and inferiority with identical or closely related musical thoughts. Included among these similarities are melodic phrases that emphasize half-step oscillations (e.g., "We are not alike" and "Younger men than I," among many others) as well as dotted rhythms and dissonant leaps to express the jitteriness and jumpiness of erratically beating hearts.

"This Nearly Was Mine," a slow waltz in keeping with Emile's sense that he has lost Nellie forever—in contrast to Nellie's "Wonderful Guy," a fast waltz of acceptance before she learns about Emile's children and former wife—shares Nellie's predilection for half-steps from the outset of the song, the tonic-leading tone oscillations in "One dream in my heart." (Note that

Nellie introduced this oscillation when she sang the word "heart" at the end of "A Cockeyed Optimist.") In another sign of dramatically meaningful musical compatibility, Emile ends most of his phrases with Nellie's "jello" rhythm (stretched to three syllables and three notes) from "A Cockeyed Optimist." In a bizarre twist of musical fate, the opening of "This Nearly Was Mine" shares the same melody and harmony—but not the rhythm, meter, character, or dramatic meaning—with "Plant You Now, Dig You Later" (see example 4.3), another one of the many songs in *Pal Joey* to feature a similar half-step oscillation (sometimes meaningfully, sometimes not).

The second "family resemblance" is a simple melodic sequence—that is, the repetition of a short musical phrase on a different scale degree, either higher or lower (see example 4.4). This common musical device gains its significance in *South Pacific*, not so much because of its ubiquity as its strategic placement. In "Dites-Moi," the song that frames the entire show, at least in its Broadway portrait, the first half of the sixteen-measure chorus consists of two four-measure phrases, the second beginning with a sequential repetition one step lower. With the opening phrase of the next song, "A Cockeyed Optimist," perhaps Nellie is telling us something musically that she doesn't know herself: her connection with and eventual acceptance of Emile's children. It is less clear why Cable sings a third variation on this sequential idea (two measures long). Perhaps it serves as a metaphor for love's innocence, whether the maternal love for a child or a young man's initial passionate love for a young woman. In any event, the musical resemblance creates a connection between Cable and Nellie that wasn't there before.[104]

The final collection of familial resemblances is rhythmic. Of course rhythmic connections figure most prominently in "Twin Soliloquies," where Nellie and Emile share their rhythms phrase by phrase. Others are more subliminal, or at least more subtle. When in the release of "A Cockeyed Optimist" Nellie sings, "hear the human race" (da-da-da-da-*dum*) and "falling on its face" (da-da-da-da-*dum*), she anticipates the central rhythmic figure that will dominate "Twin Soliloquies" (also da-da-da-da-*dum*). Add one note at the end and you have the opening rhythm of "Some Enchanted Evening" (da-da-da-da-*dum-dum*) and the dramatic culmination of a scene that began musically with "Dites-Moi" (da-da-*dum*). The fact that each song in the opening scene connects with the next contributes mightily to its escalating dramatic and musical tension released only in the epilogue to "Some Enchanted Evening," "once you have found her, never let her go!"

Example 4.4. Melodic Sequences in *South Pacific* (a) "Dites-Moi" (chorus, first 8 measures) (b) "A Cockeyed Optimist" (chorus, first 8 measures) (c) "Younger Than Springtime" (chorus, first 8 measures)

In "A Cockeyed Optimist" Nellie completes two internal phrases (on the words "yellow," "bellow," and "jello") with a quarter-note triplet, an unusual rhythm (easy to hear but hard to explain) that Emile will adopt no less than nine times in "Some Enchanted Evening" ("somehow you," "know even," and "somewhere you'll" in the first twelve measures alone).[105] In "This Nearly Was Mine" Emile will return to Nellie's distinctive rhythmic quirk on the key words of the song, "living for" and "paradise."[106] Tellingly, in light of the dialogue in the final Broadway draft when Nellie notes how much they have in common, the earlier draft offers a more pragmatic Nellie asking why Emile wants to marry her in light of the fact that they have so little in common. In the final libretto, when Nellie tells Emile that they are "the same kind of people fundamentally," her examples are somewhat prosaic: "We appreciate things! We get enthusiastic about things . . . We're not blasé."[107] If audiences are convinced at the end of the evening that Nellie would overcome her carefully taught racial prejudices and accept Emile's past, credit must be due Rodgers as much as Hammerstein for making this unlikely scenario believable and inevitable. When Hammerstein wrote that Rodgers "writes music to depict story and character and is, therefore, himself a dramatist," this is what he meant.[108]

The presence of some musical drama might be credited to Robert Russell Bennett, the principal orchestrator of *South Pacific*, who in the Entr-act playfully explores additional musical connections between songs that involve the leading tone and in the process helps audiences get a musical summary of the first act conflicts.[109] The Entr-act, like the Overture, opens with the first three notes of "Bali Ha'i," the famous ascending octave descending down by half-step to and dwelling on the leading tone (G-G-F♯ on the words "Bali Ha'i" at the beginning of example 4.2). Now, however, the ballad, formerly in duple meter, will be transformed. On the third repetition of this three-note motive, the music shifts to the waltz music associated with "I'm in love" that concluded "A Wonderful Guy." When the waltz switches back into duple meter, the musical phrase associated with "I'm in love" serves as an ingenious but natural accompaniment to "I'm Gonna Wash That Man Right Outa My Hair," a musical juxtaposition that calls attention to Nellie's conflict.[110]

Musical comedies depict life, not necessarily as it is, but as we wish it. The more we see ourselves, or prefer to see ourselves, as having grown beyond the prejudices, sexism, materialism, or the dramatic or musical style of a previous era, the more difficult it may be to accept that a work, frozen in time, actually seizes a moment and reflects that moment honestly. As we become further removed from a show's time and place, a musical that captures its moment can become a slave to that moment, despite its universality. *South Pacific* displays such striking verisimilitude to its time that future audiences might find it alienating. This is both a blessing and a curse. Because of its topicality, *South Pacific* may indeed be destined to join some Rodgers and Hart shows or other musicals of the 1920s and 1930s as a period piece, a nostalgic anachronism. More likely, *South Pacific*, a musical that daringly confronts sex, race, and war in its own time, with a libretto that challenges its characters and its audiences, and its interwoven, contrasting, and unforgettable score, will continue to challenge our own evolving values in light of filtered but nonetheless powerful memories of an increasingly distant world.

CHAPTER 5

Broadway Comes to Television:
The Three *Cinderellas*

B Y THE END OF THE 1940S, RODGERS AND HAMMERSTEIN HAD reached a plateau of success and dominance. Two remaining triumphs would launch and conclude their second and final decade, *The King and I* (1951) and *The Sound of Music* (1959). But the framing musicals of the 1940s, *Oklahoma!* (1943) and *South Pacific* (1949), were not only the two longest running musicals of their time, they would remain R&H's greatest popular successes. In their role as producers, R&H were also responsible for the third-longest-running show of the 1940s, *Annie Get Your Gun* (1946), with a book by old friends and collaborators Herbert and Dorothy Fields and music by Irving Berlin. Another of their own creations, *Carousel* (1945), turned out to be the fifth longest running. All that stood in the way of a sweep of the five longest runs and nearly total hegemony in the 1940s was the presence of Cole Porter's *Kiss Me, Kate* (1948) and the absence of R&H's innovative but less successful *Allegro* (1947), perhaps not coincidentally their only 1940s show not based on a play or a novel.

For Rodgers, the innovation and success that characterized his later years with Hart (1935–43)—the nine hits in ten attempts discussed in Chapter 3— would continue with his new partner and a string of popular and artistic victories from 1943 to 1951. A revival of *Pal Joey* in 1952, one of the first revivals to surpass its original run (which itself was more than respectable despite being branded a "foul well" by Brooks Atkinson), gave Rodgers more to celebrate before the dancing stopped. In their next show, *Me and Juliet* (1953), R&H once again risked innovation over formula by deciding not to cast ready-made stars like Mary Martin and Ezio Pinza. *Me and Juliet*, an original play-within-a-play backstager, struggled for a year, barely broke even, and promptly disappeared, unless you count *Victory at Sea* reruns that had introduced its principal song, the tango "No Other Love" (under the title "Beneath the Southern Cross"). The following year, Elaine Stritch's interpolation of "You Took Advantage of Me" and the casting of Vera Zorina (the original angel in *I Married an Angel*) as the prima ballerina Vera Barnova were not enough to rescue the Rodgers and Hart revival of *On Your Toes*—it departed after only sixty-four performances. One year later, R&H experienced the major miscalculation of their career, *Pipe Dream* (1955), an adaptation of John Steinbeck's *Sweet Thursday*, a novel filled with eccentric and occasionally uncouth characters who inhabit Cannery Row in Monterey, California—imagine a musical inhabited mainly by Bloody Marys and Billises. To add injury to insult, *Pipe Dream* opened shortly after an operation that removed a portion of Rodgers's cancerous left jaw.

Another blow to the R&H juggernaut occurred during the final months of *Pipe Dream*'s short run when Alan Jay Lerner and Frederick Loewe's blockbusting musical *My Fair Lady* arrived in town on March 15, 1956. Although neither partner publicly discussed their aborted attempt to adapt Shaw's *Pygmalion* into a Broadway musical, Lerner reported a conversation in which Hammerstein admitted that he and Rodgers had abandoned this promising property as unworkable.[1] Not only did *My Fair Lady* become the first musical to surpass *Oklahoma!*, it also gave birth to a new star in the Broadway firmament, Julie Andrews, then only twenty-one.[2]

When Andrews's agent called Rodgers to suggest that R&H compose a musical based on the Cinderella fable for a television broadcast starring Andrews in the title role, the parties quickly reached an agreement (September 5). Andrews signed on five days later, and on January 30, with much fol-de-rol and fiddledy dee, she met her Prince, the unfortunately named Jon Cypher. The remaining casting was begun on February 13, and rehearsals were launched on February 24. In lieu of out-of-town tryouts, two fully staged kinescopes were made, two weeks (what Rodgers called the New Haven tryout) and then one week before blast-off (the Boston tryout). On March 31, the first of three R&H televised versions of *Cinderella* was broadcast by CBS-TV from 8:00 to 9:30 P.M. At a time when the total U.S. population was under 180 million, an astronomical 107 million viewers saw the seventy-two-minute musical.[3] Not only did this grand event inspire what

Rodgers watching Julie Andrews on the set of the original *Cinderella*

Harold Messing described as "perhaps the greatest promotion campaign for a single show in the history of the network," it also reached the "largest single audience in the history of the television medium."[4]

Although *Cinderella* was the first R&H musical created expressly for television, by 1957 the partners were no strangers to the medium. As early as 1951 NBC had broadcast an hour-long tribute to the composer, *An Evening for Richard Rodgers*. The following year CBS devoted two one-hour programs on successive Sunday evenings of the popular *Ed Sullivan Show* to *The Richard Rodgers Story*. For six months, between October 1952 and April 1953, NBC broadcast the World War II documentary *Victory at Sea* in thirty-minute installments; the score was assembled from Rodgers's melodies by the prolific and gifted orchestrator Robert Russell Bennett. On March 28, 1954, *General Foods Twenty-Fifth Anniversary Show* offered an unprecedented ninety-minute tribute to Rodgers and Hammerstein that was broadcast simultaneously over the three major networks (and a fourth, the now defunct Dumont-TV Networks), a feat that would not be duplicated until September 2001, when the networks joined together to present a relief concert honoring the victims of the terrorist attacks on the World Trade Center and the Pentagon. The 1954 retrospective featured many of the stars who created roles in R&H shows on stage and film, including Yul Brynner, Jan Clayton, Florence Henderson, Gordon MacRae, Mary Martin, Ezio Pinza, and John Raitt. In a fabricated segment of Groucho Marx's *You Bet Your Life*, the comedian-host persisted in confusing Rodgers with the singing cowboy Roy Rogers.

Cinderella may have been the first original R&H musical to be telecast, but Rodgers at least had been testing the waters for several years. Two years before *Cinderella*, NBC-TV presented full-length and fully staged live productions of two early Rodgers and Hart musicals with all-star casts: *A Connecticut Yankee* (March 12, 1955) and *Dearest Enemy* (November 26, 1955).[5] Only a few days before *Yankee* (March 7), *Peter Pan*, starring Mary Martin, had reached 65 million viewers on NBC; its return on January 9, 1956, was seen by an estimated 50 million viewers.[6] A new Rodgers and Hammerstein musical starring *My Fair Lady* sensation Julie Andrews in another Cinderella role seemed a healthy risk.

Unfortunately, the 1957 *Cinderella*, although aired live and in color, was filmed in black and white and on kinescope, a process inferior in quality to videotape.[7] Individuals can still see the black and white kinescope of the original broadcast in The Museum of Television & Radio in New York City. According to the conventional wisdom offered by everyone from Rodgers to theater historians, it was the absence of a videotape that precluded future showings of this version. Messing's thesis refers to a black and white videotape that was used to transmit the delayed broadcast to the West Coast, but this videotape is now missing, and all that remained was the kinescope.[8] It is often assumed that kinescope cannot be shown on television. In truth, this archaic but functional form of reproduction could be broadcast, and anyone who has seen early footage from the Golden Age of television is indebted to the technology. Nevertheless, kinescope was soon replaced by color videotape, which offers sharper and clearer visual definition.

The perceived need for a videotaped *Cinderella* was a factor that led to the planning of a new version. Hammerstein had died in 1960, and Rodgers was now carrying the R&H torch for a new generation of viewers. He cast Lesley Ann Warren in her debut role at the age of eighteen, commissioned a new teleplay by Joseph Schrank, and took the legal and creative liberties of borrowing a previously unused song from the R&H catalogue to give to the Prince. First broadcast on CBS-TV on February 22, 1965 (8:30–10:00 P.M.), the new *Cinderella* was shown another eight times between 1966 and 1974. By the time Robert L. Freedman introduced the third televised *Cinderella* in 1997 on ABC-TV, Rodgers too was dead, and Walt Disney Telefilms, Storyline Entertainment, and Houston Productions commissioned a third teleplay. In this final (for now) televised *Cinderella*, three earlier Rodgers songs were recycled to take advantage of a slightly longer program. Whether by coincidence or by design, the "new" *Cinderella* songs, "Falling in Love with Love" (lyrics by Hart), "There's Music in You" (lyrics by Hammerstein), and "The Sweetest Sounds" (lyrics by Rodgers), represent the three principal stages of Rodgers's long and successful career. See table 5.1 for an overview of the song contents of the three *Cinderellas*.

The Original CBS-TV Broadcast (March 31, 1957)

Shortly before the first broadcast, Hammerstein explained that the goal of R&H was to follow the familiar legend, presumably Charles Perrault's version of 1697, rather than to make yet another in a long series of Broadway Cinderella stories.

"The traditional Cinderella has done very well. Why should we trick her up? We decided at once Cinderella would not become a shop girl from Macy's who is spotted by the proprietor's son and wafted to El Morocco. There will be absolutely no updating, no naturalistic or Freudian explanations. We wanted to do a musical version of the story that everyone remembers from childhood."[9] In other remarks, Hammerstein demonstrated his sensitivity to the expectations and interests of both children and adults: "I looked it up [the Cinderella story] in the encyclopedia. We want the kids who see it to recognize the story they know. Children can be very critical on that score. But of course, their parents will be watching too, so we have tried to humanize the characters without altering the familiar plot structure."[10]

Rodgers also emphasized R&H's desire to preserve rather than alter what he referred to as the "Cinderella story."

Table 5.1. Three *Cinderellas*

1957	1965	1997
		Prologue: "Impossible"
ACT I	ACT I	ACT I
SCENE ONE— THROUGHOUT THE KINGDOM	OUTSIDE CINDERELLA'S HOME	VILLAGE SQUARE
"The Prince Is Giving a Ball"	"Cinderella March" *"LONELINESS OF EVENING"*	**"THE SWEETEST SOUNDS"** "The Prince Is Giving a Ball"
SCENE TWO—A STREET	SCENE TWO—-THE TOWN SQUARE	
"Where Is Cinderella?" (instrumental march)	"Cinderella March" (reprise)	
SCENE THREE—INSIDE CINDERELLA'S HOME	INSIDE CINDERELLA'S HOME	ACT II
"In My Own Little Corner"	"In My Own Little Corner"	"In My Own Little Corner" **"FALLING IN LOVE WITH LOVE"**
	THE TOWN SQUARE	
	"The Prince Is Giving a Ball"	
ACT II		ACT III
SCENE ONE—THE PALACE DRESSING ROOM	INTERIOR— CINDERELLA'S HOME	STEPMOTHER'S HOUSE
	"In My Own Little Corner" (reprise)	"In My Own Little Corner" (reprise)
Act III	ACT II	
SCENE ONE— THROUGHOUT THE KINGDOM		

Table 5.1. Continued

1957	1965	1997
SCENE TWO—INSIDE CINDERELLA'S HOME	INTERIOR—INSIDE CINDERELLA'S HOME	
"Impossible"	"Impossible"	"Impossible"
SCENE THREE—INSIDE THE CARRIAGE GOING TO THE BALL		
"It's Possible"	"It's Possible"	"It's Possible"
ACT IV	ACT III	ACT IV
THE BALL	THE ROYAL BALLROOM	BALLROOM
"Gavotte"	"Gavotte" *"BOYS AND GIRLS LIKE YOU AND ME" (INSTRUMENTAL)*	"Gavotte"
"Ten Minutes Ago" "Stepsisters' Lament" "Waltz for a Ball"	"Waltz for a Ball" "Ten Minutes Ago"	"Waltz for a Ball" "Ten Minutes Ago"
		ACT V
"Do I Love You Because You're Beautiful?"	"Stepsisters' Lament" "Ten Minutes Ago" (reprise) "Do I Love You Because You're Beautiful?"	"Stepsisters' Lament" "Do I Love You Because You're Beautiful?"
ACT V	ACT IV	ACT VI
INSIDE CINDERELLA'S HOUSE	INSIDE CINDERELLA'S HOUSE	STEPMOTHER'S HOUSE
"When You're Driving Through the Moonlight" "A Lovely Night"	"When You're Driving Through the Moonlight" "A Lovely Night"	"A Lovely Night" (with abbreviated "When You're Driving Through the Moonlight")

Table 5.1. Continued

1957	1965	1997
ACT VI	ACT V	
	INTERIOR —THE PALACE	
	"Do I Love You Because You're Beautiful?" (reprise)	"Do I Love You Because You're Beautiful?" (reprise)
SCENE ONE— THE SEARCH THROUGHOUT THE KINGDOM	ACT VII	
		ALL OVER THE KINGDOM
"The Search"	"The Search"	["The Search"]
SCENE TWO—THE WEDDING IN THE MAIN BALLROOM OF THE PALACE	THE WEDDING IN THE MAIN BALLROOM OF THE PALACE	
Finale ("In My Own Little Corner," "Impossible")		**"THERE'S MUSIC IN YOU"**

Note: Additions to 1965 Cinderella in italics; additions to 1997 Cinderella in bold.

We think the Cinderella story has a pretty fair success just as it is. The plot has been used in hundreds of variations over the years, but none is better known than the original. It would be presumptuous to modernize it. . . . The newness will come from the musical treatment, but the story has not been updated. Cinderella still lives in a fairy tale kingdom with her step-mother and stepsisters. And her fairy godmother still helps her to change the mice and pumpkin into a horse and carriage. She and the prince fall ecstatically in love and are finally reunited by the search for the owner of the glass slipper.[11]

From the earliest promotional literature to the present, nearly everyone who writes about Cinderella notes that the central departure from famil-iar legend is the presence of comically selfish rather than wicked stepsis-ters. Compared to Rodgers and Hammerstein, Perrault's Stepsisters come off as somewhat harmless, albeit humorless, and the Stepmother disappears

Julie Andrews, the first Cinderella

after the first paragraph. One possible but unacknowledged point of departure might be the popular Disney animated *Cinderella* of 1950, in which
the Stepsisters and Stepmother embody the physical and moral ugliness
many had come to associate with the story. In another significant departure
from fairy tale conventions, R&H cast the beautiful and glamorous Edith
Adams—a regular on television's *Ernie Kovacs Show*, Ruth's gorgeous sister
Eileen in *Wonderful Town* (1953), and the Tony-winning supporting actress
in *Li'l Abner* (1956)—in the role of the Fairy Godmother. Also regularly
noted is Hammerstein's distaste for magic, an animus that led him to create
a Cinderella who must earn the Fairy Godmother's assistance. Like Noah's
God in *Two By Two*, Cinderella's Fairy Godmother helps those who help

themselves. As Ethan Mordden writes, "In Hammerstein, you don't just deserve happiness; you have to work for it."[12]

The R&H version departs in less immediately recognized respects from the familiar fairy tale. In Perrault, Cinderella's father is alive but powerless to spare his daughter from the dominance and cruelty of his second bride, the "proudest and most haughty woman that was ever seen."[13] Knowing that her complaints would fall on deaf ears, the original Cinderella does not even inform her father (a character who does not appear at all in R&H) of her ill treatment. The Stepmother's disappearance from the story after a single reference in Perrault's version works in a fairy tale but is arguably incompatible with the interests of riveting drama and character development on a stage. R&H's Stepmother remains an active presence. In addition to the odious labors she is forced to perform, Perrault's Cinderella willingly serves as her Stepsisters' fashion consultant and dismisses the notion of attending the ball when they ask her about it. In every way Perrault's Cinderella stands apart from her Stepsisters, both in her outer beauty and in her kindness and forbearance. Although R&H's Godmother makes Cinderella earn her magic, Perrault's Godmother makes the cinder girl fetch the pumpkin that will be transformed by magic (after the Godmother scoops its insides out) into a gilded coach. In all three televised *Cinderellas*, four white mice are found in a cage. In Perrault, the mice are trapped alive before being converted into six horses, dapple gray rather than white, as in the song.[14] Another trap captures three large rats that can be transformed into coachmen, and Cinderella fetches six lizards that the Godmother turns into footmen. The glass slippers and the strict instruction to return by midnight are, of course, nonnegotiable.[15]

Perrault's King responds immediately to Cinderella's beauty as he escorts her from the coach into the ballroom, and silence, immobility, and stupefaction greet Cinderella's arrival. The 1957 script does not indicate that the music stops, but long and conspicuous silences mark the 1965 and 1997 versions, fifty-one and twenty-one seconds, respectively. Soon Perrault's heroine demonstrates her graceful dancing, and the Prince is so stricken that he is unable to eat a morsel of the feast. Perrault's Cinderella also joins her sisters, who do not recognize her, and shares the oranges and lemons that the Prince has given her.

In numerous versions of Cinderella—including Perrault's and James Lapine and Stephen Sondheim's reworking of the Cinderella story within a larger assemblage of traditional and newly imagined fables, *Into the Woods*

—the ball lasts two or more days. After the first night, Cinderella, pretending to sleep, greets her Stepsisters upon their return, long after midnight, and learns of the beautiful and generous princess (herself). Knowing they will refuse her request, Perrault's Cinderella nonetheless asks to go to the ball to see this mysterious princess for herself. In contrast, R&H's Stepsisters boast that the Prince paid most of his attention to them and downplay the existence of an interloper.

In Perrault, Cinderella loses track of the time the second night and barely escapes the hot pursuit of the Prince. It is on this second night that Cinderella leaves her glass slipper on the palace grounds. Upon their return home, Perrault's Stepsisters report on the strange occurrence and inform Cinderella that the Prince was smitten by the unknown woman who wore the glass slipper. The search in Perrault centers on the nobility and the court rather than the kingdom at large, but the Prince nonetheless eventually locates Cinderella at the home of her sibling rivals. To the Stepsisters' astonishment, not only did the slipper fit, Cinderella was able to produce the other shoe from her pocket. It should be noted that Perrault's Prince had noticed Cinderella's great beauty, even though she was wearing rags, and was hoping the shoe would fit. Perhaps most surprisingly, Perrault's Cinderella forgives her Stepsisters for the way they have treated her. After her marriage to the Prince she even sets up her undeserving siblings in the palace and finds lords for them to wed.

Late in 1956 or early in 1957 Hammerstein drafted a "Story Outline" remarkably close to the scenario eventually adopted. At the end of the outline Hammerstein included an "IMPORTANT NOTE": "Not all of the songs have been written yet and undoubtedly, there will be others that are fitted into the above plot." The first song, "The Mother and Daughter March" (so labeled in the promotional recording performed by Rodgers that is featured as a bonus on the reissued CD), would be renamed "Where Is Cinderella?" Later, when given words, it became "Stepsisters' Lament," not noted in this first outline.[16] The only songs missing and presumably unwritten (along with the scene in which they occur) are "When You're Driving Through the Moonlight" and "A Lovely Night." More songs would appear in a scenario that corresponds to the six "sequences," later divided into acts, that framed commercial messages from Old Spice and Pepsi.

Sequence A   End of a Shopping Tour
Number 1 MARCH: WALKING HOME

[probably the same as "The Mother and Daughter March," "Cinderella March";
    retitled "Where Is Cinderella?"]
    Sequence B   At Home
Number 2 CINDERELLA!—Stepmother, Joy, Portia, and Cinderella [cut]
Number 3 TIRADE—Stepmother [cut]
Number 4 IN MY OWN LITTLE CORNER—Cinderella
    Sequence C   Montage
Number 5 THE PRINCE IS GIVING A BALL!
    Sequence D   The Godmother
Number 6 Reprise: IN MY OWN LITTLE CORNER—Cinderella
Number 7 MUSICAL SCENE [evolved into "Fol-De-Rol and Fiddledy Dee"]
Number 8 IMPOSSIBLE—Godmother and Cinderella
Number 9 I'M ON MY WAY—Cinderella and Godmother
[replaced by "It's Possible" (reprise of "Impossible")]
    Sequence E   The Ball
Number 10 WALTZ [retitled "Waltz for a Ball"]
Number 11 IF I WEREN'T KING—The King and a sextette of henchmen
[the *Fact Book* notes that this number was cut before rehearsals]
Number 12 TEN MINUTES AGO—Prince
Number 13 I HAVE A FEELING—Prince and Cinderella
[replaced by "Do I Love You Because You're Beautiful?"]
    Sequence F   The Search
Number 14 THE PRINCE IS IN A DITHER—Male Chorus [cut]
Number 15 ARE YOU BEAUTIFUL BECAUSE I LOVE YOU—Prince

The accompanying outline reveals Rodgers and Hammerstein's original
intention to include two additional songs in the first scene in Cinderella's
home, a quartet for the Stepmother, the Stepsisters, and Cinderella called
"Cinderella!" and a "Tirade" for the Stepmother. In the final version only
Cinderella's "In My Own Little Corner" remains. Doubtless some time was
spared by this action, and the change serves to keep the musical attention on
Cinderella. Nevertheless, without her "Tirade," the Stepmother vanishes as
a musical presence and so do the Stepsisters. Not yet visible is the transformation of the "Cinderella March" into the comical "Stepsisters' Lament,"
the Gavotte at the ball, and the scene in Cinderella's home after the ball
with "When You're Driving Through the Moonlight" and "A Lovely Night."
The largest change, which occurred shortly before the March 27 rehearsal,
was the removal of "Where Is Cinderella?" and its replacement with a new
opening number, "The Prince Is Giving a Ball."[17]

Messing reports that in the original script the Prince did not appear until
the ball, approximately halfway through the script. Eventually Hammerstein
introduced a scene in which the reluctant Prince prepares for this grand

event, and, at the request of his father, pretends that he is looking forward to it to please his mother. The second and third broadcasts found new ways to introduce the Prince earlier in the story and to give him a greater musical as well as dramatic presence and individuality.

Throughout most of their collaboration, R&H met in person to hash out creative problems. But Hammerstein's attendance at the 1956 Olympic Games at Melbourne (his wife, another Dorothy, was a native of Australia) meant a change from their regular modus operandi in the form of four letters that shed light on the compositional process of a song, "Do I Love You Because You're Beautiful?" Rodgers includes passages of this exchange in *Musical Stages*—two from Hammerstein's letters and two responses from Rodgers—to demonstrate the importance of details in achieving the desired artistic product. The excerpts also reveal R&H's mutual sensitivity and receptivity to respectful intrusions onto each other's turf. Thus Rodgers assures Hammerstein that he need not worry about repeating himself with the line "Am I making believe, etc." and that this sequence of words was preferable to "Am I telling my heart I see in you?" Hammerstein, in the course of the correspondence, realized that removing the word "really" in the next line, "A girl too lovely to be really true" would be "less interesting musically." Rodgers would agree that the original worked better, even if it sounded to him like a split infinitive.

Perhaps more tellingly, the exchange reveals that the idea to "stay up on the higher notes" on "Are you the sweet invention of a lover's dream?" and even the idea to conclude the song in major on the climactic line "Or are you really as beautiful as you seem?" came from Hammerstein. We learn from Hammerstein that Rodgers had originally wanted to end the song in the minor mode, then decided to move to the major mode briefly near the end before concluding on minor. In the end, Rodgers saw the dramatic (and perhaps musical) virtue of moving from A minor to C major for the final words and assured his partner that the dramatic effectiveness of this decision would not be at the expense of grammatical correctness—it was indeed kosher to provide a major mode ending to a song that began in the minor. Rodgers does not say whether he had a similar discussion with Hart many years earlier before making the same decision in "My Funny Valentine" (*Babes in Arms*). A few years later, when setting his own lyrics, he would again switch modes at the end of a song—presumably without any advice from anybody—in "The Sweetest Sounds" (*No Strings*). Perhaps not incidentally, "The Sweetest Sounds" also serves to introduce the principals in the 1997 remake of *Cinderella*, as Cinderella and her Prince once more move from A minor to C major as they do in "Do I Love You?"

Hammerstein may have convinced Rodgers of the dramatic rightness of retaining the higher notes and of the move from minor to major, but he did not convince Alec Wilder: "But for the, to me, highly inappropriate and un-related last section, I very much like 'Do I Love You Because You're Beau-tiful?' from a television play, *Cinderella*. I can't imagine what went wrong, but I feel as if someone had turned a radio dial just before the end of the song and there I was listening to an opera audition, perhaps."[18]

Because the 1957 broadcast is no longer available and is unknown out-side of its songs, a leisurely synopsis follows.

Act I

SCENE 1: Throughout the Kingdom

The broadcast opens with the production number, "The Prince Is Giving a Ball." All the women in the kingdom, eligible and ineligible, from a mar-ried woman to a grandmother to a second-grader, are hoping the Prince will propose to them. The first musical idea is nothing more than a repeated fan-fare that ascends and descends over simple arpeggiated major triads in 6/8 meter. The next music is a melody in a 4/4 meter that rises sequentially for nearly an octave as the Herald announces the Prince's seemingly endless list of given names. Each time the Herald reads a group of names, one name seems so incongruous (Herman, Maisie, Sidney) that the townspeople stop to question it. The fanfare and the music for the reading of the names both precede and follow the additional rhyming 6/8 speech-song patter of the townspeople.

SCENE 2: A Street

To the tune of the instrumental march "Where Is Cinderella?" (transformed into the "Stepsisters' Lament") this scene introduces the Stepmother (Ilka Chase), her biological offspring, Portia (Kaye Ballard) and Joy (Alice Ghost-ley), and Cinderella (Julie Andrews), who is laden with packages from their shopping expedition.

SCENE 3: Inside Cinderella's Home

The scene shifts to Cinderella's home, where her Stepmother and Stepsis-ters order their poor relation to do a host of duties, ranging from fetching

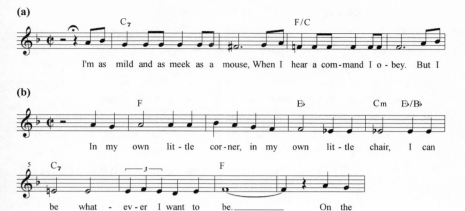

Example 5.1. "In My Own Little Corner" (a) verse (first 4 measures) (b) chorus (first 8 measures)

chairs to tending the fire. The Stepmother informs her *"own* daughters" about the ball and of her plans for them to snare the Prince in marriage, or if not the Prince, another eligible bachelor. (She is not completely deluded.) She informs them that they cannot rely merely on their great beauty and instructs them to adopt the special qualities suggested by their incongruous names, one of the few traits they share with the Prince: the intellectual Portia (named after the lawyer in Shakespeare's *Merchant of Venice*) and Joy (self-explanatory). This is the scene in which Hammerstein abandoned his intentions to include an ensemble for the four women and a solo for the Stepmother. Instead, all we hear in the scene is Cinderella's monologue about her lonely but by no means self-pitying existence ("In My Own Little Corner").

A plot synopsis may not be the best place for analytical interjection, but I cannot resist offering a few words on the deceptive simplicity of this little song (example 5.1). The dactyl (*long*-short-short) rhythms that feature prominently in the melodic line of the verse and in the opening measures of the A section of the chorus were prominent earlier in "The March of the Siamese Children" from *The King and I*.[19]

Against this rhythmic pattern are surprising juxtapositions of F-sharp and F-natural over a dominant pedal tone on C, which creates much of the underlying tension of the song. In the verse, the F-sharp on "mouse" and "house" clashes dissonantly with the supporting C7 harmony (C-E-G-B♭).

By the end of the verse the F-sharps have given away to Fs, and the harmony supports its melody by resolving to F, the key of the chorus. Clearly, Cinderella possesses the musical wherewithal to face the tensions of her life, to resolve them, and then to use her imagination to create an ideal world. The A section of this chorus offers only one further dissonant intrusion, one major departure from the conventional—or, as Rodgers might have said, one avoidance of "the pig"—when the song harmonizes the E-flat on "little chair" somewhat ambiguously as a cross between an E-flat and a C minor triad, neither of which displays the harmonic root in its bass. But this is a momentary wrinkle. In a flash the move from E-flat to E-natural gracefully returns the progression to its starting point, F, with a little written-out ornament, not unlike an eighteenth-century ornament of the classical period. In the B section, Rodgers returns to the F-sharp of the verse, first as the central note (or root) of a chord on F-sharp minor, and then in the melody as the fifth of a B major triad (B-D♯-F♯). Behind a simple rhythmic exterior dwells a capable young woman of depth and complexity.

Act II: The Palace Dressing Room

Enter the royal family. The instigator of the ball is the Queen. The King, who wants to save money for his financially strapped kingdom, remains content drinking the "wine of his country" (beer) and has the paunch to show for it. He also objects to having "chicken king" on the menu. Sometimes they speak their dialogue; sometimes they sing another 6/8 patter song on the verge of speech ("Your Majesties" in the vocal score and "Royal Dressing Room Scene" on the recording).[20] The conversational song concluded, the reluctant Prince arrives. Although certain that "the girl that I marry won't be anyone I meet at the ball!," the Prince agrees to go along with the program.

Act III

SCENE 1: Throughout the Kingdom
Another transition scene shows the royal family preparing for the ball. The King's trouser button pops and the Queen's corset snaps.

SCENE 2: Inside Cinderella's Home
Meanwhile, Cinderella is helping her Stepmother and Stepsisters with the finishing stages of their preparations and wishes them a good time. Then

back to the fireplace and the cinders for a reprise of "In My Own Little Corner." This time the words convey Cinderella's imagination that she is actually at the ball chatting with the royal family—the belle of the ball.

SCENE 3: Inside the Carriage Going to the Ball
With a "fol-de-rol and fiddledy dee" the fairy Godmother appears and taunts Cinderella with a portion of the poor girl's song. Soon she presses Cinderella on why she is not at the ball and why she does not leave her Stepmother. As previously noted, Rodgers and Hammerstein's Godmother wants her goddaughter to be self-reliant. While acknowledging that "*nothing* happens without wishing," wishing and dreaming can lead to eventual action and results. All this prepares for "Impossible," a song that states Cinderella's wishes and at the same time doubts that they will come true.[21] The point of the song is that "Impossible things are happ'ning every day!"—miracles *do* happen. The metamorphosis complete, Cinderella and her Godmother sing, "It's Possible," in which they acknowledge that "it's possible for a plain yellow pumpkin to become a golden carriage" and perhaps "for a plain country bumpkin and a Prince to join in marriage."

Act IV: The Ball

In all three telecasts the ball contains more music than any other scene, five songs in all, including the instrumental "Gavotte" and "Waltz for a Ball," two duets for Cinderella and the Prince ("Ten Minutes Ago" and "Do I Love You Because You're Beautiful?"), and the Stepsisters' big musical moment, "Stepsisters' Lament." While the Prince is about to dance the gavotte with Portia and endure her quasi-Shakespearean "quality of mercy" speech, Cinderella's Godmother deposits the belle at the ball but refuses to go in with her. "All I can do is give you your wish. How it turns out is up to you."[22] She also delivers the famous injunction to leave the ball before midnight. (At this moment the clock makes a point of showing 11:30 P.M., just long enough for the Prince to fall in love at first sight.) Cinderella's arrival stops Portia in mid-sentence, and on the word "heaven" all eyes turn to the heavenly future Princess. Ten minutes later the clock shows 11:40 P.M., and Cinderella and the Prince introduce themselves and review the historic transformation that occurred "Ten Minutes Ago," a waltz, naturally, which bears more than merely a casual resemblance to the as yet uncomposed "Do I Hear a Waltz?" in the musical of that title (see example 6.3). But unlike the central

Example 5.2. Tchaikovsky in *Cinderella* (a) "Stepsisters' Lament" (chorus, first 4 measures) (b) Tchaikovsky: Overture to *The Nutcracker* (first 4 measures)

character of *Waltz*, Leona Samish, no one can doubt that Cinderella hears a waltz. Actually she hears two.

A few seconds after "Ten Minutes Ago," the camera turns to Joy and Portia, who add words to the song associated with them from "Where Is Cinderella?" a song that shares its rhythmic contour in its opening measure ("Why would a fellow want . . . ?") and a rhythmic identity with the familiar nursery song "Who's Afraid of the Big Bad Wolf?" (compare the rhythms of "a girl like her" with "the big bad wolf").[23] As shown in example 5.2, the opening of "Stepsisters' Lament" bears a still more direct likeness to the opening of Tchaikovsky's Overture to *The Nutcracker*. Try to sing one and tap the other, and the rhythmic similarities become immediately apparent. The two pieces also share pitch contours (motive x) and the same pitches placed on different beats (motive y). The concluding three-note motive, motive z, shares both pitch and the slightest of rhythmic variants.[24]

Without borrowing or direct allusion, "Waltz for a Ball," the second waltz, captures the breathlessness and lighter-than-air quality of the occasion in its characteristic gesture of beginning most phrases of the main tune on the second rather than squarely on the downbeat of each group of three. When the Prince and Cinderella move to the center of the room less than another ten minutes later, everyone joins in a harmonized chorus of "Ten Minutes Ago" much as the folks in Iowa joined together in a refrain of "It's a Grand Night for Singing" in the original *State Fair* (another waltz, of course).

The central idea in the second duet for the Prince and Cinderella, "Do I

Love You Because You're Beautiful?" adopts as its starting point the written-out pseudo eighteenth-century ornament that concludes nearly every phrase in the main section of Cinderella's "In My Own Little Corner" (example 5.1b). On whatever level Rodgers made this connection, it is fitting to think that the Prince recognizes Cinderella for what she is and that this recognition is part of her beauty and desirability. Although he has not actually heard her song, he understands it intuitively and it is fully compatible with his music. In the spirit of the Prince's central question, careful listeners might ask whether the second song resembles the first because it is a conscious borrowing or if it is a conscious borrowing because it resembles the earlier song. In any event, the answer will have to wait, for Cinderella rushes off, and the Prince is left holding a glass slipper.

Act V: Inside Cinderella's Home

After the ball, Cinderella gives her dissembling Stepsisters an uncannily accurate description of what the ball might have been like in the song "When You're Driving Through the Moonlight." Here too, the central musical material is derived from an earlier melody, in this case the chromatic pickups to each phrase of the "Gavotte," to become the centerpiece of a new melody. To the underscored strains of "Ten Minutes Ago," Cinderella trades tales with her Stepmother and Stepsisters, with the latter offering a fictionalized account of a real encounter and Cinderella a true account of an allegedly fantastic encounter. This leads to a quartet, albeit in single file rather than contrapuntal, "A Lovely Night," in which Cinderella and the trio of harpies review and interpret the romance of the previous night from their own distorted perspectives. The song opens with a phrase that pivots off of a returning low note, but less systematically than in past uses of this device, "The Blue Room" from *The Girl Friend*, or future use in "I Do Not Know a Day That I Did Not Love You" from *Two By Two* (see examples 1.3 and 6.5, respectively). In contrast to the scalar melodic progression of these last-named songs, the central melodic contour of "A Lovely Night" consists of a major triad answered by the triad filled in by a descending chromatic scale. A noteworthy example of word painting occurs on the word "tremble," where Rodgers offers a surprising G-sharp in the melody as the top note of an augmented triad (C-E-G♯).

Act VI

SCENE 1: The Search Throughout the Kingdom
In "The Search," based on the music of "The Prince Is Giving a Ball," the
Godmother guides the Captain of the Prince's guard and two soldiers to
Cinderella. Meanwhile, the Prince discusses with his mother his desire to
find the woman who fits the slipper. The Queen asks whether Cinderella
is beautiful because the Prince loves her (or vice versa), but in the end the
answer does not matter. The shoe fits. We next observe the Stepmother and
Stepsisters scrambling to locate objects to complete Cinderella's trousseau
(something old, something new, etc.).

SCENE 2: The Wedding in the Main Ballroom of the Palace
In the final scene the Prince and Cinderella are married to the strains of "In
My Own Little Corner," transformed into a march.[25]

The Remake: *Cinderella* II on CBS-TV (February 22, 1965)

Before the new *Cinderella* was first broadcast, London audiences had had
the opportunity to see a pantomime version in 1958. This version had three
songs from *Me and Juliet*—one of the few R&H shows that didn't make it to
London—and an interpolated song with music and lyrics by Tommy Steele,
who played a newly conceived character. Mordden describes several salient
features of this short-lived production (101 performances): "A traditional pantomime, with the Stepsisters in drag, the King built up as a comedy part, a
cuddly bear character, and Tommy Steele starring as Buttons, the neglected
but dauntless servant and Cinderella's confidant. The book was of course
riddled with the shenanigans beloved of panto—bawdy humor, actors breaking out of character to game with the audience, and so on, all of this very
out of style for an R&H show."[26] Pantomimes, while popular in England,
were virtually nonexportable. A stage adaptation by Donn Driver also experienced a short run by the Cleveland Musicarnival in June 1961 and the
St. Louis Opera later that summer and led to nothing more lasting.

Rodgers, now without his partner, had the motive—to create a videotaped *Cinderella* for a new and perhaps a future generation of viewers—and
an opportunity to rethink the work. In the liner notes that accompanied the
recording of the new *Cinderella* Rodgers reinforces the mistaken assump-

tion that kinescopes could not be reshown as he addresses his intentions and argues on behalf of his second thoughts:

> Offering new productions of old favorites is a standard practice in the musi-cal theater. But a new production of a television musical is something of a rarity. Part of the reason, of course, is that there have been relatively few musicals written expressly for television. Another factor is that since most television shows are now permanently recorded on videotape, it is a relatively simple matter to rerun a popular attraction.
>
> But when Oscar Hammerstein and I wrote Cinderella in 1957, videotape had not yet been perfected. Once a show was seen, that was that: there was no way of preserving the actual performance. In a way, though, this was a lucky break so far as Cinderella was concerned. Although Oscar and I had stayed relatively close to the legendary fairy tale, there were occasions where we kidded the plot a bit. We should have known that Cinderella has been around far too long for any treatment other than the traditional one. That's why it seemed to be a good idea to try a new version for the second presen-tation. Joseph Schrank, who did the adaptation, has done a beautiful job of preserving the spirit of the familiar story, while at the same time fitting the action to the songs written for the original production. Incidentally, there is a "new" song for our "new" Cinderella. It's "Loneliness of Evening," a num-ber Oscar and I originally wrote for South Pacific, but which was cut before the show opened.
>
> Another interesting fact about doing a remake for television is that it still gets shown over the complete network to at least the same number of people who saw it before. There's no such thing as off-Broadway or summer stock tryouts so far as television is concerned. The production must be perfect the first time. Therefore, Cinderella is being treated as the brand-new produc-tion it is—original cast album and all. This is highly appropriate, because the adaptation, direction, production and cast have made it a brand-new show.
>
> Now that we have had this second chance with Cinderella, I must con-fess to a very special reason for hoping that you like it the way it is. We can't make any more changes; Cinderella—at last—is in permanent form, on videotape.[27]

Rodgers does not clarify what he means by "kidding the plot" or what steps Joseph Schrank took in "preserving the spirit of the familiar story, while at the same time fitting the action to the songs written for the original pro-duction." Indeed, the 1965 remake comes off as more earnest than its pre-decessor, and newcomer Lesley Ann Warren smudgier and more fearful in

The second Cinderella, Lesley Ann Warren, and Stuart Damon, her Prince
(1965)

the title role. On the brighter side, Warren's future Prince, played by Stuart
Damon, conveys a deadpan humor absent in his predecessor's characterization. The original Stepsisters, Kaye Ballard and Alice Ghostley, were genuinely funny. By comparison, the heavy-handed humor of Barbara Ruick's
(Esmerelda's) obsessive eyelash fluttering and Pat Carroll's (Prunella's) com-
pulsive knee creaking have the effect of one-joke comic shticks. Throughout
his ordeal Damon endures their inanities with considerable restraint, asking Esmerelda if she has something in her eye, Prunella to creak in time
to the music, and each to refrain from making personal remarks about the
weather. After his ordeal with Prunella, the Prince informs his Aide that
fatigue prompts him to sit out "the next four or five sets." Then he must face
conversation with the Stepmother, who extols her daughters' virtues to an
incredulous Prince. In his liner notes, Rodgers admits that a "special rea-

son for hoping" audiences like the new *Cinderella* was the impossibility of changing it. As far as Rodgers was concerned, the 1965 version would be the last. He forgot to consider that "impossible things are happ'ning ev'ry day." Mordden offers a vigorous indictment of the remake: "Hammerstein had died by then, and trouble began when Rodgers commissioned an entirely new script (by Joseph Schrank) that lost Hammerstein's delicate blend of romance and jest, not to mention his amusingly timeless neverland [in contrast to Schrank's self-conscious medievalisms]. . . . Gone were Hammerstein's subtle variations, the rather touching relationship between the Prince and his parents, the sardonic young Godmother. Gone as well was the simple charm of the original cast. . . . Sad to say, it is this puerile and cliché-bound *Cinderella* that survived, first in many CBS airings and lately as a commercial videotape, as kinescoped copies of the original reside only in private collections . . . a tale this audience-friendly and a score this brilliant need a truer setting than that plate of hash that Rodgers served up in 1965."[28]

One major dramatic change in the remake is the increased prominence of the Prince. In fact, the new *Cinderella* went more than a step further in the progression from the early 1957 drafts in which the Prince did not appear until the midway point of the story before being given an early exchange with his parents. In 1965, viewers meet the Prince before they meet Cinderella. Accompanied by the "Cinderella March," the Prince appears on horseback with his older Aide (in 1957 horses had been attempted and then rejected from the filming as too unpredictable). Parched after a long journey, the Prince finds himself outside Cinderella's cottage. A timid young woman responds to his distress and offers him water. In the exchange that follows we learn that the young woman's Stepmother would beat her if she found out she spoke to anyone in her absence, that her name is Cinderella (so named because she sleeps among the ashes to help keep her warmer in the cold attic), and that her father is dead. We also learn that her kindness is not contingent on her recognition of the Prince. At the beginning of the encounter he appears simply as a traveler in search of water. Only at the end of their conversation, when the Aide addresses the Prince as His Highness, does Cinderella discover his true identity. When the Prince and his entourage depart, he informs us that, despite his extensive travels, he has yet to find his "true love." He sits down and sings "The Loneliness of Evening," the second version of the number that evolved into "Twin Soliloquies" in *South Pacific*.

These changes are not insignificant. By introducing the Prince before Cinderella and especially by giving him the opening song, the balance between the two principals undergoes a permanent shift. In 1957 the first image viewers see is Cinderella and her wacky, unpleasant family, and the first song is Cinderella's ballad, "In My Own Little Corner." In 1965 viewers learn that the Prince is looking for love, that Cinderella is as kind as she is beautiful, and that the young couple have made a connection, a relationship based on something beyond romantic abstraction. Although it is difficult to suspend the suspicion that the Prince and Cinderella have begun the process that will take them from this first meeting to future romance and marriage, the new teleplay studiously avoids the direct implication of love at first sight. Like Guenevere and King Arthur in Lerner and Loewe's *Camelot* five years earlier, however, the future Princess and her Prince get a chance to learn about each other unburdened by his true identity.

Significantly, the Prince's added song is not about newfound love but about the lonely absence of love. Perhaps as a holdover from its context in *South Pacific*, some of the original lyrics also suggest that the singer is singing about an absent but known love ("I pray each day that I'll hear some word from you"). No doubt cognizant of this infelicity, Rodgers revised one lyric, "how soon will my love come home to me" to read "how soon will my love appear to me" in order to make this distinction. "Loneliness of Evening" is in the vein of Hammerstein and Kern's "Where's the Mate for Me?" from *Show Boat*. The central difference is that Ravenal meets the answer to his question during the course of the song and knows that his search is at an end, whereas the Prince meets the answer to his dreams and does not realize it.

Other modest changes in structure and character collectively produce an altered overall effect. In the 1965 version, Jo Ann Fleet as the Stepmother is demonstrably crueler than her predecessor, Ilka Chase. Now Cinderella's corner is a punishment as much as a retreat. In 1965, the King, played by Walter Pidgeon, is a less comical figure who agrees with his Queen, Ginger Rogers, that giving a ball is a good idea. The new Fairy Godmother, played by Ado Annie alumna Celeste Holm, informs Cinderella that the impossible can occur if she *wishes* hard enough. In significant contrast to Edie Adams's Godmother, Godmother Holm says nothing about the need to *earn* her dreams.

After the extended separate dialogue exchanges between Esmerelda, Prunella, the Stepmother, and the Prince, Cinderella arrives to music bor-

rowed from another discarded song from a Rodgers and Hammerstein classic, "Boys and Girls Like You and Me" from *Oklahoma!*[29] All that is heard
for the next eighty seconds (45:40–47:00 minutes) is the A section of this
song played by the orchestra and arranged as a polonaise, a Polish dance in
triple meter, to complement the Viennesy waltz flavor of the ball. Other
underscoring bears a detectable resemblance to the syncopated beginning
of Robert Schumann's Symphony No. 3 (*Rhenish*), also in triple meter. The
King sees Cinderella first, then the Queen, and the latter points her out
to the fatigued and oblivious Prince. When the young couple's eyes finally
meet, everything goes silent for just under a minute, an excruciatingly
long time for television. At the moment they touch (48:06) the orchestra
launches "Waltz for a Ball." At the completion of the "Stepsisters' Lament,"
the King and Queen notice that their son is stricken, and they rejoice by
dancing a reprise of "Ten Minutes Ago" accompanied by a chorus. This
allows those in the audience who remember Ginger Rogers's glory days with
Fred Astaire three decades earlier an opportunity to see her dance a little.

In an interesting touch, the 1965 remake conveys to viewers that the
Prince recognized his future Princess even before she tried on the slipper.
How did he know? No magic necessary, just a little prodding. When the
Prince is about to leave Cinderella's cottage, the Fairy Godmother persuades
Cinderella, who is hiding behind a corner, to offer the Prince some water
from the well. By this act of kindness that brought the two together four
score and three minutes ago, the Prince recognizes beyond any doubt that
he has found his mate.

Cinderella III on ABC-TV (November 2, 1997)

Prior to the age of videocassettes, television audiences could look forward
to annual televised showings of Julie Andrews singing from the mountain-
tops in one of Rodgers and Hammerstein's greatest and most durable successes, the film version of *The Sound of Music*. Was it mere coincidence
that *The Sound of Music* was released in theaters ten days after the *Cinderella* television remake? The 1965 *Cinderella*, without Andrews, was shown
eight more times between 1966 and 1974 on CBS and later on home video
and cable. By the 1990s the time was ripe for an updated version. The im-
petus in 1957 was the cashing in on *My Fair Lady*'s Andrews and the lure
and excitement of a new medium. The force behind the 1965 remake was
allegedly the absence of a videotape and, if we are to take Rodgers at face

value, the need to take the Cinderella story more seriously. The 1997 re-make was conceived as a vehicle to show off the singing and acting talents of Whitney Houston, who would be featured as Cinderella and also produce the project.

By the time Houston was available, CBS, which had produced the previous two *Cinderellas*, had abandoned negotiations. ABC, owned by the Walt Disney Company, stepped in, gladly agreed to produce the show, and offered it as a showcase for *Wonderful World of Disney* during the November sweeps. Houston had originally planned to play Cinderella but decided four years later that the role needed a younger talent. Houston cast herself as the beautiful and hip fairy Godmother.[30] Not surprisingly, this move led to the dramatic and musical enlargement of the role. The part of Cinderella went to Brandy Norwood, the young rhythm and blues singer and star of the popular situation comedy *Moesha*.

Robert L. Freedman was commissioned to write a new teleplay. Despite its expanded two-hour allotment, however, the new version was only five minutes longer than the 1965 remake. The remaining time was devoted to about thirty-two minutes of commercials and station identifications. The new *Cinderella* retained most of the songs from the first telecast, omitting only "Your Majesties" (also omitted in 1965), and abbreviating "When You're Driving in the Moonlight." The new version also managed to reduce the dialogue in order to make room for three new songs and considerably more dancing than either of the earlier telecasts. One of these songs, a jazzed-up version of Rodgers and Hart's "Falling in Love with Love" from *The Boys from Syracuse*, featured Bernadette Peters, a Broadway star, in the expanded role of the Stepmother.[31]

The Fairy Godmother's new status is evident from the opening. In fact, the first image viewers see is a close-up of Houston singing the first twelve measures of "Impossible" in a rhythmically free pop performance style, the pop equivalent of Sarah Vaughan's jazzy rendition of "Bali Ha'i" and "Happy Talk" on the crossover recording of *South Pacific* released in 1986.[32] It does not take long to realize that this is not going to be a conventional Julie Andrews performance of an R&H musical. After this musical preparation, Houston stops singing and addresses the audience directly. Adopting the world view of her predecessor, Edie Adams, Houston proceeds to give the plot away in an ironic spoken rhyme: "A slipper made of glass is just a shoe. And dreamers never make a dream come true."[33] She then sings another fragment of the song until she reaches the word "impossible," after which she disappears for the next forty-two minutes.

In a striking visual conceit, the first act's opening scene focuses on shoes and those who make and wear them. The outrageous pair of high heels belongs to the Stepmother. Those who have seen Peters's memorable characterization of Dot in *Sunday in the Park with George* may recognize her voice modulations as similar to those she used to parody another character, Yvonne. In this *Cinderella* we see Peters as the Stepmother on a shopping expedition with her daughters and Cinderella schlepping their purchases all over town. The Stepsisters, once again renamed, this time Calliope (Veanne Cox) and Minerva (Natalie Desselle), fight over a ridiculous hat. The honest but undiplomatic Cinderella, when asked, shares her view that the hat fails to flatter either one. When they go into the shop, Cinderella waits outside. It is now time for the first song, but instead of "In My Own Little Corner" or "Loneliness of Evening," the song is "The Sweetest Sounds," a duet for Cinderella and the Prince, who happens to be wandering aimlessly around the marketplace wondering, like *Show Boat*'s Ravenal, where's the mate for him.

The decision to recycle this important opening song from *No Strings* merits some comment. In Rodgers's career with Hart such reuse signaled a song's abandonment from a failed show—for example, the use of *Chee-Chee*'s "I Must Love You" and "Singing a Love Song" with new lyrics, "Send for Me" and "I Still Believe in You," two years later in *Simple Simon*. Although R&H had few failed shows, they usually had at least one important song that went unused and could be placed in a subsequent show, such as the abandoned "My Wife" in *Allegro* metamorphosing into Cable's "Younger than Springtime" in *South Pacific* and a discarded Cable song, "Suddenly Lovely," being set as "Getting to Know You" in *The King and I*. Earlier in this chapter I noted that Rodgers, without Hammerstein, was able to incorporate abandoned songs from *Oklahoma!* and *South Pacific* into the second *Cinderella*. What makes the use of "The Sweetest Sounds" different from these other examples is that this time Rodgers, who died in 1979, was no longer the person doing the recycling. Although *No Strings* had not received a New York revival since it first appeared in 1962, the show was successful in its own day, even earning Rodgers a Tony for best score. Any future productions of *No Strings* almost certainly would include this song.[34]

Why then reuse "The Sweetest Sounds"? One possible answer is that the 1997 telecast catered primarily to a young audience unaware that "The

Sweetest Sounds" was a reasonably popular song from an earlier generation. Who would even notice? Even less detectable is a snippet of dialogue
uttered by the 1957 Prince (*Hammerstein*'s Prince) shortly before he starts to
sing, "Do I Love You Because You're Beautiful?" that might retrospectively
be considered a possible source for Rodgers's lyric and title. Hammerstein's
line: "Why is the sound of your voice the sweetest sound in the world?"[35]

In both *Cinderella* and *No Strings*, "The Sweetest Sounds" serves as the
first complete song of the show. As in *No Strings*, the principals have not
yet met and inhabit a shared space, propless and imagined in *No Strings*,
a crowded town with outdoor markets in *Cinderella*. In both, the female
lead is African American and the male lead is white, although Paolo Mon-
talban's physical features and skin color suggest an exotic and perhaps in-
definable racial mixture, as is appropriate for the offspring of a biracial marriage (Whoopi Goldberg, an African American, and Victor Garber, white).[36]
Some things have changed between 1962 and 1997. Most visibly, the world,
even the fictional world of a Prince's kingdom, is now a multicultural one.
The Prince in the 1997 *Cinderella*, like his father before him, is destined
to marry an African American woman. The principals in *No Strings* had no
such role models, and the central female character, Barbara Woodruff, like
Jackie Robinson in his first years as a Brooklyn Dodger, was the only African
American in the game. In addition to Cinderella and her future mother-in-
law, the 1997 remake also features a black Fairy Godmother (Houston) and
a black Stepsister (Desselle as Minerva). Even the ball is a truly integrated
event.

Does this mean that Cinderella's father was African American? Was she
adopted? Abandoned? Can some of her ill treatment at the hands of the
Stepmother be due to racial prejudice (although she does seem to treat
Minerva without bias)? Should we not ask questions like this? In any event,
this line of inquiry leads to another intriguing contrast between Rodgers in
1962 and *Cinderella* without Rodgers in 1997. The Author's Note in the *No
Strings* libretto specified that Barbara Woodruff was to be portrayed "by an
American colored girl" but that "the play itself never refers to her color." The
difference between *No Strings* and other multicultural productions, such as
the London and New York *Carousel* revivals in the 1990s, is that the interracial nature of the romance in *No Strings* is a crucial reason why Barbara
could not join David Jordan in Maine. Just as Cable had to grapple with the
racial divide that separated him from Liat and Nellie Forbush had to overcome her initial resistance to Emile de Becque's biracial marriage and his

offspring, the characters in *No Strings* had to contend with the racial implications of their relationship.[37] In contrast, the characters in *Cinderella* need
not confront racial obstacles in their pursuit of happiness.

Decades after the 1950s television show *Leave It to Beaver*, things have
also changed in the gender dynamic between Cinderella and her future
Prince. Significantly, in the 1965 version it was Cinderella who fetched water
for the Prince and not vice versa. In 1997, the Prince himself helps Cinderella pick up the packages that she dropped when the royal carriage brushes
her back. And this is not all that is expected of the new Prince. He must be
quick—for example, when he readily understands the etymological meaning of her name and knows that he must treat a woman not like a Princess but
"like a *person*," "with kindness" "and respect." Considering their contrasting
socioeconomic backgrounds and cultural histories, the Prince and Cinderella have much in common. Both lead sheltered lives, experience boring
routines, and have the urge to run away. In fact, later in the evening the new
Cinderella, unlike her predecessors, prepares to leave her untenable home
life. After Cinderella's Stepmother, from a distance, interrupts the conversation between Cinderella and her future Prince, the lingering memory of
the moment just passed carries the young lovers to a partial reprise.[38] "The
Sweetest Sounds" will continue to underscore the next scene between the
Prince and his servant, Lionel, an expanded comic singing-and-dancing role
for the Crier—the man who sings out all the Prince's names in the 1957 and
1965 telecasts—now ably sung and agilely danced by Jason Alexander. In a
new scene, the Prince explains why he likes to play the role of a commoner,
and Lionel laments how this action necessitates lying to his mother. To conclude the act, the Queen announces her plans for a ball, the Prince conveys
his desire to marry for love, and Lionel conveys the invitation to the townspeople in all the Prince's names. After an elaborate dance production, "The
Prince Is Giving a Ball," Cinderella gets the last word when she *speaks* the
song's title.

The second act presents Cinderella's by now familiar "In My Own Little
Corner." Before the song, however, Cinderella exhibits a degree of assertive-
ness not found in her predecessors when she makes the point that "the proc-
lamation says that *all* of the eligible women in the kingdom are invited."[39]
This Cinderella clearly possesses a strong conviction that justice requires
social equality. Norwood's style of singing contrasts with the conventional
Broadway style. Her style allows for considerable rhythmic liberties, as in
the way she holds on to the final syllables of "all alone" and "in my own." It

should also be mentioned that, unlike her predecessors, this Cinderella must put up with several interruptions from her sisters before she has a chance to finish the song.

In a number of places the characters in the 1997 *Cinderella* offer self-referential (or self-reflexive) commentary on some of the cherished notions that belong to most tellings of this familiar story. The principal such commentator is Lionel. During his initial encounter with the Prince, after the Prince gives him his dirty peasant clothes, Lionel can't resist challenging the Prince's perversity: "Help me out here: You're rich, you live in a gorgeous palace, you've got beautiful women throwing themselves at your feet—is there something I'm not getting?"[40]

Producers, directors, and casts of previous stage or television productions usually feel no obligation to duplicate every detail of an earlier production, even if they could. With *Cinderella*, the irony is that, in contrast to other productions of 1950s musicals, the original production with the original dialogue and the original songs and the original cast has been theoretically available since 1957. In the early years of television, however, casts would reassemble and perform a show again live (as with *Peter Pan*) and did not seriously contemplate the idea of reshowing a kinescope. Rodgers, who was quite willing to add and subtract songs—provided they were his own—and to allow new scripts to be written in connection with filmed versions of his shows, was eager to do the same in 1965. Had he lived until 1997 he most certainly would have sought new solutions for a new generation (but no doubt different ones than those chosen). Like their ephemeral stage counterparts, filmed musicals reflect their time. This is as it should be. From the self-actualizing Cinderella of 1957 to the kind and generous Cinderella of 1965 to the Cinderella of 1997 who will settle for nothing less than equal rights and a prince of a Prince, the three *Cinderellas* offer road maps for their respective eras.

The Rodgers and Hammerstein Organization has been in serious negotiations for a video release of the original *Cinderella*. Perhaps by the time you read this paragraph such a videotape or DVD will be available, and interested viewers will no longer need to journey to the Museum of Television & Radio in New York City to see the first R&H *Cinderella* for themselves with Julie Andrews in her prime. Surely such a product would complement the two sequels currently available on videocassette, the modified 1957 version currently distributed by the Rodgers and Hammerstein Organization for regional theaters and school productions, and the modified 1997 tour version starring Eartha Kitt as the Fairy Godmother. Although less responsive than the 1997 *Cinderella* to evolving sensibilities on the nature of mature versus romantic love, the original broadcast, with its light touch and memorable performances, remains the *Cinderella* of choice for those who have seen them all and lived to write about them.

Cinderella may have begun as a television broadcast rather than a Broadway musical, but for the past several decades it has been doing quite well impersonating a Broadway musical. And like *Show Boat*, there are many possible *Cinderellas*. In transferring *Cinderella* to the stage, the shorter duration of the televised broadcasts (the first acts of some R&H stage shows last as long) combined with the flexibility of the story itself creates abundant opportunities and a perceived license to modify the plot and characterizations and to add recycled Rodgers songs for short-changed characters. Whatever its future, even in the absence of a fourth *Cinderella*, the show will no doubt continue to transcend the sum of its three televised versions. After nearly a half century, it ranks securely along with *The King and I* and *The Sound of Music* as one of Rodgers and Hammerstein's great *stage* legacies of the 1950s.

CHAPTER 6

After Hammerstein

THE LEGEND OF RICHARD RODGERS CONTINUED TO GROW AND prosper after the death of Oscar Hammerstein, Rodgers's partner from *Oklahoma!* to *The Sound of Music*—eighteen years of mostly bright, golden haze on the meadow. Five years after Hammerstein died of stomach cancer in 1960, a film version of *The Sound of Music* arrived with two new songs, words and music by Rodgers ("I Have Confidence in Me" and "Something Good"). The film would reign as box office champion for the next four years, and it remains the highest grossing film musical of all time.[1] Overlapping its initial release was the first *Cinderella* television re-make, the version that would be shown in each of the next five years, twice in 1971, and again in 1974 and later on home video and cable. Through these reincarnations of familiar work, the magical name of Rodgers and Hammerstein continued to receive wide exposure for Rodgers's nineteen remaining years.

During these years, Rodgers continued to compose musicals, first with himself as a lyricist and then with a succession of partners—Stephen Sondheim, Martin Charnin, Sheldon Harnick, Martin Charnin again, and Raymond Jessel (the latter for only four lyrics). With striking unanimity, biographers and critics have characterized Rodgers's final musicals, especially the four he composed after *No Strings* (1962), his first and only attempt as a composer-lyricist for an entire show, as a sad epilogue to the glorious careers with Hart and Hammerstein. Mary Rodgers's assessment is representative of prevailing attitudes: "My father never again found a compatible partner although he doggedly continued to grind out musicals (flawed and lacklustre work, for the most part) until his own death in 1979."[2]

The musicals Rodgers wrote after the death of Hammerstein, from the relatively successful *No Strings* to the four problematic shows that followed — like Tolstoy's unhappy families, each unhappy in their own way — have not received the attention they deserve. Most who have looked at these shows tend to focus on problems and unfavorable comparisons with Rodgers's work with Hart and Hammerstein. Given the escalating status and prestige of the parties involved, few writers neglect to emphasize the acrimonious collaboration between Rodgers and his co-creators on *Do I Hear a Waltz?* (1965): Arthur Laurents (librettist) and Sondheim (lyricist), the latter Hammerstein's protégé, virtual son, and close friend of R&H's children, contemporaries James Hammerstein and Mary Rodgers. Another problem, actually a series of problems, orbits around the difficult stars who undermined the process (and in most cases the results) of Rodgers's final trio of shows: Danny Kaye in *Two By Two* (1970), Nicol Williamson in *Rex* (1976), and Liv Ullmann in *I Remember Mama* (1979). In addition to the tepid initial popular reception of *Waltz, Rex,* and *Mama* — the star status of Kaye helped *Two By Two* earn a profit — the perception remains that Rodgers's legendary infallible theatrical intuition and even his seemingly inexhaustible melodic gifts suffered irreversible decline after *No Strings.* What really went wrong with these shows? Does the fault lie in their stars or in themselves? Should we blame Rodgers's creative partners or Rodgers? Did Rodgers raise the bar so high in his previous work that these shows suffer by comparison? Do William Hyland's remarks about *Rex* apply to other post-Hammerstein shows as well: "It was good by Broadway standards but not by the standards Rodgers himself had established over the years"?[3] Can future audiences and critics find something to appreciate in these seemingly flawed and little-known musicals?

The Tyranny of the Zeitgeist

Steven Suskin's "Broadway Scorecard" offers a useful summary of how some (but by no means all) major New York daily papers received Rodgers's final shows.[4]

Review response to Rodgers's late shows

	Rave	Favorable	Mixed	Unfavorable	Pan
No Strings (580 performances)	1	3	2		1
Do I Hear a Waltz? (220 performances)		2	1	3	

	Rave	Favorable	Mixed	Unfavorable	Pan
Two By Two (343 performances)	1	1	2	1	1
Rex (49 performances)				1	5
I Remember Mama (108 performances)		1			5

Before its long-awaited premiere at the 54th Street Theatre (March 15, 1962), *No Strings* had generated considerable buzz, much of which concerned what Rodgers was going to do after the death of his illustrious partner. Would he try to find another collaborator, or would he strike out on his own? To prepare for the latter possibility, Rodgers spent several months after Hammerstein's death writing some of his own lyrics to match the new songs he needed for the film remake of *State Fair*. After testing these waters, Rodgers was ready to try writing lyrics for a complete show. While no one seemed to find Rodgers's lyrics as clever as Hart's or as inspiring as Hammerstein's, they were generally acknowledged as competent and praised for their craftsmanship. And they demonstrated that Rodgers had indeed learned something from each of his predecessors. *No Strings* was lauded for its chic depiction of high Parisian fashion, its modern story, if not for Samuel Taylor's book, which is typically described as "heavy-handed and sluggish." The innovative staging, in which the cast moved props and scenery (and were often themselves the props and scenery), was praised. Also much appreciated was the way its chamber jazz orchestra, which incidentally contained no strings, participated directly but unobtrusively on stage.[5]

For the final time, Rodgers participated in an award-winning show that enjoyed a successful run.[6] Although the show lost to Frank Loesser's *How to Succeed in Business Without Really Trying* for Best Musical, Rodgers's acclaimed score won a Tony Award for Best Music, Diahann Carroll shared the Best Actress honors with *Carnival*'s Anna Maria Alberghetti, and the show lasted a respectable 580 performances, far fewer than *The Sound of Music* but only twenty fewer than *Flower Drum Song* four years earlier. Like the many now-forgotten shows with Hart, Rodgers's *No Strings*, an unequivocal popular and artistic success in its time, introduced at least one lasting song, "The Sweetest Sounds," which opened and closed the show. As we saw in the previous chapter, the *Cinderella* remake of 1997 reused this song—which bears a familial melodic and rhythmic resemblance to the main theme of

the finale of Brahms's Second Piano Concerto—in a similar dramatic context for a national television audience, most of whom would presumably be
unfamiliar with the by then obscure *No Strings*.

Despite its acclaim and the personal triumph for Rodgers, *No Strings*
continued to be overshadowed by other shows. Loesser's *How to Succeed*
(October 14, 1961) won not only the Tony but the Pulitzer Prize as well,
and it went on to a highly acclaimed revival in the late 1990s. Less than
two months after *No Strings opened*, Sondheim's *Funny Thing Happened
on the Way to the Forum* arrived (May 8, 1962). *Forum* earned a Tony for
Best Musical, and, although the nominating committee overlooked Sondheim (the composer-lyricist) at the time, he has belatedly received much of
the credit for the show's initial success and timeless hilarity, and for its boffo
revival in the 1990s. Meanwhile, although *No Strings* appeared as part of
the New York City Center's prestigious *Encores!* series in 2002, the musical
is still awaiting its first staged Broadway revival.

Rodgers's late quartet of shows were similarly fated to go up against
more popular and most often critically better-received shows. *Do I Hear
a Waltz?* had the misfortune of appearing one season after Jerry Herman's
blockbuster, *Hello, Dolly!* (January 16, 1964), and Jule Styne and Bob Merrill's *Funny Girl* (March 26) and, worse, the same season that opened with
the hit of the decade, Bock and Harnick's *Fiddler on the Roof* (September 22). Rodgers and Sondheim shared a nomination for Best Score (the
award went to *Fiddler*'s composer, Jerry Bock, and lyricist, Sheldon Harnick),
but *Waltz* was passed over even as a *candidate* for Best Musical—that award
also went to *Fiddler*. Other contemporary musicals by rising creative stars
included the underrated *Golden Boy* by Charles Strouse and Lee Adams,
originally starring Sammy Davis Jr. (October 20, 1964), and John Kander and
Fred Ebb's *Flora, the Red Menace* (May 11, 1965), the show that launched
the Broadway career of Liza Minnelli. Before it closed, *Waltz* would have
to contend with *Man of La Mancha* (November 22).

Sondheim's own modernist presence would continue to cloud and sometimes overshadow Rodgers' subsequent achievement. In the 1970–71 season
Two By Two (November 10, 1970) fell critically short of Sondheim's path-
breaking but unprofitable *Follies* (April 4, 1971) and the still-running *Company* from the previous season (April 26, 1970). *Rex* (April 25, 1976) had
the bad luck of following Marvin Hamlisch's *A Chorus Line* (May 21, 1975),
the musical megahit of the 1970s, by less than a year. But it also followed
on the heels of Sondheim's relatively unpopular but strikingly innovative

Pacific Overtures (January 11, 1976) and has since been overshadowed by the belated success of another contemporary show, Kander and Ebb's *Chicago* (June 1, 1975). The close and shocking juxtaposition of Sondheim's *Sweeney Todd* (March 1, 1979) and Rodgers's *I Remember Mama* (May 31, 1979) makes the aging composer's nostalgic swansong appear more traditional than it was intended to be. In all these cases, Rodgers must bear the wrath of what pianist Glenn Gould termed the "tyranny of the zeitgeist." Perhaps some of Rodgers's late musicals would have fared better had they appeared in an earlier decade, perhaps the 1940s or 1950s. But on second thought, perhaps not, for they would then have been forced into a more direct comparison with Rodgers and Hammerstein.

No Strings

In *No Strings*, Barbara Woodruff (Diahann Carroll), a gorgeous, elegant, and stylish black American model working in Paris for a prestigious magazine, meets David Jordan (Richard Kiley), a white Pulitzer Prize–winning novelist who has been bumming around Europe, unable to settle down and write something worthwhile. Barbara and David meet at a photography shoot and fall in love in act I. In act II David remains unable to abandon the high life and concentrate on his writing, at least while in Europe, despite Barbara's willingness to curtail her own career and help him through his creative crisis. In the end they painfully realize that David must return to his home state of Maine in order to work, and Barbara must remain in Paris. David promises to return. To assuage the pain and loneliness during an indefinite separation he suggests they pretend that the "sweetest sounds" of their powerful but uncommitted love (a bond with no strings) "is still inside" their heads "waiting to be said" and that their romance "never happened." To the strains of "The Sweetest Sounds," David and Barbara sing of the "dearest love in all the world" that awaits them "somewhere" in the future.[7]

What goes unsaid is that racial differences and social responses to these differences were instrumental (but without strings) in Barbara and David's decision not to settle down together in bucolic bliss in rural Maine. In the Author's Note in the published text, Samuel Taylor includes the following statement: "The part of Barbara Woodruff in *No Strings* is designed to be played by an American colored girl in her early twenties. It is proposed that she also be beautiful, have style, and wear clothes well; be intelligent, witty, warmly human, and wise. The play itself never refers to her color."

Diahann Carroll (Barbara Woodruff) and Richard Kiley (David Jordan) in
No Strings (1962)

When planning *No Strings*, Taylor and Rodgers decided on a Paris location in part because in an era before supermodels like Tyra Banks and Naomi
Campbell, it seemed implausible that a black fashion model would succeed
in the United States. It should also be recalled that the action in *No Strings*
occurs during a turbulent and momentous period in the American civil
rights movement, one year before the first blacks were admitted to the University of Mississippi and before Martin Luther King's "I Have a Dream" ora-
tion, two years before the Civil Rights Act was passed, and three years before
the Voting Rights Act was passed. Despite the events swirling around them
and an emerging racial consciousness and pride, direct references to race are
minimal. Barbara tells David she attended George Washington High "uptown . . . way uptown." The song "Maine" refers to the racial divide, when
we learn that Barbara hails from "up North of Central Park," a place where
"there's a sidewalk symphony of song and shout" (perhaps a reference to

the African American ring shout), which must be Harlem. It is also possible to interpret Barbara's response when David accuses her of anti-American prejudice (she responds with "some of my best friends are American") as a reference to racial prejudice, a twist on a familiar phrase. In their farewell conversation Barbara suggests they attend one Saturday-night dance in Maine "to show we're not cowards," another possible allusion to the racial implications of their romance.[8]

Although Carroll and Kiley tried to persuade them to explain *why* Barbara cannot join David in Maine, Rodgers and Taylor considered the matter nonnegotiable. Thirteen years earlier, when composing *South Pacific*, Rodgers, with Hammerstein, faced the matter of race head on, not only in "Carefully Taught" but also as a central theme of the show. Although the presence of "Carefully Taught" was controversial, Rodgers and Hammerstein insisted that it remain in the show, and for Hammerstein especially, "Carefully Taught" constituted "what the play is about."[9] Rodgers, however, later dismissed the political meaning of the song as a factor in his decision to include it in the show. From Rodgers's perspective "Carefully Taught" simply was the right song for a particular dramatic situation and "was never written as a 'message' song."[10] When Rodgers conceived the idea of a black actress in a starring role for *No Strings* after watching the talented and poised Carroll perform on the *Tonight Show*, hosted by Jack Paar in April 1961, he felt that the casting spoke for itself and made any specific references to race in the play unnecessary. In Rodgers's view, "rather than shrinking from the issue of race, such an approach would demonstrate our respect for the audience's ability to accept our theme free from rhetoric or sermons."[11] Rodgers acknowledged that "the reason for the breakup is clearly because of anticipated racial prejudice." Perhaps Hammerstein would have persuaded Rodgers to be more explicit, but Carroll and Kiley could not.

Barbara and David's unwillingness to openly discuss race, at least on stage, remained a source of controversy. Rodgers biographer Hyland sides with Rodgers and Taylor, given the racial sensitivities of the time.[12] Although the decision to make the whole play a dream struck some critics as overly facile and unsatisfying, Carroll considered this matter "an absolutely brilliant solution."[13] If they never really met, then Barbara's race would not be an issue in David's decision to return to Maine. An interracial romance, even one that does not lead to marriage and children and a move to Maine, was bold in 1962. Later it became too tame.

It is unusual for Rodgers to make specific musical allusions to shows by others, but *No Strings* offers two examples. The first occurs at the conclusion of David's "How Sad," a song that laments the sorry state of a world in which "women are stuck with men." If the twist on "A Hymn to Him," in which Alan Jay Lerner and Frederick Loewe's Henry Higgins asks "Why can't a woman be more like a man?" goes unnoticed, Rodgers makes the connection to *My Fair Lady* explicit when David adopts the rhythm of Higgins's musical question asked in the song "Why Can't the English?" to inquire "How can a woman / Be like a woman?" Instead of Higgins's "learn to speak," however, Rodgers offers a new punchline, "What does she see in men?"[14] A more striking connection with an earlier classic appears in the instrumental portions of "Eager Beaver," where Rodgers uses the same unison three-note rhythmic figure that figures prominently in the "Prologue" to *West Side Story* (♩♪♪). Like Bernstein, Rodgers follows the figure with dramatic silences. Although Rodgers softens the potential musical violence by descending a major third rather than Bernstein's harsher major second (spelled as a diminished third), the effect is remarkably similar and likely intentional. It is also notable that when Rodgers uses a rhythmically altered version of this figure as an accompaniment to the verse of the song, his starting note is B-natural, a tritone (*West Side Story*'s ubiquitous interval) above the key of the song (F minor).[15]

Two different phrases in two separate *No Strings* songs actually quote from Rodgers and Hammerstein's "You'll Never Walk Alone," albeit in dissimilar contexts and without demonstrable dramatic meaning.[16] More often, Rodgers and Rodgers mark a discernible return to the days of Rodgers and Hart. Those who prefer the earlier partnership to the work with Hammerstein typically lament Rodgers's abandonment of the jazz vernacular that characterized his work with Hart. Blue notes and jazzy rhythms can be found sporadically in *State Fair* ("It Might as Well Be Spring"), *South Pacific* ("Honey Bun"), *Me and Juliet* ("The Way It Happens"), and *Flower Drum Song* ("Grant Avenue"), but for the most part Rodgers's musical style took a turn with his second partner. *No Strings* marks a welcome homecoming to the jazz world of Rodgers and Hart, especially in Barbara's three solo songs "Loads of Love," "You Don't Tell Me," and "An Orthodox Fool." "Be My Host" and "Eager Beaver" are also stylistically dissimilar to the vast majority of the songs Rodgers composed with Hammerstein. In at least two cases, "La-La-La" and "Loads of Love," Rodgers borrows literally from Hart songs:

"There's a Small Hotel" and "I Like to Recognize the Tune." In other cases, the resemblance is subtler, fleeting, and more a matter of tone than specific reference.

What brings *No Strings* stylistically beyond the Rodgers and Hart era are all those tritones (augmented or raised fourths—for example, A to D-sharp) that were so prevalent in the bop recordings of Dizzy Gillespie and Charlie Parker in 1945, first released about two years after Hart's death, and in the following decade, in Bernstein's score to *West Side Story*. From almost the first note of the opening song Rodgers offers a bittersweet tritone D-sharp on "sweet" against the tonic A to introduce the opening separate but equal duet, "The Sweetest Sounds." Other tritones will follow on "-side," "kind-," "most," and "me." The flute that follows Barbara and David's clarinet, instruments more associated with cool than bop, lend additional jazzy flair to an accompaniment figure otherwise not unlike *Oklahoma!*'s "I Can't Say No" and any number of Rodgers and Hammerstein tunes. Bop tritones, hidden and overt, will continue to characterize Barbara throughout the show.

In "Loads of Love" Barbara takes the tritone hints in "The Sweetest Sounds" and uses this expressive interval to proclaim her jazzy and hip persona (and perhaps indirectly her race). Though slightly obscured by Rodgers's subtle chord voicings, the A sections offer a succession of ii-V-I cadences (see example 6.1), the harmonic staple of jazz from the later years with Hart and a progression that would be welcome in many jazz ensembles in the 1950s and early 1960s:

I never have been handed much,	C7-F, Bb-Eb
I never have demanded much,	Am-D, Gm7-C7
I just want money,	G7-E dim.
A nice position,	Eb6-G7
And loads of lovely love.	C7-F7-Bb

On the second "much" ("demanded much") Barbara hits her longest and highest note so far, an F-sharp, a tritone above the C chord that underlies the harmony. When in the next measures the F-sharp resolves up to a G, actually twelve Gs, Rodgers will change the harmony at least twice a measure until a final ii-V-I cadence brings the tune solidly back to B-flat, which is just a little past Rodgers's harmonic starting point (on "handed much"). Rodgers will also begin his release (B section) with an F-sharp, an augmented second above the E-flat major chord that supports it, on his gradual way to the longest and highest note of all, an A-natural on the word "how" (and later, when

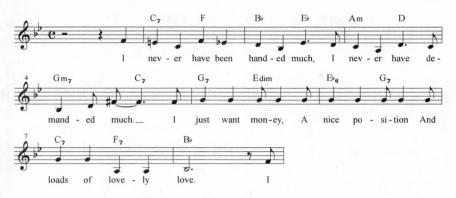

Example 6.1. "Loads of Love" (chorus, first 8 measures)

the song is repeated on another key word, "heart"). In both cases, Rodgers will delay the resolution of this A, the leading tone in the central key of B-flat, until the word "bliss," two measures later. In fact, Rodgers will not firmly resolve the A and establish the tonic B-flat until the last note of the song, one octave higher than the first and less conclusive B-flat resolution.

Although I will not attempt to unravel the intricate cross-fertilization between Rodgers's music and lyrics, his musical workshop alone provides a fascinating glimpse into his creative mind and helps shed light on what is probably the most persistent Rodgers legend: his swiftness as a tunesmith. Few profiles neglect to mention how quickly he was able to compose "Bali Ha'i" (which, according to Joshua Logan, who claimed to be present, was tossed off in about five minutes) or some other hit song. Somewhat defensively, Rodgers would publicly emphasize the amount of preparation and discussion that preceded the few minutes it took him to set a Hammerstein lyric or, earlier, to write a melody for Hart to set. I have noted Rodgers's argument that a composer cannot create a song in a half-hour any more than a woman can produce a baby within this time frame, since both creations require conception and gestation. While Rodgers's extant sketches do not contradict the legend, they do modify it. Although many songs seem to have sprung fully formed, others underwent substantive melodic revision before becoming the melodies we recognize today. *No Strings* offers two examples of the latter process ("Loads of Love" and the title song), and the title song of *Do I Hear a Waltz?* offers yet another (see example 6.3a). Whether or not he was working from a lyric, Rodgers's first musical draft follows the rhythms

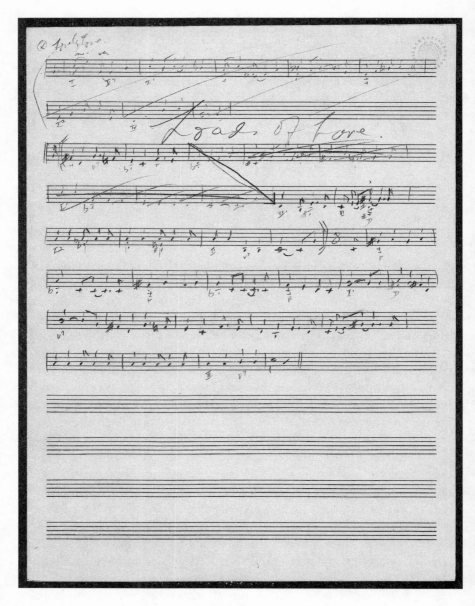

Rodgers's musical sketch for "Loads of Love" (*No Strings*)

Example 6.2. "Loads of Love" (sketch, chorus, first 8 measures)

of the eventual lyrics, even when the pitches are barely similar. Here is how he began to sketch "Loads of Love," first in facsimile and then partially transcribed (see opposite page and example 6.2).

In a second draft, Rodgers begins as he would in the final draft, but after two measures he breaks away into something unexpected and eventually unused. At the moment Rodgers reaches the tritone (G-sharp against a D in the sketch), six measures later, he gets back on track and continues where he left off on the future words "never have." From then on the song looks as it does today.

Do I Hear A Waltz?

Each of Rodgers's final four shows brought together considerable and much-tested talent. After working with Hart, an outstanding craftsman, Rodgers was not at all timid about trying to collaborate with the best of all possible lyricists and librettists—from Hammerstein, who served as both for *Show Boat* and for many of the most acclaimed operettas of the 1920s and early 1930s, to Harnick, the acclaimed lyricist of *Fiddler on the Roof*.[17] The playwright and librettist Arthur Laurents, in tandem with lyricist Sondheim, had happily joined composers Bernstein for *West Side Story* and Jule Styne for *Gypsy*, two enormous critical and popular successes. The year before *Waltz*, however, Laurents and Sondheim had experienced one of the worst commercial flops of their careers in *Anyone Can Whistle*, and for the next six years Sondheim was unable to mount a show in his preferred dual role as composer-lyricist. Despite this setback, the potential of a Laurents-Sondheim combination with Rodgers, who was fresh from a personal triumph with *No Strings*, was encouraging. Unfortunately, the singular collaboration of this talented triumvirate ended unhappily. Although a number of thoughtful critics, especially in recent years, have found much to praise in the result, all involved agree that the process was difficult and often unpleasant. In fact, the process may have led the central creators to overlook the merits and strengths of their unwanted and maligned offspring. Sondheim thought the whole idea was a mistake. Laurents (it was his play) and Rodgers thought the show a good idea gone awry. Few shows have been so disdained by their creators as *Do I Hear a Waltz?*

As with *No Strings*, the plot of *Do I Hear a Waltz?* concerns a "perfectly lovely couple" from diverse cultures, this time an unmarried American secretary for a high-powered advertising firm, Leona Samish (Elizabeth Allen), a "brightly attractive woman lost in her thirties" on vacation in Venice, and Renato di Rossi (Sergio Franchi), a middle-aged Italian shop owner, married with children. Leona and Renato meet and become infatuated with one another, but in the end their cultural values clash and they separate. The source of incompatibility changes from *No Strings* to *Waltz*, but in each case differences in cultural background and attitudes lead to the same conclusion. In contrast to the earlier musical, in which the principals at least contemplated a life together, it soon becomes clear in *Waltz* that Renato had in mind a no-strings relationship from the beginning, or, to use a later Sondheim lyric, a "moment in the woods," and that Leona has no interest in sustaining a relationship as the other woman (even if Renato is trapped in a loveless marriage in a culture that precludes divorce as an option). By the time Leona decides to momentarily settle for less and to "eat the ravioli," Renato has lost his appetite and is no longer emotionally receptive to a woman who could not "Take the Moment."

Throughout Rodgers's career, process as well as the results really mattered, and although he himself was sometimes considered demanding, critical, chary with praise, and unresponsive, even before Hammerstein's death, Rodgers was able to sustain productive and lasting relationships with a range of quirky creative collaborators. Florenz Ziegfeld and George M. Cohan stand virtually alone among the personalities who successfully thwart Rodgers's attempt at diplomacy in *Musical Stages*. It must not have been easy for Rodgers when he learned that the ghost of Hammerstein, Laurents, and Rodgers's daughter Mary, Sondheim's longtime friend, succeeded in making Sondheim feel he would be disloyal if he declined to work with another living composer legend. In the beginning, Sondheim's reluctance can be attributed to his desire to compose his own music. After the quick demise of *Anyone Can Whistle*, however, he was less likely to get such an opportunity. In the meantime he could, reluctantly, work with Rodgers. The result was a conflict of wills, egos, personalities, creative ideologies, and generational attitudes.

Most of this has been discussed, especially in the growing literature on Sondheim.[18] Here I focus on the contradictory artistic visions and values that divided the trio. Despite Sondheim's reluctance, however, the collaboration did get off to a good creative start. Even Rodgers recalled that he "worked closely and well" with Sondheim in the beginning and that they were able to work either words first or occasionally melody first. For his part, Sondheim publicly expressed the view that "the best man for this score is Dick."[19] Also at the beginning the lyricist and composer shared a common goal with the playwright and lyricist, in particular the decision to "purposely avoid the clichés that we could easily fall into with a story about an American tourist in Venice."[20] Musically this meant no tarantellas or other signifiers of Italian popular music—for example, the kind of music Porter wrote for the Renaissance portions of *Kiss Me, Kate,* or the music from the prominent Italian-American component in Loesser's *Most Happy Fella.*[21]

Problems began when the unified vision began to break down and the show fell below expectations. The main corrective action was the decision to add choreography to what had been a nondancing show. Thus the walking song, "Two By Two" (unrelated to the title song of Rodgers's next show *Two By Two*), was replaced by "Here We Are Again," a dance number staged by newly acquired choreographer Herbert Ross. A principal area of conflict reached a peak during the final stages: Elizabeth Allen's performance as Leona. Laurents thought that previous portrayals of this character in the original play *The Time of the Cuckoo* (Shirley Booth) and the film *Summertime* (Katharine Hepburn) were miscast—the actresses were older and more "spinsterish" than desirable. Although Allen fit what he was looking for visually, from the outset Laurents did not want to cast the vocally strong actress, the choice of Rodgers, who was the producer, and of John Dexter, the director. In Laurents's view, Allen's "acting sufficed but her persona was as cold as a knife and humorless."[22] Later, Rodgers too decided that Allen did not convey the necessary vulnerability and considered replacing her, but in the end he concluded that the fault rested more with the play than the actress.[23] Leona's unlikable predilection for alcohol and her eventual intoxication in *Cuckoo* also stayed. But Leona made herself unredeemably unsympathetic when, in this drunken state and out of anger and moral turpitude, she informed fellow American guest Jennifer (June in the play), Eddie's pretty young wife, that her husband had had a sexual encounter with the proprietress of their pensione, Signora Floria (Carol Bruce), on a gondola the night before.

In Rodgers's view, Leona's disclosure was the "fundamental problem with the story that I never realized until too late." Rodgers continues: "It wasn't only that Elizabeth Allen, the actress playing the heroine, was younger and less spinsterish than either Miss Booth or Miss Hepburn; it was simply that in a crucial scene in the second act the girl gets drunk and tells a young wife [Jennifer, played by Julienne Marie] that her husband [Eddie, played by Stuart Damon, Antipholus of Syracuse in the 1963 Off-Broadway revival of *The Boys from Syracuse* and *Cinderella*'s second television Prince] has had a dalliance with the owner of their *pensione*. I felt that this made the heroine unsympathetic and that audiences would not accept it, no matter what the provocation might have been, but despite my objection, Sondheim and Laurents were adamant about retaining the scene."[24]

In his autobiography, *Original Story By,* Laurents revisited the evolution of his work from *Cuckoo* (play) to *Summertime* (film) to *Waltz* (musical) and shed some new light on the show's history that helped explain his confrontation with Rodgers. In *The Time of the Cuckoo* the problem was Shirley Booth, a magnificent actress with one dramatic "flaw": an insatiable need for audiences to like her. For this reason Booth was unable, or at least unwilling, to unleash the fury that makes Leona so viciously expose Eddie and June's affair. Thirteen years later, much to Laurents's chagrin, this was the scene Rodgers wanted to take out. The script writers for *Summertime,* who did not include Laurents, left out the entire party scene. Hepburn fans could see an inhibited but likable woman make a quick exodus from romantic Venice to spare future involvement and hurt, but they did not see her drink too much or tell tales on her neighbors.

For Laurents, Leona's public embarrassment and "agony," made more piercing by her inebriated condition, explain and justify her outburst, making the party scene necessary and right. For Rodgers, the outburst led to the withdrawal of audience sympathy and interest in this character. Although I normally seek to avoid bias in favor of Rodgers, in this case he needs a public defender. Rodgers has frequently been accused of abusing his authority as the show's producer, but nobody mentions that in this case the producer allowed himself to be outvoted and agreed to keep the scene. In *Cuckoo,* June confronts Eddie about whether he has had an affair. At first Eddie lies, then he tells the truth, but in such a way that his wife has the option of believing

Librettist Arthur Laurents and lyricist Stephen Sondheim, with the composer at the piano, during the creation of *Do I Hear a Waltz?* (1965)

what she wants to believe. By omitting this scene in the musical, Leona's informing, now less prepared, is all the more despicable and devastating.

A major theme of both *Cuckoo* and *Waltz* is the collision between American and Italian attitudes.[25] Leona is depicted as a woman who appreciates the monetary value and status of a goblet. Signora Fioria appreciates its beauty: "But it is so lovely, what's the difference?" (if it is real or not). Renato may be an opportunistic lover, but he does know how to seize the moment and has long since concluded that when one can't have beefsteak, ravioli is not so bad, especially in Italy. Leona (Renato's latest meal) isn't that hungry, and in the end, metaphorically, she will end up going hungry when it comes to romance.

It was important to Laurents that Leona Samish *not* earn our sympathy. In *Anyone Can Whistle*, Laurents's previous collaboration with Sondheim, the librettist clashed with Angela Lansbury, who played a corrupt mayor. As Ethan Mordden phrased it, "She wanted to find some humor in the role, some style, but Laurents wanted only a creep."[26] Leona is more than a creep, and she does possess a sense of humor, but she is not especially endearing. Even without her drunken outburst it might have been a challenge to gain audience sympathy for a beautiful woman with romantic problems. Sondheim may have characterized Leona as a woman who can't sing (see below), and as we have already observed, a woman who knows only the cash value of a goblet and a woman who when in Rome (or Venice) will not do what the Italians do and "eat the ravioli."

Before leaving Leona, it may be relevant to note that informing and informers are central themes in Laurents's life and art. As late as *Jolson Sings Again* in the early 1990s, Laurents was grappling with why people like Elia Kazan and Jerome Robbins informed and how they rationalized their betrayals.[27] Leona, as played by Allen, may be an inhibited beauty, but more seriously she is an informer, and it for this reason Laurents felt that she deserves to lose our sympathy.

The clash between Laurents and Rodgers raises a number of difficult questions. How far should the creators of a play or musical be willing to go to allow a main character to show their flaws, their poor character, and unlikable deeds? Why do we have more tolerance for flawed characters in a play than for their musical counterparts? In his famous review of Rodgers and Hart's *Pal Joey* Brooks Atkinson asked "whether one could draw sweet water from a foul well."[28] Although it took a studio cast album and a revival in the early 1950s for the show to fully catch on, the original *Pal Joey* was actually a hit when it arrived on Christmas Day 1940 and held the Broadway stage for most of 1941. Seventeen years later, however, it still had to be sanitized in order to satisfy a Hollywood Production Code that did not look kindly on adultery, blackmail, run-of-the-mill two-timing, seedy nightclubs, or upscale dens of iniquity. That said, it is also arguable that Rodgers and Hart's Joey Evans had more socially redeeming values (and less offensive sexist language) than John O'Hara's *New Yorker* Joey and his exploitable "mice" (i.e., female prey). Rodgers and Hammerstein's Billy Bigelow is an accomplice to murder who hits his wife, but compared to his unrepentant, bullying, and nonmarrying literary counterpart in Molnár's *Liliom*, the musical Billy has some redeeming personal qualities (and is eventually redeemed in the afterworld). Furthermore, to his credit, in contrast to the insufferably pompous and "over bearin'" Enoch Snow, Billy never interrupts Julie Jordan in a song. In *No Strings*, the likable but weak David Jordan leaves the woman of his dreams, mainly because he can't discipline himself to work in Europe. Before *Waltz*, musical characters were expected to generate audience sympathy, or in any event more sympathy than their counterparts in a play. All this would change a few years later with the neurotic and self-absorbed characters that inhabit Sondheim's *Company*. But Rodgers in 1965 could not cross this line any more than Shirley Booth could in 1951.

Opening-night critics were not unfavorably disposed. At the same time, they were far from effusive. When a score is described as "agreeable but certainly short of world-shaking," one immediately senses that it is not regarded as another *Fiddler*. Howard Taubman concludes his opening-night review by faintly praising the work for its "self-restraint" and the "courage to abjure garishness and stridency." One week after proclaiming that *Waltz* lacked boldness and freshness and "is not a great musical," Taubman still thought that the work "is not a distinctive, new creation."[29] Walter Kerr clearly has some reservations about this "entirely serious and very dry musical about an American tourist who goes to Venice and doesn't have any fun." In his follow-up review, Kerr praises Rodgers for "his restiveness, his continued unwillingness to redo the last show that had succeeded, his voluntary surrender of the devices traditionally used to wake customers up" but concludes that "if a musical is going to be as serious as *Do I Hear a Waltz?* it has got to be more serious than *Do I Hear a Waltz?*—still richer in its insights, still more uncompromising in its way with words." In Kerr's view, Rodgers's "musical-comedy songs," while "generally of a high order," are out of place in a show that lies outside this genre.[30] As with so many musicals that fail to take flight, the book received the brunt of the criticism, even in the midst of laudatory remarks for everything else. Richard Watts's review in the *New York Post* exemplifies this view: "So winning in its score, lyrics, setting, cast, production, spirit and general atmosphere that it offers an evening of charming and tasteful entertainment despite certain strong reservations I have concerning the libretto by Arthur Laurents."[31]

A generation later, Sondheim authority Stephen Banfield, who devotes to *Waltz* only one paragraph of his monumental 450-page study of *Sondheim's Broadway Musicals*, writes that Rodgers "was past his prime and produced music that is generally unmemorable, more than once veering toward the wrong European country, overendowed with sententious parallel thirds rather than freely soaring melody, and almost entirely starved of the compound time gaiety its setting called for."[32] For Banfield, Leona's opening number, "Someone Woke Up," was rich in unfulfilled promise, and for the most part Rodgers substituted a "lackluster" score when the expressed intention was to produce something "touching and intimate." Judging *Waltz* by Sondheim's standards, Banfield sees the show as a failure.

A growing number of recent critics and historians express more positive assessments. Suskin considers the score as a whole "quite charming," singles out four songs that "all accomplish what they set out to with charm and grace" ("Moon in My Window," "Here We Are Again," "Take the Moment," and "Someone Woke Up"), and praises the "final sweeping waltz" of the title song.[33] Ken Mandelbaum, who discusses *Waltz* in his "Not Bad" chapter in his book of flops, thinks that unhappy memories harbored by Laurents, Rodgers, and Sondheim obscured their judgment and caused them to condemn the show unfairly. For Mandelbaum, "the score was excellent, with Rodgers in generally fine form and Sondheim in altogether superb form," and he cites five songs that "have never really received the recognition they deserve."[34] Martin Gottfried in *Sondheim* concludes that *Waltz* was "a dispirited affair, an unnecessary and processed musical, safe and predictable and heartless," but praises Rodgers for composing "some of his best songs in years."[35] According to Kurt Gänzl, in *Waltz* Rodgers "turned out one of the most appealing romantic-comic scores of his career."[36] Mordden, who proclaimed *No Strings* a "great show," finds *Waltz* to be "a wonderful show with a really lovely score."[37] In a more recent study Mordden, seconding Mandelbaum, concluded that *Waltz* "has suffered a bad rap from its surviving authors, lyricist Stephen Sondheim and book writer Arthur Laurents, and that their dissatisfaction seems based more on the miserable time they had work-ing with composer Richard Rodgers and director John Dexter than with any flaw in the composition."[38]

After thirty-five years of neglect and abuse of the show, Laurents, with the cooperation of Sondheim and the Rodgers and Hammerstein Organi-zation, created a revised and well-received *Do I Hear a Waltz?* that was produced at the George Street Playhouse in New Jersey in 2000. Another performance based on this new version at the Pasadena Playhouse the next year directed by David Lee led to a new recording with "warm hearted" and effusive notes by Lee and R&H Organization President Theodore S. Chapin.[39] The production and recording deleted "Bargaining," reordered "Here We Are Again" and "Someone Like You," and reinstated "Everybody Loves Leona," dropped during the tryouts.[40]

Peter Filichia, who also considers Rodgers's "very fine score" as first among the show's assets, suggests that people thinking of producing the show acquire Sondheim's original lyrics to "We're Gonna Be All Right," since they are "far more acerbic, witty, and interesting."[41] In an interview with his biog-rapher Meryle Secrest, Sondheim recalled that Rodgers, presumably at the urging of his wife, Dorothy, rejected the first draft for this song.[42] Sondheim gave him another lyric that was used in the show, the recording, and the vocal score. The original rejected lyrics turned up a decade later in *Side by Side by Sondheim* (1976) and can be heard in the cast recording of that show, as well as on the Pasadena Playhouse recording.[43] Both recordings also include the music and lyrics for a snappy verse that was regrettably dropped from the Broadway version. In the interview with Secrest, Sondheim ex-plains more about why Rodgers asked for a new lyric. "I wrote lyrics which had some bite to them and Dick Rodgers thought the song was wonderful. Next day he called a lunch and kept slamming the lyrics against his forearm and saying, 'This will not do, this will not do,' and I kept asking, 'Why?' The truth was, he'd shown the lyric to his wife and she did not like it. He prob-ably showed it to her out of enthusiasm. But you know, it's got stuff about sexuality in it." Secrest goes on to explain that to appease the "strait-laced" Dorothy Rodgers, Sondheim "had to remove the offending lines, but they were subsequently restored, and these are the ones that are always heard." In all likelihood the main offending lyric occurs in the final stanza:

> Sometimes she drinks in bed,
> Sometimes he's homosexual,

> But why be vicious?
> They keep it out of sight.
> Good show—
> They're gonna be all right.

Sondheim's original lyric is indeed funnier and more acerbic than the lyric that went into the show and was recorded on the cast album, and in my view constitutes an improvement that enriches Rodgers's catchy tune. At the same time, the depiction of Eddie as a bisexual seems misplaced. The problem faced by Jennifer and Eddie is that the latter has had an affair with Signora Fioria, a sensual woman who cheated on her husband with his best friend and was not loath to seize a no-strings sexual moment. The line in the song about Eddie's alleged homosexuality seems designed more to get a laugh than to add meaningfully to audience understanding.[44] As written, "We're Gonna Be All Right" seems perfect for a couple in *Company* (perhaps for the couple who sing of their askew marriage in "The Little Things You Do Together"). It is not necessary to bring Dorothy Rodgers into the picture to understand Rodgers's point. In any event, especially with the restored verse and lyrics, the song is a winner and a great Sondheim-Rodgers tune, and even in its original Broadway form full of the mischievous lyrical fun and musical insouciance that recall the good old days of Rodgers and Hart, and a welcome respite from an otherwise earnest evening.

To encapsulate the central artistic conflict and its resolution: over Rodgers's objections, Laurents and Sondheim insisted that Leona remain faithful to Laurents's original vision and inform on Eddie and Fioria. The librettist and lyricist prevailed over the composer-producer, who allowed himself to be outvoted. For good or ill, audiences would confront a deliberately unsympathetic Leona—not vulnerable enough, too pretty, too Ethel Merman. In his work with Hammerstein, Rodgers was often willing to incorporate unlikable aspects into their central characters. Leona may come across as morally sanctimonious, suspicious, and irritating (she can't resist calling everyone "Cookie"), but it is her purposefully hurtful action toward a troubled young married couple that seems especially destined to trouble future audiences. An informer's lot is not a happy one, and not "Everybody Loves Leona."

In contrast to *No Strings*, which marks a modernized return to the jazzier world of Rodgers and Hart, the music of *Do I Hear a Waltz?*, with the exception of "We're Gonna Be All Right," more often suggests the musical language of Rodgers with Hammerstein.[45] In particular, Renato's music, especially as sung by the trained operatic voice of Sergio Franchi, might be characterized as an Italianate tenor version of the quasi-operatic baritone of Billy Bigelow in *Carousel* and of course the full operatic basso of Ezio Pinza in *South Pacific*. And when audiences hear Leona sing "Someone Woke Up," they immediately know that this central character possesses a voice to match her mouth. This is not a song designed for Nellie Forbush.

The title song of *Waltz* (sketched in example 6.3a, final form in example 6.3b) captures the one Cinderella moment in the show.[46] Renato has given Leona the garnet necklace she desired, and instantly she hears and then sings a Viennese waltz (although geographically she remains in Venice). Although the feeling will soon perish, for a few minutes she has found her prince. To capture these feelings, Rodgers offers a song that does not simply sound like the waltz Cinderella's Prince sang shortly (very shortly) after meeting his future bride, "Ten Minutes Ago." In several crucial rhythmic, melodic, and harmonic respects Rodgers approximates not only the feeling but the music itself. By transposing "Do I Hear a Waltz?" in the same key as "Ten Minutes Ago" it should be easier to see as well as hear these connections (see example 6.3b–c).

Not only do both waltzes begin with a perfect fourth to mark the opening downbeats, the first phrase of both songs shares the entire pitch pool (D-G-D-C♯-D), albeit differently placed. The songs depart in several pitch and rhythmic details over the first A section, but by playing the bracketed material it should be possible to recognize the underlying fundamental similarities. In fact, "Do I Hear a Waltz?" constitutes more an ingenious transformation of a previous Rodgers song—that is, a stylish new model of a song classic.

Both songs also adopt a similar approach and set of musical ideas in the second A section. Instead of repeating their related opening eight-bar phrases, both present a string of quarter notes (nineteen in "Ten Minutes Ago" and twelve in "Waltz"), preceded in each case by an upbeat and a leap (an ascending major sixth and an ascending minor seventh, respectively) and concluding in each case with a held note of various lengths (four beats and nine beats) on the fifth degree of the scale. Especially telling is the unusual shared A minor seventh with an added eleventh on identical melodic resting places in measure seven of both songs. The differences are also revealing. His feelings secure, Cinderella's Prince is rhythmically solid, and his accents

Example 6.3. Leona Samish and Cinderella (a) "Do I Hear a Waltz?" (sketch, chorus, first 10 measures) (b) "Do I Hear a Waltz?" (chorus, first 8 measures [transposed from F major to G major]) (c) "Ten Minutes Ago" (chorus, first 8 measures)

occur in all the strong beats. Leona's feelings may be momentarily liberated, but her irregular accentuation belies an uncertainty and an inability to succumb to the accents of a traditional Viennese waltz. She is singing the Prince's song, but her latent neuroses make it her own.

In later years, Laurents acknowledged that it was a mistake for him to have persuaded Sondheim, his younger colleague and friend, to work on a show that he did not want to do. Laurents admits that he "behaved quite badly also," especially when he angrily left the first run-through to purchase a coat. But for Laurents, Rodgers remains the central villain. Laurents especially faults Rodgers's treatment of Sondheim, whom Rodgers had known since 1942, when the talented young lyricist was twelve years old, before he metamorphosed "from an attractive little boy to a monster."[47] Laurents was also genuinely disappointed with the results. His main criticism was what he perceived to be the show's blandness and absence of style. When Laurents writes that the lyric Rodgers described as "shit" in front of everyone ("Perfectly Lovely Couple") surpassed the tune in quality, one can infer he that thought Sondheim would have profited from a more forward-looking composer, no doubt Sondheim himself.[48] The bottom line for Laurents was that a good score could have redeemed the show, faults and all, but that Rodgers had failed to produce one. Laurents: "There was a song in *Waltz* called 'Stay' that always sounded to me like a lament from the Russian steppes. The first *note* bored me." It also probably did not help that Rodgers eventually barred Laurents from the theater when he tried to offer suggestions. Laurents concludes that everyone involved worked below their best and that the "whole thing was a mistake all the way around."[49]

Sondheim went on the record with the comment that he never thought the play should be musicalized, because "it's about a lady who, metaphorically, can't sing," a description that Laurents took issue with.[50] For Sondheim, *Do I Hear a Waltz?* falls into the category of "what Mary [Rodgers] calls a 'why' musical."[51] The kindest words he could muster about *Waltz* were that it was a "workmanlike, professional show." In the end Sondheim concluded with uncharacteristic harshness that "it deserved to fail." Sondheim got his wish. The show opened at the 46th Street Theatre on March 18 and closed 220 performances later.[52]

Two By Two

Not long after *Do I Hear a Waltz?* Rodgers returned to television for the third time in a decade.[53] The project on this occasion was a ninety-minute broadcast of *Androcles and the Lion*, based on Shaw's play. The broadcast featured Norman Wisdom as Androcles, Geoffrey Holder as the Lion, and Rodgers's old friend Noël Coward as Caesar. Unlike the oft-repeated telecast of the *Cinderella* remake two years earlier, the show aired one time only, on NBC, November 15, 1967. For the final time, Rodgers wrote the lyrics as well as the music for the required eight songs, and although the show was generally well received, from Rodgers's perspective the broadcast "didn't come off well, I'm afraid."[54] History seems to agree with Rodgers. As of this writing the published songs and original cast recording are out of print and no commercial videotape has been released.

Sometime in 1969, Martin Charnin, a lyricist who had not yet scored his success of a lifetime with *Annie* (1977), brought to Rodgers the idea of adapting Clifford Odets's final completed play, *The Flowering Peach* (1954), a retelling of the biblical story of Noah and the flood in which the characters expressed themselves with a modern sensibility and Yiddish repartee. As an actor, Charnin played Big Deal in the original Broadway production of *West Side Story*. He then wrote lyrics for several Off-Broadway revues and various unsuccessful projects, including *Hot Spot* (1963) with Mary Rodgers, through whom he met Rodgers. For the Noah libretto, Rodgers hired Peter Stone, who gained recognition for his screenplays for Cary Grant's last films *Charade* (1963) and *Father Goose* (1964) before writing the teleplay for *Androcles*. His major work on Broadway was the excellent book for the multi-award-winning historical musical *1776* (1969).[55]

Over the past dozen years the familiar Noah story had been the basis for Benjamin Britten's one-act children's opera, *Noye's Fludde* (1958), and Stravinsky's final work for the stage, *The Flood*, with miming, singing, dancing, and narration, broadcast on CBS television in 1962 and staged the following year. When Odets wrote his play it was a time when worried Americans were building bomb shelters in their yards and basements, and the parallels between the flood and potential nuclear destruction were palpable and immediately understood. In Stone's conception, adapted from Odets but with the Jewishness and Yiddishkeit toned down for a broader Broadway audience, the idea was to create a story that would appeal to an audience less fearful of a nuclear or other World War II–type holocaust.

In 1970, the generation gap (which is what Danny Kaye saw as the theme when he first discussed the idea of starring in the show), the nature of faith, and man's relationship with God provided opportunities for drama and humor. The success of *Fiddler on the Roof*, still running strong after six years, in which Tevye the Dairyman converses one-on-one with God, may have also been a factor in the decision to set the ancient biblical story. In any event, Kaye, as Noah, talks and sings to God every bit as much as Zero Mostel and his successors in the earlier role. Not long into the show, for example, the 600-year-old, somewhat hard-of-hearing Noah asks God to clarify his messages: "You want us to build a *what?*" "Forty days and forty *what?!!*" In the opening song, "Why Me?," Noah runs through the other possible candidates to build an ark and round up two of every species, and in the course of the song he reluctantly comes to understand that God is right. To his surprise and chagrin Noah realizes that, strange as it may seem, he is "the best of the lot."

The biblical Noah had three married sons, Shem (Harry Goz, formerly a Tevye), Ham (Michael Karm), and Japheth (Walter Willison). In *Two By Two* the characters have stronger individual profiles than they did in the Bible, and both Odets's and Stone's book take liberties with the biblical Ur-text. In Stone's version, only the spiritually challenged Shem is happily married, and his wife, Leah, joins him in hoarding manure on the boat for future profit. The middle son, Ham, is unhappily married to Rachel (Tricia O'Neil). Rachel secretly loves the rebellious youngest son, Japheth, who challenges God's morality and Noah's authority and has to be literally knocked out before his family can get him onto the boat. Before the flood, Japheth meets Goldie (Madeline Kahn), a gentile, whom he invites on board as a possible mate. Also before the flood, which begins at the end of act I and, through sound effects, continues during intermission, Japheth lets Rachel know that he loves his brother's wife in "I Do Not Know a Day I Did Not Love You" and discovers that she returns his love. During the course of the deluge and its aftermath, Ham and Goldie fall in love. Given the blessing of Noah's wife, Esther (Joan Copeland), shortly before her death ("Hey, Girlie"), Ham and Rachel resolve to divorce amicably, paving the way for a marriage between Japheth and Rachel.

Noah may get all the laughs in such comic numbers as "Why Me?" and "Ninety Again!," the latter celebrating the fact that God restored a portion of Noah's youthful vigor, but Rodgers's musical sympathies seem to lie with Rachel and Japheth's love for one another. Midway through act I, Rachel, married for 5 years, shares her unhappiness with Esther, Noah's bride of 121 years, who replies that 5 years is a "long time to be unhappy." Rachel then sings her big number, "Something Doesn't Happen," a song about her loveless marriage.[56]

The song is simple, direct, and effective. The A sections of the chorus (A-A-B-A) introduce a repeated two-bar melody, each beginning with the word "something" ("Something isn't there / Something isn't good / Something doesn't happen"), and each moving down a step from the previous phrase before culminating in a cadence on the repeated "that should, that should" (see example 6.4a). As throughout his career, Rodgers offers a surprise note here and there, even within this predictable pattern. The G-sharp on the second measure forms the third degree of a dominant seventh on E to cre-

Example 6.4. "Something Doesn't Happen" (a) chorus, first A section (mm. 1–9) (b) chorus, final A section and extension (mm. 25–36)

ate the kind of II-V-I (E-A-D) progression reminiscent of "Loads of Love" but without the syncopation. In the final A section (see example 6.4b) the E functions as its own dominant preparation and makes this note itself a point of arrival and the climax of the song on the word "day" in the eighth measure. The song concludes, unusually, with a four-measure extension that returns to the G-sharp and a conventional II-V-I progression in the key of D major.

It is late in act I that Japheth informs Rachel that, to protest God's merciless decision to destroy human life, he will not join his family on the ark. He then shares the real reason: the burden of having to live in close quarters with her. Japheth's song to Rachel, "I Do Not Know a Day I Did Not Love You," is the song most often singled out as attaining Rodgers's previous standards. Walter Kerr goes as far as to rank it as "one of the very best, surely, that Mr. Rodgers has ever written."[57] One striking feature in the song

Example 6.5. "I Do Not Know a Day I Did Not Love You" (chorus, first 8 measures)

recalls a technique that Rodgers employed in "The Blue Room," from *The Girl Friend* (1926) (see example 1.3). In the earlier song, the downbeat of the first five measures of each A section falls on middle C. On measures 2, 3, and 4 of the first A Hart offers the rhyming "*blue* room," "*new* room," and "for *two* room." For the other A sections Hart selects a new rhyme to mark the downbeats on repeated pitches. Rodgers follows each pivot tone with a rising scale starting on F. By the fifth measure the scale catches up to the pivot and every note is a high C to match the line "ev'ry day's a hol-(i-day)." Interestingly, by the time Rodgers returns to the middle C in the eighth measure, it sounds fresh. In the A section, the scale occurs on the offbeat surrounded by the C wedge. The B sections are devoid of any such subterfuge.[58]

"I Do Not Know a Day I Did Not Love You" (example 6.5) offers its variant of "Blue Room" within an expansion of the standard thirty-two-bar form, now a forty-eight-bar melody, A-B-A'-A'-B-A', in which each letter represents eight bars. In the first half of each A section, the wedge notes on B-flat fall twice each measure while the words "not," "a," "I," and "not" again all fall on the offbeats 2 and 4. The scale descends mainly by half steps, G-flat on "do," F on "know," E-flat on "day," E-double flat on "did," ending on D-flat for "love you." The second half of each A keeps the B-flats on the offbeats but reverses the ascending scale, this time unwaveringly by half steps, Db-D-Eb-E ending the section on a prolonged F.

Other points of contrast between "Blue Room" and "I Do Not Know" include the absence of internal rhymes throughout and repeated notes at the climax in the latter song. Since it takes four measures simply to sing "I Do Not Know a Day I Did Not Love You," opportunities for rhyming are few, despite the extended length ("there" and "hair" between the first A and

B, "spent" and "meant" between the next pair of A's, and "song" and "along" between the final B and A'). In "Blue Room," Rodgers uses repeated note C's as a climax to the wedged C's and the ascending scale. In "I Do Not Know" Rodgers uses repeated notes prominently only in the B section to create a broader sectional contrast. Although Rodgers is clearly borrowing from a long-familiar technique, he is trying to do and say something new in his advanced age.

Perhaps to a greater degree than even *The Sound of Music*, throughout *Two By Two*, especially in Noah's music, Rodgers writes with a simplicity that borders on the simplistic. Case in point is the three-note pattern that pervades the verse of "You Have Got to Have a Rudder on the Ark," a song in which Noah, at the outset a strict constructionist, does not allow for a human interpretation of the word of God, especially in the song's verse: "If God would have wanted a rudder, / Then God would have said 'Make a rudder,'" and since he didn't, "There ain't gonna be any rudder." In act II, when the ark is certain to sink (if matters were left up to God), Noah finally decides that God wants humans to assume some responsibility for their own safety and asks his son Japheth to put on a rudder.

The simple but dynamic conclusion of Noah's final song, "The Covenant," bears a strong melodic, rhythmic, and harmonic resemblance and evokes the boisterous tone of the coda of "There's Nothing Like a Dame." In contrast, Noah in "Hey, Girlie" expresses his grief at the imminent loss of Esther with a simplicity and reverence that evokes the hymnlike songs that Rodgers wrote with Hart, especially "Nobody's Heart" from *By Jupiter*, and the anthems that he wrote with Hammerstein, like *Carousel*'s "You'll Never Walk Alone." For the first sixteen measures, the supporting harmony is an unwavering pedal tone on G, and the melody in the second half of each A section consists entirely of scales and repeated notes. Rodgers introduces each A section with a downward leap of a minor seventh (B down to a C-sharp) resolving upward by a half step to the sixth (D). Throughout his long career Rodgers frequently followed a large descending leap with an ascending half-step resolution. The technique appears as early as Rodgers's first published song, "Auto Show Girl" in 1917 (see example 1.1a) and as late as the verse of "Ev'ry Day" (*I Remember Mama*), one of the composer's final songs. After avoiding the practice through most of thirty-five years, however, Rodgers would return to this device regularly in each of his final quintet of shows (for example, "Nobody Told Me" in *No Strings*, "Take the Moment" in *Waltz*, and *Rex*'s "Away from You," in which Rodgers inserts intervening pitches to obscure and soften the fall of the leaps), in addition to "Hey, Girlie," to name only the most prominent examples.[59]

Despite these musical high points, some of which were acknowledged by reviewers, not everyone was satisfied. As expected, the book received most of the critical abuse. Not surprisingly, the book writer, Stone, offered another explanation of why "the show didn't work": "Every one of us was working on a different show. Charnin and I were doing one show, which was the Odets concept of Noah's family being a lower-middle-class Jewish family from Queens. Rodgers wanted something less Jewish, less lower class, more lyrical, which was his experience. Layton [director Joe Layton] wanted stage magic and brought in concepts that only hurt the show. And Danny Kaye was interested in being Danny Kaye, and why shouldn't he be? That's where his security was, right? He wanted up-front, downstage Danny Kaye numbers, so he never really played too well with the rest of the company."[60]

Kaye was a successful movie singer and comedian in the 1940s and '50s. Among his most memorable comic film roles was the lead in *The Court Jester*; he also memorably played leading roles in Loesser's *Hans Christian Andersen* and Berlin's *White Christmas*. In the late 1960s Kaye hosted a popular television variety series. But he had not appeared on Broadway since 1941, the year he played the androgynous photographer Russell Paxton and sang, with astonishing rapidity, a list of rhyming Russian composers in *Lady in the Dark* ("Tschaikowsky," with lyrics by Ira Gershwin and music by Weill). Later that year he played in Porter's *Let's Face It* and sang "Let's Not Talk About Love" and special material provided by his wife, Sylvia Fine Kaye, "Melody in Four F."

Largely on the basis of Kaye's star quality—his name was placed in capital letters above the title—ticket sales for *Two By Two* were exceptionally strong. Most of the opening-night critics praised Kaye above all else. Clive Barnes called it "Mr. Kaye's show," and Richard Watts advised his readers that the show was "worth seeing if only for his memorable performance." Future Kaye biographer Martin Gottfried, who had nothing positive to say about Rodgers's "unmemorable" score, expressed the minority view that Kaye, although "unusually credible as Noah," lacked "charisma" and presence and was vocally "weak."[61]

In *Musical Stages* Rodgers devotes less than a full page to *Two By Two*, at the time his most recent musical. After recalling his initial confidence in the show, which "called for a bravura performance" that Kaye could provide, Rodgers focuses on the sad saga of a performer who behaved unpro-

Joe Layton (the director) with Danny Kaye (the star) and the composer on the set of *Two By Two* (1970)

fessionally after a torn ligament forced him to perform from a wheelchair for most of the show's run. Among Kaye's stage antics (not all mentioned by Rodgers) were attempts to run down fellow actors with his wheelchair, unzipping Esther's dress, goosing other female cast members with his crutch, ad-libbing, taking inappropriate tempo liberties, and even making derogatory speeches to the audience after the curtain. Since Kaye's response to criticism was to sulk and slow down, which was even worse than the cutting up, Rodgers "reluctantly said nothing."[62] Just as Rodgers's experience with *I'd Rather Be Right* had been sullied by the ad-libbing and disrespectful behavior of George M. Cohan thirty-three years earlier, the residue of *Two By Two* was a "sour taste," and "not because of the mixed reception (it ran almost a year and showed a small profit), but because of Danny's behavior after the show had opened in New York." Had Kaye been dismissed the show would have almost certainly closed before it had time to make its money back. In any event, the show closed when Kaye did. It was grim consolation, but thanks to Kaye, *Two By Two*, alone among Rodgers's final four shows, escaped a place in Ken Mandelbaum's critical survey of failed shows, *Not Since Carrie: Forty Years of Broadway Musical Flops*.

The fate of *Two By Two* (and later *Rex* and *I Remember Mama*) is not dissimilar to that of even the popular shows that Rodgers wrote with Hart. Shows almost invariably introduced two or more songs that would enter the repertory, and perhaps gain canonic status, while the book was dismissed as serviceable but mediocre. As with Rodgers's final trilogy, a number of Rodgers and Hart shows—for example, *Simple Simon* with Ed Wynn or *I'd Rather Be Right* with Cohan—also attained some of their ephemeral popularity by featuring stars. After first casting relative unknowns in *Oklahoma!* and *Carousel*, Rodgers and Hammerstein were not averse to building a show around one or more stars, Ezio Pinza and Mary Martin in *South Pacific*, Gertrude Lawrence in *The King and I*, Martin again in *The Sound of Music*. But although the perfection of *South Pacific*'s original cast may have been a factor inhibiting New York stage revivals, these shows do not rely on a star the way *Simple Simon* depended on the special zany talents of Wynn. After fifty years in the business, Rodgers had gone a full cycle. Once again his shows featured great songs and a great star in a show that was destined to be forgotten.[63]

Rex

On April 25, 1976, six years after Danny Kaye celebrated the final performance of *Two By Two* by throwing away his crutch and bounding out of the Imperial Theatre, *Rex* made its ill-fated debut at the Lunt-Fontanne with Nicol Williamson, another talented but extraordinarily difficult actor, in the central role of Henry VIII. According to director Edwin Sherin, Williamson, who was experiencing marital and drinking problems, participated only halfheartedly in rehearsals and showed "contempt for the writing, which was perhaps justified." His most notorious action, however, occurred on stage during curtain calls, when he heard Jim Litton's "it's a wrap" as "it's crap" and hit the dancer in the face in front of the audience.[64] Before *Rex*, Williamson had been nominated for a Tony Award in *Inadmissible Evidence* (1966) and had achieved acclaim as Hamlet, also on stage. The same year as

Rodgers rehearsing *Rex* (1976) with Nicol Williamson (King Henry VIII)

Rex he appeared as Sherlock Holmes in the popular film *The Seven-Per-Cent Solution.*

In addition to Williamson, *Rex* offered a promising new collaboration with Sheldon Harnick (b. 1924), the lyrical half of Bock and Harnick, the team that created the Pulitzer Prize–winning musical biography of LaGuardia, *Fiorello!* (1959), the frequently revived *She Loves Me* (1963), and one of the most successful musicals of the post–Rodgers and Hammerstein era, *Fiddler on the Roof* (1964). After a famously troubled tryout period in Wilmington, Delaware (February 23–29), Washington, D.C. (March 4–20), and Boston (March 23–April 10), *Rex* closed within weeks of its New York opening on April 25, after only forty-nine performances. It was Rodgers's worst failure since *Chee-Chee* in 1928.

What went wrong? All fingers point to the producer, Richard Adler (b.

1921), best known as the co-lyricist–composer responsible for the back-to-
back hits with Jerry Ross (1926–55): *The Pajama Game* (1954) and *Damn
Yankees* (1955). In his autobiography *You Gotta Have Heart,* Adler acknowledges culpability and explains how a promising idea metamorphosed into
a disaster.[65] Aside from not closing the show in Wilmington, Adler reflects
that his biggest mistake was the decision not to pay director-choreographer
Michael Bennett his asking price. Unfortunately, Hal Prince and Jerome
Robbins were unavailable at any price. If one accepts the notion that Rodgers
and Harnick had the potential to succeed with a musical depiction of Henry
VIII's dramatic life, the absence of a director with the experience and imagination of Bennett, who directed *A Chorus Line* instead, proved to be an
insurmountable obstacle. Since the Shuberts' offer to invest $150,000 was
contingent on hiring him as director, the decision not to pay the full sticker
price for Bennett ended up costing Adler financially as well as artistically.
Adler ended his search by hiring Ed Sherin, who had successfully directed
the play *The Great White Hope* in 1968. Three years before *Rex,* in his first
and last attempt at a musical, *Seesaw,* Sherin had been replaced by Bennett. Jerome Lawrence and Robert E. Lee, authors of the popular historical
play about the Scopes "Monkey" Trial, *Inherit the Wind* (1955), and Jerry
Herman's hit musical *Mame* (1966), had failed in the their next Herman
outing, *Dear World* (1969). Unable to complete a book for *Rex* to Adler's
satisfaction, Lawrence and Lee were replaced by Sherman Yellen, whose
previous credits included an appearance among the contributors to the revue *Oh! Calcutta!* and most recently *The Rothschilds,* the troubled musical
that permanently severed the working relationship of Bock and Harnick in
1970. At the end of the preproduction phase Adler was able to assemble his
first choice of composer and lyricist, his second choice of librettist, his third
choice of director, and, according to Suskin, his fifth choice of star (after
Richard Burton, Peter O'Toole, Albert Finney, and another Rex, Rex Harrison, turned him down).[66]

The choice to base a musical on Henry VIII, King of England from 1509
to 1547, was ostensibly a good idea. Henry was a handsome, athletic, and
brilliant man, and his life had more than its share of political and romantic entanglements. He was also a successful part-time composer, a talent
that could be put to use in a musical ("No Song More Pleasing"). After
forty years, Charles Laughton's famous characterization in *The Private Life
of Henry VIII* (1933) remained unforgettable. Thirty years later, Henry VIII
(played by Robert Shaw) had figured prominently in the Academy Award–

winning film *A Man for All Seasons* (1966), which revolved around the king's stormy relationship with Sir Thomas More (Paul Scofield). Another popular film, *Anne of the Thousand Days* (1969), based on Maxwell Anderson's 1948 Broadway play with Rex Harrison, had focused on the romance between Henry (Burton) and Anne Boleyn, played by the young Oscar-nominated French-Canadian actress Geneviève Bujold. A six-part series featuring Keith Michell, *The Six Wives of Henry VIII*, appeared with much fanfare on public television in 1972. While not quite approaching the sheer number of *Titanic* spin-offs in the late 1990s (books, movies, television specials, and a Tony Award–winning musical), Henry's prospects remained bright for musical treatment, especially with a Rodgers and Harnick score. On the other hand, Henry VIII's behavior made Leona Samish look positively saintly in comparison. Although Henry—the character, not the actor playing him— became progressively nicer during the tryout period, the task of transforming an adulterer, murderer, and sexist pig into a character audiences would want to cheer remained one of several unsolvable problems for Henry VIII, the musical, known as *Rex*.

Although *Rex* explores Henry's troubled relationships with Wife No. 1, Catherine of Aragon, and her successor, Anne Boleyn, the central issue of the musical is the king's desire for a son. The historical Henry had reason to worry that the absence of a legitimate male could put the still relatively short-lived Tudor dynasty in jeopardy. A disputed succession was at the heart of the War of the Roses (1454–85) between the houses of York and Lancaster that preceded the reign of his father, Henry VII. Long before the end of the sixteenth century it was clear that a woman, Elizabeth I (reigned 1558–1603), who figures prominently but arguably too late in act II of *Rex*, could lead England to a political and cultural peak. Before Elizabeth I, Catherine the Great of Russia, England's Queen Victoria, and India's Indira Gandhi, the latter reigning contemporaneously with Nicol Williamson's Henry, political pragmatists did not give women much of a chance to lead a country unchallenged. Unfortunately, *Rex*'s Henry failed to make a case to support his fears. In the aftermath of Kate Millett's *Sexual Politics* and Germaine Greer's *The Female Eunuch* and a growing consciousness of social and political equality for women, a man who recognizes the superiority of his daughter to govern but who remains unable to think outside the box is clearly at odds with 1970s sensibilities. Despite attempts to transform Henry into a nice guy, his fundamental misogyny would prove overwhelming.

Reviewers found much to malign. The highest mark earned among Suskin's six New York critics was an "unfavorable," and the rest were "pans." Again the book took the greatest hit, but few involved escaped unscathed. Several critics mentioned the unsuccessful attempt at capturing the presumed earthy (gross) humor of Renaissance England. Here is a sample of some dialogue that appears in the mouth of Henry's fool, Will Somers, in the "unrevised first rehearsal script" from December 23, 1975.

A punny riposte to Cardinal Wolsey:

> WILL: Everyone knows that lechery is a *cardinal* sin. (I-3)

A randy rhyme:

> HENRY: Give me the chance to talk and test their wits.
> WILL (to his hand puppet): Give him the chance to gawk and grab their tits. (I-2)

And some ribald locker-room talk:

> COMUS [Court Wizard and Astrologer]: The Magic Heart cannot deceive. It cannot flatter. It will not lie. It may tell you the three words every ardent lover longs to hear from his lady—"She loves me." Or it may tell the four dreaded words a lover fears most from his mistress—
> HENRY: "She loves me not." (HE counts words on his four fingers)
> WILL: No, Harry—(HE throws himself suggestively against COMUS' table and in the high-pitched voice of a wanton wench:) "Is it really in?" (I, 18–19)

Most critics did not blame the failure of *Rex* on the musical messenger. Barnes is the exception rather than the rule when he accused Rodgers of composing "airy-fairy madrigals, lute-songs jazzed up for a Broadway orchestra, a sort of mixture of Benjamin Britten and Irving Berlin"—in the postmodern era such a combination might be viewed more favorably—"with the somewhat sad result that we appear to be hearing an anthology of songs from *Camelot* that were ditched on the road."[67] More typical is Kerr, also of the *Times*, who found "at least two sweet songs that seem to have escaped the show's textbook blight" ("No Song More Pleasing" and "Elizabeth"). Kerr blamed Yellen and Harnick for "loading Rodgers down with expository work, asking him to fashion into chorded structures all of the information that ought to have been incorporated into the book, or sent back, its dust intact, to the British Museum."[68] At least three reviewers, including two who probably were not taken into account in Suskin's Scorecard, were laudatory about the Rodgers and Harnick score. Writing in *Newsday*, George Oppenheimer characterized the music as "supremely melodic, helped enormously by the literate lyrics of Sheldon Harnick" and "the finest music Rodgers has composed since *The Sound of Music.*"[69] Martin Gottfried, past leader of the opposition to Rodgers and Hammerstein and, like most reviewers, critical of *Rex*'s book, proclaimed that Rodgers "has provided his finest score since *No Strings*" and that "here, once more, were lilting, surprising melodies, singing out with no apologies to current musical theater sophistication, nor any need for them."[70] Theodore E. Kalem in *Time* wrote that "Rodgers is incapable of writing an uningratiating tune," but he faulted the music's suitability for the show at hand.[71]

Howard Kissel in *Women's Wear Daily* is the only critic who mentioned the striking dissonant harmonic clash (A-flat against an A-natural, the major and minor thirds in F major), ironically on the alternating French and English words "eternal harmony/l'harmonie éternelle," "unending concord/la concord immortelle," "abiding amity/l'amitié continuelle," and "lasting peace/la paix perpetuelle" before additional bilingual contrapuntal lines bring "The Field of Cloth of Gold" to an exciting conclusion. It is possible that Kissel's review appeared beneath Suskin's radar screen. In any event, it certainly does not fall into the "unfavorable" or "pan" category. In fact, it is close to a "rave" and certainly "favorable." Although Kissel accuses Yellen's book of conventionality, "full of easy laughs and, probably to set a 16th-Century tone, some phony bawdiness," he also finds much to praise in the book in addition to the other dimensions of this show, including the lyrics, cast, sets, and costumes. This is what Kissel wrote about Rodgers's music, which he describes as "a score with integrity": "As for the beautiful and dramatically knowing score, it has two songs worthy of inclusion in the canon of Rodgers classics—'Away from You' and 'As Once I Loved You.' It has a ballad, 'No Song More Pleasing,' that shows Rodgers is still the master of the long, haunting melodic line and a choral number ["The Field of Cloth of Gold"] that shows his skill at creating dramatic dissonance."[72]

In a striking group portrait of three unusual contemporaries, Sondheim's *Pacific Overtures*, Bernstein and Lerner's *1600 Pennsylvania Avenue*, and *Rex*, Irving Kolodin seems to have seen a different show from most of the New York critics quoted above. Actually, he did see a different show, the Wilmington preview, before Prince and other doctors tried to cure what was perceived as a seriously ailing patient. His only significant criticism was the "over-extended first act." Kolodin most definitely thought the show was destined to succeed. In fact, he went out on a critical limb when he prophesied that "it will, without question, be a reputation-maker for many in the large cast." He devoted particular attention to "one sustained stretch, a gush of vintage Rodgers from the vintner's own private stock, in a setting of prime Harnick verse." The first song in a trio of the "best individual items the composer has written in years" was "From Afar," the song in which "Henry laments the separation from his daughter, and recognizes that she is probably better suited to rule England than is the softer, childish Edward." Next came "In Time," in which Elizabeth shares Henry's private thoughts. With a breathtaking absence of prescience Kolodin predicted that the final song, "The Pears of Anjou," "is destined, certainly, for inclusion in Rodgers's own Top 40."[73] What happened instead was that "The Pears of Anjou," included in the "unrevised first rehearsal script" the previous December, soon vanished from Rodgers's Top 900 songs. Because it died on the road it was understandably but unfortunately omitted from the cast recording and also from the vocal score that was prepared in early 1976. The death of a king, even a king who manages to sing while dying, might strike some as uncomfortably close to the death of Siam's leader at the end of *The King and I*. Nevertheless, "The Pears of Anjou" makes a powerful finale to *Rex*, and it poetically prepares for the future rule of his daughter Elizabeth, fruit of Henry's kingship, a true renaissance.

Rex offers a fairly reliable historical portrait worthy of Will Durant's *Story of Civilization*, as well as many accurate dramatic details suitable for the stage, such as when Francis throws Henry in a wrestling match at the Field of Cloth of Gold. But does Henry need to give a history lesson in the song "Why?," which in any event shares an unfortunate rhythmic resemblance, minor mode (always unusual for Rodgers), and even pitch contour with the eighteenth-century Christmas carol "God Rest You Merry Gentlemen"? The show might also profit from the deletion of "The Chase," sung by Comus, Will, Smeaton, and Gentlemen of the Court. We know that Henry is a womanizer. Why rub it in? In any event, the musical weight of the show already skews dangerously away from Henry and toward his fool and other minor characters.

Near the end of his confessional, Adler expressed his recognition, "in hindsight, that Elizabeth was *the* fascinating person about whom the musical should have been written about in the first place." Perhaps a revised libretto could make Elizabeth more central. Although she gets the last word (and song, "In Time"), her dramatic confrontation with Henry unfortunately goes unsung and therefore conveys much less emotional impact.

Sheldon Harnick (*Rex*'s lyricist) and Rodgers

Anne Boleyn in act I and Elizabeth in act II are not only played by the same actress, Penny Fuller, but they also share musical material. The first of these songs, however, "So Much You Loved Me," a love duet between Anne and Henry, was, according to Stanley Green's R&H *Fact Book* and a typed song list in the Library of Congress Collection, dropped before the New York opening (although it appears on the cast recording). In act II, the song reprises with a new set of lyrics that express Henry's love and respect for his spirited daughter Elizabeth, privately and "From Afar," lyrics that do not bear a meaningful relationship to the dramatic context of "So Much You Loved Me." It might have helped if Elizabeth could have sung this reprise to or with Henry, but what Elizabeth really needs is another song of her own. The undernourished second act could definitely support more music for her. Years later Harnick came to the view that the problem with "The Pears of Anjou" and two other songs could be traced to their musical accompaniments.[74] Despite these wrong notes, the by no means problem-free *Rex* nonetheless remains worthy of the name Rodgers and Harnick. The show might have profited from the services of Bennett or Hammerstein, but even without them the endangered show deserves to be saved—with some creative editing—from extinction.

Unfortunately, as of this writing no script or score of *Rex* is available for purchase or rental.[75] All that remains is the Original Cast recording, transferred to CD in the 1990s with a reprint of Mort Goode's detailed summary notes from the original LP and a reliable new overview by Bert Fink, vice president for public relations at R&H, who admits to having seen *Rex* at the Boston tryouts. Twice.[76] While my purpose here is not to defend *Rex* as a neglected masterpiece, I do feel that Rodgers's penultimate Broadway musical contains some excellent material, including a potentially workable book, and that the show merits a concerted effort to salvage it.

I Remember Mama

In 1943, Kathryn Forbes published her autobiographical short stories about her immigrant Norwegian family struggling to survive during hard economic times in the San Francisco of 1910 and 1911, first in *Reader's Digest* and then as a book, *Mama's Bank Account*. Shortly thereafter, Dorothy Rodgers came up with the idea of adapting the stories for the stage. The resulting play by John Van Druten, *I Remember Mama* (1944), the first production of Rodgers and Hammerstein Inc., starring Mady Christians as Mama, Oscar Homolka as Uncle Chris, and Marlon Brando in his stage debut as Nels, enjoyed an extremely long run for a play, 714 performances. A successful tour, a film (1946), and a long-running television series (1949–56) followed.

The Broadway version of these stories, *I Remember Mama*, which premiered on May 31, 1979, at the Majestic, was Rodgers's last new musical. It was preceded by a tryout hell that surpassed those of Lew Fields in the 1920s at his most desperate. Mandelbaum astutely summarizes some of these travails in *Not Since Carrie*.[77] One day after the Philadelphia tryout the producers Alexander H. Cohen and Hildy Parks fired the director, Charnin (replaced by Cy Feuer), and the lyricist, who also happened to be Charnin (replaced by Raymond Jessel). Soon, Danny Daniels replaced the original choreographer, Graciela Daniele (no relation). Unfortunately, neither personnel changes nor changes in the book and score could salvage deeper artistic and production problems, which for many critics started with the Swedish actress Liv Ullmann in the title role. By nearly all accounts Ullmann,

Liv Ullmann (Mama), lyricist Martin Charnin, and Rodgers during the
creation of *I Remember Mama* (1979)

who had captivated moviegoers in a series of films by the great Swedish director Ingmar Bergman, could neither sing nor dance, and she appeared
generally uncomfortable in a musical. Gerald Bordman writes: "Anyone remembering Mady Christians or Charlotte Greenwood (who headed the road
company) or Irene Dunne (of the film version) had to blanch watching this
new Mama, who was not only patently too young and beautiful, but con-
veyed nothing of the warmth, wisdom or selfless dedication her predecessor had broadcast across the footlights."[78] Ironically, only a few years before
the decision to cast her in *I Remember Mama*, Rodgers saw Ullmann in
A Doll's House at Lincoln Center. On this occasion Dorothy Rodgers apparently asked her husband when its author, Henrik Ibsen, had died. The
composer replied, "Tonight."[79]

To smooth the episodic short stories into a continuous dramatic narrative, Thomas Meehan developed the idea of creating a marital and family
conflict at the end of the first act.[80] In Meehan's scenario, Papa leaves his

family without consultation to take a job in Norway, but Mama and the children refuse to join him there. In contrast to most musical romances, classically embodied in the story of *Oklahoma!*'s Curley and Laurie, who manage to resist each other until the second act, Mama and Papa Hansen clearly and demonstrably love each other at the outset ("You Could Not Please Me More"). Before the musical is over, the adoring Norwegian pair, however, touchingly and independently realize they must be together, even if they have to cross the Atlantic Ocean to accomplish this. The principal conflict is thus poverty and joblessness rather than character and personality. The Hansen home is full of harmony—the children miraculously abstain from internecine sibling rivalry, and every day we hear the sound of music ("Ev'ry Day [Comes Something Beautiful]" and "Mama Always Makes It Better").[81]

Uncle Chris is patriarchal, a bigot, and a drunk, but he is also funny and fundamentally good-hearted. Musical characters almost invariably are kinder, gentler, warmer, and fuzzier versions of their sources. The exception is Uncle Chris (George Irving). In the musical, as in the play and stories, he is quick to help Dagmar get to the hospital for her appendicitis, but in the musical Chris dies embittered, having squandered his wealth. In the stories and the play (but not the musical) readers and audiences learn along with his family that for years Chris has devoted a considerable portion of his wealth to operations that cure handicapped children.

The music of *I Remember Mama* goes beyond the simplicity standard set by certain songs in *The Sound of Music* or *Two By Two*. Most of the melodies, written either for children or for an actress who could not sing, fall within narrow ranges and avoid extremes of high and low. Many of the songs contain repetition of rhythms and single notes ("A Little Bit More") or short sequential phrases with slight chromatic alterations ("You Could Not Please Me More"). With the exception of "Easy Come, Easy Go," which evokes ragtime, the melodies carefully eschew the American vernacular. Two second-act songs mark a return to traditional old-world (but not necessarily Norwegian) waltzes, "Fair Trade" and "Time." In a striking example of coming full circle, one song was reported to have been borrowed from the opening number of Rodgers's first amateur show, *One Minute Please*, which opened and closed at the Akron Club on December 29, 1917. No specific song has been identified, but by a strange stroke of cyclic history "Auto Show Girl," Rodgers's first published song, shares some noticeable rhythmic and melodic features with the ersatz Norwegian "Lullaby" (sung in Norwegian to the music of "Ev'ry Day").[82]

We earlier mentioned two musical allusions to non-Rodgers shows in *No Strings*. Perhaps inadvertently but not less intriguingly, *I Remember Mama* pointedly recalls the lyrics to two recent and more successful Broadway shows. Although neither was composed by Rodgers, the references suggest Rodgers's later lyricists, Harnick and Charnin himself. Near the end of the evening, Mama realizes that her seventeen-year-old daughter, Katrin, is ready to strike out on her own to pursue her dreams of being a writer.[83] This prompts Mama's nostalgic sentiments in "Time" ("When did you happen? / Where was I looking?"), a song that will probably recall for many *Fiddler on the Roof*'s "Sunrise, Sunset" ("Is this the little girl I carried?"). One song earlier, Uncle Chris toasts death in "It's Going to Be Good to Be Gone," a tune more Russian than Norwegian. One of the many fringe benefits of dying is that he can look "forward to no tomorrow!" — possibly an oblique allusion to Charnin's *Annie* (and if so, a delicious one). In any event, in the lyrics to "Good to Be Gone" Charnin offers an antidote to the aggressive optimism he championed in the then still-running show with its ubiquitous anthem "Tomorrow."[84]

Rodgers's last musical with Hammerstein, *The Sound of Music*, inspired considerable criticism that was retrospectively used to dismiss earlier shows: R&H were excessively sentimental. In his Columbia University interviews Rodgers vigorously defended the concept of sentiment in general and as it applied to their work: "Surely vast numbers of the theatre-going public and the motion picture public are deeply interested in sentiment. And I'm tired of this semantic nonsense about the difference between sentiment and sentimentality. I still don't know what that means. But most of us live on sentiment. We feel it towards our parents when we're very young. We feel it toward our wives and husbands and certainly toward our children. It's a way of life all over the world. And to reject this, I think is ridiculous."[85]

The inherent sentimental nature of *I Remember Mama*, especially in the wake of contemporary musicals such as *Sweeney Todd* and *Evita*, frequently inspired a critical tone that more than occasionally degenerates into condescension and hostility. *I Remember Mama* was not the first time critics had accused Rodgers of failing to produce a "great score according to Richard Rodgers standards" (John McClain reviewing *The King and I*).[86] The difference was that nearly everyone felt this way about *I Remember Mama*. Richard Eder's biting review of *I Remember Mama* in the *New York Times* represents the prevailing critical epiphany that this "tedious failure" displays "a mass of clichés and a pervading, forced cuteness," "sugary simplicity," and "stale wit and mobilized sentiment." About the nicest thing Eder can say about Rodgers's "fairly bland" score is that it "includes several nice pieces."[87] For Kissel, the critic who wrote *Rex*'s most positive review, Rodgers should be excused for his inability to translate the "simplemindedness" of the lyrics, in particular those of replacement lyricist Raymond Jessel, with anything other than a "score of unimaginable thinness."[88]

Yet again the book (this time by *Annie* librettist Meehan), lyrics, casting, and production rather than Rodgers's music prompted the most critical wrath. Douglas Watt considered Rodgers's final score "better on the whole than those from either of his last two shows" (Mama might call this "dratting" with faint praise), although it exhibited only "teasing echoes of the grand years with Oscar Hammerstein."[89] Few could offer truly encouraging words, although John Beaufort came close when he concluded that the show "wins its welcome" for many features, in addition to Rodgers's "several choice musical numbers."[90]

Only Clive Barnes exhibited a high tolerance for a "simple, sentimental play with music, embellished with the ageless freshness of Rodgers." Suskin placed Barnes in the "favorable" column. One suspects that Barnes might have had more company if *I Remember Mama* had appeared a couple of decades earlier, but in the late 1970s he alone appreciated the "touching" and "old-fashioned" themes, the "exquisite performance" of its nonsinging star, the "nuances" of George Irving as Uncle Chris, and Cy Feuer's success in "giving an intimate play something of the scope and punch of a musical spectacular." And after all the hedging and tepid praise by other contemporary critics, one is stunned to read Barnes's response to Rodgers's music: "I loved the score. It is simple on the mind, but easy on the heart."[91]

Barnes had no critical coattails, however, and the show died ignominiously after 108 performances on September 2, 1979, a few months before Rodgers himself died. Although *I Remember Mama* improved slightly on *Rex*'s dismal run, it suffered an indignity that was spared its immediate predecessor when it became the first Rodgers show since *By Jupiter* to go unrecorded in its original production. As with *Rex*, no libretto or vocal score was published. Five years later, this humiliating situation was partially remedied when the original Papa (George Hearn) and Uncle Chris (Irving) joined a newly assembled cast headed by Sally Ann Howes as Mama and Ann Morrison as Katrin for a nearly complete commercial recording, orchestrated and conducted by Bruce Pomahac.[92]

The Rodgers & Hammerstein Organization created a rental perform-

ing version of the script and score that included several discrepancies between this recording and what audiences had originally heard. The Broadway *Mama* included four songs with lyrics by replacement lyricist Jessel
("A Little Bit More," "Uncle Chris," "Easy Come, Easy Go," and "Lars,
Lars"). For the recording, the last of these, a song for Mama, was replaced
by Mama's "When," a Charnin song cut during the tryouts. Another deleted
song by Charnin, "A Most Disagreeable Man," paired on the recording with
"Uncle Chris," was not separately listed despite its presence in the script and
score as well as on the recording. Besides the one substitution and the one
addition, the recording and rental score adheres closely to the Broadway
version.

The Legacy

It is sad but probably true that the vast majority of composers, in whatever
style, outlive their period of greatest impact. Few composers besides Haydn
and Verdi created music into their seventies that achieved, much less surpassed, the lasting popular and critical favor of earlier triumphs. Even "the
great Stravinsky," one of the celebrities the reporter Melba recalls having
interviewed in the course of her striptease number "Zip" in *Pal Joey*, received half-hearted support, even from his fans, for the music he composed
in his seventies and early eighties, and his final works remain widely unknown to all but experts. In the Broadway arena, Sondheim, on the eve of his
seventieth birthday, shared his "observation that Broadway composers past
the age of 50 never turned out anything good."[93] Of course, Sondheim himself, soon to deliver a new musical, *Bounce*, at the age of seventy-three, had
already created *Sunday in the Park with George*, *Into the Woods*, *Assassins*,
and *Passion* after reaching the magic number designed to trigger an auto-
matic invitation into the American Association of Retired Persons (AARP).
The innovative *No Strings* appeared a few months before Rodgers turned
sixty. Despite such exceptions, Sondheim's statement sadly contains more
than a few grains of truth.

By the death of Hammerstein, Rodgers and Hammerstein themselves
had long since completed their revolution, a series of musicals that served
as models for more than a generation. New writers, new teams, and new
styles almost inevitably leave past masters behind, even R&H. During the
nineteen years after Hammerstein's death, however, Rodgers continued to
grow. He wrote the lyrics to an entire musical for the first time, he formed

partnerships with some of the most tested and promising lyricists of his day, he continued to tackle unusual subjects, including an interracial romance, Noah and the flood, and King Henry VIII's relentless desire for a male heir. He also approached traditional subjects in less conventional ways— for example, by studiously avoiding Italian popular music in a musical that takes place in Venice.

Although we may not know how to assess these final shows or what we should do with them, perhaps it is unnecessary to dismiss a musical like *Do I Hear a Waltz?* simply because it falls short of either Rodgers or Sondheim at their best. Must we discard *I Remember Mama* because it lacks the cutting edge of *Oklahoma!* or *Sweeney Todd?* Most Broadway composers either die (Gershwin, Kern), gradually fade away (Loewe, Porter, Berlin), or fail in their struggle to mount one last successful show (Loesser, Bernstein, Strouse).[94] Virtually alone among his contemporaries, Rodgers stayed the course and staggered to the finish line. With time, I think we will become increasingly thankful that he did.

A few months after the close of *I Remember Mama* and a little more than two weeks before Rodgers died on December 30, 1979, a joyously received new production of *Oklahoma!* came to town. Another highly touted production of *Oklahoma!* from Britain's Royal National Theatre, produced by Cameron Mackintosh, directed by Trevor Nunn, and choreographed by Susan Stroman arrived at Broadway's Gershwin Theatre in March 2002 in time for the Rodgers centennial. In earlier chapters I have noted other revivals of Rodgers and Hart and Rodgers and Hammerstein since Rodgers's death. The end of Rodgers's parade has not passed by. In fact, it is not yet in sight.

In the fall 2001 issue of *Happy Talk,* Bert Fink (the man who saw *Rex* twice in 1976) recalled a conversation between Mary Rodgers and Katie Couric that took place in a segment of the *Today Show* designed to commemorate the fiftieth anniversary of *Oklahoma!* in 1993. "Katie Couric asked Mary Rodgers: 'Isn't it great having all this wonderful music back?' Mary's response: 'It never left.'"[95]

Many people would lose their money on *Who Wants to Be a Millionaire?* or *Jeopardy* if asked who composed "Blue Moon," but they could readily sing or hum it. Others who would draw a blank at the name Richard Rodgers know about Rodgers *and* Hart or Rodgers *and* Hammerstein. People may know nothing about the theatrical contexts of the songs they hear in jazz clubs, cabarets, or Nordstrom's, but they know Rodgers's songs and want to hear them again. Rodgers still reaches us. Some may prefer Berlin, Kern, Gershwin, Porter, Harold Arlen, or Paul Simon, but Rodgers's place as one of America's major popular songwriters is secure.

The essence of a great song remains mysterious. Fools give us reasons, some writers like Alec Wilder and Allen Forte can explain them (up to a point), but it is not easy to capture the magic of a great song without actually singing or playing or listening to the song. I have identified some idiosyncratic Rodgers touches, including the "Rodgers leap" (example 1.5), the unexpected notes at the end of a phrase, and the seemingly infinite possibilities that Rodgers can exploit with a simple scale. But this is only the beginning. As Wilder wrote in *American Popular Song: The Great Innovators, 1900–1950*, "Of all the writers whose songs are considered and examined in this book, those of Rodgers show the highest degree of consistent excellence, inventiveness, and sophistication."[96]

Rodgers was proud of his song legacy, but what meant the most to him was writing shows. At a late stage in his career (only two musicals to go), he revealed to what extent his daughter Mary's observation was right on the mark: "Theatre was his hobby. And his life."[97] Here is Rodgers speaking: "And I like the actual work. I like being given a lyric, and taking it and trying to work out the problem, trying to get a good idea for a song—the music—that pleases me. I enjoy the transfer from my head to somebody else's throat—the whole process. Even the terror of taking the thing out of town. It looks awful then, even if it's good. You don't know whether you're going to get it fixed or not. I like the whole process."[98]

A partial summary of what Rodgers was trying to accomplish can be found in his essay entitled "Opera and Broadway" that appeared in *Opera News* in 1961.[99] Rodgers acknowledges that most musicals of the 1920s, including by implication most of the musicals he composed with Hart, lacked maturity in their books. Nevertheless, almost from the start he thought of himself as a musical dramatist who, along with Berlin, Kern, the Gershwins, and Vincent Youmans, was "breaking ground for a native American musical theater." Writing shortly after Hammerstein's death, Rodgers emphasized that the "rejection of pat formula exemplifies a reaching out for new subjects and ideas that is the very keynote of our growing lyric theater" and that "it has become clear that 'plays with music' or musical comedies of our Broadway theater might be called, without apology or self-consciousness, American opera." These remarks do not mean that Rodgers was "aspiring" to opera, but they convey his conviction that the best of American musical

Table 6.1. Musical Program for *No Strings*

The action of the play takes place in Paris, Monte Carlo, Honfleur, Deauville, and St. Tropez

PROLOGUE
"The Sweetest Sounds" (Barbara and David)

ACT I
"How Sad" (David)
"Loads of Love" (Barbara)
"The Man Who Has Everything" (Louis)
"Be My Host" (David, Comfort, Mike, Luc, Gabrielle, and Dancers)
"La La La" (Jeanette and Luc)
"You Don't Tell Me" (Barbara)
"Love Makes the World Go" (Mollie, Comfort, and Dancers)
"Nobody Told Me" (David and Barbara)

ACT II
"Look No Further" (David and Barbara)
"Maine" (David and Barbara)
"An Orthodox Fool" (Barbara)
"Eager Beaver" (Comfort, Mike, and Dancers)
"No Strings" (David and Barbara)
Reprise: "Maine" (Barbara and David)
Reprise: "The Sweetest Sounds" (David and Barbara)

---

theater offers an equal alternative to European opera, a "product of American know-how," and a "marriage not only of the arts but also of the technical aspects of modern stage-craft."

Between the time "Any Old Place with You" was interpolated in Lew Fields's *A Lonely Romeo* in 1919 to the closing of *I Remember Mama* a few months before Rodgers's death in 1979, musical theater was a passion that would not yield to sickness, depression, incompetent producers, unruly stars, or the occasional inevitable failure. The legacy of what Rodgers accomplished during his sixty years on the wicked stage was enormous. His songs and musical stories have indeed "never left." Every day is Rodgers's day, and he walks alone.

Table 6.2. Musical Program for *Do I Hear a Waltz?*

ACT I

SCENE 1: Venice
"Someone Woke Up" (Leona)

SCENE 2: Garden of Pensione Fioria
"This Week Americans" (Fioria)
"What Do We Do? We Fly?" (Leona, Mrs. McIlhenny, Mr. McIlhenny, Eddie, Jennifer)

SCENE 3: Di Rossi's Shop
"Someone Like You" (Di Rossi)
"Bargaining" (Di Rossi)

SCENE 4: Piazza San Marco
"Here We Are Again" (Leona; danced by Vito and Ragazzi [Steve Jacobs, Sandy Leeds, Joe Nelson, Nancy Van Rijn, Mary Zahn])

SCENE 5: Interior of Pensione Fioria
"Thinking" (Di Rossi and Leona)

SCENE 6: Garden of Pensione Fioria
"No Understand" (Fioria, Eddie, Giovanna)
"Take the Moment" (Di Rossi)

ACT II

SCENE 1: Facade of Pensione Fioria
"Moon in My Window" (Jennifer, Fioria, Leona)

SCENE 2: Outside the Garden of Pensione Fioria
"We're Gonna Be All Right" (Eddie, Jennifer)
"Do I Hear a Waltz?" (Leona, Company)

SCENE 3: Piazza San Marco
"Stay" (Di Rossi)

SCENE 4: Garden of Pensione Fioria
"Perfectly Lovely Couple" (Leona, Di Rossi, Mr. McIlhenny, Mrs. McIlhenny, Jennifer, Eddie, Giovanna, Fioria)

SCENE 5: The Same
Reprise: "Take the Moment" (Di Rossi)
"Thank You So Much" (Di Rossi and Leona)

Table 6.3. Musical Program for *Two By Two*

TIME: Before, during, and after the Flood.

ACT I
IN AND AROUND NOAH'S HOME

"Why Me?" (Noah)
"Put Him Away" (Shem, Ham, Leah)
"The Gitka's Song" (The Gitka)
"Something, Somewhere" (Japheth, Family)
"You Have Got to Have a Rudder on the Ark" (Noah, Shem, Ham, Japheth)
"Something Doesn't Happen" (Rachel, Esther)
"An Old Man" (Esther)
"Ninety Again!" (Noah)
"Two By Two" (Noah, Family)
"I Do Not Know a Day I Did Not Love You" (Japheth)
Reprise: "Something, Somewhere" (Noah)

ACT II
ON THE ARK AND ATOP MT. ARARAT, FORTY DAYS AND
FORTY NIGHTS LATER

"When It Dries" (Noah, Family)
Reprise: "Two by Two" (Noah, Esther)
"You" (Noah)
"The Golden Ram" (Goldie)
"Poppa Knows Best" (Noah, Japheth)
Reprise: "I Do Not Know a Day I Did Not Love You" (Rachel, Japheth)
"As Far as I'm Concerned" (Shem, Leah)
"Hey, Girlie" (Noah)
"The Covenant" (Noah)

Table 6.4. Musical Program for *Rex*

ACT I

SCENE 1: Greenwich Palace
"Te Deum" (Company)

SCENE 2: King Henry's Tent
"No Song More Pleasing" (Smeaton)

SCENE 3: The Field of Cloth of Gold
"Where Is My Son?" (Henry)
"The Field of Cloth of Gold" (Company)

SCENE 4: French Pavillion
Basse Dance (Company)

SCENE 5: Comus' Chambers

SCENE 6: Hever Castle
"The Chase" (Comus, Will, Smeaton, Gentlemen of the Court)

SCENE 7: Hampton Court Palace
"Away from You" (Henry)

SCENE 8: Chapel
"As Once I Loved You" (Catherine)

SCENE 9: The Throne Room

SCENE 10: Hampton Court Corridor

SCENE 11: Queen Anne's Bedroom
"Elizabeth" (Smeaton, Lady Margaret, Lady in Waiting)

SCENE 12: Comus' Laboratory
"Why?" (Henry)

SCENE 13: The Palace
Reprise: "No Song More Pleasing" (Jane, Henry)
Reprise: "Away from You" (Anne)

SCENE 14: The Tower of London

SCENE 15: The Coronation

SCENE 16: The City of London
Reprise: "Te Deum" (Company)

ACT II

SCENE 1: Hampton Court Palace, Ten Years Later
"Christmas at Hampton Court" (Elizabeth, Edward, Mary)

Table 6.4. Continued

SCENE 2: The Great Hall at Hampton Court Palace
"The Wee Golden Warrior" (Will, Edward, Elizabeth, Mary)
Sword Dance and Morris Dance (Sword and Morris Dancers)
"The Masque" (Ladies and Gentlemen of the Court)

SCENE 3: The Throne Room
"From Afar" (Henry)

SCENE 4: Hampton Court Corridor
"In Time" (Elizabeth, Will)

SCENE 5: Comus' Laboratory

SCENE 6: Henry's Laboratory

SCENE 7: The Throne Room
Reprise: "In Time" (Elizabeth, Edward)
Reprise: "Te Deum" (Company)

Table 6.5. Musical Numbers in *I Remember Mama*

The action takes place in and near San Francisco.

ACT I

Summer and Fall 1910

"I Remember Mama" (Katrin) [lyrics by Martin Charnin]

Kitchen of the Hansens' House, Steiner Street
"A Little Bit More" (Mama, Papa, and Children) [lyrics by Raymond Jessel]
"A Writer Writes at Night" (Katrin and Mama) [lyrics by Charnin]

Parlor of the Hansen House
"Ev'ry Day (Comes Something Beautiful)" (Mama, Papa, Family, and Guests)
   [lyrics by Charnin]
"The Hardangerfjord" (danced by The Company)

Front Porch of the Hansen House
"You Could Not Please Me More" (Papa and Mama) [lyrics by Charnin]

The Kitchen
"Uncle Chris" (Aunt Jenny, Aunt Sigrid, Aunt Trina, Mr. Thorkelson) [lyrics by
   Jessel]

The Hospital
"Lullaby" (Mama) [lyrics by Charnin]

The Parlor
"Easy Come, Easy Go" (Uncle Chris and Friends; danced by Dagmar and Uncle
   Chris) [lyrics by Jessel]

The Kitchen
"It Is Not the End of the World" (Papa, Mama, and Children) [lyrics by Charnin]

Table 6.5. Continued

ACT II

Spring 1911

Back Porch of the Hansen House
"Mama Always Makes It Better" (Children) [lyrics by Charnin]

The Parlor
"Lars, Lars" (Mama) [lyrics by Jessel]

Palace Hotel Lobby
"Fair Trade" (Dame Sybil, Mama, and Admirers) [lyrics by Charnin]

Uncle Chris's Ranch
"It's Going to Be Good to Be Gone" (Uncle Chris) [lyrics by Charnin]

The Kitchen
"Time" (Mama) [lyrics by Charnin]

Works by Richard Rodgers

Rodgers and Hart Broadway and London Musicals, Original Films, and Miscellaneous Works

Unless otherwise noted, all works are Broadway musicals.

1920	*Poor Little Ritz Girl*
1924	*The Melody Man*
1925	*The Garrick Gaieties, 1925*
	Dearest Enemy
1926	*Fifth Avenue Follies* [night club]
	The Girl Friend
	The Garrick Gaieties, 1926
	Lido Lady [London]
	Peggy-Ann
	Betsy
1927	*One Dam Thing After Another* [London]
	A Connecticut Yankee (Original)
1928	*She's My Baby*
	Present Arms
	Chee-Chee
1929	*Spring Is Here*
	Heads Up!
1930	*Simple Simon*
	Ever Green [London]
1931	*America's Sweetheart*
	The Hot Heiress [film]
1932	*Love Me Tonight* [film]

The Phantom President [film]
1933   *Hallelujah, I'm a Bum* [film]
        Dancing Lady [film]
1934   *Hollywood Party* [film]
1935   *Mississippi* [film]
        Jumbo
1936   *On Your Toes*
        Dancing Pirate [film]
        All Points West [symphonic narrative]
1937   *Babes in Arms*
        I'd Rather Be Right
1938   *Fools for Scandal* [film]
        I Married an Angel
        The Boys from Syracuse
1939   *Too Many Girls*
        Ghost Town [ballet (without Hart)]
1940   *Higher and Higher*
        Pal Joey
1941   *They Met in Argentina* [film]
1942   *By Jupiter*
1943   *A Connecticut Yankee* (Revised)

Rodgers and Hammerstein Broadway Musicals, Original Films, and Television Broadcasts

1943   *Oklahoma!*
1945   *Carousel*
        State Fair [film]
1947   *Allegro*
1949   *South Pacific*
1951   *The King and I*
        Victory at Sea [television (without Hammerstein)]
1953   *Me and Juliet*
1955   *Pipe Dream*
1957   *Cinderella* [television]
1958   *Flower Drum Song*
1959   *The Sound of Music*

Broadway Musicals and Television Broadcasts After Hammerstein

1960   *The Valiant Years* [television]
1962   *No Strings*
       State Fair [film remake]
1965   *Do I Hear a Waltz?*
       Cinderella [television remake]
1967   *Androcles and the Lion* [television]
1970   *Two By Two*
1976   *Rex*
1979   *I Remember Mama*

Notes

ABBREVIATIONS

Bordman   Bordman, Gerald. *American Musical Theatre.* New York:
                            Oxford University Press, 2001.

Complete Hart Lyrics   Hart, Dorothy, and Robert Kimball, eds. *The Complete
                            Lyrics of Lorenz Hart.* New York: Knopf, 1986; rev. and
                            expanded, New York: Da Capo, 1995.

Enchanted Evenings   Block, Geoffrey. *Enchanted Evenings: The Broadway Musi-
                            cal from "Show Boat" to Sondheim.* New York: Oxford
                            University Press, 1997.

Ewen   Ewen, David. *Richard Rodgers.* New York: Henry Holt,
                            1957.

Hyland   Hyland, William G. *Richard Rodgers.* New Haven: Yale
                            University Press, 1998.

Mordden *R&H*   Mordden, Ethan. *Rodgers & Hammerstein.* New York:
                            Abrams, 1992.

Musical Stages   Rodgers, Richard. *Musical Stages: An Autobiography.* New
                            York: Random House, 1975; repr. New York: Da Capo,
                            1995, 2000. All Mary Rodgers quotations from 1995 edition.

New York Critics' Reviews *New York Theatre Critics' Reviews.* New York: Critics'
                            Theatre Reviews, 1940–1996.

Opening Night   Suskin, Steven. *Opening Night on Broadway: A Criti-
                            cal Quotebook of the Golden Era of the Musical Theatre,
                            "Oklahoma!" (1943) to "Fiddler on the Roof" (1964).* New
                            York: Schirmer, 1990.

R&H Fact Book   Green, Stanley, ed. *Rodgers and Hammerstein Fact Book:
                            A Record of Their Works Together and with Other Collabo-
                            rators.* New York: Lynn Farnol Group, 1980.

Reminiscences   *Reminiscences of Richard Rodgers.* Oral History Collection
                       of Columbia University, 1968.

Rodgers Reader   Block, Geoffrey. *The Richard Rodgers Reader.* New York:
                       Oxford University Press, 2002.

Secrest   Secrest, Meryle. *Somewhere for Me: A Biography of Richard
                       Rodgers.* New York: Knopf, 2001.

Wilder   Wilder, Alec. *American Popular Song: The Great Innova-
                       tors, 1900–1950.* New York: Oxford University Press, 1972.

INTRODUCTION

1. Mary Rodgers Guettel, "Introduction," in *Musical Stages,* vii–ix, reprinted in *Rodgers Reader,* 255–58. Mary dates her remarks September 1994.

2. *Musical Stages,* 293–94.

3. Hyland, 240–42.

4. Arthur Laurents, *Original Story By: A Memoir of Broadway and Hollywood* (New York: Knopf, 2000), 213–14. See also interviews with Mary Rodgers Guettel and Linda Rodgers Emory on *American Masters: "The Sweetest Sounds,"* produced for PBS by Thirteen/WNET New York, 2001.

5. Interview in *Music by Richard Rodgers,* produced for PBS by Thirteen/WNET New York, 1990.

6. Frank Rich, "Oh, What a Miserable Mornin'," *New York Times Magazine,* October 28, 2001, 58–61; quote on page 60.

7. Mary Rodgers, *Musical Stages,* vii.

8. Secrest, *passim.*

9. The fall 2001 issue of *Happy Talk: News of the Rodgers & Hammerstein Organization* offers a more comprehensive list of Rodgers centennial productions. See also *www.rr2002.com.*

CHAPTER 1. From Apprentice to Musical Dramatist

1. Shortly after arriving in America, where they settled in the unlikely town of Holden, Missouri, the Rogozinskys changed their surname to Abraham. In New York in 1892, Richard's father, William Abraham, legally changed his name to William Abraham Rodgers (Secrest, 16–17).

2. According to William G. Hyland, only Mortimer was bar mitzvahed (Hyland, 7); Meryle Secrest concludes that both brothers went through this rite of passage (Secrest, 25).

3. For more on the perceived "Jewish" qualities of American popular song, see Jeffrey Magee, "Irving Berlin's 'Blue Skies': Ethnic Affiliations and Musical Transformations," *Musical Quarterly* 84, no. 4 (Winter 2000): 537–80.

4. Nijinsky's North American tour occurred in 1916. Hofmann appeared in America nearly every year after 1898. Rodgers also regularly attended performances of the New York Philharmonic during his youth.

5. *Musical Stages,* 15. A more legible version of "Camp-Fire Days" appears in

Deems Taylor, *Some Enchanted Evenings: The Story of Rodgers and Hammerstein* (New York: Harper, 1953), 23.

6. *Musical Stages*, 20. See also Rodgers, "Jerome Kern: A Tribute," *New York Times* (October 7, 1951); reprinted in *Rodgers Reader*, 268–71.

7. Rodgers, "How to Write Music in No Easy Lesson: A Self Interview," *Theatre Arts* (October 1939), 741–46, quotation on 742, reprinted in *Rodgers Reader*, 261–65, quotation on 262. *Musical Stages*, 28.

8. *Musical Stages*, 28.

9. *One Minute Please* also included "At the Movies," with lyrics by Dr. Milton G. Bender, Hart's controversial companion and associate until his death, songs with lyrics attributed to book writer Ralph G. Engelsman, and songs with lyrics by Rodgers himself.

10. Oscar Hammerstein II, Foreword, *The Rodgers and Hart Song Book* (New York: Simon and Schuster), 1951, ix–xiii, quotation on ix; reprinted in *Rodgers Reader*, 79–83, quotation on 79. Although the character Hart played was clearly based on Pickford, the name had been changed to Mrs. Rockyford. I thank Frederick Nolan for this information.

11. Rodgers, "Hammerstein: Words by Rodgers," *New York Times Magazine* (July 10, 1960), 26, 54, reprinted in *Rodgers Reader*, 284–89 (Rodgers's side of the short pants vs. long pants debate appears on 285).

12. Rodgers, "The Broadway Audience Is Still There, Waiting for More Good Shows," *Dramatists Guild Quarterly* (1971), 12; reprinted in *Rodgers Reader*, 326–34, quotation on 328.

13. Ewen, 81.

14. Rodgers may have met Herbert the same day he met Lew and the rest of the Fields clan (Joseph, Dorothy, and Frances), but Herbert and Hart had known each other for several years. For a thorough and comprehesive study of Lew Fields's long career, including material on the eight shows with music by Rodgers and Hart, see Armond and L. Marc Fields's excellent *From the Bowery to Broadway: Lew Fields and the Roots of American Popular Theater* (New York: Oxford University Press, 1993).

15. According to Armond and L. Marc Fields, the audition took place in late July or early August.

16. *Musical Stages*, 37–38.

17. Fields and Fields, *Bowery to Broadway*, 392.

18. *Musical Stages*, 50.

19. A few years later Schwab co-wrote the book, with B. G. DeSylva, for Ray Henderson, De Sylva, and Lew Brown's *Good News!* (1927), one of the greatest hits of the 1920s.

20. Rodgers and Hart liked "I Want a Man" (not yet heard in New York) enough to use it again in *America's Sweetheart* as late as 1931. One other *Winkle Town* song, "If I Were King," made it to Rodgers and Hart's amateur show of that name and to their final amateur revue, *Bad Habits of 1925* (February 8, 1925). *Complete Hart Lyrics*, 29–34.

21. Fields and Fields, *Bowery to Broadway*, 418. Even after the success of *The Garrick Gaieties*, word of Lew Fields's reluctance to support *Dearest Enemy* would create similar problems for obtaining a producer. Several years *before* the disastrous and humiliating meeting with Max Dreyfus, Rodgers had had an audition with his brother

Louis, the owner of T. B. Harms, the company that published the scores of Rodgers's model theater composer Jerome Kern. The meeting, arranged by a mutual acquaintance, occurred shortly after the performance of Rodgers's second amateur effort, *Up Stage in Down*, in 1919. In *Musical Stages* Rodgers describes how Kern's publisher "listened attentively" before encouraging him to finish high school (*Musical Stages*, 25–26).

22. Fields and Fields, *Bowery to Broadway*, 422. Armond and L. Marc Fields continue: "After only seven weeks, *Variety* was at a loss to explain the failure, finally attributing it to its late arrival and the summer heat" (423).

23. Ted Goldsmith, "One Hart Would Not Stand Still," *Theatre Magazine* (April 1931), 37.

24. "The Boys from Columbia," *Time* (September 26, 1938), 35–39, quotation on 36, reprinted in *Rodgers Reader*, 47–53, quotation on 50.

25. Ibid.

26. Magee, "Irving Berlin's 'Blue Skies,'" 539–40; *Musical Stages*, 88.

27. The creative process by which the concluding phrase of "Do I Love You Because You're Beautiful?" in *Cinderella* was transformed from minor to major is discussed in Chapter 5.

28. The absence of the B section in "Manhattan," composed in 1922 and the earliest Rodgers standard, may have less to do with formal tinkering than it does with the lack of formal consolidation before 1925, when the A-A-B-A and A-B-A-C forms began to dominate (*Musical Stages*, 80). But this historical clarification does not detract from the point that Rodgers did not feel constrained by standard forms any more than Shakespeare felt constrained by the sonnet. On the evolution of song forms in the 1920s, see Graham Wood, "The Development of Song Forms in the Broadway and Hollywood Musicals of Richard Rodgers, 1919–1943," Ph.D. diss., University of Minnesota, 2000, chapter 2.

29. *Musical Stages*, 128.

30. Rodgers, "How to Write Music," 741–42; *Rodgers Reader*, 262.

31. *Musical Stages*, 206.

32. "Cleverest of Our Lyricists Are Seldom Big Hit Writers," *New York Herald Tribune* (May 31, 1925).

33. Rodgers, "Introduction," *Rodgers and Hart Song Book*, 1–4, quotation on 4, reprinted in *Rodgers Reader*, 265–68, quotation on 268. "Any Old Place with You" was also included in *Rediscovered Rodgers & Hart* (1992) and *Rodgers and Hart: A Musical Anthology* (1995). As recently as 1999, this historical milestone was included in a television broadcast devoted to the songs of Rodgers and Hart, *Thou Swell, Thou Witty: The Rodgers & Hart Story* (PBS).

34. The song also contains a disproportionately long verse (thirty-two bars) typical of songs composed prior to the mid-1920s.

35. The two songs from the short-lived *Melody Man* (1924), "Moonlight Mama" and "I'd Like to Poison Ivy," were published in their own time but have so far eluded rediscovery in sheet music and recorded anthologies.

36. In "Auto Show Girl" and "Love's Intense in Tents," the note on which the turn revolves is the third of the triad. In "Any Old Place with You," like "Auto Show Girl" also in C major, the starting point is the fifth.

37. Another memorable use of the diminished seventh occurs throughout "You Took Advantage of Me" on the first and third measures of the A sections (beats 3 and 4).

38. Charles Hamm, ed., *Irving Berlin: Early Songs* (*Music in the United States of America*), 3 vols. (Madison, Wis.: A-R Editions, 1994).

39. Berlin is in good company. A collection of Franz Schubert's first 190 songs (roughly one-third of his total) would leave all but the most knowledgeable Schubert lover similarly befuddled. "Gretchen am Spinnrade" and "Heidenröslein" are there, but "Erlkönig," perhaps the most famous song of Schubert's youth, would remain a few songs in the future.

40. Green places Rodgers at the institute between 1921 and 1923 but does not specify semesters (*R&H Fact Book,* 3); Secrest states that he enrolled "in the late spring of 1921" (46). Many thanks to Jeni Dahmus, archivist at The Juilliard School, for informing me that Rodgers enrolled in the fall of 1920 and for other information about Rodgers's student record during his years at the institute.

41. Writing in 1959, Ferdinand Davis states that Goetschius's books "were the first text-books written by an American to be published in America" and, "moreover, there was not then as there is not now, a single text-book in English on the classical method." Ferdinand Davis, "The American Way, or How Not to Teach Music," *Caecilia* (1959), 7–11, quote on 7. As the title of his article suggests, Davis, like Nicholas Slonimsky, takes a dim view of Goetschius's so-called classic method. For Davis, "All that Goetschius has done is to compound the obscure with the impossible" (11).

42. Percy Goetschius, *The Theory and Practice of Tone-Relations: An Elementary Course of Harmony with Emphasis upon the Element of Melody* (New York: G. Schirmer, 1931).

43. Ibid., 14–15.

44. The year after Rodgers enrolled marked the long-awaited English version of Thayer's *Life of Beethoven*, which Krehbiel had revised and completed. Krehbiel died on March 20, 1923.

45. Hyland, 22–23.

46. At the institute Rodgers did learn how to use roman numeral analysis, a technique that he would apply in labeling his private sketches for the rest of his career. See Hyland, 24.

47. *Musical Stages,* 46.

48. For Hamm, both Tin Pan Alley songs and European classical music exhibit a "sense of forward thrust, achieved through the pervasive use of melodic sequence and functional harmony intensified through frequent chromatic alteration"; Charles Hamm, *Yesterdays: Popular Song in America* (New York: Norton, 1979), 371.

49. Wilder, 192–93.

50. Gerald Mast, *Can't Help Singin': The American Musical on Stage and Screen* (Woodstock, N.Y.: Overlook, 1987), 170. Mast's chapter on Rodgers and Hammerstein is reprinted in *Rodgers Reader,* 87–104.

51. Three successive notes of the scale, G-A-B♭ (mm. 2–4) share the same word, "room."

52. Wilder, 164.

53. See also the discussion of "Bewitched" in *Enchanted Evenings,* 109–10.

54. In 2001, the soundtrack of the dance section heard in the Tony Award–

winning hit musical *Contact* ("Swinging") was jazz violinist Stéphane Grapelli's recording of this perennial tune.

55. *Musical Stages*, 101, 103. This passage on the origins of "My Heart Stood Still"
and the comments by Furia (see note 56) are reprinted in *Rodgers Reader*, 21–24.

56. Philip Furia, *The Poets of Tin Pan Alley* (New York: Oxford University Press,
1990), 109.

57. In an ascending melodic F minor scale, the sixth degree (D-natural) would
normally *ascend* to the seventh (E-natural). By descending back to C, Rodgers thwarts
our expectations of D-flat while at the same time managing to save the melodic climax
for the *leap* to D natural on the word "thrill." For a rich theoretical discussion of "My
Heart Stood Still," including an explanation of the musical connections between the
chorus (discussed here) and the preceding verse, see Allen Forte's *American Popular
Ballad of the Golden Era, 1924–1950* (Princeton, N.J.: Princeton University Press, 1995),
182–88, most of which is reprinted in *Rodgers Reader*, 26–30.

58. "The Boys from Columbia," 35–39, reprinted in *Rodgers Reader*, 47–53; Mar-
garet Case Harriman, "Words and Music: Rodgers and Hart," *New Yorker* (May 28 and
June 4, 1938), rev. and repr. in Harriman's collected profiles, *Take Them Up Tenderly*
(New York: Knopf, 1945), 166–85, and in *Rodgers Reader*, 53–68.

59. Rodgers, "How to Write Music," 743; *Rodgers Reader*, 263.

60. *Musical Stages*, 118.

61. Brooks Atkinson, "The 'Girl Friend' is Captivating," *New York Times* (March
18, 1926).

62. "Redcoats and Patriots," *New York Times* (September 19, 1925).

63. Ethan Mordden, *Make Believe: The Broadway Musical in the 1920s* (New
York: Oxford University Press, 1997), 114–19 and 197–200, quotation on p. 118; reprinted
in *Rodgers Reader*, 11–19, quotation on p. 16.

64. Rodgers, *Rodgers and Hart Song Book*, 2; *Rodgers Reader*, 266. Wilder also
singles out "You Can't Fool Your Dreams" for its musical innovation. After pointing
out harmonic features of interest in this song, Wilder, unaware that "Manhattan" was
composed in 1922, goes on to include that "nothing of consequence was written for five
years" (Wilder, 165).

65. *Musical Stages*, 66.

66. Frederick Nolan, *Lorenz Hart: A Poet on Broadway* (New York: Oxford University Press), 246–49.

67. *Musical Stages*, 91.

68. Secrest, 95.

69. Fields and Fields, *Bowery to Broadway*, 402.

70. Robert Benchley, *Life* (November 26, 1925). Quoted in *R&H Fact Book*, 27.

CHAPTER 2. A Tale of Two *Connecticut Yankees*

1. Though one London critic described *Lido Lady* as the "best musical comedy
for years," Rodgers himself did not think much of it and made no attempt to bring the
show to New York.

2. Lew, not enamored of costume dramas, even one with the sensibility of a 1920s
musical comedy, would not agree to produce *Dearest Enemy*. Two years later, even with

the successes of *Dearest Enemy, The Girl Friend,* and *Peggy-Ann* behind Rodgers, Hart, and Herbert Fields, the senior Fields resisted producing *A Connecticut Yankee* until his son showed him a finished script. For additional material on the Rodgers and Hart shows produced by Lew Fields, see Armond and L. Marc Fields, *From the Bowery to Broadway: Lew Fields and the Roots of American Popular Theater* (New York: Oxford University Press, 1993), and Jason Rubin, "Lew Fields and the Development of the Broadway Musical," Ph.D. diss., New York University, 1990.

3. "Mr. Rodgers' Yankee," *New York Times* (November 21, 1943). According to *Mark Twain A to Z*, the film began with Twain's Hank Morgan (now named Martin Cavendish) "reading Mark Twain's novel and dreaming about introducing 20th-century technology to Camelot." R. Kent Rasmussen, *Mark Twain A to Z: The Essential Reference to His Life and Writings* (New York: Facts on File, 1995), 98. The Internet Movie Data Base offers a slightly more detailed plot summary: "In 1921, a young man, having read Mark Twain's classic novel of the same title, dreams that he himself travels to King Arthur's Court, where he has similar adventures and outwits his foes by means of very modern inventions including motorcycles and nitroglycerine."

4. The Richard Rodgers Collection, Library of Congress, Washington, 1995, compiled by Mark Eden Horowitz.

5. *Musical Stages,* 107.

6. Ibid., 105.

7. *Rediscovered Rodgers & Hart* (Secaucus, N.J.: Warner Bros., 1992), 144–47.

8. *Musical Stages,* 107.

9. Sid Silverman, "Connecticut Yankee," *Variety* (November 9, 1927), 49.

10. Charles Brackett, "Twitter, Tragedy, and a Yankee," *New Yorker* (November 12, 1927), 33.

11. Wells Root, "The Connecticut Yankee," *Time* (November 14, 1927), 40.

12. Percy Hammond, "'The Connecticut Yankee,' a Rich Song and Dance Thing with a Dubious Libretto," *New York Herald Tribune* (November 4, 1927), 16.

13. Robert Benchley, "Undue Enthusiasm," *Life* (November 24, 1927), 23.

14. Ethan Mordden, *Make Believe: The Broadway Musical in the 1920s* (New York: Oxford University Press, 1997), 199.

15. Hammond, "'Connecticut Yankee,'" 16.

16. Root, "Connecticut Yankee," 40.

17. Silverman, "Connecticut Yankee," 49.

18. In Twain's novel the rescue vehicle is the bicycle.

19. Concerning the meaning of the novel Everett Carter writes: "The available evidence, then, external and internal, suggests that the meaning of *A Connecticut Yankee* is, as the author repeatedly said it was, that the American nineteenth century, devoted to political and religious liberalism and to technology, was better than the traditional past." Carter, "The Meaning of *A Connecticut Yankee,*" from *American Literature* 50 (1978): 418–40; reprinted in Samuel Langhorne Clemens (Mark Twain), *A Connecticut Yankee in King Arthur's Court,* ed. Allison R. Ensor, Norton Critical edition (New York: Norton, 1982), 434–52 (quotation on p. 454).

20. 1927 libretto (act II, scene 3, p. 36).

21. Twain, *A Connecticut Yankee in King Arthur's Court,* 83–84.

22. Ibid., 85.

23. Mordden, *Make Believe*, 123.

24. Martin Rubin, *Showstoppers: Busby Berkeley and the Tradition of Spectacle* (New York: Columbia University Press, 1993), 47–57 (especially pp. 48–51).

25. Hammond, "Connecticut Yankee," 16. Silverman also singled out the "novelty routines" created by Berkeley and performed by a chorus of twenty-four in appealing costumes. *Variety* (November 9, 1927), 49.

26. Bordman, 482.

27. John Martin, "The Dance: New Musical Comedy Talent," *New York Times* (July 22, 1928).

28. The revival of *Show Boat* in New York (October 2, 1994), directed by Hal Prince, is the most successful hybrid to date. For earlier stage and film versions see Miles Kreuger, *"Show Boat": The Story of a Classic American Musical* (New York: Oxford University Press, 1977) and *Show Boat*, conducted by John McGlinn, EMI CDS 7 49108 2.

29. See the collection of songs, *Vocal Selections from "A Connecticut Yankee"* (New York: Warner Bros., 1984).

30. Tommy Krasker and Robert Kimball, *Catalog of the American Musical* (Washington, D.C.: National Institute for Opera and Musical Theater, 1988), 327. See also *Complete Hart Lyrics*, 110.

31. Sketches for "Someone Should Tell Them" appear with other sketches for *One Dam Thing after Another*, and there is no documented evidence that this song was among those dropped from this show.

32. "Someone Should Tell Them" is included in the *Vocal Selections from "A Connecticut Yankee*," 12–15.

33. *Complete Hart Lyrics*, 111.

34. The deleted "I Blush" and "Someone Should Tell Them" are among the nine songs published in the Vocal Selections from *A Connecticut Yankee* (Warner Bros., 1984). The others are "My Heart Stood Still," "Thou Swell," "On a Desert Island With Thee," and "I Feel at Home With You" from 1927 and "To Keep My Love Alive," "Can't You Do a Friend a Favor," and "You Always Love the Same Girl" from the 1943 revival.

35. Rodgers, *Richard Rodgers: Letters to Dorothy, 1926–1937*, ed. William W. Appleton (New York: New York Public Library, 1988), 41.

36. Richard Rodgers Collection, Music Division of the Library of Congress, Box 4, Folder 15. The idea of transforming a duple-metered melody into triple meter is also found in "Joey Looks into the Future," the ballet music that concludes act I of *Pal Joey*, where the music of "Bewitched" is featured as a waltz. Although Rodgers was capable of composing independent ballet music (e.g., "Slaughter on Tenth Avenue"), Rodgers usually was not the one to do this. In later years dance arrangements would be worked out by Trude Rittmann (also spelled Rittman). In the absence of a sketch or score in Rodgers's hand it is likely that Oscar Kosan and not Rodgers should be credited for the ballet music recorded on the 1950 cast album and published in the 1962 piano-vocal score. This doesn't mean, however, that the metamorphosis of "Bewitched" from a duple ballad to a sweeping Rodgers-type waltz in three-quarter time was not the composer's idea.

37. Krasker and Kimball, *Catalog*, 327. I thank Frederick Nolan for sharing his copy of the long unavailable 1927 piano selections published by Harms.

38. Steven Suskin, *Berlin, Kern, Rodgers, Hart, and Hammerstein: A Complete Song Catalogue* (Jefferson, N.C.: McFarland, 1990), 20. In *Show Tunes: The Songs, Shows, and Careers of Broadway's Major Composers*, 3rd ed. (New York: Oxford University Press, 2000), 93, Suskin praises Rodgers's "Nothing's Wrong" as "the first of his breathtaking waltzes."

39. For more on *Betsy* see Jeffrey Magee, "Irving Berlin's 'Blue Skies': Ethnic Affiliations and Musical Transformations," *Musical Quarterly* 84, no. 4 (Winter 2000), 552–57.

40. Brooks Atkinson, "'Betsy' Presented: Elaborately Staged," *New York Times* (December 29, 1926).

41. Dwight Blocker Bowers, Notes to the Smithsonian Collection of Recordings, American Songbook Series (Smithsonian Institution, 1992), 7. The anthology includes Dennis's 1954 recording of "This Funny World" among its elite list of twenty-four Rodgers and Hart songs.

42. *Heads Up!* (1929), no doubt hit by the Depression, would receive a still more tepid reception and close after only nineteen performances in May 1930.

43. The previous year, Carpenter was a bit player and understudy for Gertrude Lawrence in *Oh, Kay!*, a Gershwin show. Rodgers told Dorothy that he "enjoyed it more than any other musical show" he had "ever seen" (*Letters to Dorothy*, 9).

44. "My Heart Stood Still" was replaced by Vivian Ellis and Desmond Carter's "I Don't Know How." Also for this London production Ellis and Carter wrote a new song for Merlin (a nonsinging role on Broadway), "I Never Thought of That" (*R&H Fact Book*, 75). Despite Rodgers and Hart's impressive talent, hits like "My Heart Stood Still" didn't grow on trees. "Here in My Arms," the big song of *Dearest Enemy*, had already been interpolated into Rodgers and Hart's London hit, *Lido Lady*, and *Peggy-Ann* had songs that were familiar from the London production of that show in 1927.

45. "Mr. Rodgers's Yankee," 1.

46. Secrest, 227.

47. *Reminiscences*, 218; reprinted in *Rodgers Reader*, 307–8.

48. For a reliable account of Hart's last month, see Secrest, 229–34.

49. The title "Here's Martin the Groom," absent from the working 1943 libretto (which has the text of "A Ladies' Home Companion") and according to Robert Kimball from New York playbills as well, surfaces in the 1943 rental libretto and score. To confuse matters further, both opening numbers begin with the familiar melody "For He's a Jolly Good Fellow." See *Complete Hart Lyrics*, 295.

50. For other examples of possible gay readings in Hart's lyrics see John M. Clum, *Something for the Boys: Musical Theater and Gay Culture* (New York: St. Martin's, 1999), 58–68, and Jeffrey Smart, "Lorenz Hart: This Can't Be Love," in *Staging Desire: Queer Readings of American Theater History*, ed. Kim Marra and Robert A. Schanke (Ann Arbor: University of Michigan Press, 2002), 167–93.

51. According to Robert Kimball, the continuation of "Ye Lunchtime Follies" (designated "Elaine" in the appendix to *Complete Hart Lyrics*, 333) was dropped, although it does appear in the Tams-Witmark Piano Score rental. The same appendix printed a newly discovered continuation of "Ye Lunchtime Follies," a sung dialogue between Merlin and Fay (designated "I Won't Sing a Song") that never made it into either the librettos or the score. In the expanded edition of *Complete Hart Lyrics*, Robert Kim-

ball and Dorothy Hart identify "I Won't Sing a Song," an incomplete lyric dropped from *Yankee* discovered by Hart's doctor shortly before the lyricist's death, as a likely candidate for Hart's final lyric (*Complete Hart Lyrics*, 333).

52. The dramatic modernity of "You Always Love the Same Girl" is addressed by William Everett in "King Arthur in Popular Musical Theatre and Musical Film," in *King Arthur in Music (Arthurian Studies, 52)*, ed. Richard W. Barber (Woodbridge, U.K.: Boydell & Brewer, 2002).

53. Wilder, 174.

54. The overture, seven songs, and the second-act finale were recorded by the original 1943 cast (four songs originally from 1927 and three new ones) (Decca 440-13 560-2). A considerably more complete version of the 1943 version, however, was recorded from the television broadcast of 1955 (AEI-CD 043).

55. By Suskin's Scorecard the next major Rodgers and Hart revival, 1952's *Pal Joey*, earned five raves and two favorables. It ran for 542 performances, longer than any revival up to that time. See *Opening Night*, 540.

56. The discovery of "I Won't Sing a Song" (see note 51) has only recently begun to challenge "To Keep My Love Alive" as a candidate for Hart's last song.

57. Louis Kronenberger, "Sir Galahad to the Rescue," *New York Newspaper PM* (November 18, 1943), reprinted in *New York Critics' Reviews*, vol. 4, 219; John Chapman, "'Connecticut Yankee' Beautiful in a New Version at the Beck," *New York Daily News* (November 18, 1943), reprinted in *New York Critics' Reviews*, vol. 4, 220.

58. Wilella Waldorf, "'A Connecticut Yankee' in a New 1943 Version," *New York Post* (November 18, 1943), reprinted in *New York Critics' Reviews*, vol. 4, 221.

59. Vera-Ellen can be seen dancing in "Slaughter on Tenth Avenue" in the Rodgers and Hart biopic *Words and Music* (1948), as well as singing and dancing in *On the Town* (1949), *Three Little Words* (1950), *Call Me Madam* (1954), and *White Christmas* (1954), among others.

60. Burton Rascoe, "Connecticut Limps Back," *New York World-Telegram* (November 18, 1943), reprinted in *New York Critics' Reviews*, vol. 4, 220.

61. John Chapman, "'Connecticut Yankee' Beautiful in a New Version at the Beck," *New York Daily News* (November 18, 1943), reprinted in *New York Critics' Reviews*, vol. 4, 220.

62. Some familiar names associated with this broadcast include Eddie Albert (Martin), Janet Blair (Sandy), and Boris Karloff (King Arthur). The songs (and some dialogue) for this recording are available on AEI-CD 043. The *Dearest Enemy* broadcast (November 26, 1955) has been released on AEI-CD 042.

63. Ben Brantley, "'A Connecticut Yankee,'" *New York Times* (February 10, 2001). Nytoday.com/scri.

CHAPTER 3. Hits, Long Runs, and a Musical Comedy of Errors

1. *Musical Stages*, 148–53. *Love Me Tonight* is currently unavailable on video-cassette or DVD. The scene with "Isn't It Romantic" can be seen in *American Masters: "The Sweetest Sounds,"* produced for PBS by Thirteen/WNET New York, 2001.

2. *Musical Stages*, 148.

3. Ibid., 164.

4. Ibid., 172.

5. Of the twelve longest-running book musicals of the 1930s, Rodgers and Hart contributed four: #7 *I Married an Angel* (338 performances); #8 *On Your Toes* (315 performances); #11 *I'd Rather Be Right* (290 performances); and #12 *Babes in Arms* (290 performances). The top six were Gershwin's *Of Thee I Sing* (441), Porter's *Anything Goes* (420) and *DuBarry Was a Lady* (408), Kern and Harbach's *Cat and the Fiddle* (395), Henderson, DeSylva, and Brown's *Flying High* (357), and Kern and Hammerstein's *Music in the Air* (342). The revues, *Hellzapoppin* (music by Sammy Fain, among others) and *Pins and Needles* (music and lyrics by Harold Rome), surpassed all book shows at 1,404 and 1,108 performances, respectively.

6. This was the season that *Porgy and Bess* closed after 124 performances.

7. Margaret Case Harriman, "Words and Music: Rodgers and Hart," *New Yorker* (May 28 and June 4, 1938), 9–23 and 21–25; reprinted in *Take Them Up Tenderly* (New York: Knopf, 1945), 166–85. "The Boys from Columbia," *Time* (September 26, 1938), 35–39. Both profiles are reprinted in *Rodgers Reader*, 47–53 (*Time*) and 53–68 (*New Yorker*).

8. As in the summer of 1937, not much else was running on Broadway during this period. Gerald Bordman points out that in 1941 the appearance of *Best Foot Forward* was separated from its popular predecessor, *Lady in the Dark*, by eight months (Bordman, 578).

9. It has long been public knowledge that Hugh Martin was the man responsible for the uncredited famous jazzy vocal trio arrangement of "Sing for Your Supper." The following year he received official credit as the vocal arranger of *Too Many Girls*.

10. *Musical Stages*, 178.

11. Mielziner's musicals (other than those with Rodgers and Hart or Hammerstein) include the following: *Annie Get Your Gun, Guys and Dolls, Gypsy, 1776*; plays include *Strange Interlude, Street Scene, Winterset, Abe Lincoln in Illinois, The Glass Menagerie, A Streetcar Named Desire, Mister Roberts, Death of a Salesman, Tea and Sympathy,* and *Cat on a Hot Tin Roof*. For an illustrated survey of Mielziner's career, see Mary C. Henderson, *Mielziner: Master of Modern Stage Design* (New York: Back Stage Books, 2001).

12. After designing only the sets for *Carousel*, Mielziner would provide sets and lighting for *Allegro, South Pacific, The King and I, Me and Juliet,* and *Pipe Dream*.

13. Although Rodgers and Hart profited from *Jumbo*, the extraordinary expenses created a loss for its producers, Billy Rose and Jock Whitney.

14. In order to avoid the appearance of difficulties with Hart, Rodgers's production of *Best Foot Forward* was both uncredited and unpublicized.

15. Brooks Atkinson, "'On Your Toes,' Being a Musical Show with a Book and Tunes and a Sense of Humor," *New York Times* (April 13, 1936), and "On Your Toes," *New York Times* (October 12, 1954).

16. In 1996, the 1955 *Connecticut Yankee* broadcast was released on compact disc (AEI-CD 043).

17. Spialek died on November 20, 1983, a few months after the *On Your Toes* revival opened on April 11.

18. *The Ultimate Rodgers & Hart, Volume 1* (Pearl GEM 0110) offers a selection of period recordings, particularly British, of Rodgers and Hart shows, from *Dearest Enemy* through *Hallelujah, I'm a Bum* (1925–33). *The Ultimate Rodgers & Hart, Volume 2* (Pavillion/Pearl/U.K. 114) starts with *Mississippi* and, excluding *I'd Rather Be Right* and *The Boys from Syracuse*, continues through "You're Nearer" from the film version of *Too Many Girls* (the original cast recordings for this and presumably later Rodgers and Hart shows will appear in volume 3). See table 3.5.

19. *Ben Bagley's Rodgers and Hart Revisited*, vols. I–V (Painted Smiles: I, PSCD-116 [1990]; II, PSCD-139 [1992]; III, PSCD-106 [1989]; IV, PSCD-126 [1991]; V, PSCD-140 [1992]).

20. *Musical Stages*, 175.

21. *Enchanted Evenings*, 89–90.

22. For additional historical discussion and analysis of *On Your Toes*, see *Enchanted Evenings*, 87–103.

23. Harriman, *Take Them Up Tenderly*, 177. Rodgers repeated this claim in *Great Performances: Richard Rodgers*, produced by PBS, Thirteen/WNET, New York, 1990.

24. *Musical Stages*, 189.

25. Musicals based on Shakespeare remained few and far between until a flurry of Shakespearean rock musicals appeared in the late 1960s and early 1970s. After Rodgers and Hart the major musicals based on Shakespeare are *Kiss Me, Kate* (1948) and *West Side Story* (1957) (see *Enchanted Evenings*, 179–96 and 245–73).

26. Lehman Engel, *The American Musical Theater* (New York: Collier Books, 1975), 15.

27. *Musical Stages*, 194–95.

28. Brooks Atkinson, "Christmas Night Adds 'Pal Joey' to the Musical Stage," *New York Times* (December 26, 1940), 22. See also Atkinson's partial retraction when reviewing the revival, "At the Theatre," *New York Times* (January 4, 1952), 17. Both reviews are reprinted in *Rodgers Reader*, 68–70 (1940 review) and 158–59 (1952 review).

29. For additional history, criticism, and analysis of *Pal Joey*, see *Enchanted Evenings*, 104–14.

30. Vito Russo, *The Celluloid Closet* (New York: Harper & Row), 39.

31. "Sing for Your Supper," "He and She," "Falling in Love with Love," and "This Can't Be Love" were the four songs that survived from stage to screen.

32. Rodgers regretted being persuaded to use an early song with Hart, "Mountain Greenery," for the college prom music in *Allegro* in 1947 (see *Musical Stages*, 252).

33. Tommy Krasker, "*Babes in Arms*: History and Synopsis," notes to New World Records NW 386–2, 1989, 11.

34. Theodore S. Chapin, "*Babes in Arms*: Circa 1999," notes to City Center Encores! (DRG 94769), 1999, n.p.

35. Constance Valis Hill, *Brotherhood in Rhythm: The Jazz Tap Dancing of the Nicholas Brothers* (New York: Oxford University Press, 2000), 127. Fayard Nicholas made the same point in an interview that appeared in the outtakes for *American Masters: "The Sweetest Sounds"* on the web (see note 1).

36. 1937 libretto, act I, scene 4, p. 26.

37. The libretto also contains a chicken-stealing scene (act I, scene 4, p. 27), a

direct descendant from the nineteenth-century minstrel show tradition. I would like to thank Thomas Riis for pointing this out to me.

38. *Complete Hart Lyrics*, 28. The other parodies in "Shakespeares of 1922" are *Merchant of Venice, King Lear, Julius Caesar,* and *Romeo and Juliet.*

39. Komisarjevsky might have been a familiar name to Rodgers and Hart, since he had directed the Theatre Guild's production of Henrik Ibsen's *Peer Gynt* two seasons before their *Garrick Gaieties.*

40. *Musical Stages*, 191. See also Rodgers, "A Night Out with the Boys," *New York Herald Tribune* (April 14, 1963).

41. See Lawrence W. Levine, *Highbrow, Lowbrow: The Emergence of Cultural Hierarchy in America* (Cambridge, Mass.: Harvard University Press, 1988).

42. Bordman, 44.

43. Winton Dean, "Shakespeare and Opera," in *Shakespeare in Music: A Collection of Essays,* ed. Phyllis Hartnoll (London: Macmillan, and New York: St. Martin's, 1964), 100. In Dean's view the depiction of a shipwreck provides a "brilliant opening scene" and the "smooth contrivance of the ensembles proclaim the master librettist." In *The Concise Oxford Dictionary of Opera* (London: Oxford University Press, 1983), Harold Rosenthal and John Warrack note that *Equivoci* enjoyed several revivals in the 1970s.

44. For a discussion of Shakespeare's probable and possible sources for *The Comedy of Errors,* see *Narrative and Dramatic Sources of Shakespeare I: Early Comedies, Poems, Romeo and Juliet,* ed. Geoffrey Bullough (London: Routledge and Kegan Paul, and New York: Columbia University Press, 1957), 3–11.

45. *The Reader's Encyclopedia of Shakespeare,* ed. Oscar James Campbell (New York: Thomas Y. Crowell, 1966), 130.

46. Kenneth Muir, *Shakespeare's Sources I: Comedies and Tragedies* (London: Methuen, 1957; repr. 1965), 20.

47. George Abbott, *"Mr. Abbott"* (New York: Random House, 1963), 179.

48. Ibid., 179–80.

49. Ibid., 180.

50. *Time,* September 26, 1938, 35 (*Rodgers Reader,* 49).

51. *Musical Stages*, 191. Shakespeare V, i, 69–70.

52. Harry Levin, *"The Comedy of Errors* on Stage and Screen," in *William Shakespeare: "The Comedy of Errors,"* ed. Harry Levin (New York: Signet, 1989), 182.

53. *Reader's Encyclopedia of Shakespeare,* 133.

54. Harold Bloom, *Shakespeare: The Invention of the Human* (New York: Riverhead, 1998), 21.

55. In the 1963 Off-Broadway revival (of which more later) Comedy and Tragedy are replaced by the two Dromios: Dromio of Syracuse (first line), Dromio of Ephesus (second line), and both Dromios for the third line.

56. "Table II: Comparative Analysis," in *William Shakespeare: The Complete Works,* ed. Alfred Harbarge (New York: Penguin, 1969), 31. Thanks to Shakespeare scholar Peter Greenfield for calling my attention to this source.

57. In several cases Shakespeare frames a prose scene with a poetic couplet. See, for example, the opening and closing couplets of act I, scene 1.

58. Walter Kerr, "A Line I'd Call Pretty," in *Thirty Plays Hath November: Pain and Pleasure in the Contemporary Theater* (New York: Simon and Schuster, 1969), 192–95, reprinted in *Rodgers Reader*, 231–34.

59. Theodore S. Chapin, "Rodgers and Hart: What Can Time Do?" Notes to *The Boys from Syracuse*, 1997 City Center's *Encores!* (DRG 94367), n.p.

60. In the 1963 Off-Broadway revival the song is assigned to the Courtesan.

61. Brooks Atkinson, "The Play in Review," *New York Times* (November 24, 1939).

62. Alan Brien, *London Daily Telegraph* (November 8, 1963), quoted in Secrest, 369. For Secrest, the London production conclusively demonstrated that in comparison to Sondheim's *Funny Thing Happened on the Way to the Forum*, still running after a more than a year, Rodgers and Hart's dinosaur "was obviously far less clever, witty, and pointed."

63. Abbott, "*Mr. Abbott*," 187.

64. In a surprising turn of fate, all was forgiven (or perhaps forgotten) when, two years later, Ebb was preparing his first Broadway show with composer John Kander, *Flora, the Red Menace*. The librettist and director of *Flora* was Abbott.

65. This is, of course, a takeoff on Porter's "I Get a Kick Out of You" from *Anything Goes* (1934).

66. The 1963 libretto sets this up when Luce says, "I married him for life, and, by God, he's going to show some" (p. 26).

67. Diana E. Henderson, "A Shrew for the Times," in *Shakespeare, The Movie*, ed. Lynda E. Boose and Richard Burn (London: Routlege, 1997), 148.

68. Douglas Brode, *Shakespeare in the Movies: From the Silent Era to "Shakespeare in Love"* (Oxford: Oxford University Press, 2000), 15.

69. Levin, "*Comedy of Errors* on Stage and Screen," 187.

70. Ibid., 188.

CHAPTER 4. World War II, the Musical: *South Pacific*

Epigraphs: Richard Watts, Jr., "A Grand Musical Play Called 'South Pacific,'" *New York Post*, April 8, 1949, reprinted in *New York Critics' Reviews*, vol. 10, 315. Margaret M. Knapp, "*South Pacific*," in *Cambridge Guide to American Theatre*, ed. Don B. Wilmeth and Tice L. Miller (Cambridge: Cambridge University Press, 1993), 440. Although in this chapter I take issue with its interpretation of Cable's response to Liat, this pithy summary is a port of entry for those new to *South Pacific*. For a more detailed plot summary that includes the dramatic placement of the songs, see Kurt Gänzl and Andrew Lamb, *Gänzl's Book of the Musical Theatre* (London: The Bodley Head, 1988), 679–83.

1. *Oklahoma!* reigned in London for 1,548 performances (April 29, 1947–October 21, 1950), in later months moving from the Drury Lane to the Stoll Theatre to make way for the first of *Carousel*'s impressive but less spectacular 566 performances at the Drury (June 7, 1950–October 13, 1951). *South Pacific* followed in close succession on November 1 and played at the Drury until September 26, 1953. See *R&H Fact Book*, 526–29, 540–43, and 571–75.

2. *R&H Fact Book*, 568–71.

3. Both the 78s and 33 rpm albums present the fourteen main songs as well as

the Overture and the Finale. To accommodate all this material on fourteen sides, two pairs of songs songs, "Dites-Moi" and "Cockeyed Optimist," and "Honey Bun" and "Carefully Taught," share rather than own a separate side.

4. *South Pacific* won a total of eight Tony Awards for the 1949–50 season, including Best Musical, Best Book (Hammerstein and Joshua Logan), Best Score (Rodgers), Best Direction (Logan), and a quartet of best performances (Ezio Pinza and Mary Martin) and supporting performances (Myron McCormick and Juanita Hall). The previous year *South Pacific* had garnered Donaldson Awards (offered between 1944 and 1955) in virtually the same categories. The only discrepancies were that Hammerstein received a separate Donaldson award for his lyrics and Pinza won for Best Debut Performance rather than Best Performance.

5. Since the Pulitzer committee did not at the time subscribe to the notion of the composer as dramatist, it excluded George Gershwin from the award. Rodgers therefore became the first composer to receive the Pulitzer Prize for Drama. *Oklahoma!* received a special citation from the Pulitzer committee in 1944 but did not actually win the prize.

6. Howard Barnes, "Pearls, Pure Pearls," *New York Herald Tribune*, April 8, 1949, reprinted in *New York Critics' Reviews*, vol. 10, 313.

7. In a lap dissolve in film, one shot is fused with another; in the stage equivalent, new scenes enter as the old disappear. Ethan Mordden notes that the dissolve was used in *Allegro* but that it was overwhelmed by the show's many other innovative staging devices. He also acknowledges the obvious fact that the bare stages of *Allegro* virtually created a necessity for dissolves. See Mordden *R&H*, 119.

8. Brooks Atkinson, "At the Theatre," *New York Times*, April 8, 1949.

9. Barnes, "Pure Pearls," 313. Although Robert Garland thought that Rodgers had produced a score destined for considerable wear in jukeboxes, he does not name any songs by name. Robert Garland, "Fine Music, Smooth Lyrics, Prize Story," *Journal American*, April 8, 1949, reprinted in *New York Critics' Reviews*, vol. 10, 312.

10. Robert Coleman, "'South Pacific' a Solid Hit, with Great Cast, Score," *Daily Mirror*, April 8, 1949, reprinted in *New York Critics' Reviews*, vol. 10, 313.

11. Ward Morehouse, "'South Pacific' Is Stunning," *The Sun*, April 8, 1949, and John Chapman, "'South Pacific' a Beautiful, Big Musical, and Pinza Dominates It," April 8, 1949, reprinted in *New York Critics' Reviews*, vol. 10, 314–15.

12. Watts, "Grand Musical Play," 315.

13. According to Steven Suskin's "Broadway Scorecard," New York critics gave *South Pacific* nothing less than eight raves (*Opening Night*, 639–43).

14. It is not entirely coincidental that Nellie Forbush's home town of Little Rock, Arkansas, would become the locus of American racial conflict in 1957. Nevertheless, *Baltimore Sun* theater critic J. Wynn Rousuck refutes undocumented but persistent rumors that *South Pacific* was banned throughout the South in the 1950s: "After the initial touring production played Atlanta in 1953, some Georgia legislators introduced legislation aimed at banning entertainment with 'an underlying philosophy inspired by Moscow.' Only South Africa appears to have successfully outlawed the show. However, here in Baltimore, community activist A. Robert Kaufman recalls that local civil rights workers won the support of Rodgers and Hammerstein when they asked the producers to boycott the city's former Ford's Theatre, which had segregated seating. 'We got a

letter from Rodgers and Hammerstein confirming that [*South Pacific*] would not play Baltimore,' Kaufman says. As a result, the show didn't reach Baltimore until the fifth and final year of its first national tour—1955, by which time Ford's was integrated." J. Wynn Rousuck, *Baltimore Sun*, February 11, 2002. www.sunspot.net/entertainment.

15. New York City Center Light Opera, 1955, 1957, 1961, and 1965; St. Louis Municipal Opera, 1955; San Francisco and Los Angeles Civic Light Opera (with Mary Martin and Giorgio Tozzi), 1957; Kansas City Starlight Theatre, 1957; Dallas State Fair Music Hall, 1957 and 1962. *R&H Fact Book*, 569–70.

16. John Rockwell, "A New 'South Pacific' by the City Opera," *New York Times*, March 2, 1987.

17. Manuela Hoelterhoff, "City Opera's 'South Pacific,'" *Wall Street Journal*, March 5, 1987, reprinted in *New York Critics' Reviews*, vol. 48, 372.

18. Mordden *R&H*, 124.

19. Ethan Mordden, *Beautiful Mornin': The Broadway Musical in the 1940s* (New York: Oxford University Press), 269.

20. James A. Michener, *Tales of the South Pacific* (New York: Macmillan, 1947). See John P. Hayes, *James A. Michener: A Biography* (Indianapolis: Bobbs-Merrill, 1984), 59–71.

21. A short list of Michener's historical novels includes *The Bridges at Toko-ri* (1953), *Sayonara* (1954), *Hawaii* (1959), *The Source* (1965), *Centennial* (1974), *Space* (1982), *Texas* (1985), and *Alaska* (1988); among his many nonfiction writings are *Iberia* (1968), *Kent State: What Happened and Why* (1971), *Sports in America* (1976), and an autobiography, *The World Is My Home: A Memoir* (1992).

22. Michener, "Happy Talk: Tribute to the Writers of 'South Pacific,'" *New York Times*, July 3, 1949.

23. In the film, Harbison serves as Nellie's date after the Thanksgiving show and is given some lines that don't appear in the final film script. This decision further reduces Dinah's already truncated appearance (compared to her role in Michener's novel). Instead of Nellie asking if Dinah is ready, she says to Harbison, "Bill. Bill. Bill. Can we go now please?"

24. Michener, "Our Heroine," in *Tales of the South Pacific*, 51.

25. Michener, "Fo' Dolla'," in *Tales of the South Pacific*, 154.

26. Billis is in fact a conflation of at least three characters, Bus Adams, Tony Fry, and Atabrine Benny, two of whom are totally subsumed by Billis and his antics.

27. Michener, "Dry Rot," in *Tales of the South Pacific*, 126.

28. Mordden, *Beautiful Mornin'*, 263.

29. *Musical Stages*, 258–64. In Rodgers's *Reminiscences*, the story of *South Pacific* also begins when Rodgers met Logan at the party, but in this earlier source Rodgers remembered, weeks later, that Logan had suggested a book for a possible musical and then called him (in *Musical Stages*, Logan called Rodgers). See *Reminiscences*, 291–305, reprinted in *Rodgers Reader*, 311–17.

30. Although not named, this third story was "A Boar's Tooth." The selective use of other stories will be discussed in connection with the adaptation of Michener's *Tales*.

31. Mordden *R&H*, 116.

32. Ibid. *South Pacific* was not the first to modify these rules. To take one example, Frank Loesser's first Broadway show, *Where's Charley?* (1947), introduced audiences

to the idea that secondary characters can be lyrical principals in contrast to the comic leads.

33. *Musical Stages*, 260.

34. Ibid., 260; Mary Martin, *My Heart Belongs* (New York: William Morrow, 1976), 160, reprinted in *Rodgers Reader*, 149.

35. *Musical Stages*, 262.

36. Ezio Pinza, with Robert Magidoff, *An Autobiography* (New York: Rinehart, 1958), 244.

37. *Reminiscences*, 291–305, reprinted in *Rodgers Reader*, 311–17. Near the end of his recollections of *South Pacific* Rodgers discusses the negative British critical response, not only to *South Pacific* but to all R&H musicals after *Oklahoma!*—a response that Rodgers attributes to the jealousy generated by the absence of quality native British artistic products (*Reminiscences*, 302–3; *Rodgers Reader*, 316).

38. *Musical Stages*, 261. Rodgers's disclaimer marks a pattern of thought that would reemerge during the production of *No Strings*. In this self-evidently interracial musical, Rodgers, over the questions and objections of nearly everyone involved, asserted repeatedly that race had nothing to do with why the white and African-American couple could not lead a life of happiness and fulfillment in Maine (see chapter 6).

39. Joshua Logan, *Josh: My Up and Down, In and Out Life* (New York: Delacorte, 1976), 220–46, reprinted in *Rodgers Reader*, 133–46. For a more recent account, see Hyland, *Richard Rodgers*, 179.

40. Logan, *Josh*, 228. Before *South Pacific* Logan had directed *On Borrowed Time* and *Knickerbocker Holiday* (1938), *Morning's at Seven* (1939), *This Is the Army* (1942), and *Mr. Roberts* (1948). After *South Pacific* he directed *Picnic* (1953), *Fanny* (1954), *Middle of the Night* (1956), and *Mr. President* (1962), in addition to several films, including *Picnic* (1955), *Bus Stop* (1956), *Sayonara* (1957), *South Pacific* (1958), *Camelot* (1967), and *Paint Your Wagon* (1969).

41. Trude Rittmann was Rodgers's dance arranger from *Carousel* until the 1970s.

42. Logan does not mention that he and Hayward tried to fire Pinza but were overruled by R&H.

43. Logan mistitles "Suddenly Lovely" as "Suddenly Lucky," an error that set in motion decades of confusion. See the discussion later in this chapter. The lyrics of "Suddenly Lovely" are reprinted in Frederick Nolan, *The Sound of Their Music: The Story of Rodgers & Hammerstein* (New York: Applause Theatre & Cinema Books, 2002), 189.

44. *Musical Stages*, 264.

45. Rodgers's sketches and holograph scores are located in the Richard Rodgers Collection, Music Division, Library of Congress. For a comprehensive catalogue and description of the contents, see Guides to Special Collections in the Music Division of the Library of Congress, The Richard Rodgers Collection, Library of Congress, Washington, 1995, prepared by Mark Eden Horowitz.

46. The January 21, 1949, libretto is also housed in the Library of Congress.

47. The "Bright Canary Yellow" holograph is in D major, the same as "Twin Soliloquies," which follows later in the scene. For a published version of the untitled lyric, see also *Lyrics by Oscar Hammerstein II* (Milwaukee: Hal Leonard, 1985), 198.

48. Since Rodgers also sketched "A Cockeyed Optimist," it was presumably part of

the original conception of the scene. In any event, the canary yellow image appears in the January draft for both "Bright Canary Yellow" and "A Cockeyed Optimist."

49. "Loneliness of Evening" was published, along with "Now Is the Time" and "My Girl Back Home," in *Rodgers and Hammerstein Rediscovered* (Williamson Music, 1992). The lyrics can also be found under the title "Will My Love Come Home to Me?" in *Lyrics by Oscar Hammerstein II*, 198.

50. Both Martin and Pinza in their memoirs recall hearing and sharing their response to "A Wonderful Guy." Martin, *My Heart Belongs*, 160; Pinza, *An Autobiography*, 238.

51. The autopsy on Emile's bully also changed from the novel to the musical in a manner designed for their respective audiences. Michener's bully succumbed to Emile's willful attack with a knife.

52. Both numbers can be heard in the complete recording conducted by John Owen Edwards (Jay Productions Ltd., CDJAY2 1246, 1997). "Now Is the Time" can also be heard prior to "This Nearly Was Mine" in the 2001 Royal National Theatre London production.

53. Martin's is the only contemporary account to mention "Will You Marry Me?" In contrast to the interpretation offered here, however, she places the song originally in act II before it was replaced by "This Nearly Was Mine." According to Martin, "Will You Marry Me?" was "lovely, but it didn't have the dramatic intensity for the scene" and "This Nearly Was Mine" replaced it the week before the New York opening. Martin, *My Heart Belongs*, 167.

54. *Musical Stages*, 261.

55. Stanley Green credits Rodgers's daughter Mary with remembering the tune. Stanley Green, *The Rodgers and Hammerstein Story* (New York: John Day, 1963; repr., New York: Da Capo, 1980), 135–36. According to Hugh Fordin, the only other *South Pacific* song in which the music preceded the words was "This Nearly Was Mine." See Fordin, *Getting to Know Him: A Biography of Oscar Hammerstein II* (New York: Random House, 1977), 279.

56. Stephen Citron, *The Wordsmiths: Oscar Hammerstein 2nd and Alan Jay Lerner* (New York: Oxford University Press, 1995), 199, and Fordin, *Getting to Know Him*, 279. Offering neither a title nor a lyric, Rodgers's first major biographer David Ewen mentions that "'Younger Than Springtime' had originated in *Allegro* but had been discarded" and that "Hammerstein had always been fond of it" (Ewen, 254).

57. According to the Library of Congress guide to the Rodgers Collection, no sketches or holographs are extant for "My Wife," nor does the Rodgers and Hammerstein Organization have a copy. Tom Briggs, the Director of the R&H Theater Library, informed me that the Library of Congress possesses a "music-only sheet with 'My Wife' written in Rodgers's hand at the top" (personal communication, August 2, 1999). Steven Suskin lists "My Wife" as an unpublished song for *Allegro* that contains the first lyric for "Younger Than Springtime" (see Suskin, *Berlin, Kern, Rodgers, Hart, and Hammerstein: A Complete Song Catalogue* [Jefferson, N.C.: McFarland, 1990], 161 and 247).

58. Citron, *Wordsmiths*, 199. In a personal communication October 4, 2001, Citron informed me that he had seen this sheet in the *Allegro* file ten years ago, and

that it was this manuscript that he used to make the connections between "My Wife" and "Younger Than Springtime" in *Wordsmiths*.

59. Logan, *Josh*, 233.

60. Ibid.

61. A similarly effective reworded reprise of "If I Loved You" had been the only major tryout change in the *Carousel* score. See *Enchanted Evenings*, 164.

62. It is possible that Hammerstein needed additional time after January to work out the lyrics to "Honey Bun." The libretto, however, includes the following description and opening lyric line before noting "lyric coming later": "Nellie dressed as a sailor, sings a verse about a wonderful girl, the refrain stating that she is a 'hundred and one pounds of fun, that's my little honey-bun.'"

63. Paul Osborn's screenplay of *South Pacific* (Final Script, June 10, 1957) is in the *South Pacific* boxes of the uncatalogued Oscar Hammerstein II Collection, Music Division, Library of Congress.

64. *Reminiscences*, 304–5, reprinted in *Rodgers Reader*, 317.

65. The Zeitlin memo and other memos discussed below are found in the Joshua Logan Papers, Manuscript Division, Library of Congress.

66. In the end they settled for blue filters, perhaps as a metaphor for Cable's blue Philadelphia blood.

67. Joshua Logan, "Inglorious Technicolor," in *Movie Stars, Real People, and Me* (New York: Delacorte, 1978), 138. Gerald Mast also ultimately blames Rodgers for allowing the production of a film with few rivals in "sheer bad taste." After noting Juanita Hall's fuchsia face in "Bali Ha'i," Mitzi Gaynor's and Rossano Brazzi's ash-gray faces against the silver-blue sky in "Some Enchanted Evening," and of course the bright canary yellow that fills the screen in "A Cockeyed Optimist," Mast recalls that "a younger Richard Rodgers had written a parody of conveying emotion by turning colors—'That Terrific Rainbow' for *Pal Joey*." Gerald Mast, *Can't Help Singin': The American Musical on Stage and Screen* (Woodstock, N.Y.: Overlook, 1987), 217.

68. Ethan Mordden, *The Hollywood Musical* (New York: St. Martin's, 1981), 207.

69. Scene 2 in the staged version. See *Six Plays by Rodgers & Hammerstein* (New York: Modern Library, 1959).

70. The final film script opened the plantation scene with a chorus of "Dites-Moi," but this too was removed during the filming.

71. *Six Plays*, 298.

72. Screenplay, Final Script, p. 33.

73. Some other less significant departures: Cable's inquiry about the identity of Bloody Mary is omitted in the film, and his questions to Billis about whether he knows de Becque are transferred to the film's opening shot on the airplane. The Latin business with the Professor, perhaps a little esoteric for a film audience—just as in scene 9 the French natives who sing "Bali Ha'i" in French become bilingual French natives who sing only in English—is omitted from the film; the knowledge that Cable is a Princeton man would suffice. Toward the end of the scene the exchange in which Mary thanks Cable for kicking her off Navy property is absent from the June script but nonetheless inserted into the film. See *Six Plays*, 293, 296–99.

74. Ibid., 306–7.

75. Ibid., 308–9.

76. The brief added exchange does not appear where expected in the Screenplay, Final Script, p. 49.

77. *Six Plays*, 312–16.

78. Once again the actual film departs from the final film script, which, like the stage version, is abbreviated. Moving ahead to the 2001 television broadcast, when Emile in the reworked script first tells Nellie he killed a man, he offers no reason, not even that he killed a wicked bully.

79. *Six Plays*, 329.

80. In both stage and film versions Emile sings "going" in contrast to Nellie's "gonna."

81. In the stage version we don't really know why Cable was in the hospital; in the film Cable refers to the "darn malaria" he contracted on "Bali Ha'i."

82. Leonard J. Leff and Jerold L. Simmons, *The Dame in the Kimono: Hollywood, Censorship, and the Production Code from the 1920s to the 1960s* (New York: Grove Weidenfeld, 1990), passim; quotation on p. 220.

83. Logan does not mention in his memoirs the perhaps still more suggestive gesture that before the blackout "the lights fade slowly as his hand slides her blouse up her back toward her shoulder." *Six Plays*, 323.

84. Section II4 of the Code prohibits miscegenation. Although it selectively defines this activity as "sex relationships between white and black races," one can assume that the Code would frown on sexual relationships between any two different races.

85. *Six Plays*, 323; Screenplay, Final Script, p. 72.

86. Between the moment when Cable picks up Liat and the next morning is a scene with Billis waiting for Cable at the pier.

87. Frank McCarthy to Buddy Adler with a carbon copy to Logan (May 28); Geoffrey M. Shurlock to McCarthy (June 4); Shurlock to McCarthy (June 21); McCarthy to Adler with a carbon copy to Logan (July 8); and Shurlock to McCarthy (July 17).

88. Unfortunately, a script labeled Temporary Revised Script did not surface in my examination of the Logan and Hammerstein Collections in the Library of Congress.

89. Bert Fink, "ABC Scores Some Enchanted Evening with *South Pacific*," *Happy Talk* 8/3 (Summer 2001), 1, 5.

90. Moorea: "Volcanic island (1988 pop. 7,059), c. 50 sq mi (130 sq km), South Pacific, second largest of the Windward group of the SOCIETY ISLANDS, FRENCH POLYNESIA" (*The Columbia Encyclopedia*, 5th ed. [New York: Columbia University Press, 1993], 1826).

91. Attentive listeners can hear "Happy Talk" in the background at the Officer's Club (along with "You Never Had It So Good," cut from *Me and Juliet*, and "Loneliness of Evening," cut from *South Pacific*).

92. "ABC Scores," 5.

93. Interestingly, the current Royal National Theatre production for the most part adopts the running order of the television version.

94. *Six Plays*, 347.

95. Jeanne Crain had just turned twenty when *State Fair* was released; Shirley Jones twenty-one in the film version of *Oklahoma!*; Julie Andrews twenty-two in the televised *Cinderella*; Mitzi Gaynor a youthful and attractive twenty-eight in the *South*

Pacific film; and Lesley Ann Warren an eighteen-year-old in her debut role in the *Cinderella* remake.

96. Julie Salamon, "'South Pacific': Being Corny as Kansas Isn't So Simple Anymore," *New York Times*, March 26, 2001. <www.nytimes.com/2001/03/26/arts/26 SALA.html>

97. *Musical Stages*, 219 and 236.

98. Quoted in Theodore S. Chapin, "Rodgers and Hart: What Can Time Do?" Notes to *The Boys from Syracuse*, 1997 Original New York Recording, City Center's *Encores!* (DRG 94767), n.p.

99. Another presumably self-aware example of Rodgers inverting the opening A section material in the B section can be found in "Bewitched" (see *Enchanted Evenings*, 109).

100. Richard Rodgers, "How to Write Music in No Easy Lessons: A Self Interview," *Theatre Arts* (October 1939), 741–46; all quotes from p. 743, reprinted in *Rodgers Reader*, 261–65, quotations on p. 263.

101. For additional analytical discussion of thematic origins and unities (among other critical issues) in *Carousel*, see Joseph P. Swain, *The Broadway Musical: A Critical and Musical Survey* (New York: Oxford University Press, 1990), 99–127, and *Enchanted Evenings*, 159–78.

102. Martin, *My Heart Belongs*, 160.

103. *Enchanted Evenings*, 109–12.

104. Cable is also tangentially connected to Nellie and Emile through "Bali Ha'i." Although "Bali Ha'i," with its emphasis on the leading tone, doesn't literally belong to Nellie and Emile, leading tones also beckon them to their own equally special island in the South Pacific.

105. For more on the quarter-note (and half-note) triplet, see *Enchanted Evenings*, 55–57.

106. Bloody Mary and Cable also share a prominent rhythm between "Bali Ha'i" and "Younger Than Springtime." Cable's verse (the musical foreplay that preceded the main chorus of the song) transforms the rhythm of Mary's verse into a new melody.

107. *Six Plays*, 328–29.

108. Hammerstein, "Foreword" to *Rodgers and Hart Song Book*, xi, quoted in *Rodgers Reader*, 81.

109. My thanks to Bruce Pomahac of the Rodgers and Hammerstein Organziation for clarifying the extent of Bennett's contribution (personal communication, October 9, 2001).

110. The insertion of fragments of "Some Enchanted Evening" and "Wonderful Guy" in the orchestration of "This Nearly Was Mine" is probably also Bennett's idea, although it is possible they were inserted at the suggestion of Rodgers.

CHAPTER 5. Broadway Comes to Television

1. Lerner recalled a conversation with Hammerstein in which Rodgers's partner said that *My Fair Lady* "can't be done. . . . Dick and I worked on it for over a year and gave it up." Alan Jay Lerner, *On the Street Where I Live* (New York: Norton, 1978), 38.

2. Less than two years before *My Fair Lady*, Andrews had made a successful

debut in the New York production of the London import *The Boy Friend* (September 30, 1954).

3. The figure of 107 million was 37 million more than the number of viewers who tuned in to see the Beatles on *The Ed Sullivan Show* in the early 1960s. In a later, more fragmented television world the *South Pacific* broadcast in March 2001 reached an estimated 16 million viewers and was rightly considered a huge success.

4. Harold Messing, "The CBS Television Production of *Cinderella*," M.A. thesis, Stanford University, August 1957, 1–2.

5. The music and some introductory dialogue from these broadcasts have been released on CDs: *Dearest Enemy* (AEI-CD 042) and *A Connecticut Yankee* (AIE-CD 043).

6. The *Peter Pan* version distributed on videotape is the final broadcast of 1960 (Goodtimes VHS 7001, 1990).

7. The "New Haven" and "Boston" kinescopes were presumably destroyed.

8. Messing's source is an April 2, 1957, interview with Paul Davis, who is listed on various original documents as the compiler (Messing, "CBS Television Production of *Cinderella*," 58). In his notes to the City Center production of 1995, Richard Traubner, citing Messing, mentions the videotape but erroneously assumes that it was filmed in color. The first known color videotape dates from October 1957. I would like to thank Jane Klain, the manager of research services at the Museum of Television & Radio, for clarifying the history of kinescope and videotape. If the videotape is ever discovered—and Klain is working on this—it would be possible to naturally restore the original color without resorting to "colorization."

9. Ewen, 303. Quoted also in Hugh Fordin, *Getting to Know Him* (New York: Random House, 1977), 332–33.

10. Stanley Green, "'Cinderella' on a Coaxial Cable," *Saturday Review* (March 30, 1957), 24–25, quoted in Messing, "CBS Television Production of *Cinderella*," 9–10. Although the broadcast was intended to reach viewers of all ages, several critics pointed out that the relative lateness of the presentation, 8:00 to 9:30 P.M., precluded young children from watching.

11. CBS Color Television News, March 7, 1957, quoted in Messing, "CBS Television Production of *Cinderella*," 10.

12. Mordden *R&H*, 182.

13. Alan Dundes, *Cinderella: A Folklore Casebook* (New York: Garland, 1982), 16.

14. In the copy lent to me by the R&H Organization, a handwritten emendation, "white," replaces the gray mice specified in the typescript.

15. Perhaps to allow for the possibility that the singer portraying the title role of Rossini's *La Cenerentola* (1816) would possess more than a petite shoe size, this Italian Cinderella loses one of her matching bracelets at the ball.

16. Sony Classical (SK 60889).

17. Messing, "CBS Television Production of *Cinderella*," 53.

18. Wilder, 221–22.

19. The main melodic content of the verse also strongly evokes, without literal quotation, a passage from Adolphe Adam's ballet *Giselle* (1841).

20. "Your Majesties" was the only song dropped from both the 1965 and 1997

broadcasts in favor of dialogue. I think this was a mistake. It might not be memorable as a song, but it presents important dialogue in a believable musical conversation.

21. Near the end of "Impossible," the words "[And be-] cause these daft and dewy-eyed dopes keep building up impossible hopes" share the basic rhythmic profile and bear a recognizable melodic resemblance to an analogous portion of "I Whistle a Happy Tune" from *The King and I*, another song about wishes, on the words "For when I fool the people I fear, I fool myself as well!"

22. 1957 Script, p. 69.

23. Once Rodgers gets the point across, he keeps the basic rhythmic pattern for the next phrase. Compare the next "big bad wolf" with *Cinderella*'s slightly elongated "a frail and fluf [-fy]."

24. It was noted in Chapter 1 that hearing Josef Hofmann play Tchaikovsky's Piano Concerto No. 1 was a highlight of Rodgers's youth (*Musical Stages*, 18–19). In his recollection of *Chee-Chee*, Rodgers recalls using Tchaikovsky for mischievous purposes, one of the few times he directly quoted someone else's tune: "One special pleasure I derived in composing the score for *Chee-Chee* was a musical joke that I used toward the end of the second act. As the son of the Grand Eunuch was being led off for his emasculation operation, he was accompanied by a triumphal march, in the middle of which I inserted several bars of Tchaikovsky's *Nutcracker Suite*. I found it gratifying that at almost every performance there were two or three individuals with ears musically sharp enough to appreciate the joke" (*Musical Stages*, 119).

25. The libretto (K 126) indicates that the processional music is "Do I Love You Because You're Beautiful?" Does this represent a change or an error?

26. Mordden *R&H*, 184.

27. Richard Rodgers, Notes to the *Cinderella* remake (Columbia OL 6330).

28. Mordden *R&H*, 185.

29. The published vocal score includes "Boys and Girls Like You and Me" as a song for the King and Queen, an addition adapted for stage productions that could use a few more songs than could fit into an eighty-minute television broadcast. The song, incorporated into the stage version of *State Fair*, is one of the few R&H songs praised by Wilder.

30. When Glenn Close wanted to produce *South Pacific* as a starring vehicle, the versatile actress had no other credible options. Liat is not only Tonkinese, she is also considerably younger than Nellie and needs to remove at least some of her clothes. Worse, she does not have much of a speaking role and nothing to sing. And one can only imagine the furor if Close cast herself as Bloody Mary.

31. Both Peggy Lee's "Lover" and Peters's "Falling in Love with Love" convert a waltz into a somewhat frenetic Latin-tinged duple meter.

32. CBS 42205. Vaughan (1924–90), widely regarded as one of the leading jazz singers of her generation, sang and recorded with Billy Eckstine, Dizzy Gillespie, and Charlie Parker in the 1940s and remained near the top of her form throughout the 1980s. The *South Pacific* crossover also offered the operatic voices of Kiri Te Kanawa (Nellie Forbush) and the Spanish tenor José Carreras (Emile de Becque), who had appeared the previous year as Maria and Tony in an operatic *West Side Story* conducted by its composer, Leonard Bernstein. Among the major roles in the *South Pacific* cross-

over recording, only that of Cable was sung by an artist associated with Broadway, the tenor Mandy Patinkin.

33. 1997 Script, p. 1.

34. The entire *No Strings* Original Broadway Cast album was a hit. According to the CD liner notes, it "debuted on the *Billboard* charts on April 21, 1962, reached #5 and remained on the charts for 274 weeks" (Angel ZDM 0777–7–64694). See also Hyland, 271.

35. 1957 Script, p. 85.

36. Freedman tries to take advantage of Goldberg's comic delivery—for example, when she quips, "It's very difficult to cancel once you've got the ball rolling." 1997 Script, p. 29.

37. These issues will be revisited in Chapter 6.

38. The Stepmother's off-stage calls are reminiscent of the meeting scene in *Show Boat*, when Magnolia's mother, Parthy, shrilly calls her daughter's name and interrupts the underscoring to "Make Believe."

39. 1997 Script, p. 25.

40. Ibid., p. 12.

CHAPTER 6. After Hammerstein

1. Thomas Vinciguerra, "Do You Really Call That Sound Music?" *New York Times*, August 20, 2000.

2. *Musical Stages*, ix; Mary Rodgers's entire introduction is reprinted in *Rodgers Reader*, 255–59, quotation on p. 257.

3. Hyland, 305.

4. *Opening Night*, 488–92, and Steven Suskin, *More Opening Nights on Broadway: A Critical Quotebook of the Musical Theatre, 1965 Through 1981* (New York: Schirmer, 1997), 235–41, 461–67, 769–75, 929–34.

5. Twelve years before *No Strings*, Taylor's play *The Happy Time*, adapted from a novel by Robert Fontaine, was produced by Rodgers and Hammerstein and enjoyed a long run. Taylor also wrote the play and screenplay versions of *Sabrina Fair* (the film title shortened to *Sabrina*) and *The Pleasure of His Company*, the latter with Cornelia Otis Skinner. Alfred Hitchcock buffs know Taylor for his screenplay for *Vertigo*. *No Strings* was Taylor's first musical libretto.

6. The London export of *No Strings*, however, closed after a disappointing 135 performances (December 30, 1963, to May 9, 1964). Instead of Carroll and Kiley, the production featured Beverly Todd and Art Lund (the original Joey in Frank Loesser's *The Most Happy Fella* [1956]).

7. Including the two duet reprises in act II, David and Barbara virtually monopolize the musical proceedings. Barbara sings two solo songs in act I and one in act II. David sings only one solo ("How Sad") but joins Barbara for seven songs. After being featured in five of the nine songs in act I, the musical couple sings six out of the seven songs and reprises in act II. With a little revision *No Strings* could probably be converted into a two-character show along the lines of *I Do! I Do!*

8. *No Strings*, Script, p. 118.

9. James A. Michener, *The World Is My Home: A Memoir* (New York: Random House, 1992), 295.

10. *Musical Stages*, 261–62.

11. Ibid., 307.

12. Hyland, 269. Hyland also reports that protests forced an early closing of the road tour (Hyland, 272). In a televised interview Kiley recalls observing audience members walk out, presumably in response to an on-stage kiss with Carroll (*Music by Rodgers*, Produced for PBS by Thirteen/WNET New York, 1990).

13. Diahann Carroll, with Ross Firestone, *Diahann: An Autobiography* (Boston: Little, Brown, 1986), 114; Carroll's recollections of Rodgers and *No Strings* are reprinted in *Rodgers Reader*, 217–24, quotation on p. 221.

14. When Barbara's platonic but hopeful gigolo Louis sings "I can ask for anything more" in "The Man Who Has Everything," Rodgers, the lyricist, is surely making a verbal allusion to an Ira Gershwin line in "I Got Rhythm," "who could ask for anything more."

15. The tritone, or augmented fourth (in this case F-B♮), is the same dissonant interval that permeates *West Side Story* and bebop.

16. In "The Man Who Has Everything," Louis de Pourtal, Barbara's rich and, at least for a little while longer, undemanding boyfriend, sings two musical lines, "The girl whom I've chosen for my quarry" and later "But sit on the terrace sipping scotch," which depart only minimally from Nettie Fowler's phrase, "sweet silver song of a lark," in *Carousel*'s anthem, "You'll Never Walk Alone." Coincidentally, the music to David's "blissful to be there" in "How Sad" approximates the same phrase.

17. On the unfulfilled collaboration with Lerner, see *Musical Stages*, 314–15, and Hyland, 277–79.

18. See especially Craig Zadan, *Sondheim & Co.* (New York: Harper & Row, 1986), 99–111, reprinted in *Rodgers Reader*, 224–30; and Meryle Secrest, *Stephen Sondheim: A Life* (New York: Knopf, 1998), 173–79.

19. Louis Calta, "Rodgers and Sondheim Preparing a Musical," *New York Times*, November 6, 1964.

20. *Musical Stages*, 318.

21. In *Waltz*, the song that exploits the limits imposed by language, "No Understand," or, in Italian, "Non capisco," bears a familial textual resemblance to Masetto's aria "Ho capito" in Mozart's *Don Giovanni*. In the unlikely event that the resemblance was intentional, it would stand out as one of the few conscious debts to an Italian musical source in this studiously non-Italianate score.

22. Arthur Laurents, *Original Story By: A Memoir of Broadway and Hollywood* (New York: Knopf, 2000), 214.

23. Several opening-night reviewers wondered why a woman as beautiful as Allen had trouble finding eligible men. Richard Watts suggested one explanation: Allen's "loathsome habit of calling them 'Cookie.'" Richard Watts, *New York Post*, March 19, 1965, reprinted in *New York Critics' Reviews*, vol. 26, 360.

24. *Musical Stages*, p. 319.

25. Laurents, *Original Story By*, 195. For Laurents's complete account of the origins of *Cuckoo* and its film and musical adaptations, see pages 185–219.

26. Ethan Mordden, *Open a New Window: The Broadway Musical in the 1960s* (New York: St. Martin's, 2001), 108.

27. Laurents, *Original Story By*. See especially 300–24.

28. Brooks Atkinson, "Christmas Night Adds 'Pal Joey' to the Musical Stage," *New York Times*, December 26, 1940, reprinted in *Rodgers Reader*, 68–70.

29. Howard Taubman, "Theater: 'Do I Hear a Waltz?' Opens," *New York Times*, March 19, 1965, reprinted in *New York Critics' Reviews*, vol. 26, 359; Taubman, "'Cuckoo' into 'Waltz,'" *New York Times*, March 28, 1965.

30. Walter Kerr, "Walter Kerr Reviews 'Do I Hear a Waltz?'" *New York Herald Tribune*, March 19, 1965, reprinted in *New York Critics' Reviews*, vol. 26, 359–60; Kerr, "Sobriety in Venice," *Thirty Plays Hath November: Pain and Pleasure in the Contemporary Theater* (New York: Simon & Schuster, 1969), 189–92, reprinted in *Rodgers Reader*, 237–40, quotation on p. 239.

31. Richard Watts, Jr., "Americans in a Musical Venice," *New York Post*, March 19, 1965, reprinted in *New York Critics' Reviews*, vol. 26, 360.

32. Stephen Banfield, *Sondheim's Broadway Musicals* (Ann Arbor: University of Michigan Press, 1993), 45.

33. Steven Suskin, *Show Tunes: The Songs, Shows, and Careers of Broadway's Major Composers* (New York: Oxford University Press, 2000), 113. In an earlier book Suskin wrote that "virtually every song is interesting and appealing"; see *Berlin, Kern, Rodgers, Hart, and Hammerstein: A Complete Song Catalogue* (Jefferson, N.C.: McFarland, 1990), 34.

34. Ken Mandelbaum, *Not Since "Carrie": Forty Years of Broadway Musical Flops* (New York: St. Martin's, 1991), 255; Mandelbaum's commentary on *Do I Hear a Waltz?* is reprinted in *Rodgers Reader*, 250–52, quotation on p. 251.

35. Martin Gottfried, *Sondheim* (New York: Abrams), 74.

36. Kurt Gänzl, *The Encyclopedia of the Musical Theatre, L–Z* (New York: Schirmer, 1994), 1227.

37. Mordden *R&H*, 214.

38. Mordden, *Open a New Window*, 70.

39. Fynsworth Alley 302 062 126 2.

40. Another title absent from the original cast recording, "We're Going to the Lido," is based on the "La la la la la" music that introduced "Here We Are Again."

41. Peter Filichia, *Let's Put on a Musical!* (New York: Back Stage Books, 1993), 178.

42. Secrest, *Sondheim*, 176 and 178.

43. *Side by Side By Sondheim* (RCA CBL2-1851) and *Do I Hear a Waltz?* (Fynsworth Alley 302 062 126 2). The Broadway lyric can be heard on the Original Broadway Cast album of *Do I Hear a Waltz?* (SONY SK 48206) only.

44. One of the relatively few lyrics by Hart that contained an overt reference to homosexuality, albeit sung by a woman to a man ("I was a queen to him. / Who's goin' to make me gay now?" in "He Was Too Good to Me"), was dropped from *Simple Simon*. The possibility of a gay interpretation was later removed when the song was reworked as "He Looks So Good to Me" for the film musical *The Hot Heiress* before this song too was dropped.

45. In some cases Rodgers returns to musical fragments that originally appeared

in his work with Hammerstein. For example, a phrase in "Bargaining" and a phrase in "Take the Moment," two Renato songs, duplicate phrases originally found in Billy Bigelow's "Soliloquy."

46. Most interestingly, Sondheim himself set an alternate lyric to "Do I Hear a Waltz?" (almost identical to the lyric of Rodgers's sketch). Sondheim's version, also remarkably close to the *rhythm* of Rodgers's sketch shown in example 6.3a, was copyrighted in 1998 and published in *All Sondheim*, vol. 4 (Miami: Warner Bros., 1999). Above the title is the caption "from the unproduced TV musical *Do You [not I] Hear a Waltz?"*

47. "Rodgers and Sondheim," 29.

48. Meryle Secrest, *Sondheim*, 178.

49. Zadan, *Sondheim & Co.*, 100–1.

50. Zadan, *Sondheim & Co.*, 100. On another occasion Sondheim suggested that *My Fair Lady* was also unnecessary and need not have been musicalized.

51. Secrest, *Sondheim*, 178.

52. Several *Waltz* lyrics foreshadow ideas that Sondheim returned to in his own shows. The idea of building a city "in the middle of that sea" in Leona's opening song, "Someone Woke Up," anticipates the title of the opening song in *Pacific Overtures*, "The Advantages of Floating in the Middle of the Sea." The end of the song, "Just so Leona could come here / And stand like a lump dripping wet / With no shoes on at noon on a Monday and cry" parallels the conclusion of the opening (and title) song in *Sunday in the Park with George*, albeit with a change of day. A lyrical phrase in the title song, "An old lady is waltzing in her flat, / Waltzing with her cat!" metamorphoses into "At my tiny flat there's just my cat," a lyric from "Broadway Baby" in Sondheim's *Follies*.

53. Rodgers wrote the incidental music for the twenty-six-part documentary series *Winston Churchill—The Valiant Years*, based on the former prime minister's memoirs (November 27, 1960, to May 21, 1962); on February 22, 1965, CBS first broadcast the television remake of *Cinderella*, which included a song, "Loneliness of Evening," that had been deleted from *South Pacific*.

54. *Musical Stages*, 331.

55. Stone's best known Broadway credits after *Two By Two* include *Sugar* in 1972 (music by Styne and lyrics by Merrill), *Woman of the Year* in 1981 (Kander and Ebb), *My One and Only* in 1983, an adaptation of Gershwin's 1927 hit *Funny Face*, and the Tony Award–winning *Will Rogers Follies* in 1991 (music by Cy Coleman and lyrics by Betty Comden and Adolph Green).

56. All the songs discussed here as well as most of the rest of the score can be heard on the Original Broadway Cast album (SONY SK 30338).

57. Walter Kerr, "Golden Boy in a Different Play," *New York Times*, November 22, 1970, reprinted in *New York Critics' Reviews*, vol. 31, 162–63, quotation on p. 162.

58. Rodgers discusses "Blue Room" and includes a musical example of the first A section in his own hand in *Musical Stages*, 80.

59. Rodgers also frequently favored half steps without leaps in a number of songs in his final shows—for example, "The Sweetest Sounds" and "Nobody Told Me" in *No Strings*, "Take the Moment" and "Stay" in *Do I Hear a Waltz?* and "A Writer Writes at Night" and the verse of "Ev'ry Day (Comes Something Beautiful)" in *I Remember Mama*. For striking earlier examples one can turn to the main melodic idea of Hart's

"With a Song in My Heart" from *Spring Is Here* (1929), recognizably transformed (and with a leap) in Hammerstein's "Some Enchanted Evening."

60. Marty Bell, *Broadway Stories: A Backstage Journey Through Musical Theatre* (New York: Limelight, 1993), 150.

61. Martin Gottfried, "'Two By Two' . . . 'a plain re-telling of Noah's story,'" *Women's Wear Daily*, November 12, 1970, reprinted in *New York Critics' Reviews*, vol. 31, 161.

62. *Musical Stages*, 323. For a fuller account of Kaye's performance antics in *Two By Two*, see Martin Gottfried, *Nobody's Fool: The Lives of Danny Kaye* (New York: Simon & Schuster, 1994), 288–300.

63. Having seen a production of *Two By Two* in the Rodgers centennial year, I am almost prepared to hypothesize that Kaye may have actually shortened the run of the show and hurt its posthumous reputation. In any event, I am convinced that the show does not need Kaye in order to succeed. The show has held up, as Mel Brooks might say, "surprisingly well."

64. Secrest, 392. Barbara Andres (Queen Catherine) continues where Sherin leaves off: "The wives tried to get Nicol offstage and away from Jimmy [Litton], who was on the floor. At first the audience thought it was all part of the curtain call, but they soon realized it was real. There was a terrible feeling in the company against Nicol, the serfs against the king, as it were."

65. Richard Adler, *You Gotta Have Heart: An Autobiography* (New York: Donald I. Fine, 1990), 266–69, reprinted in *Rodgers Reader*, 240–43.

66. Suskin, *More Opening Nights*, 774.

67. Clive Barnes, "'Rex' By Rodgers Stars Williamson," *New York Times*, April 26, 1976, reprinted in *New York Critics' Reviews*, vol. 37, 286.

68. Walter Kerr, *New York Times*, quoted in Suskin, *More Opening Nights*, 772–73.

69. George Oppenheimer, *Newsday*, May 9, 1976, quoted in *R&H Fact Book*, 679.

70. Martin Gottfried, "'Rex'—From a Time Past," *New York Post*, April 26, 1976, reprinted in *New York Critics' Reviews*, vol. 37, 287.

71. T. E. Kalem, "Imperator Submersus," *Time*, May 10, 1976, reprinted in *New York Critics' Reviews*, vol. 37, 289.

72. Howard Kissel, "Rex," *Women's Wear Daily*, April 26, 1976, reprinted in *New York Critics' Reviews*, vol. 37, 288.

73. Irving Kolodin, "Music Returns to the Musical," *Saturday Review* (April 3, 1976), 43–45; quote on p. 44. In the "unrevised first rehearsal script," "The Pears of Anjou" appears after "In Time" in a musically sparse second act.

74. Personal communication, October 17, 2001. Micheal F. Anders's reconstructed performance (April 11–13, 16–20, 2002) and Sheldon Harnick's preperformance lecture, "Musical Out-Takes" (April 14), at the University of Findlay, Ohio, addressed some of these perceived infelicities.

75. To remedy this lapse, the Rodgers & Hammerstein Organization is preparing a rental score as well as a libretto revised under Harnick's artistic supervision. Personal communication, Micheal Anders (April 19, 2002).

76. Bert Fink, "A Requiem for *Rex*," 5–7, and Mort Goode, "Synopsis," 8–14 (RCA Victor CD 09026–68933–2).

77. Mandelbaum, *Not Since "Carrie*," 102–4, reprinted in *Rodgers Reader*, 248–50. For a thorough account of *Mama*'s genesis and production history see Robert Fishman, "The 'Mama' Chronicles," *Show Music* 7/4 (Winter 1991–92), 19-28 and 8/1 (Spring 1992), 19–25.

78. Bordman, 757.

79. Mordden *R&H*, 215. In her autobiography, *Choices*, Liv Ullmann recalls her musical theater debut (New York: Knopf, 1984), 9–17. This is how she described the first time she sang for Rodgers:

> "Could you please sing a little tune," Richard Rodgers asks politely. "It will make it so much easier for me when I compose your songs."
>
> "I don't dare to."
>
> "Sooner or later you will have to sing anyway," the old genius says mildly. "This is a musical."
>
> "Oh, please wait—I am so ashamed of my voice."
>
> "I have heard it all. Nothing would surprise me," he comforts me. "Don't be afraid. I just need to know your key. Sing anything. Sing 'Happy Birthday to You.'" The lovely man takes my hand and looks at me encouragingly.
>
> I sing.
>
> Before my eyes he ages twenty years. (10)

80. Meehan had previously written the libretto to *Annie* (1977). In 2001 he won his second Tony Award, for the libretto to *The Producers*, which he wrote with Mel Brooks.

81. It is hard to resist contemplating the notion that Rodgers was struck with the contrasts between the happy Hansens and the often-brooding and silent New York City household in which Rodgers grew up at about the same time.

82. See also example 1.1a and the previous discussion of *Two By Two*'s "I Do Not Know a Day I Did Not Love You" (example 6.5). "Sixteen Going on Seventeen" from *The Sound of Music* displays many half steps that precede rather than follow a leap.

83. Although Green spells her name Katrine in the *Fact Book*, she is Katrin on the rental script and studio cast recording.

84. "Easy Come, Easy Go" (a Jessel lyric) bears a readily perceptible *musical* resemblance to *Annie*'s "Easy Street" (a Charnin lyric). Howard Kissel implies that George Irving was primarily responsible for the misplaced national identity when he writes that "Irving, as Uncle Chris, doesn't seem the least Norwegian—unless there were shtetls in Norway." Howard Kissel, "I Remember Mama," *Women's Wear Daily*, June 1, 1979, reprinted in *New York Critics' Reviews*, vol. 40, 230.

85. *Reminiscences*, 352; *Rodgers Reader*, 320.

86. John McClain, "Another Great Hit for Dick and Oscar," *Journal American*, March 30, 1951, reprinted in *New York Critics' Reviews*, vol. 12, 304.

87. Richard Eder, "I Remember Mama," *New York Times*, June 1, 1979, reprinted in *New York Critics' Reviews*, vol. 40, 227.

88. Kissel, "I Remember Mama"; reprinted in *New York Critics' Reviews*, vol. 40, 230.

89. Douglas Watt, "'Mama' Not All That Memorable," *Daily News*, June 1, 1979, reprinted in *New York Critics' Reviews*, vol. 40, 228–29.

90. John Beaufort, "'I Remember Mama': An Aura of Good Feeling," *Christian Science Monitor*, June 4, 1979, reprinted in *New York Critics' Reviews*, vol. 40, 229–30.

91. Clive Barnes, "Liv & Rodgers Will Make You Remember 'Mama,'" *New York Post*, June 1, 1979, reprinted in *New York Critics' Reviews*, vol. 40, 228.

92. TER CDTER 1102.

93. Frank Rich, "Conversations with Sondheim," *New York Times Magazine*, March 12, 2000, 89. Also in this interview Rich reports Sondheim's retrospective view that "the only project he regrets was his collaboration with Richard Rodgers on *Do I Hear a Waltz?* after Hammerstein's death." Rich continues: "Sondheim attributes that production's rancid atmosphere to his sense that 'Dick was afraid that his well had run dry.'"

94. Some selective details: George and Ira Gershwin ended their traditional Broadway careers with two flops, *Pardon My English* and *Let 'Em Eat Cake* in 1933 (*Porgy and Bess* [1935], of course, is a special case). Kern ended his long and illustrious years on Broadway anticlimactically in 1939 with *Very Warm for May*, which closed after fifty-nine performances; he died before he could begin *Annie Get Your Gun* in 1945. Berlin finished his Broadway career with a failure, *Mr. President* (1962). Loesser's *Pleasures and Palaces* (1965) closed out of town in Detroit. Bernstein and Lerner's *1600 Pennsylvania Avenue* (1976) lasted a week, six weeks fewer than *Rex*. After *Annie*, Strouse's remaining six shows ran a total of thirty-six performances—none longer than seventeen performances, and two closing after opening night. Two Off-Broadway shows, *Mayor* (1985) and the *Annie* sequel *Annie Warbucks* (1993), however, were modestly successful.

95. Bert Fink, "Announcing the 2002 Richard Rodgers Centennial," *Happy Talk* 8/1 (Fall 2001), 2.

96. Wilder, 163.

97. *Musical Stages*, ix.

98. Richard Rodgers, "The Broadway Audience Is Still There, Waiting for More Good Shows," *Dramatists Guild Quarterly* (1971), 6, 11–17,reprinted in *Rodgers Reader*, 326–34, quotation on p. 334.

99. Richard Rodgers, "Opera and Broadway," *Opera News* (February 25, 1961), 9–11, reprinted in *Rodgers Reader*, 289–93. The remaining quotations in this paragraph are taken from this article.

Permissions

Hammerstein II. Copyright Renewed. WILLIAMSON MUSIC owner of publication and allied rights throughout the world. International Copyright Secured. All Rights Reserved.

With LORENZ HART

"All Dark People" (from BABES IN ARMS): Words by Lorenz Hart. Music by Richard Rodgers. Copyright © 1937 (Renewed) by Chappell @ Co. Rights for the Extended Renewal Term in the U.S. Controlled by Williamson Music and WB Music Corp. o/b/o The Estate Of Lorenz Hart. International Copyright Secured. All Rights Reserved.

"He Was Too Good to Me" (from SIMPLE SIMON): Words by Lorenz Hart. Music by Richard Rodgers. Copyright © 1930 (Renewed) by Chappell & Co. Rights for the Extended Renewal Term in the U.S. Controlled by Williamson Music and WB Music Corp. o/b/o The Estate Of Lorenz Hart. International Copyright Secured. All Rights Reserved.

"Shakespeares of 1922": Words by Lorenz Hart and Morrie Ryskind. Music by Richard Rodgers. Copyright © 1986 Williamson Music, WB Music Corp. o/b/o The Estate Of Lorenz Hart and The Estate Of Morrie Ryskind. International Copyright Secured. All Rights Reserved.

"You Have Cast Your Shadow on the Sea" (from THE BOYS FROM SYRACUSE): Words by Lorenz Hart. Music by Richard Rodgers. Copyright © 1938 (Renewed) by Chappell & Co. Rights for the Extended Renewal Term in the U.S. Controlled by Williamson Music and WB Music Corp. o/b/o The Estate Of Lorenz Hart. International Copyright Secured. All Rights Reserved.

With RICHARD RODGERS

"The Man Who Has Everything" (from NO STRINGS): Lyrics and Music by Richard Rodgers. Copyright © 1962 by Richard Rodgers. Copyright Renewed. WILLIAMSON MUSIC owner of publication and allied rights throughout the world. International Copyright Secured. All Rights Reserved.

With STEPHEN SONDHEIM

"Someone Woke Up" (from DO I HEAR A WALTZ?): Music by Richard Rodgers. Lyrics by Stephen Sondheim. Copyright © 1965 by Richard Rodgers and Stephen Sondheim. Copyright Renewed. Williamson Music and Burthen Music Co., Inc., owner of publication and allied rights throughout the world. International Copyright Secured. All Rights Reserved.

"We're Gonna Be All Right" (from DO I HEAR A WALTZ?): Music by Richard Rodgers. Lyrics by Stephen Sondheim. Copyright © 1965 by Richard Rodgers and Stephen Sondheim. Copyright Renewed. Williamson Music and Burthen Music Co., Inc., owner of publication and allied rights throughout the world. International Copyright Secured. All Rights Reserved.

Music and Lyrics

RODGERS AND CHARNIN

"I Do Not Know a Day I Did Not Love You" (from TWO BY TWO): Lyrics by Martin Charnin. Music by Richard Rodgers. Copyright © 1970 by Richard Rodgers and Beam One, Ltd. Copyright Renewed. WILLIAMSON MUSIC, owner of publication and allied rights of Richard Rodgers throughout the world. EDWIN H. MORRIS &

RODGERS AND HAMMERSTEIN

RODGERS AND HART

RODGERS AND RODGERS

RODGERS AND SONDHEIM

Prose

Photography

CBS Photo Archive: 5.1, 5.2, and 5.3

Jerry Ohlinger's Movie Material Store: 4.4, 4.5

Library of Congress (Music Division): 6.2

Ross Mulhausen: 3.2

Museum of the City of New York: 1.1, 1.2, 1.3, 3.1, 6.5, and 6.6

Courtesy of the The Rodgers and Hammerstein Organization: frontispiece, 2.1, 2.2, 2.3, 4.1, 4.2, 4.3, 6.1, 6.3, 6.4, and 6.7

General Index

Page numbers in italic type refer to photographs

Index of Rodgers's Works